Organization Design for International Construction Business

Lu Chang Peh · Sui Pheng Low

Organization Design for International Construction Business

Springer

Lu Chang Peh
School of Science and Technology
SIM University
Singapore, Singapore

Sui Pheng Low
School of Design and Environment
Department of Building
National University of Singapore
Singapore, Singapore

ISBN 978-3-642-35163-1   ISBN 978-3-642-35164-8 (eBook)
DOI 10.1007/978-3-642-35164-8
Springer Heidelberg New York Dordrecht London

Library of Congress Control Number: 2012954671

© Springer-Verlag Berlin Heidelberg 2013

This work is subject to copyright. All rights are reserved by the Publisher, whether the whole or part of the material is concerned, specifically the rights of translation, reprinting, reuse of illustrations, recitation, broadcasting, reproduction on microfilms or in any other physical way, and transmission or information storage and retrieval, electronic adaptation, computer software, or by similar or dissimilar methodology now known or hereafter developed. Exempted from this legal reservation are brief excerpts in connection with reviews or scholarly analysis or material supplied specifically for the purpose of being entered and executed on a computer system, for exclusive use by the purchaser of the work. Duplication of this publication or parts thereof is permitted only under the provisions of the Copyright Law of the Publisher's location, in its current version, and permission for use must always be obtained from Springer. Permissions for use may be obtained through RightsLink at the Copyright Clearance Center. Violations are liable to prosecution under the respective Copyright Law.

The use of general descriptive names, registered names, trademarks, service marks, etc. in this publication does not imply, even in the absence of a specific statement, that such names are exempt from the relevant protective laws and regulations and therefore free for general use.

While the advice and information in this book are believed to be true and accurate at the date of publication, neither the authors nor the editors nor the publisher can accept any legal responsibility for any errors or omissions that may be made. The publisher makes no warranty, express or implied, with respect to the material contained herein.

Printed on acid-free paper

Springer is part of Springer Science+Business Media (www.springer.com)

Contents

1 **Introduction** 1
   1.1   Background 1
   1.2   Research Problem 2
   1.3   Knowledge Gap 3
   1.4   Aims and Objectives 4
   1.5   Research Hypotheses 4
   1.6   Contribution to Practice 4
   1.7   Research Scope and Limitations 5
   1.8   Research Stages 5
   1.9   Expected Significance and Contribution of the Research
         to Knowledge and Practices 6
   1.10 Problems Encountered and the Actions Taken
         to Overcome Them 7
   1.11 Structure of the Research 8
   References 10

2 **Flight-Time, Geographical Distance and Related Issues** 13
   2.1   Introduction 13
   2.2   The Associated Attributes of Distance 13
   2.3   Flight-Time and Distance 14
        2.3.1   Time 14
        2.3.2   Flight Routes 15
        2.3.3   The Aircraft's Speed 16
        2.3.4   Climate 17
        2.3.5   Time-Zones 17
        2.3.6   Jet-Lag and Circadian Rhythm 17
   2.4   Globalization and Geography 18
   2.5   Manifestations of Distance 18
        2.5.1   Cultural Distance 19
        2.5.2   Administrative/Attributional Distance 21

		2.5.3	Geographical Distance, Gravitational Distance and	
			Topological Distance	22
		2.5.4	Economic Distance	25
		2.5.5	Technological Distance	26
		2.5.6	Socio-demographical Distance	27
		2.5.7	Relational/Affinity Distance	27
		2.5.8	Organizational Distance	28
	2.6	Summary		33
	References			34
3	**Core and Peripheral System of Cities**			37
	3.1	Introduction		37
	3.2	Human and Economic Geography		37
	3.3	Geo-politics		38
	3.4	Geo-economics and Spatial Economics		39
	3.5	Transportation		40
	3.6	Location		41
	3.7	Localization		42
		3.7.1	Virtual Clusters	46
		3.7.2	Paradox of Globalization and Localization	46
	3.8	Agglomeration		47
	3.9	Centrality		49
	3.10	Complementarities of Services		50
	3.11	System of Cities		50
	3.12	Firm's Behavior		52
	3.13	Summary		54
	References			55
4	**Internationalization of Singaporean A/E Firms**			59
	4.1	Introduction		59
	4.2	Discontinuities or Inter-connectivity		59
	4.3	Economics and Internationalization		60
	4.4	MNE and FDI		61
		4.4.1	FDI	66
		4.4.2	Trade-Agreements	66
		4.4.3	Borne Global	67
		4.4.4	Embeddedness	67
		4.4.5	Barriers to Entry	67
	4.5	International Construction		68
	4.6	Singapore-Domiciled Service Firms		68
		4.6.1	Singapore's Construction Industry	69
		4.6.2	Singapore's Construction Exports	70
		4.6.3	Architectural and Engineering Services	71
		4.6.4	A/E Communications	71
		4.6.5	Supply-Chain of A/E Consultancy Services	71
		4.6.6	Role of the Government	72

	4.7	Internationalization Risks	73
		4.7.1 Risks and Uncertainty	73
		4.7.2 Country or City Risk	74
		4.7.3 Forecasting	74
		4.7.4 Risk Management	74
	4.8	Market Entry	75
		4.8.1 Entry Mode	75
		4.8.2 Progression of Entry Modes	76
	4.9	Eclectic-Diamond Framework	77
		4.9.1 Eclectic Paradigm	77
		4.9.2 Diamond Theory	79
		4.9.3 Combining the Eclectic Paradigm with Diamond Theory	79
	4.10	Distance and Internationalization	79
	4.11	Conclusion	82
	References		83
5	**Business Strategies and Organization Design**		87
	5.1	Introduction	87
	5.2	Military Strategies and Formations	87
	5.3	Theory of the Firm	88
		5.3.1 Resource-Based Theory	89
		5.3.2 Transaction-Costs Theory	89
		5.3.3 Behavioural Theory	93
		5.3.4 International Product Life-Cycle Theory	93
		5.3.5 Uppsala Model	94
		5.3.6 Networks Theory	94
	5.4	Issues on Strategic Management	95
		5.4.1 New Economy	95
		5.4.2 Complexity and Flexibility	96
		5.4.3 Intelligence	96
		5.4.4 Psychoanalyzing the Organization	96
		5.4.5 Competency	96
		5.4.6 Internationalization	97
		5.4.7 Strategies and Systems	97
		5.4.8 Entry Strategy	97
		5.4.9 Organization Structure	97
		5.4.10 Leadership	98
		5.4.11 Human Resource	98
		5.4.12 Partnering	98
		5.4.13 Communications	98
		5.4.14 Marketing	99
		5.4.15 Value Creation	99
		5.4.16 Learning and Knowledge Management	99
		5.4.17 Cultural Management	99

	5.5	Strategic Analysis, Planning, Matching and Implementation	99
	5.6	Entry Strategy and Entry Mode	100
	5.7	Organization Design	102
	5.8	Inter-dependence of Strategy and Organization Structure	104
	5.9	McKinsey 7S	105
	5.10	A/E Firm's Business Strategies	106
	5.11	Summary	107
	References	107
6	**Theoretical and Conceptual Framework**	111
	6.1	Introduction	111
	6.2	Theoretical Framework	111
		6.2.1 Flight	112
		6.2.2 Gravity Model	113
		6.2.3 Agglomeration in Core Locations and Back-Washes in Periphery Locations	114
		6.2.4 Venturing Overseas	114
		6.2.5 Embeddedness	115
		6.2.6 Risks, Business Strategies and Organization Structures	115
		6.2.7 Dynamic 8S Framework	115
		6.2.8 Organization Design of an A/E Firm	116
		6.2.9 Isomorphism	117
	6.3	Relationship Between Key Elements	118
	6.4	Conceptual Model of Study	119
	6.5	Parameters for Measurement	120
	6.6	Implications of Study	122
		6.6.1 Interpolation and Extrapolation of Organization Design	122
		6.6.2 Location Theory and Research Design	122
	6.7	Summary	129
	References	131
7	**Research Design and Methodology**	133
	7.1	Introduction	133
	7.2	Research Framework	133
	7.3	Pilot Study	134
	7.4	Population and Sampling	135
	7.5	Data Collection Instruments	135
		7.5.1 Questionnaire Surveys and Interviews	137
	7.6	Data Collection	137
		7.6.1 Fieldwork	138
	7.7	Statistical Analysis	141
	7.8	Content Analysis	143
	7.9	Case-Based Reasoning (CBR)	144
	7.10	Validation, Reconciliation and Adaptation	145
	7.11	Summary	146
	References	146

8 Data Collation and Results ... 149
- 8.1 Introduction ... 149
- 8.2 Profile of Questionnaire Replies and Interviewees ... 149
- 8.3 Content Analysis ... 151
  - 8.3.1 Content Analysis Methods ... 151
  - 8.3.2 Differences in Perceptions Between Private Firms and Government-Linked Firms ... 160
- 8.4 Statistical Analysis ... 162
  - 8.4.1 Factor and Reliability ... 162
- 8.5 Integration of Content Analysis and Statistical Analysis ... 162
- 8.6 Summary ... 173
- References ... 173

9 Background of Internationalizing Construction Firms and Cities ... 175
- 9.1 Introduction ... 175
- 9.2 Singapore's A/E firms' Traits and Characteristics ... 176
  - 9.2.1 Firm A ... 176
  - 9.2.2 Firm B ... 177
  - 9.2.3 Firm C ... 177
  - 9.2.4 Firm D ... 177
  - 9.2.5 Firm E ... 178
  - 9.2.6 Firm F ... 178
- 9.3 Corporatized or Privatized Firms ... 179
- 9.4 Motivations and Objectives ... 180
- 9.5 Competitiveness and Competitive Strengths of Singapore's A/E Firms ... 181
- 9.6 Internationalization of Singapore's A/E firms ... 183
  - 9.6.1 Reasons for Internationalizing ... 184
  - 9.6.2 "Hot-Spots" and "Cold-Spots" ... 184
  - 9.6.3 Preferred Locations to Venture Overseas ... 186
  - 9.6.4 Countries and Cities ... 188
- 9.7 Difficulties of Internationalization ... 197
- 9.8 Management of Risks ... 199
- 9.9 Prerequisites and CSF ... 204
- 9.10 Summary ... 205
- References ... 206

10 Findings and Synthesis of Themes ... 207
- 10.1 Introduction ... 207
- 10.2 7-h Flight-Radius ... 207
- 10.3 Core and Periphery Locations ... 212
- 10.4 Gravitational Distance ... 215
  - 10.4.1 Globalization and Virtual Collocation ... 219
  - 10.4.2 Importance of Physical Presence ... 220

	10.5	Double-Octagonal Perspective of Distance	222
		10.5.1 Changes	226
		10.5.2 Spillages	227
		10.5.3 Time-Lags and Differences	228
		10.5.4 Psychic Distance	228
		10.5.5 Communications	229
		10.5.6 Networks	230
		10.5.7 Cost-Value	231
		10.5.8 Control	232
	10.6	Eclectic Diamond Framework	233
		10.6.1 Factor Conditions	234
		10.6.2 Demand Conditions	234
		10.6.3 Related and Complementary Industries	236
		10.6.4 Strategies Due to Competition	238
		10.6.5 Government Interference	239
		10.6.6 Chance	241
		10.6.7 Ownership Qualities	242
		10.6.8 Locational Factors	243
		10.6.9 Internalization	244
	10.7	The 8S Framework	246
		10.7.1 Business Strategies	246
		10.7.2 Organization Structure	256
		10.7.3 Organization Systems	259
		10.7.4 Leadership Styles	262
		10.7.5 Skills and Staff	263
		10.7.6 Shared Values	265
		10.7.7 Supply-Chain	266
		10.7.8 Dynamic Strategies	268
	10.8	Synthesis of Findings and Themes	270
		10.8.1 Generalization of Findings from Content Analysis	271
		10.8.2 Generalization of Findings from Statistical Analysis	277
	10.9	Decision-Support Systems and Management Information Systems	277
	10.10	Summary	278
	References		279
11	**CBR-DSS and Validation**		283
	11.1	Introduction	283
	11.2	Management of an A/E Firm	283
	11.3	Sharing and Learning from Others in the Industry	285
	11.4	Discussion on Findings in Content Analysis and Statistical Analysis	286
	11.5	The CBR-Logic	288
	11.6	Step-by-Step Demonstration of the CBR-DSS	289

	11.7	Validation		295
		11.7.1	Feedback	297
		11.7.2	Recommendations and Modifications	298
	11.8	The Completed CBR-DSS Prototype		299
	11.9	Conclusion from Validation		301
	References			303
12	**Conclusion**			305
	12.1	Introduction		305
	12.2	Major Contributions of the Study		306
		12.2.1	Major Findings of the Study	307
		12.2.2	Validation of Hypotheses	318
		12.2.3	Contribution to Knowledge	319
		12.2.4	Contribution to Practice	320
		12.2.5	Innovations of the Study	321
	12.3	Limitations of the Research		322
	12.4	Recommendations for Future Research		323
	References			324

Appendix A: Internationalization of Architectural and Engineering (A/E) Firms 325

Appendix B: Internationalization of Architectural and Engineering (A/E) Firms 329

Appendix C: Validation Form 337

Bibliography 339

Chapter 1
Introduction

1.1 Background

Singapore's present Prime Minister Mr. Lee Hsien Long, when he was then Chairman of the Economic Review Committee recommended that businesses domiciled in Singapore should consider venturing into overseas market in order to sustain business growth (Economic Review Committee Report 1986). Mr. Goh Chok Tong, then the Prime Minister of Singapore in 2001, extended this view during his National Day Rally speech, when he advised Singaporean indigenous and foreign companies with their headquarters or regional headquarters set up in Singapore to make use of their geographical and cultural proximities to reach out to countries or cities that are within 7-h flight-time from Singapore Changi International Airport because these hinterlands contain 2.8 billion people and millions of middle-income consumers which would provide Singapore with enormous and numerous opportunities. Minister Mentor Lee Kuan Yew (2005) thus exhorted Singaporeans to jump on the bandwagon of China, India and South-east Asia's growth as Asia enters into a new era of renaissance. In order to do that, Singapore would need to be able to play the international game: to build a brand-name, reputation, networks, contacts, and project the influence of Singapore through both government and also private organizations.

Since then, Singapore-domiciled businesses have taken off in a huge way to invest and operate in regional countries and cities. Of particular interest to this study is the recommendation prescribed by Mr. Goh Chok Tong. The rationale for internationalization to keep within 7-h flight-time is because flight-time is directly proportionate to geographical distance. The longer the flight-time, the further the business would be away from home, i.e. Singapore. Mr. Goh's recommendation focused on the need for Singapore-based businesses to venture overseas into regional countries and cities that are not too far away as doing otherwise would sap their access to home-based resources and impose logistical constraints. In addition, countries and cities that are in close geographical proximity to Singapore are likely to be those that possibly share some historical, cultural (assimilation and acculturation) and language affinities (migration and mass-media) with Singapore which Singapore-based businesses are cognizant of and can benefit from.

1.2 Research Problem

Some 2,000 years ago, Sun Tzu said that "time spent in reconnaissance is seldom wasted" (Giles 1910). Insight and market intelligence are necessary when businesses venture into foreign markets. Likewise, Backman and Butler (2004) who studied the complexity of the Asian business environment, stressed the importance of having good information because it gives choices, power, leverage in negotiations and a sustainable business. There are many other common challenges for the transnational manager.

Indigenous and transnational firms with their Head-quarters (HQ) or Regional HQ domiciled in Singapore need to have good strategic plans and management when extending their operations or services to neighbouring or other overseas countries. However, geographical separation can influence many environmental elements, which in turn, affect the management of these overseas businesses. For example, "The Tyranny of Distance" by Geoffrey Blainey (1977) pointed out the inconveniences incurred and costs required to bridge distance. It was thought that resources would be sapped with distances, discontinuities or dislocations at countries and city borders. Obviously, proximity would eliminate or minimize such disjointedness and disconnectedness. The dictum of "proximity" suggests that being nearer to the home environment allows access to and knowledge of resources, networks and markets, whilst being farther would erode the firm's comparative advantages. Allen (1977) postulates that spatial arrangement has a significant impact on communications between colleagues within an organization. Root (1998) considered geographical distance away from base to affect the selection of an appropriate entry mode. Ghemawat (2001)'s Cultural, Administrative, Geographical and Economical (CAGE) Framework and Lojeski and Reilly's (2007) Virtual Distance Model suggest that there could be several facets of distance. Phukan (2003) put forward that remote or distance management can be affected by distance, time-zone differences and cultural issues. All these suggest that flight distance could affect business strategies and organization structures. Virtual or perceived distance is important because it affects innovation, the level of trust, job satisfaction, team performance and team leader's effectiveness (Lojeski 2007). Paradoxically, The Death of Distance (Cairncross 1997), Borderless World (Ohmae 1999) and The World is Flat (Friedman 2005) have been suggesting that globalization has made physical distance irrelevant.

Singapore's construction-related businesses are impeded due to the inherent economic constraints of Singapore as a small country (Asad and Lee 2008). On the other hand, the burgeoning demand for A/E consultancy services from emerging markets like China, South-east Asia, India and the Middle-east have profound implications for Singapore's businesses. Venturing out has been recognized as a key and strategic pillar for economic growth for the island-country.

Firms that seek to endeavour into international markets would have to contemplate how to organize themselves to work efficiently and effectively.

Barlett and Ghoshal (1998) saw an organization in these terms: the anatomy – the organization structure that defines the distribution of assets and resources and the allocation of roles and responsibilities; the physiology – the flows of goods, resources, people and information around the organization and the processes and relationships such flows create; and the psychology – the culture, shared vision and values that give the organization a meaning and glues all things together. Markides (1999) described the organization as being made up of four elements: culture, structure, incentive systems and workforce. This organizational model is very similar to the Peters and Waterman (1982) McKinsey 7S strategic model that considers strategy, structure, systems, shared values, style, staff and skills, whereby strategy, structure and systems are deemed to be the hard-wares; style, staff and skills are considered to be the soft-wares of the organization; and shared values bind these features together. According to Markides (1999), the headquarters would coordinate and command activities across geographically and functionally dispersed establishments within the organization.

The key problem is that: a business strategy that applies across all cities or a one-size-fit-all organization design is unlikely to work effectively and efficiently given the specific positional, multi-dimensional and varying conditions. Therefore, the study seeks to find out what appropriate business strategies and organization designs the A/E firm should implement in each city, and how flight-time or geographical distance influence such a phenomenon. The study would, in the process, uncover (i) whether geographical distance could erode the competitiveness of an internationalizing A/E firm; (ii) and whether private and government-linked firms should implement different business strategies and organization designs.

1.3 Knowledge Gap

There have been studies conducted to find out business strategies used by transnational A/E/C firms (Ling et al 2005; Ofori et al 2006); and how geographical distance affects an internationalizing organization (Ghemawat 2001; Lojeski and Reilly 2007), but no studies have been committed to establish any relationship between business strategies and organization design with geographical distance.

Moreover, even though Singapore-domiciled A/E firms have been venturing overseas, it is presently still obscure what are the best or common entry strategies adopted to gain and maintain the all-important beach-heads or footholds to expand the overseas venture; and how these firms organize themselves structurally in various host cities. It is unclear if there is a relationship between flight-time (as a proxy for geographical distance) and these strategies and organization. It is also uncertain if Singapore's A/E firms are competitive in overseas markets. The purpose of this study is to provide answers to this lacuna in knowledge as well as to develop a framework for organizational learning through a Knowledge-based

Decision Support System (KBDSS) using the Knowledge and Case-based Reasoning (CBR) approach.

1.4 Aims and Objectives

The aim of the study is to enhance the understanding of internationalization efforts by transnational A/E firms. The objectives of the research are to:

1. Evaluate the competitiveness of Singapore-domiciled A/E consultancy firms using Porter's Diamond Theory (Porter 1990) and Dunning's Eclectic Paradigm (Dunning 2000) templates;
2. Highlight the discontinuities in environment and in access to resources due to borders and geographical distances;
3. Analyze if geographical distances alters an organization's risk perception of its overseas market; and analyze the relationship between flight-time (proxy for geographical distance) and organization designs adopted by Singapore-domiciled A/E consultancy firms when they export their services;
4. Compare and contrast the organization designs of private and government-linked A/E organizations that export their services; and
5. Develop and test a KBDSS using the CBR approach that would help companies planning to venture overseas to decide on an appropriate organization design.

1.5 Research Hypotheses

It is hypothesized in this research that flight-time affects institutional risks, business risks and cultural risks – the three key aspects of an environmental scan and these in turn influence organization design (see Fig. 1.1). Using Singapore Changi International Airport as the point of origin, the study hypothesizes that there is a significant relationship between flight-time (proxy for geographical distance) and organization structures adopted by Singapore-owned A/E consultancy firms when they export their services abroad.

1.6 Contribution to Practice

The internationalization of A/E consultancy firms would make an interesting study because of their mobility and exportability. Moreover, Singapore has the talent-pool and infrastructure to support fast-growing regional cities in terms of A/E competencies or capabilities. Furthermore, the research on government-linked and private A/E firms has been disproportionately modest in comparison to studies

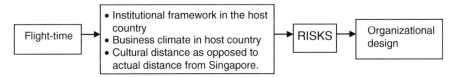

Fig. 1.1 Factors to consider for organization design

committed on construction firms in the construction industry. The investigation of A/E consultancy services in overseas markets would be attractive because of A/E's adaptability and exportability properties.

This research is innovative because no one has yet attempted to establish flight-distance with different business strategies and organization designs. This study looks into decision-management for overseas ventures by Singapore-domiciled firms. The research would also explore how the companies alter their strategic thrusts when they work in different cities to "acclimatize" to the business climates. One more attractive approach is the study of the transitions made by public-turned private firms as they re-align their business strategies and organization design. Another new finding is to link all these re-posturing to flight-time or flight-distances.

1.7 Research Scope and Limitations

The focus of this research is on A/E consultancy firms domiciled in Singapore and their business strategies and organization structures. Due to financial and time constraints, only the cities that are along the North-eastern flight-route via Singapore are examined. These cities are namely: Kuala Lumpur, Ho Chi Minh, Hong Kong, Shanghai and Beijing. The above cities are chosen because of their progressive intervening distance and flight-time away from Singapore. These cities are favourite destinations of Singaporean A/E firms, and are within 7-h flight-time flying out from Changi International Airport.

A study would also be conducted to sieve out aspects of business strategies and organization designs that transnational companies perceive as most important and critical because strategies and organization designs can too often be overly all-encompassing. The understanding of business strategies is important because business strategies are very strongly interlinked to organization designs.

1.8 Research Stages

The study has five distinct stages. The first stage is the literature review to form the theoretical underpinnings. The second stage is a pilot study of A/E consultancy firms to identify strategic and organizational issues; and cities perceived to have more strategic relevance and significance to their businesses. The third stage includes case studies and surveys incorporating questionnaires and interviews with A/E consultancy firms. The fourth stage is the data collation, analysis and interpretation. The fifth and last stage is the validation of findings. The targets of the field study are Singapore-domiciled A/E consultancy firms. Details are as follows:

1. Literature review on internationalization theories, strategic management and organizational studies;
2. Conducted pilot study to identify (a) business strategies and organization structures implemented by transnational companies, and to identify (b) overseas cities which Singapore-domiciled A/E consultancy firms have an active presence in;
3. Collated market intelligence of the countries and cities identified to gain a better understanding of their business climates. This formed part of the knowledge-based decision support system (DSS) based on Cased-based Reasoning (CBR);
4. Local and overseas surveys and observations were conducted to obtain inputs for the DSS; and
5. The CBR-DSS was validated.

1.9 Expected Significance and Contribution of the Research to Knowledge and Practices

The study contributes to knowledge because no one has yet so far attempted to establish the relationship between flight-time with different business strategies and organization structures. The study would also be a contribution to social sciences and is important to the field of proxemics because it studies how distance affects business strategies and organization design. The study is significant to industrial practices because Singapore is a small country with limited resources for the economy to be self-sufficient in the long run. The construction industry in Singapore is fraught with limitations due to the fluctuating peaks and troughs within a small domestic market. To avoid stagnated economic growth in the domestic market, forays should be made into booming industrializing countries in the surrounding regions like China, India, Vietnam, the United Arab Emirates, etc. to ride on the expanding business opportunities in these countries. Construction-based companies must therefore expand their operations and export their services and/or products overseas. A/E consultancy firms have a major role to play in this thrust. They possess good mobility and there exists a good talent pool and professional infrastructure in Singapore to support the fastest-growing cities in China, India, Vietnam, the United Arab Emirates, etc. As a matter of fact, many Singaporean A/E firms have already established offices in major cities like Shanghai, Bangalore and Dubai. It is anticipated that more would be joining them in the near future as part of portfolio diversification.

However, venturing overseas can involve complex issues with possibly many unforeseen risks and difficulties. This is especially so when the company is a newcomer to the overseas operating environment. Learning from the experience of other companies and foreign investors is imperative to help shorten the learning curve. The knowledge, expertise and experience garnered from the "first-movers" can provide invaluable business intelligence to those following suit later. Blomstermo and Deo Sharma (2003) notably suggested that trial and error, learning by doing, and the development of experiential knowledge accumulated are major factors that may be used to explain the behaviour of international firms. The set-up of a knowledge base would enable the filtering and sharing of advice, concerns, information, and intelligence for adaptation by companies for their future endeavours. They may also point out the difficulties and suggest how to circumvent around them to participate more competently. This would help firms that are or would be attempting to venture abroad, avoid the pitfalls previously encountered by the first-movers. Such opportunities can also help to facilitate upgrading across the board. This form of cross-learning and collaboration may also go a long way towards forging better relationships with complementary firms from allied supporting industries to improve the efficiency of the entire supply-chain through collaboration and strategic alliances (Handfield and Nichols 2002).

Public-turned-private entities or Government-linked companies (GLCs) were examined to understand how they re-align their business strategies and organization structures when they export their services overseas into regional markets. This study is also innovative because based on expert inputs, it would develop a case-based reasoning system for use in decision-making and rationalization of the appropriate business strategies and organization designs that would function more efficiently and effectively if firms plan to foray into previously unchartered blue-ocean territories and markets of overseas cities. The study seeks to provide useful information on the appropriate business strategies and organization structures that may be adopted as part of the organizational-learning based model. Furthermore, the study, although having its emphasis on the A/E consultancy firms, would lay good foundation for possibilities to explore Singapore's other forms of exports to other countries; as well as explores beyond the 7 h frontiers, to further locations in South America, Africa and East Europe.

1.10 Problems Encountered and the Actions Taken to Overcome Them

Although utmost care was taken in designing the research methodology, it was inevitable that the study encountered several problems such as:

Problem (i) Firms were wary about inviting competitors if they were to share their intelligence and formulae for success to facilitate other firms to internationalize. These firms regarded their know-how as a strategic asset, and preferred to guard such knowledge to maintain their competitive edges over other firms. Thus, these firms were reluctant to divulge information and contribute to the study.

Problem (ii) Firms, their senior management and employees were not always available to respond to questionnaires, interviews and case studies. This problem was exacerbated because the study requires fieldworks in several cities, and data collection could not be arranged to fit perfectly.

Problem (iii) Long-tail Syndrome and description of business strategies and organization structures can be subjective and hard to define.

The respective proposed solutions were:

Solution (i and ii) To approach firms with reputation of knowledge transfer to other firms or collaboration with academia and research institutions.

Solution (iii) The 20–80 Pareto Principle were applied, so that the myriad of issues pertaining to business strategies and organization structures could be trimmed, streamlined, and made concise for manageability, but yet robust for the study's requirements. Furthermore, knowledge-based inputs were introduced into the CBR to provide useful qualitative analysis.

1.11 Structure of the Research

The structure of the book is shown in Fig. 1.2. The figure shows how the chapters in the book relate to each other. Essentially, the book comprises of four parts – (i) research problem; (ii) theoretical underpinning; (iii) investigation; and (iv) findings, application and conclusion.

This chapter provides the research background including the research problem, aims and objectives, research hypotheses and research significance and contributions. It is hypothesized that flight-time, as a proxy for geographical distance, influences the organization design of an internationalizing A/E consultancy firm.

Chapter 2 appraises on the physical dimensions of flight-time and geographical distance. Flight-time causes changes in climate, time-zones, culture, administration, geography (e.g. topography), economy, technology, demography, historical links and organizational distance. A firm has to deploy appropriate business strategies and organization designs to internalize these distance-rooted variations.

Chapter 3 reviews literature on agglomeration and centrality. When centripetal forces of localization outweigh the centrifugal forces of dispersion in a location, agglomeration in the location occurs. Over time, the location grows to become a "black-hole" that sucks up the most economic potential in the region, but causes "back-wash" or draining effects to other cities in its vicinity. The firm has to consider how such phenomena shape the global or regional mosaics.

Chapter 4 reviews literature on organization design. Organization design must complement business strategies, and encompasses organization structure, organization systems, leadership style, skills of firm, characteristics of staff and shared values. Firms have to re-posture themselves or realign their business strategies and organization designs when they internationalize.

1.11 Structure of the Research

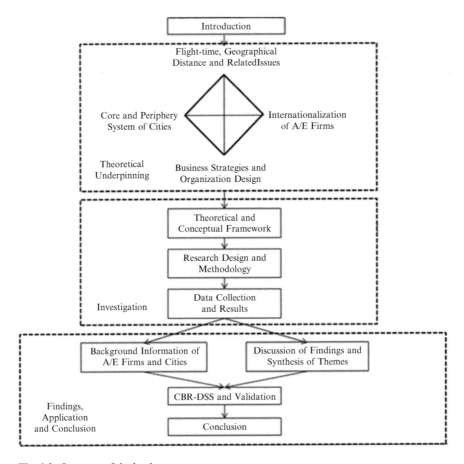

Fig. 1.2 Structure of the book

Chapter 5 reviews literature on internationalization. When a firm ventures overseas, it is exposed to unfamiliar conditions and situations. A firm has to internalize these changes so that it stays efficient and competent. The study suggests that the Eclectic Diamond Framework, an integration of Dunning's (1988) Eclectic Paradigm and Porter's Diamond Framework (1990), provides a comprehensive and succinct framework to consider the risks of internationalization.

Chapter 6 explains the theoretical and conceptual framework of the study. The relationships between flight-time, geographical distance, different manifestations of distance, gravitational distance, a city's role in the system of cities, business opportunities and risks, business strategies and organization designs of A/E firms were established.

Chapter 7 lays out the research design and methodology to fulfill the research objectives. The study uses statistical and content analyzes to interpret data collated from questionnaire surveys, interviews and case studies. The information, collected from Singapore, Johor Bahru, Kuala Lumpur, Penang, Ho Chi Minh City, Hanoi, Shanghai, Beijing and Tianjin, were then inputted into a CBR-DSS.

Chapter 8 displays the collation of data, stratified in terms of firms and cities, and analyzes them using Statistical Analysis and Content Analysis. The purpose of the analyses is to identify important factors, their correlations and co-occurrences with one another, pertaining to the research's central theme of flight-time and its influences on organization designs of Singaporean A/E firms when they venture into regional overseas markets.

Chapter 9 presents the background information of the A/E firms and cities involved in the case studies. The characteristics, motivations, competitive strengths, choice of markets of firms, and the difficulties and risks, prerequisites and critical success factors of the firms' ventures into overseas markets are discussed.

Chapter 10 discusses the synthesis of the study's themes. It was found that flight-time (as a proxy for geographical distance) alters the environment and affects an A/E firm's access to strategic home-based location-specific resources. Therefore, the A/E firm has to internalize these distance-rooted implications with business strategies and organization designs.

Chapter 11 validates to authenticate the CBR-DSS. The CBR-DSS was engineered based on inputs from the study's content analysis, and then attested by four senior industry practitioners. The CBR-DSS was ascertained to be a useful checklist and toolkit for an internationalizing A/E firm, to obtain preliminary guidance, advices and recommendations on business strategies and organization designs.

Chapter 12 discusses the conclusions and summarizes the book. The competitiveness of Singapore's A/E firms was evaluated using Strength, Weakness, Opportunities and Threats (SWOT) analysis; strategies adopted by A/E firms in different stages were shared; the internationalization efforts of private and government-linked A/E firms were compared; and the implications of flight-time on discontinuities in environment, access to home-based resources, perception of risks, decisions on business strategies and organization designs were explicated. The chapter also suggests how the study contributes to existing knowledge, and recommends areas for future research.

References

Allen TJ (1977) Managing the flow of technology. MIT Press, Cambridge, MA
Asad L, Lee PO (2008) Introduction. In: Asad L, Lee PO (eds) Regional outlook – Southeast Asia 2007–2008. Institute of Southeast Asian Studies, Singapore
Backman M, Butler C (2004) Big in Asia – 25 strategies for business success. Palgrave Macmillan, New York
Barlett CA, Ghoshal S (1998) Managing across borders: the transnational solution, 2nd edn. Harvard Business School Press, Boston
Blomstermo A, Sharma DD (2003) Learning in the internationalization process of firms. Edward Elgar, Cheltenham
Cairncross F (1997) The death of distance. Harvard Business School Press, Boston

References

Dunning JH (1988) The eclectic paradigm of international production: a restatement and some possible extensions. J Int Bus Stud 19(1):1–31

Dunning JH (2000) The eclectic paradigm as an envelope for economic and business theories of MNE activity. Int Bus Rev 9:163–190

Friedman T (2005) The world is flat. Straus and Giroux, New York

Ghemawat P (2001) Distance still matters: the hard reality of global expansion. Harv Bus Rev 79:137–147

Giles L (1910) The art of war by Sun Tzu. El Paso Norte

Handfield RB, Nichols EL Jr (2002) Supply chain redesign – transforming supply chains into integrated value systems. Prentice Hall, Upper Saddle River

Lim L (2005) Asia experiences new era of renaissance – keynote speech by Lee Kuan Yew at the Official Opening of the Lee Kuan Yew School of Public Policy and conference on managing globalization: lessons from China and India. The Straits Times. 5 April 2005

Ling YY, Ibbs CW, Cuervo JC (2005) Entry and business strategies used by international architectural, engineering and construction firms in China. Constr Manag Econ 23(3):509–520

Lojeski KS (2007) The collapsing corporation and the rise of virtual distance: the challenges of driving innovation in a world without leaders. In Conference on managing virtual distance, Anaheim, CA, 14–16 Nov 2007

Lojeski KS, Reilly RR (2007) Multitasking and innovation in virtual teams. In: Proceedings from the 40th annual Hawaii international conference on system sciences. Howe School of Technology Management. IEEE Computer Society, Hoboken

Markides C (1999) All the right moves: a guide to crafting breakthrough strategy. Harvard Business School Press, Boston

Ministry of Trade and Industry, Singapore (1986) Economic review committee report

Ofori G et al (2006) Strategies for penetrating engineering and construction markets in South-east and East Asia. Final report on research project RP296 000-012-112, Department of Building, National University of Singapore, Singapore

Ohmae K (1999) The borderless world: power and strategy in the interlinked economy (Revised edition). Collins, London

Phukan PJ (2003) Why project managers need lessons on distance management. Business Publications Division of the Indian Express Group of Newspapers, Mumbai. http://www.expressitpeople.com/20030728/cover.shtml. Accessed Feb 2007

Porter ME (1990) The competitive advantage of nations. Free Press, New York

Root FR (1998) Entry strategies for international markets (Revised edition). Jossey- Bass, San Francisco

Chapter 2
Flight-Time, Geographical Distance and Related Issues

2.1 Introduction

This chapter discusses the paradox of the world-flattening effects of globalization and the perpetual influences of geography. It is postulated in this chapter that flight-time can act as a proxy for geographical distance, and that flight-time is a causal factor for other facets of distance, namely cultural distance, administrative distance, geographical distance, gravitational distance, topological distance, economical distance, technological distance, socio-demographic distance, relational or affinity distance, and organizational distance. Organizational distance is further explained by changes, spillages, psychic distance, networks, communications, net cost-benefits, control and friction.

2.2 The Associated Attributes of Distance

Distance can be the causal factor for many other elements (Lojeski and Reilly 2007). Lojeski and Reilly (2007) categorized geographical distance, temporal distance and organizational distance under physical distances. Face-to-face interaction, technical skills and support, and team size were classified under operational distances. Lastly, interdependence distance, cultural distance, relationship distance and multi-tasking were considered under affinity distances. If these aspects of distances are not managed properly, the team might become dysfunctional and exhibit symptoms such as an unwillingness to collaborate, a lack of connection to the common mission, too much time spent managing the team rather than getting work done et cetera.

Ghemawat (2001) summed up the barriers created by distance with the CAGE framework, acronym for Culture distance, Administrative or political distance, Geographical distance and Economic distance. Thus, the CAGE looks into religious and ethnic make-up, social norms, languages, colonial links, trade arrangements, physical distance between markets, size of market, access, internal topography, transportation and communication infrastructures and economic disparities between the markets and so on. When an A/E firm venture into an overseas market, it could be hampered by a different language, unfamiliarity of building codes and regulations, access to home-based resources, and difficulty in finding suitable human resources. Ghemawat (2001) used the CAGE framework to describe how companies routinely overestimate the attractiveness of foreign markets while ignoring the costs and risks of doing business in a new market. Ghemawat (2001) also propounded how dramatically an explicit consideration of distance can change a company's outlook of its strategic options.

2.3 Flight-Time and Distance

The amount of flight-time or flight-distance could be the causal factor for variation of a spectrum of factors, such as climate, time-zone, bodily adjustments, cultural distance, administrative distance, geographical distance, economical distance, technological distance, socio-demographical distance, relational distance and organizational distance. Table 2.1 shows how either virtual communication, commuting between cities or the organization structure of a transnational firm could be affected by flight-time.

2.3.1 Time

Flight-time does not equate to trip-time. Other than normal checking in-and-out procedures and waiting, a person on a social or business travel may also be concerned about transportation time to- and-fro from airports, transfer-to-transit-time if the location is not a direct destination and so on. Therefore, a journey to an outlying location may consume more time because of the need to transfer-to-transit or/and a longer commuting-time from the arrival to the outlying location. For instance, Singapore's Prime Minister Lee Hsien Loong (2009) has encouraged Singaporean firms to seek outlying or second-tier provinces like Ningbo, of Zhejiang Province, China. However, the Singapore Airlines has no direct nor connecting flights to Ningbo. To get to Ningbo from Singapore, one could choose to get to Xiamen or Beijing, and then take a connecting flight from either Xiamen or Beijing to fly to Ningbo. A trip to Shanghai from Singapore which is a location that is geographically further away, takes only 5 h. If we interpolate, a flight from Singapore to Ningbo should take slightly less than 5 h. Yet, as Ningbo is not a first-tiered city of China, most national airliners do not fly direct to the city and domestic transit flights are needed to reach the city. A layover and transit flight can be very time-consuming, shown in the flight schedules below:

Singapore to Xiamen (4:05) + Layover (6:00) + Xiamen to Ningbo (1:15) = 11:20 via Air China

2.3 Flight-Time and Distance 15

Table 2.1 Impact of flight-time on communication, the employee and the firm

Nature of interaction	Action	Barriers
Communication	In general	Costs of communication infrastructure
	Communication between expatriate and local	Language, culture, work ethics
	Inter-city communication	Time-differences and time-lags
		Unfamiliarity
		Reduction in frequency of interaction
		Loss of information
		Misunderstanding
		Communication and Coordination
	Communication with clients abroad	Lack of face-to-face contacts
		Deceit
Employee	Commuting	Jet-lag
	Temporary posting (shuttling frequently)	Sense of belonging
	Permanent posting	Reluctance to be away from home-city
Firm	Transportation	Travelling and freight costs
	Resources	Sap of resources
	Due diligence	Understanding of the environment
	Establishment	Networks
	Management	Control

Singapore to Beijing (6:15) + Layover (3:15) + Beijing to Ningbo (2:05) = 11:35 via Air China

Note: These two flight-schedules are considered the shortest in terms of time-duration.

2.3.2 Flight Routes

Sometimes, the flight may not take the most direct route. There have been many cases of airspace ban. For example, the European Union warned a list of nearly 4,000 airlines that it says should reduce their impact on the environment from 2012 or face a ban from European airports (Global Times 2009).

Direction of flight is incidental with jet-streams. Jet-streams are fast flowing, narrow air currents found at the tropopause, the transition between the troposphere where temperature decreases with height, and the stratosphere where temperature increases with height. Routes may also change as planes save energy and fuel consumption when they fly with a jet-stream. Conversely, airplanes would encounter significant air resistance if they had to fly against it. Flight-time can also be affected by head or tail-winds and air-traffic control.

Table 2.2 Geodesics of cities and distances of cities away from Singapore

City	Latitude Degree minutes	Longitude Degree minutes	Distance away from Singapore (km)	Flight-time (hours: minutes)
Singapore	1′14N	103′55E	–	–
Kuala Lumpur	3′8N	101′42E	307	0:55
Penang	5′4N	100′23E	598	1:25
HCM City	10′46N	106′43E	1,085	2:05
Hanoi	21′03N	105′85	2,197	2:30
Shanghai	31′10N	121′28E	3,769	5:05
Beijing	39′55N	116′25E	4,457	6:00
Tianjin	39′14N	117′18E	4,411	9:15 (with transit)

Geographical distance refers to the distance between two geographic points. There are essentially three abstract ways of calculating geographical distance between two locations on earth, depending on whether the surface is flat, spherical or ellipsoidal. The distance between two points in Euclidean space is the length of a straight line from one point to the other. In non-Euclidean geometry, straight lines are replaced with Geodesics. The great-circle distance or orthodromic distance is the shortest distance between any two points on the surface of a sphere measured along a path on the surface of the sphere. However, the earth is ellipsoidal. The distance of two locations on the surface of earth can be computed using Vincenty algorithm and the WGS84 ellipsoid model of the earth, which is a GPS "as the crow flies" technology. Table 2.2 shows the distance away from Singapore and the geodesic coordinates of the various cities that the study is trying to examine. The latitudes give the location of a place on earth north or south of the equator, whereas the longitudes give the location in terms of east or west of the Prime Meridian. To encapsulate, climate changes with latitude and time-zones changes with longitudes.

2.3.3 The Aircraft's Speed

There are five major manufacturers of civil transport aircraft, namely Airbus from France, Boeing from the United States of America (USA), Bombardier from Canada, Embraer from Brazil and Tupolev from Russia. The Singapore Airlines' (SIA) fleets consist mainly of wide-body aircrafts from these five aircraft families: Airbus A380, Airbus A340, Airbus A330, Boeing 747 and Boeing 777. These aircrafts have different traits in terms of its engine, seat configuration, flying range, seating and cargo capacity, maximum cruise speed and so on. As such, they cater to different hauls and routes. For instance, an Airbus A380-841 has a Rolls Royce Trent 970 engine and a 471 seat capacity, cruises at a speed of 0.85 Mach, and is used by SIA to reach destinations like London, Paris, Sydney and Tokyo. On the other hand, the Boeing 777-312 has a Rolls Royce Trent 892 engine and a 332 seat capacity, cruises at 0.84 Mach, and reaches places like Bangalore, Bangkok, Dubai and Shanghai.

2.3.4 *Climate*

Climate encompasses the temperature, humidity, atmospheric pressure, winds, rainfall, atmospheric particle count and numerous other meteorological elements in a given region over long periods of time. It is affected by its latitude, altitude, terrain, ocean currents, as well as the presence of persistent snow or ice. The Köppen classification includes climate regimes such as rainforest, monsoon, tropical savanna, humid subtropical, humid continental, oceanic climate, Mediterranean climate, steppe, subarctic climate, polar ice cap and desert.

2.3.5 *Time-Zones*

A time-zone is defined as a region of the earth that has uniform standard time, usually referred to as local time. Conventionally, time-zones compute their local time as an offset from Coordinated Universal Time (UTC). Time-zones are divided into standard and daylight saving. Daylight saving time-zones or summer time-zones include an offset for daylight saving time. Standard time-zones are defined by geometrically subdividing the earth's spheroid into 24 wedged-shaped sections called lunes, bordered by meridians each 15° of longitude apart. Therefore, local time of neighbouring zones would differ by 1 h. However, it must be noted that political boundaries, geographical practicalities, and convenience of inhabitants can result in irregularly-shaped zones. Time-zones and the international date-line can confuse travelers and work matters that traverse between different cities. Communication and coordination can be made complicated too.

2.3.6 *Jet-Lag and Circadian Rhythm*

Jet-lags occur due to rapid long-distance transmeridian (east-west or west-east) travel. When traveling across time zones, the body clock will be out of synchronization with the destination time, as the body experiences incoherence with the daylight and darkness contrary to the bodily, circadian rhythms it has grown accustomed. The circadian rhythm dictates the times for sleeping, waking, eating, hormone regulation and body temperature variations. Jet-lag is a physiological condition as a consequence of a disruption to normal circadian rhythms of the traveler, resulting in symptoms like loss of appetite, nausea, digestive problems, headaches, sinus irritation, fatigue, irregular sleep patterns, insomnia, disorientation, grogginess, irritability and mild depression. The aftermath of a long-distance transmeridian journey can cause jet-lags lasting several days, and recovery rate from this approximates at 1 day per eastward time zone or 1 day per 1.5 westward time zones. Therefore, a working trip which requires long-distance fly-commuting would have a negative impact on productivity and health, and should be considered by the firm when dispatching its staff abroad.

2.4 Globalization and Geography

Globalization is the term used to describe how people around the world are unified into a single society via economic, political and socio-cultural integration. It was thought that such integration would be brought about by trade, foreign direct investments, capital flows, migration and the spread of technology, resulting in the transnational diffusion of ideas, language and culture.

In the past few decades, the elimination of tariffs, creation of free trade zones, reduced transportation costs due to improved transportation technologies and containerization of goods, subsidies for global corporations, reduction of capital controls, harmonization and supranational recognition of intellectual property, and digitization have enabled geographic dispersion and have flattened the earth (Friedman 2005).

It seems that technology, communication and market advances have fundamentally changed the global perspectives of time, distance and spatial boundaries. The "death of distance" was therefore espoused by Frances Cairncross (1997), who was then a senior editor at the Economist. However, Kitchin and Dodge (2002) thought that "boundary-less" is an illusion. Instead, Olson and Olson (2000) and Kitchin and Dodge (2002) lauded the triumph of geography and suggested that the submission on the fracturing of geographies due to telecommunications is misleading and overstated, and that the proposition of the death of distance is greatly exaggerated.

Distance, with its associated attributes such as culture, time-zones, geography and language affects how humans interact with one another. Consequently, it is immortal in several essential respects (Olson and Olson 2000). Distance is enduring in the business world despite the proliferation of information and communication technology because communication is the life-blood of any organization; and that regardless of how globalization and technology have bridged the tyranny of distance, there still remain facets of organization communication that could be impaired and distorted by distance (Allen 1977).

2.5 Manifestations of Distance

Distance is not uni-dimensional as there can be many facets of distance. For example, culturally and economically similar countries such as New Zealand and Norway may lie far away in geographical terms (Reid and OhUllachain 1997). Successive innovations in information and transport technology may have made the world seemingly a smaller place (Friedman 2005). However, Olson and Olson (2000) pointed out that like before, transport or distance continues to shape society and space in myriad practical ways. Likewise, similarity in cultural and economic distance reduces uncertainty and allows for easier management of a subsidiary because closeness may alleviate problems in conducting actual business operations as it is easier to monitor, coordinate and market activities of particular importance in the early stages of internationalization when firms are often small and face severe

2.5 Manifestations of Distance

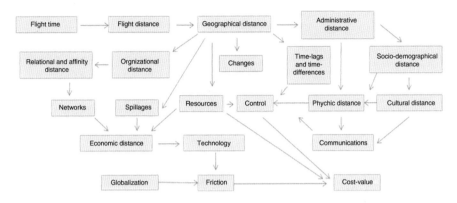

Fig. 2.1 Manifestations of distance

resource constraints (Davidson 1983). The "tentacles" of Distance (refer to Fig. 2.1) provide a lucid illustration of the different forms of distances which include:

(i) Cultural distance;
(ii) Administrative distance;
(iii) Geographical distance;
(iv) Economic distance;
(v) Technological distance;
(vi) Socio-demographical distance;
(vii) Relationship and affinity distance; and
(viii) Organizational distance – changes, spillages, time-lags and time differences, psychic distance, networks, communications, net cost-benefit, and control + friction with globalization, improvement of communications and transportation technologies.

2.5.1 Cultural Distance

Thomas Friedman's *Longitudes and Attitudes* (2001) depicts how civilizations in different parts of the world have different social norms. They think, behave and act differently. Differences between countries or cities of different societal value systems increase the cost of entry for international business, decrease operational benefits, and hamper the firm's ability to transfer core competencies to foreign markets (Barlett and Ghoshal 1998). This results in an additional burden for multinational companies to adapt to local cultural values that can be transmitted through the difference in political and economical systems, religion, education and languages et cetera (Tihanyi et al. 2005).

Transnational firms tend to find it easier to transfer their technologies, human resource practices, and operating procedures and to achieve internal consistency through standardization when the cultural values between the host and home

Table 2.3 Cultural indexes between selected countries

Countries	Singapore	Malaysia	Vietnam	Hong Kong	China	Japan	UK	US
Singapore	–	1.7	1.9	1.22	2.66	4.81	3.33	3.47
Malaysia	1.70	–	0.23	4.49	6.27	6.12	4.07	3.98
Vietnam	1.9	0.23	–	4.39	6.29	5.17	2.90	2.73
Hong Kong	1.22	4.49	4.39	–	0.36	2.67	4.38	4.21
China	2.66	6.27	6.29	0.36	–	2.68	6.54	6.19
Japan	4.81	6.12	5.17	2.67	2.68	–	3.95	3.40
UK	3.33	4.07	2.90	4.38	6.54	3.95	–	0.08
US	3.47	3.98	2.73	4.21	6.19	3.40	0.08	–

Edited from Chen (2005)

Table 2.4 Hofstede's cultural index score

Country	Power distance	Uncertainty avoidance	Individualism	Masculinity	Long-term orientation
Singapore	74.0	8.0	20.0	48.0	48.0
Malaysia	104.0	36.0	26.0	50.0	–
Vietnam	89.0	48.3	37.5	43.8	–
Hong Kong	68.0	29.0	25.0	57.0	96.0
China	80.0	40.0	20.0	66.0	118.0
Japan	54.0	92.0	46.0	95.0	80.0
UK	35.0	35.0	89.0	66.0	25.0
US	40.0	46.0	91.0	62.0	29.0
Sign of relationship	No	No	No	Yes	Yes

Implication: Only certain dimensions of cultural distance are affected by flight-distance

countries are more alike than different (Earley and Ang 2003). Therefore, ceteris paribus, firms would prefer entering into markets which have less cultural differences from their home-city. Cultural distance affects a firm's entry mode choice, international diversification and performance (Tihanyi et al. 2005). Table 2.3 shows the aggregates of cultural distances between countries, and reveals that cultural similarities between two countries are generally stronger when (i) the countries are geographically nearer to each other; (ii) the countries are administratively more similar; and (iii) the countries have more historical, relational and language affinities (or similarities). In Table 2.4, Chen (2005) applied Hofstede's (1980) Framework for assessing culture containing these five dimensions: Power Distance, Individualism versus Collectivism, Masculinity versus Femininity, Uncertainty Avoidance and Short versus Long term Orientation. There are also other ways to measure culture, for example, Trompenaars and Hampden-Turner (1998) listed Universalism versus Particularism, Individualsim versus Collectivism, Neutral versus Emotional, Specific versus Diffuse, Achievement versus Ascription, Sequential versus Synchronic and Internal versus External Control. However, the premise is all the same – people and organizations from countries with greater cultural differences think, behave and work less similarly.

2.5 Manifestations of Distance

Table 2.5 Communism around the world

Communist states	Elected communist party	Formerly communist
PR China, North Korea, Laos, Vietnam, Cuba	Cyprus, India, Moldova, Nepal	Afghanistan, Albania, Angola, Benin, Bulgaria, Cambodia, Congo, Czechoslovakia, East Germany, Ethiopia, Mongolia, Mozambique, Poland, Romania, Somalia, South Yemen, Soviet Union, Yugoslavia

2.5.2 Administrative/Attributional Distance

Geopolitics and local politics can be affected by attributional distance. Attributional distance is the measure of how distant or how near two countries are, owing to their political or cultural characteristics (Henrikson 2002). Different forms of government have different attributes in terms of democracy, state-society relationship, identity and ethnic policies, social movements, institutional make-up, political economies and foreign policies. Table 2.5 shows a list of communist countries, or countries with communist parties, or formerly communist countries before their change of regimes. It is apparent that the spread of communism was and is still, concentrated in a few parts of the world. Before the collapse of the Soviet Union and Eastern Europe's communist bloc, communism was wide-spread, from North Korea, to China, Cambodia, Mongolia, Afghanistan, Czechoslovakia, Romania, Poland, East Germany, Congo, Angola, Cuba and so on, so much so that its adversary, USA, the leader of nations who champions democracy and capitalism, had to apply the "containment strategy" to limit and prevent Soviet Union's expansionism.

"Global politics and local politics, though interlinked today by processes of globalization, remain separated by the phenomenon of distance. Sheer physical distance, with its associated geography, assumes mainly a causal importance (Henrikson 2002, p. 437)." Dwight Eisenhower once famously explained on the "falling domino" principle, saying "You have a row of dominoes set up, you knock over the first one, and what will happen to the last one is the certainty that it will go over very quickly. So you could have a beginning of a disintegration that would have the most profound influences." (Eisenhower 1954, p. 382). The Domino Effect set off by the bankruptcy of Soviet Union resulted in a chain reaction, causing its neighboring or nearby allies to fail as well, and this occurred in a linear sequence, as communist countries fell one by one, leaving China, North Korea, Laos, Vietnam and Cuba the only country-level survivors of the communism's ideology. The above development suggests that the administrative characteristics of a country may be influenced by its neighboring countries. Different forms of governments encourage different levels of capitalism, laissez-faire and state intervention. Countries therefore, vary in the level of openness to foreign direct investments – there are differences in foreign ownership restrictions, investment promotion, pre-establishment procedures, access to land, currency convertibility, expropriation and international arbitration. The ease of

Table 2.6 Country openness

Country	Government type	Country openness	Ease of doing business (ranking)	Investment risk ratings (2002)	Distance away from Singapore (km)
Singapore	Parliamentary republic	89.98	1	84.8	–
Malaysia	Constitutional monarchy	76.06	20	55.3	KL – 307
Vietnam	Communist state	38.07	83	29.3	HCM City – 1,085
Hong Kong	Limited democracy	83.95	4	66.5	HK – 2,588
China	Communist state	31.65	92	57.6	Shanghai – 3,796 Beijing – 4,457

conducting a business can also vary – there are differences in the ease of starting a business, dealing with licenses, employing workers, registering properties, getting credit, protecting investors, paying taxes, trading across borders, enforcing contracts and closing of business. The host government plays a big role in creating an ambient environment for foreign direct investments. It is therefore no mere coincidence that Singapore, which is well-known to have an efficient and capable government, has a very high investment risk rating, whereas Vietnam, with a reputation of haphazard foreign-investment policies, has a much lower investment risk rating, as seen in Table 2.6.

The form of administration or government also affects the country's legal system. Generally, there are a few types of legal systems in the world today, namely: civil law, common law, customary law and religious law. Table 2.7 shows the various differences between these legal systems. For example, Singapore and Malaysia apply Common law; Vietnam draws on a mix of Civil law and Communist legal law; while China uses Communist legal law. An international firm might prefer to draw up a contract based on international law or in a law that it is familiar and comfortable with, or call for international arbitration when a conflict cannot be resolved.

2.5.3 *Geographical Distance, Gravitational Distance and Topological Distance*

Distance can be measured in its actual or functional sense. For example, actual geographical distance can be operationalized as the air distance in 1,000 km; while functional distance can take the form of driving or flight-time (Reid and OhUllachain 1997). It should be noted that distance need not always be a straightforward measurement of separation between two points. Distance can take on new

2.5 Manifestations of Distance

Table 2.7 Major legal systems of the world (Neubauer and Meinhold 2007)

	Common law	Civil law	Socialist law	Islamic law
Source of law	Judicial interpretation and legislation	Code	Code	Sacred religious document
Lawyers	Control courtroom	Judges dominate trials	Judges dominate trials	Secondary role
Judges' qualifications	Former practicing lawyers	Career bureaucrats	Career bureaucrats, Party members	Religious as well as legal training
Degree of judicial independence	High	Insulated from regime	Very limited	Very limited
Juries	Often available at trial level	Mixed tribunals in serious cases	Often used at lowest level	Not allowed
Policy-making role	Courts share in balancing power	Courts have equal but separate powers	Courts are subordinate to the legislature	Courts and other government branches are subordinates to the Shari'a
Examples	Australia, England, USA, Canada, India, Singapore	France, Germany, Mexico, Japan	Russia	Saudi Arabia

dimensions, especially when there are barriers or a lack of facilitation. An instance would be how a taxi-driver in Manhattan, New York, would have to drive his car around the surrounding blocks instead of going straight from point A to point B. Similarly, a business traveler might have to go to his local airport, take a plane from country A to country B, and then board a shuttle-bus from airport B to get to his destination in the city to meet his business partner. Transportation infrastructure like airports, sea-ports, water-channels and highways are important to bridge distances between places or to improve the accessibility of a location, and has been the emphasis of governments in order to attract more FDIs.

The desire of a market is dependent on its market size and geographical proximity (Johanson and Vahlne 1977). A transnational firm's internationalization often follows a proximate to distant sequential pattern. This shows that distance affects the relationship of two entities. The interaction between two locations can decrease because of intervening opportunities between them. Indeed, the First Law of Geography suggests that, "Everything is related to everything else, but near things are more related than distant things" (Tobler 1970, p. 234). Spatial interaction between a pair of locations decreases when the intervening distance increases. Spatial interaction, the realized movement of people, freight or information between two places underlines that the costs incurred by a spatial interaction is less significant than the benefits gained from it. There are basically three types of interaction model – the gravity model, the potential model and the retail model. The gravity model measures the interaction between any possible pair of location. The potential model measures interaction between one location and every other location. The retail model measures the boundary of the market areas between two locations competing over the same market. The Gravity model follows Issac Newton's Law of Gravity, which states that: "Any two bodies attract one another with a force that is proportional to the product of their masses and inversely proportional to the square of the distance between them". Therefore, the spatial interaction between two locations is dependent on their market sizes and intervening distance.

Topological distance suggests how two countries may seem more remote from one another if there are other countries or seas located in between them. The configuration of the number and arrangement of these intervening country-spaces is the key variable. For example, Switzerland is like the melting pot of the many cultures of Europe because it is located centrally in the continent; ancient China was much sheltered from the influence of other civilizations because of its natural barriers of mountainous plateaus in the west and seas in the east; Japan was able to isolate itself to stay as a closed economy and country because of its Sakoku (locked) policy and the distortion factor of oceans or seas (Beckmann 1999) until the arrival of Commodore Matthew Perry to force the opening of Japan to foreign traders; landlocked countries like Austria, Serbia, Afghanistan, and Bhutan or doubly-land-locked countries like Liechtenstein and Uzbekistan may have disadvantages in transportation and trade; while enclaves like San Marino in Italy and the Vatican City in Rome may become reliant on the countries surrounding them et cetera. Demand is more likely to be similar in geographically proximate markets (Burenstam-Linder 1961; Luostarinen 1979).

2.5.4 Economic Distance

Economic distance refers to the disparities between countries in terms of living standards and development of infrastructure (Reid and OhUllachain 1997). Geography and wealth has long been perceived as correlated attributes of nations. In fact, it has been observed that nations furthest away from the equator are the wealthiest, e.g. Canada and Nordic countries (Low 1990). Even within wealthy continents and large countries, wealth increases with distance away from the equator, e.g. southern Europe and south USA are relatively poorer than their northern neighbours. This global North–south divide is called the Brandt line (Mackinnon and Cumbers 2007). The CID also found that only three tropical economies were high-income – Hong Kong, Taiwan and Singapore while all countries within temperate zones have either middle or high income industries with few exceptions.

Strictly put, economic distance is defined as the distance a commodity may travel before transportation costs exceed the value of the freight. Hence, countries try to improve their road, railways, in-land waterways in order to reduce their economic distance to transnational firms or potential investors.

From NASA's satellite photographs on earth, the concentration of the night-lights appears to be around North America, Western Europe and East Asia. Upon closer scrutiny on the maps of Europe and USA, there appears to be brighter and bigger nodal points at the whereabouts of London, Paris, Milan in Europe, and New York-Boston in the eastern coast, Chicago in the middle and San Francisco-Los Angeles in the western coast of USA. Night-lights are useful tools that transcend national borders to indicate economic development and the presence of commercial activities. From the images, we can be informed of economic and wealth-disparities around the world. The shiniest nodes represent the cities that possess the highest concentration of commercial activities while the less bright or dark patches reveal relative inactivity. Affluence inequality can have a stratification effect – people who are already well-to-do can benefit from wealth-condensation to get richer, but for the less privileged, opportunities are limited and they find it hard to elevate themselves out of poverty. International inequality is the economic differences between countries. Advanced developed countries enjoying high Gross Domestic Product in Purchasing Power Parity (GDP-PPP) while severely underdeveloped countries only have meager Gross Domestic Product in PPP (GDP-PPP). The G-20 also have a disproportionately 85% of the world's Gross National Product (GNP), consistent with the Pareto 20-80 rule. Wealth is geographically determined and wealth of a country has spillover effects on its neighboring countries.

Let's take Canada as an example. Canada's partners of free-trade agreements are mostly countries in close geographical proximity to itself. Having a free-trade agreement allows easier imports and exports, or other transfers between the countries in such a concord, and this relationship may bridge the two countries in terms of economic development and progress.

Table 2.8 highlights several countries and their top exporting markets. Similarly, Germany's 15 largest export markets are namely France, USA, UK, Italy, Netherlands, Belgium, Austria, Switzerland, Spain, Poland, Sweden, Czech Republic,

Table 2.8 Top exporting markets

Top exporting markets					
Singapore	Malaysia	Vietnam	China	Japan	USA
Malaysia	USA	USA	USA	USA	Canada
USA	Singapore	Japan	HK	China	China
China	Japan	Australia	Japan	South Korea	Mexico
Indonesia	China	China	South Korea	Taiwan	Japan
Japan	Thailand	Singapore	Germany	Hong Kong	Germany

Source: CIA website

Japan, Denmark and Hungary. These include all eight German neighbours, the majority of which are rather small countries. It shows that countries tend to export to countries in closer geographical proximity to themselves, barring the exception of strong economic power-houses like USA and Japan. It definitely seems that countries enjoy more intimate economic ties with countries nearby.

2.5.5 Technological Distance

Moore's law has suggested that computer power roughly double every 18 months. This has smoothed the progress of digitization and has radically lowered the cost and raising the speed of moving data and information, dramatically favouring geographic dispersion (Barkema et al. 2002). However, there is still much technological disparity between developed and developing countries.

Technological distance between two countries is the difference in their technical, industrial, scientific and managerial knowledge. According to the Economic Intelligence Unit (EIU 2008), the top ten technologically advanced countries in terms of e-readiness are namely Denmark, USA, Sweden, Hong Kong, Switzerland, Singapore, UK, Netherlands, Australia and Finland. Japan is at 22nd, Malaysia is 36th, China is 56th, and Vietnam is 65th; whereas in applied technology, USA, Japan and Germany would be the leaders.

Akamatsu's (1962) Flying Geese Paradigm seek to explain the spread of growth in the East-Asia-ASEAN region and the spillover effects of technology transfer, the process of sharing of skills and knowledge of Japan's applied technology to intermediately advanced countries like Korea, Singapore, Taiwan and Hong Kong, which in turn transferred these technologies to third-tiered countries like Indonesia, Malaysia, Thailand and Philippines. Similarly, Canada and Mexico benefitted from USA while Belgium and Switzerland benefitted from Germany. These suggest that learning, knowledge and innovation spillover are influenced by geographical distance and technological distance (Asheim and Gertler 2005).

2.5.6 Socio-demographical Distance

Demography measures a population's size, structure and distribution. Demography includes the study of age, gender, marital status, education and literacy, language, employment status and occupation, nationality or citizenship, religion, ethnic, et cetera. According to Huntington (1996), several cultures are inherently disagreeable while others are agreeable with each other. For example, the Sinic civilization is close to Japanese civilization, but it is distant from Western civilization; and Western civilization is close to Japanese and Latin civilization, but it is distant from Sinic and Islamic civilization. As the first law of geography suggests, every country influences or has an effect on its adjacent countries. The Bogardus Social Distance Scale (Bogardus 1926), a psychological test to empirically measure people's willingness to interact with others from a specific group type, has also shown that people are more willing to intermingle, inter-relate, communicate and cooperate with those who are more socio-demographically similar to themselves.

2.5.7 Relational/Affinity Distance

Ravenstein's (1885) law of migration proposes that (i) every migration flow generates a counter migration; (ii) the majority of migrants move a short distance; (iii) migrants who move longer distance tend to choose big-city destinations; (iv) urban residents are less migratory than inhabitants of rural areas; and (v) families are less likely to make international moves than young adults. Migration could be due to push factors such as lack of opportunities as well as pull factors such as better opportunities, living conditions, education, security, et cetera.

History has recorded great migrations during the Roman Empire Period due to "barbarian invasions" and the Transatlantic Migration of poor Europeans to the Americas et cetera. There have also been many Diasporas since recorded history, such as the Jewish Diaspora during biblical times and Chinese Exodus which drove 50 million Chinese worldwide during its civil war in the 1950s, mainly to countries such as Thailand, Malaysia, Indonesia, Singapore, Philippines, Vietnam, Myanmar, USA and Canada. Singapore is a multi-racial and multi-religious country, with many immigrants from China, Arab Peninsula, Malaysia, Indonesia, India, et cetera, and thus inherits much relationship and affinity with these countries. Colonial ties can also pass down legacies in law, culture, traditions, et cetera. Many Commonwealth countries that used to be colonies of Great Britain stay influenced by England.

The theory of intervening opportunity suggests that "the number of persons going a given distance is directly proportional to the number of opportunities at that distance and inversely proportional to the number of intervening opportunities (Stouffer 1940, p. 846)." Zipf's (1946) Inverse distance law, on the other hand, suggests that movement or interaction across space is inversely proportional to distance. Nonetheless, both imply that people and firms tend to re-locate themselves to proximate places (Stouffer 1940).

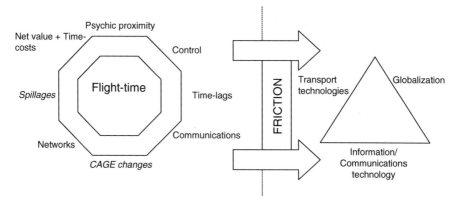

Fig. 2.2 Time-space compression, friction and fission effect of distance

2.5.8 Organizational Distance

Organizational distance includes changes, spillages, time-lags, psychic distance, networks, communications, net cost-benefit, control and friction between globalization, improvement of communications and transportation technologies. Out of these factors, changes and spillages are external factors while the others are internal factors. Figure 2.2 shows the influences and friction of distance on a firm and its organization design despite the time-space compression and bridging forces of information and communications technologies, transport technologies and globalization. The study therefore, seeks to investigate how flight-time affects these relationships, which will in turn influence the business strategies and organization designs of an internationalizing A/E firm.

2.5.8.1 Distance and Changes

Jared Diamond (1997)'s *Guns, Germs and Steel* proposed that Eurasian civilizations' hegemony is not due to intellectual, moral or inherent genetic superiority, but rather due to environmental differences and endowments, which were able to provide a positive feedback loop. Masters and McMillan (2001) agreed that there is better soil fertility and more resources in temperate regions, and propounded that people are more vigorous in cold climate, thus creating a positive and reinforcing loop that enhances the development of the colder regions.

Flight-time also dealt internationalising firms with Cultural, Administrative, Geographical, Economical, Technological, Socio-demographic and Relational changes. Some examples are the differences in workdays and work-hours, time zones, and climatic changes that would necessitate assimilation training on the part of the firms. The functions of buildings – to provide shelter from the weather and a comfortable living and working environment are essentially the same worldwide, but there are very significant differences in the requirements for buildings in the hot and temperate climates (Seeley 1995). For instance, designs for thermal capacity (expansion and contraction) and insulation may have to differ for energy savings and comfort while materials used may have to differ due to agents like moisture and solar radiation.

2.5.8.2 Distance and Spill-Over

State failure and the resulting chaos of a neighbouring country can underline a country's stability as well, as refugees, armed conflicts, and diseases spill across borders (Bremmer 2006). Distance also affects migration, inter-city movement, bilateral trade, human interaction et cetera (Rosenberg 2004). Neighbouring countries or cities influence one another's macro, industry and task environment in the socio-cultural, political, economical, and technological spheres. Countries or cities, which are geographically positioned near to each other, interact and assimilate to each other's influence more than countries that are spaced apart. An example of an economical spill-over would be the Sijori Growth Triangle partnership arrangement between Singapore, Johor of Malaysia and Riau Islands of Indonesia. Conley and Ligon (2002) also highlighted that the rates of long-run economic growth are not independent across countries, and found that there are often significant spill-over that account for the spatial covariance in growth rates of neighbouring countries.

2.5.8.3 Distance and Time Lag

In this Digital Age, time is becoming more important (Lojeski and Reilly 2007). Evans and Harrigan (2003) emphasized that timely delivery may be more critical in some industries than others. For instance, instantaneous communication would be paramount for financial services like foreign exchange trading but less so for others. Tolerance of time lags may vary for different industries as illustrated in Fig. 2.3. Generally, services are non-storable, non-transferrable and non-standard, and involve more complicated contacts, negotiations, and monitoring. Therefore, the consideration of having an overseas office, which may affect the time-lag of communications between the clients, work-partners and the organization, is important for transnational firms.

2.5.8.4 Distance and Psychic Distance

Psychic distance may often be misunderstood as cultural distance but it is actually a measure of understanding and ability to adapt to a host environment. For example, China, Taiwan, Hong Kong, Japan, Korea, Vietnam and Singapore could be categorized in the Sinic civilization because of their common Confucianism values,

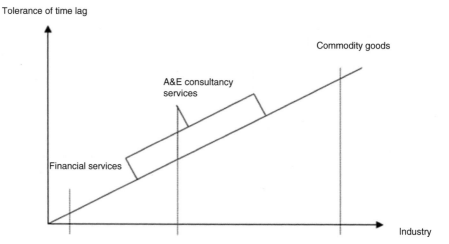

Fig. 2.3 Time-lag tolerance of different industries

traits and virtues (Huntington 1996). A firm or its employees should be able to adapt faster and better when venturing or re-locating into a new environment with prior understanding or trained adaptability. Cultural distance is different from psychic distance because there can be psychic distance asymmetries between two countries (Ellis 2008). An USA firm in Japan and a Japanese firm in USA would have similar cultural distances, but Japanese firms may have less psychic distance of the American market than Americans have of the Japanese market. American and European investors used to hold a mono-centric mind-set, assuming that what is being accepted in their home markets would be equally accepted in Asia to their own detriment. Now, these firms have acknowledged that every market has its own peculiarities and preferences, and have customized their solutions for each market.

2.5.8.5 Distance and Networks

The small world experiment conducted by Stanley Milgram (1967) suggested that human society is a small world and that people in USA seemed to be interconnected by three friendship links; while the "six degree of separation" suggests that the whole world could be interconnected by six friendship links. Social network portals like Friendster, MySpace and Facebook have become hugely popular because users are able to keep in touch with pals and also get to know one another's friends.

Networks are very important in business – an overseas office seeks to be connected and integrated with its home-office/ head-quarters and other branch-offices to share information and resources; a firm seeks business networks to get in touch with business opportunities. Singapore's Minister Mentor, Mr Lee Kuan Yew

2.5 Manifestations of Distance

once said in 1988, that East Asia share many characteristics derived from a common cultural base which is Chinese in origin (Barr 2000). This is why communities or cartels like the Singapore Chinese Chamber of Commerce and Industry have been formed, to link Singaporean Chinese up with fellow Chinese businessmen in the region who prefer to network and collaborate with Chinese counterparts that share common Sinic culture and values. Networks are probably more important in Asia than other parts of the world, and this can be exemplified by the prominences of Chaebols in Korea, Keiretsu in Japan, and "Guan-Xi" or "bamboo networks" in China. Like how distance between collaborators affects the efficiency of Just-in-time (JIT) techniques, e.g. co-manufacturing of automobiles and their parts by car manufacturer Toyota and its suppliers, distance affects a firm's networks, the fluidity and efficiency of its work processes, and how a firm can leverage on its partners' resources and strengths.

2.5.8.6 Distance and Communications

Brown and Duguid (2000) suggested that there is a social life of information. Information is best transferred or understood when there is spatial proximity and face-to-face interaction. In fact, it was proven statistically that there is a significant relationship between a country's physical location and language similarities and the structure of global communication networks – telecommunications, written or face-to-face, represented by telephone, mail, trade and transportation networks (Ro and Gu 1995).

Furthermore, Allen (1977) found that communications are adversely affected with increased distance. Collocated and synchronous interaction provides advantages like rapid feedback, multiple and flexible channels, personal and nuance information, shared context, informal time for bonding, co-reference, individual control, implicit cues and the spatiality of reference (Olson and Olson 2000). Olson and Olson (2000) also found that participants working face-to-face encounter less confusion and misunderstanding and feel less disoriented or without context. This is because communications can be distorted by noise, barriers and filters as they go through the process of idea generation and encoding, transmitting through the channels, receiving, decoding, understanding and response. Hence although people recognize the greater flexibility and access enabled by technology, they still prefer face-to-face interactions for most purposes as these new technologies have their limitations as well as the need for operational protocol. Being near instead of away from the point of demand also allows for the flexibility in communications which is vital to understand about the market, practise due diligence and implement market strategies strategically to appeal to the right clientele, get businesses, deliver the project and be sustainable in the market. It seems that codified knowledge has become increasingly global in organizational reach, while tacit knowledge remains local, relying on geographical proximity to foster communication and interaction between firms (Maskell and Malmberg 1999).

2.5.8.7 Distance, Costs and Benefits

Luostarinen (1979) and Ghemawat (2001) highlighted the importance of benefits, costs, and risks evaluation using frameworks that consider socio-cultural, administrative and political, geographical, physical and economical factors. An internationalising A/E firm would have to evaluate the benefits and costs of different entry modes, organization structure and communication, and rewarding systems in the target-market. Entry modes would in turn affect organization structures and systems. Hu and Chen (1993) suggested that there are three factors which may affect the transaction costs of services: (1) geographical distance; (2) difference in culture, business customs and economic systems; and (3) government policies and possible political risks. Setting up a wholly-owned subsidiary incurs higher costs and requires more commitment, though it also gives the firm a higher level of control than exporting.

Distance matters because telecommunication and commuting costs significantly depend upon distance, whereas geographical proximity provides greater convenience for communication and transportation that facilitates more business opportunities and promotes the convergence of cultural and business customs.

2.5.8.8 Distance and Control

Globally dispersed organizational processes require teams to make effective time pacing and synchronization (Barkema et al. 2002). However, this is made complicated by the work-days and work-hours of cities around the world that may be different. For example, Arab countries may have a Friday to Wednesday work-week; some European countries, like Germany, have a four and a half day work-week, from Monday to Friday noon; whereas most other countries have a Monday to Friday work-week. Some countries also stipulate maximum working hours. Countries and cities may also have contrasting normal working-hours – some from 8 to 6, some 9 to 5, or 9 to 6. Some have short lunch-breaks; others may be entitled to longer lunch-breaks plus morning and afternoon teas, or reading newspapers and chit-chatting before real-work. Some cultures may "force" employees to stay back at least by an hour after the official working-hours or to leave only after their superior has left; while some can leave on the dot or even before the end of the day. Countries and cities may have different public holidays. Some companies allow their employees to bring work home or work else-where without turning up for work at the office as long as they fulfil their responsibilities and complete their tasks. Different regions may have different time zones too. Furthermore, time zones may change with seasons, making coordination even more complicated. Distance away from a home-market may also bring about climatic changes. The northern and southern hemispheres have opposite climates during the year. It can be spring time in February, summer in May, autumn in September and winter in November in Europe and North America but the exact reverse in Australia and South America. The international manager would have to manage all these diversities and misfits (Drucker 1973).

Digitization might have revolutionized inter-city communications, but an organization that ventures overseas has to put the above-mentioned into consideration to decide on the appropriate level of control for the head-quarters to rein over the overseas office (Barkema et al. 2002). Firms would have to search for the fit between dominant strategic requirements of its business and the firm's dominant strategic capability to streamline itself away from the organizational quagmire (Barlett and Ghoshal 1998).

2.5.8.9 Friction

There would be friction due to distance incurred and friction due to the interaction between proximity and distance. Both Sun Tzu (sixth century BC) and von Clausewitz (1832) wrote much about how friction would affect warfare. Only practice and experience could enable the commander to make the right decisions for major and minor matters in the pulse-beat of war (Clausewitz 1832).

The same principle should also apply to international business management. Friction separates real war from war on paper. Every element has its potential of friction, and the effects each brings cannot be accurately measured, as suggested by the Black Swan phenomenon and Butterfly Effect. Thus, friction is the force that makes the apparently easy difficult. Friction of distance postulates that distance requires efforts, money and time to overcome. Friction covers factors such as temporal distance when team members are separated by work schedule differences and considerations such as team size, distribution asymmetry and face-to-face interaction which affects team-work; whether or not the team member has been multi-tasking; and technical skills and support provided by other team members.

2.6 Summary

This chapter debates on whether globalization and technologies have made distance and geography irrelevant or have exacerbated their importance. Figure 2.4 shows the dynamic relationship of flight-time, distance, environmental factors, and how firms organize themselves in overseas markets. Flight-distance is postulated to be a causal factor that affects Cultural distance, Administrative distance, Topographical distance, Gravitational distance, Economical distance, Technological distance, Sociodemographic distance, Relational distance and Organizational distance. To an internationalizing business entity, increasing flight-time implies changes in the physical environment, transportation, communications and opportunity costs, control of resources, extensiveness of useful networks, time-lags, physical, political, economic,

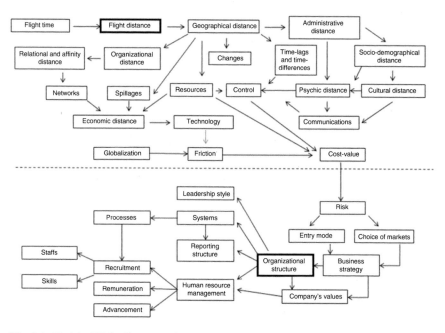

Fig. 2.4 Model of flight-distance and organization structure relationship

social and technological environment, spillages of influences and the resulting value-costs evaluation. A firm would then have to internalize these distance-rooted factors, by means of choice of markets, entry modes, business strategies and organization design.

References

Akamatsu K (1962) A historical pattern of economic growth in developing countries. The Developing Economies, Tokyo, Preliminary Issue no. 1, pp 3–25
Allen TJ (1977) Managing the flow of technology. MIT Press, Cambridge, MA
Asheim BT, Gertler MS (2005) The geography of innovation: regional innovation systems. In: Fagerberg J, Mowery D, Nelson R (eds) The Oxford handbook of innovation. Oxford University Press, Oxford, pp 291–317
Barkema HG, Baum JA, Mannix EA (2002) Management challenges in a new time. Acad Manage J 45(5):916–930
Barlett CA, Ghoshal S (1998) Managing across borders: the transnational solution, 2nd edn. Harvard Business School Press, Boston
Barr MD (2000) Lee Kuan Yew and the "Asian values" debate. Asian Stud Rev 24(3):309–334
Beckmann MJ (1999) Lectures on location theory. Springer, Berlin
Bogardus ES (1926) Social distance in the city. Proc Pub Am Sociol Soc 20:40–46
Bremmer I (2006) The J curve – a new way to understand why nations rise and fall. Simon & Schuster, New York
Brown JS, Duguid P (2000) Social life of information. Harvard Business Press, Boston

References

Cairncross F (1997) The death of distance. Harvard Business School Press, Boston
Chen C (2005) Entry strategies for international construction markets. Doctorate thesis, Department of Architectural Engineering, The Pennsylvania State University, University Park
Conley TG, Ligon E (2002) Economic distance and cross-country spillovers. J Econ Growth, Springer 7(2):157–187
Davidson WH (1983) Market similarity and market selection: implications for international marketing strategy. J Bus Res 11:439–456
Diamond J (1997) Guns, germs and steel: the fate of human societies. Norton, New York
Drucker P (1973) Management: tasks, responsibilities, practices. Harper Business, New York
Earley PC, Ang S (2003) Cultural intelligence: individual interactions across cultures. Stanford University Press, Stanford
Economist Intelligence Unit (2008) E-readiness Ranking 2008. The Economist, London
Ellis PD (2008) Does psychic distance moderate the market size–entry sequence relationship? J Int Bus Stud 39(3):351–369
Evans CLL, Harrigan J (2003) Distance, time and specialization. FRB International Finance discussion paper, no. 766, Washington, D.C.
Friedman T (2001) Longitudes and attitudes. Farrar, Straus and Giroux, New York
Friedman T (2005) The world is flat. Straus and Giroux, New York
Ghemawat P (2001) Distance still matters: the hard reality of global expansion. Harv Bus Rev 79(8):137–147
Global Times (2009) Airlines face EU airspace ban. Global Times. 24 Aug 2009
Henrikson AK (2002) Distance and foreign policy: a political geography approach. Int Polit Sci Rev 23(4):437–466
Hofstede G (1980) Culture's consequences: international differences in work-related values. Sage, Beverly Hills
Hu MY, Chen H (1993) Foreign ownership in Chinese joint ventures: a transaction cost analysis. J Bus Res 28(2):149–160
Huntington SP (1996) The clash of civilization. Free Press, New York
Johanson J, Vahlne JE (1977) The internationalization process of the firm: a model of knowledge development and increasing foreign market commitments. J Int Bus Stud 8(1):23–32
Kitchin R, Dodge M (2002) Virtual reality, space and geographic visualisation. In: Fisher P, Unwin D (eds) Virtual reality in geography. Taylor & Francis, London, pp 341–361
Lewis M (1989) Liar's Poker. Hodder & Stoughton, London
Linder SB (1961) An essay on trade and transformation. Almqvist & Wicksell, Stockholm
Lojeski KS, Reilly RR (2007) Multitasking and innovation in virtual teams. In Proceedings from the 40th annual Hawaii international conference, Waikoloa, 2007
Low SP (1990) The organization of construction export marketing. Avebury Press, Singapore
Luostarinen R (1979) Internationalization of the firm. Published dissertation. International Business, Helsinki School of Economics, Helsinki
Mackinnon D, Cumbers A (2007) An introduction to economic geography – globalization, uneven development and place. Pearson Education, Harlow
Maskell P, Malmberg A (1999) Localised learning and industrial competitiveness. Cambridge J Econ 23(2):167–185
Masters WA, McMillan MS (2001) Climate and scale in economic growth. J Econ Growth 6(3):167–186
Milgram S (1967) The small world problem. Psychology Today 2:60–67
Neubauer DW, Meinhold SS (2007) Judicial process: law, courts and politics in the United States. Cengage
Olson GM, Olson JS (2000) Distance matters. Hum Comput Interact 15:139–179
Public papers of the president Dwight Eisenhower, 1954, pp 381–390
Ravenstein E (1885) The laws of migration. J Stat Soc 46:167–235
Reid NO, OhUllaChain B (1997) Acquisition versus greenfield investment: the location and the growth of Japanese manufacturers in the United States. J Reg Stud Assoc 31:403–416

Ro T, Gu C (1995) The effect of social and physical distance on the global communication networks. Int Commun Gaz 54(2):163–192, Sage Publications

Rosenberg MT (2004) Gravity model: predict the movement of people and ideas between two places. http://geography.about.com/library/weekly/aa031601a.htm. Aug 2004

Seeley IH (1995) Building technology, 5th edn. Palgrave, New York

Stouffer SA (1940) Intervening opportunities: a theory relating to mobility and distance. Am Sociol Rev 5(6):845–867

Tihanyi L, Griffith D, Russell C (2005) The effect of cultural distance on entry mode choice, international diversification, and MNE performance: a meta-analysis. J Int Bus Stud 36:270–283

Tobler W (1970) A computer movie simulating urban growth in the Detroit region. Econ Geogr 46(2):234–240

Trompenaars, F. and Hampden-Turner, C. (1998). Riding the Waves of Culture - 2nd Edition. McGraw-Hill

Von Clausewitz K (1832) On war (trans: Howard M, Paret P, 1984). Princeton University Press, Princeton

Zipf GK (1946) The P_1P_2/D hypothesis: on the intercity movement of Persons. Am Sociol Rev 2:677–686

Chapter 3
Core and Peripheral System of Cities

3.1 Introduction

This chapter discusses topics in human and economic geography such as geo-politics, geo-economics, spatial economics, complementarities of regions, trade agreements, central and peripheral locations and agglomeration. This chapter explains why and how countries play the geo-political game. It seeks to demarcate why and how countries enter into alliances with other nations to maximize their economic efficiency for development. It shall also answer why in the system of cities, some cities assume central locations while others become periphery. Lastly, it will explain what are the forces of agglomeration and why firms choose to cluster themselves together; and how all these factors affect the internationalization of a transnational firm.

3.2 Human and Economic Geography

Human geography focuses on the study of patterns and processes that shape human interaction with the built environment, with particular reference to the causes and consequences of the spatial distribution of human activities on earth's surface. The branches of human geography include political geography, socio-cultural geography and economical geography.

Economic geography is therefore a subset of human geography. It is the study of the spatial variation on the earth's surface of activities related to producing, exchanging, and consuming goods and services (Hartshorn and Alexander 1988). Notably, economic geography and scale economies stress the role of physical and economic geography in influencing city size, emphasizing on three aspects of geography – natural attributes of landscape such as topography, weather, and raw resource deposits; the role of neighbors; and internal historically developed aspects of cities such as transport infrastructure and culture.

One of the foci of human and economic geography is spatial interaction, which refers to the movement process demonstrated by the flows of goods and services over space. Fundamentally, interaction is directly proportionate to mass or attraction, but inversely proportional to distance. It has been suggested by the geographer Ullman (1956) that for spatial interaction to occur, three interrelated conditions must be satisfied – complementarities, intervening opportunity, and transferability. Complementarity occurs when there is a situation of reciprocity, in terms of demand and supply between two locations. Intervening opportunity describes the phenomenon that spatial interaction is more likely with a location that is proximate that offers the same characteristics, than with a location that is distant. Transferability suggests that transport infrastructures, i.e. modes and terminals, must be present to support an interaction between two locations.

The principle of least effort generally accounts for the length and intensity of this movement and interaction. This principle is based on the idea that one minimizes distance and selects the shortest path when moving between the two points. Underlying this is the notion of friction of distance, which refers to the resistance to movement over space (Ullman 1956).

3.3 Geo-politics

The concept of geo-politics was introduced by Halford Mackinder's (1904) Heartland Theory which proposed that whichever empire in hold of the pivotal and strategic vast areas of north and central Asia would become the world's hegemony-power. Geo-politics is like a game of tug-of-war between countries which have to decide who to partner or oppose, or to remain neutral. But it is also more than that because sometimes, nations loom in "grey areas" of "coop-petition" – an in-between of cooperation and competition. An example would be the rise in prominence of China. In his book *The World is Flat*, Friedman (2005) told a proverb about a gazelle waking up every morning knowing it must run faster than the fastest lion and a lion waking up knowing it must outrun the slowest gazelle. Everyone is wary of China, but they also understand that they have to tap into the abundance of opportunities that China offers. China is running, and all have to join in the race, both a 100 m dash against it and 4 × 100 m relay with it, concurrently. Other examples would be how USA seeks to retain its stranglehold on petroleum to preserve its own world-power and economic interests when they station their military troops around the globe; European nations formed the European Union (EU) to get more clout in geo-political matters; African countries are exchanging their oil and gas for financial aids and technology transfer; North Korea insists on the development of nuclear technology so that they would be able to hold more chips on the international game-table despite the risk of incurring economic sanctions in the shorter term; Australia and New Zealand are trying to affiliate themselves with Asia more and more instead of only inclining towards the West (Asad and Lee 2008); while Singapore uses a hedge-diplomacy strategy so that there would be some allies from somewhere to bail the small island-country out of trouble whenever the need arises.

The world has always been divided into many parts in terms of politics, economics and culture. In modern times, globalization has formed a new mosaic of regions and it is likely to result in many deepening predicaments. For instance, within Asia, there remain several fault-lines that may ignite strong conflicts or even waging of wars, disrupting stability and common welfare between states. Examples of these fault-lines or problem-areas include the Korean Peninsula which separates the capitalism of South Korea and communism of North Korea, the wrestling to claim sovereignty of several South-China Seas islands, pro-independence ambitions of Taiwan, Tibet and Xinjiang, Indian-Pakistan's territorial conflict in Kashmir and the Middle-East's terrorism and sectorian conflicts. There are also other possible flash-points. Examples are the verbal spates between the leaders of Malaysia and Singapore over racial issues and China's agitated protests against the Japanese for their resistance to officially apologise and to renounce their rights to weaponry for their role in the provocation of war-fare during World-War 2. At the same time that countries such as Thailand and Sri Lanka are recovering from military coups and civil wars, many countries, such as Macau, Angola, Azerbaijian, Qatar and China are surging forward with technology leaps and fast paces of growth.

Bilateral ties and the planning and strategizing of geo-politics remain separated by the phenomenon of distance in the form of gravitational distance, topological distance and attributional distance. Gravitational distance suggests that a country's political power over another country decays with increasing distance although the mass or size of countries can modify this assumed attenuation of influence. Topological distance may make any two countries seem more remote from one another if there are other countries located in between them. Topological distance is also influenced by the number and arrangement of these intervening country-spaces. Attributional distance is the perception of which countries seem more distant from or, conversely, nearer to one another owing to their political or cultural characteristics (Henrikson 2002). Distance's impact on geo-politics could be profound. There is a Chinese proverb that goes – "when the lips die, the teeth suffer". Neighboring countries often collaborate together to solve problems or create win-win results. However, there have also been many cases of strained relationships between adjacent countries as mentioned earlier.

3.4 Geo-economics and Spatial Economics

Geo-economics or international economics is the study of spatial, temporal and political aspects of economies and resources, and is intrinsically linked to geo-politics. Krugman and Obstfeld (2000) observed that seven themes occur throughout the study of international economics. These are namely – the gains from trade, the patterns of trade, protectionism, the balance of payments, exchange rate determination, international policy coordination and the international capital market. Spatial economics, on the other hand, focuses on location theory, spatial competition and regional/urban economics (Fujita et al. 1999). It has been observed that a great deal of today's world trade takes place in the three key regional trading blocs – Western Europe, Asia and North America, called the Triad market. These large world trade regions emerged mainly due to the active pursuit of regional free trade areas, technological changes and the changing ways of which firms operate. (Kohno et al. 2000). Therefore, judgment by analysts who predicted the imminent demise of the nation-state and the advent of the borderless world seems unduly precipitating in view of the continued robust presence of behemoths like the USA, Germany, Japan and China (Scott 1998).

3.5 Transportation

While an efficient transport network is a necessary pre-condition for economic growth, it does not guarantee economic growth. It is not sufficient on its own to encourage economic growth but is interdependent on a series of factors which determine the location and expansion of economic activity (Cole 1998).

Transportation is a vital activity in moving both freight and passengers around the world (Coyle et al. 2000). Hubs in transportation networks enjoy a similar advantage to central places (Krugman 1996). Fujita and Mori (1996) argued that this may help explain why so many large cities are port cities. Cities in strategic locations are chosen to become aviation hubs due to the selection of optimum or refraction routes after considering the principles of minimization and traffic. More flights and vessels converge at these transportation hubs. Outlying locations, in contrast, are serviced by transit (feeder) flights or vessels. Therefore, cities in strategic locations, such as Atlanta, Chicago, Amsterdam, Hong Kong and Singapore which are key air-transportation nodes as well as port cities benefit and prosper from their advantageous strategic positions; whereas less accessible countries, such as landlocked countries or countries which are not strategically located are harder to commute to and from, incur higher transportation costs and have less propensity to attract FDIs etc.

In Der Isolierte Staat, Von Thünen (1826) introduced the Location Theory which propounded that the costs of transporting goods consume some of Ricardo's economic rent. The total costs of an economic activity and its distribution must take in consideration land costs and transportation costs. According to the Central Place Theory by Christaller (1933), transportation costs and economic rents vary across goods, leading to different land uses and use intensities as a result of distance from the marketplace. The trade-off between fixed production costs and transport costs is central to the geographical organization of any industry in that its solution determines the spatial packing of firms. Hence, firms may set up an off-shore facility, where land costs and labour costs are cheaper to produce lesser-value products or services, but retain higher-value products or services in central locations where land costs and labour costs are more costly. Transportation costs of products or services generally increase over distance. In fact, the Launhardt-Weber model (Weber 1929) postulated that transport cost minimization was the dominant consideration in firm location, and that downstream costs was a function of the location of upstream firms. This function explains the Just-in-time benefits and why top car manufacturer Toyota has its numerous suppliers clustered around its main facilities to reduce transportation costs. However, the transportation cost of a product or service is also subjected to the type of the product or service – a heavier or bulkier product would be more expensive to transport, whereas a service, being intangible and helped by the proliferation of the world-wide-web and advances in communication technologies, has a much lower transportation cost.

The costs or revenue of a firm is sensitive to distance. According to Smith (1981), a firm is likely to choose a location where total revenue would exceed total costs by the greatest amount for the highest profit. The figure shows how marginal unit of cost and revenue affects total costs, total revenue and total profits. Dissimilar products or services have different marginal cost and marginal revenue implications across distance. The figure has shown that distance can affect a firm's total costs, revenue and profits. The firm would therefore have to consider how and where to locate its facilities (e.g. plant or overseas office).

Most consumers are indifferent to small variations in price, travel, distance and even quality. However, when these differences become large, the consumers will react. Devletoglou (1965) assumed that the consumer decides based on distance. Figure 3.1 shows the sphere of influence of a firm and the zone of indifference whereby consumers within the area would not have any preference over firm A or firm B selling similar goods (Devletoglou 1965). It has been suggested that consumers located in area A tend to go to firm A while consumers in area B tend to go to firm B to get a non-differentiated good or service whereas consumers who do not fall into the sphere of influence of firm A nor the sphere of influence of firm B are located in a zone of indifference – they do not have preferences. In other words, it was suggested that in the zone of indifference, firms compete not on location and proximity to consumers or clients, but in terms of price or product differentiation.

3.6 Location

"Location, location, location!" has always been the maxim of marketing geography, the study of where to locate a store or retail chains to maximize target exposure. This dictum not only apply to retailing, agriculture, manufacturing and recreational activities, but also on the location of consultancy firms. Location deals with "what is where" for the firm. "What" refers to the type of economic activity and "where" refers to the other activities in that environment that interact with the activity under consideration.

The location of firms is at the very heart of location theory. According to, there are three primary types of trading area models that can be used to analyze store location potential and trading area: analogous, regression, and gravity. An analogous model uses revenues of similar stores in the market area, the competitors' positions, the new store's expected market share, and the size and density of the trade area to estimate new store sales. On the other hand, a regression model employs a number of mathematical equations to relate potential store sales as the dependent variable, with a number of independent variables such as population

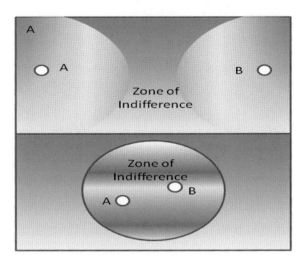

Fig. 3.1 Zone of indifference

size, average income, the number of households, close competitors, traffic patterns, etc. Lastly, a gravity model is based on the assumption that a certain radius or a group of customers within a radius are drawn to stores in a particular area on a number of factors such as distance to market, distance between markets, relative market population, store's image, etc.

Factors important to a start-up or relocating firm when choosing an office space include availability of labor with specific skills, relative low cost of office rental and recruiting suitable employees, low taxes or subsidies, infrastructure, amenities and facilities, accessibility through transportation, and the flexibility of the office-space. The Weberian Triangle (Weber 1929) that proposes that the optimal location for a firm is the one that has the best middling accessibility to key resources or distribution points, so that the total distance from resources and markets is minimized. The Hotelling Phenomenon (Hotelling 1929) is very similar to the Weberian Triangle, in that it suggests that a firm tries to locate itself in between customers or clients or in a location that can cater to the most number of customers or clients. Arising from the literature review undertaken in this study, a summary of the theoretical underpinnings of the firm's location is shown in Table 3.1.

3.7 Localization

Localization can be a self-reinforcing process – the presence of more firms can make markets larger, and the demand fosters supply in a positive-loop relationship (Pred 1966). Alfred Marshall (1890) identified three reasons for localization, namely: (i) the concentration of several firms in a single location that offers a pooled market for

3.7 Localization

Table 3.1 Brief description of important theories on location

Concepts	Description	Authors
Classical theories		
Land-use model/Locational rent	Market processes and economic activities determine how locations with different land rents would be used	Von Thünen (1826), Weber (1929), Predoehl (1925) and Christaller (1933)
Location triangle/Optimal industrial location	Firms would choose optimal locations that minimize their total costs. It suggests that a firm considers distance and transportation costs when deciding to locate.	Launhardt (1885) and Weber (1929)
Spatial competition/ Hotelling phenomenon/ Distance inelasticity of demand	Explains the "rush to the middle" phenomenon for a firm's optimal location. It suggests that a firm tends to locate itself in a middle location.	Hotelling (1929)
Central place theory	A type of gravity model that defines a hierarchy of central places. The theory suggests that economic activities and talents tend to agglomerate in central places.	Christaller (1933)
Neo-classical applications		
Centrifugal and centripetal forces	Forces of centralization and decentralization due to economies of scale and positive spillovers, or competition and higher costs of operations	Hurd (1911), Colby (1933), Mydral (1957) and Krugman and Venables (1995)
Localization economies	Firms of the same industry locating in close proximity to each other to benefit from economies of scale.	Marshall (1890)
Gravitation	Larger cities have larger spheres of influence than smaller ones. This is a model that follows Newton's theory on gravity.	Reilly (1931) and Zipf (1946)
Retail location/Market area	Accessibility of location for consumers to buy their merchandise. A more accessible place tends to attract more customers.	Christaller (1933) and Huff (1963)
Spatial pricing	Pricing of a good or service depending on customer's location. A firm has to consider transportation costs to deliver its goods or services to the customer.	Hoover (1937)
City rank-size	Hierarchy of cities with different sizes of population and economic activities. The core	Zipf (1946)

(continued)

Table 3.1 (continued)

Concepts	Description	Authors
	city of a region is called the primate city.	
Breaking-point of trade	It is used to define the breaking-point of trade between two cities such that a customer residing at the location of this trade breaking-point would be indifferent to the two trade areas for a non specialty good.	Converse (1949)
Intervening opportunities	Distance ventured is directly proportional to number of opportunities but inversely proportional to the number of intervening opportunities at that distance	Zipf (1946)
Optimal distribution of public services among regions	Location of public services to cater to the most people in the population. Public services seek to maximize their positive utility to the community.	Samuelson (1954)
General equilibrium	Explains the spatial equilibrium of demand and supply. Location of industries tends to consider the spatial general equilibrium.	Isard (1956)
Space margin of profitability	The choice of industrial location after the evaluation of cost and revenue. A firm tends to locate in a place where it can derive maximum profits.	Rawstron (1958)
Optimal location	An industry's optimal location varies with the levels of input it requires and output generated. Therefore, when an industry's production volume increases or decreases, there should be a re-evaluation of its location.	Moses (1958)
Incrementalism	Firms expand into nearby markets first, then incrementally move into further markets when they have accumulated knowledge and experience	Braybrooke and Lindblom (1963)
Location networks	Locations are connected so that resources and markets can be shared. Central places tend to be the most connected and accessible.	Hakimi (1964)
Multi-plant location	Discusses the best choice and arrangements for multiple plants. A transnational firm may	Dewey (1969)

(continued)

3.7 Localization

Table 3.1 (continued)

Concepts	Description	Authors
	have to consider the concept to prevent cannibalism between offices.	
Agglomeration	Describes the benefits that firms obtain when clustered around one another, or how these firms are interdependent on each other	Krugman (1991)
Urban spatial structure		
Mono-centric cities, polycentric cities and edge cities	Mono-centrism is the organization of economic activities around a core centre; polycentrism is the organization of economic activities of a region around several centre; and edge city is the organization of economic activities outside a traditional urban area	Marshall (1890)
Urban spatial structure	Describes how activities are arranged in a city, e.g. in concentric, sector theory or multiple nuclei zones.	Weber (1899)
Core and periphery	Describes how high-level economic activities are concentrated in one area surrounded by areas of less dense and less important activities.	Predoehl (1928)
Suburbanization	The process of population movement from cities to the rural–urban fringe. However, the reverse trend is much stronger in most places.	Harris and Ullman (1945)
Urban density	Population density declines exponentially with distance from the city. Economic activities and talents tend to agglomerate in urban cities.	Clark (1951)
Growth poles	Economic development or growth is not uniform over an entire region – it instead takes place around a specific pole.	Perroux (1955) and Hirschman (1958)
Sticky places	Explains why with free trade, information technology, globalization and capital mobility, certain places manage to anchor productive activities while others cannot (Markusen 1996).	Markusen (1996)

workers with industry-specific skills, ensuring both a lower probability of unemployment and a lower probability of labour shortage; (ii) localized industries that support the production of non-tradable specialized inputs; and (iii) informational spillovers that give clustered firms a better production function than isolated producers. Isard (1956) grouped location factors into three categories: (i) transfer costs; (ii) labour, power, tax costs etc.; and (iii) agglomeration economies and diseconomies due to forward and backward linkages.

One conspicuous feature of the new locational models seems to be that under certain circumstances, agglomeration takes place such that activities of firms concentrate into geographically well-defined areas. The driving forces behind agglomeration, or clustering, allude to the type and degree of scale of economies in production (Braunerhjelm and Svensson 1998).

Localization is different from agglomeration in that it refers to the concentration of a single type of firm or industry in a location, whereas agglomeration includes external economies and refers to the clustering of a variety of activities that may complement one another in a location.

3.7.1 Virtual Clusters

Localization theory before globalization and virtual collocation take on a global scale, emanates from works by Von Thünen (1826) and Marshall (1890). According to Marshall (1890), three sources of localization can be defined – pooling of labor markets, access to specified intermediate inputs, and localized technologically spillovers. Most importantly, Marshall (1890) stressed that technological spillovers were confined to geographically concentrated regions.

In today's world, the proximate and the distant may seem almost equally familiar due to the advancement of transport and communication technology (Scott 1998). There is a potential spatial dispersal of clustered firms and a reduction in geographic clustering as a result of more efficient means of transport (Bergman and Feser 1999). Whether cluster advantages can be transferred from spatially defined entities to non-spatial or virtual clusters rests mainly on how learning takes place in electronic networks and whether tacit knowledge can be exchanged in electronic communications systems (Passiante and Secundo 2002). It does seem that the clustering phenomenon can go beyond geographical boundaries through electronic networks, and that input–output linkages between companies need not imply a need for geographical co-location anymore (Porter 1990).

3.7.2 Paradox of Globalization and Localization

Socio-economic activities are subject to centripetal or centrifugal forces and these polarization and de-polarization forces form the contours of a mosaic of regions scattered across the globe because of the globalization-localization paradox (Scott 1998). The paradox suggests that extraordinary improvements in modern transportation and communication technologies that have occurred over the last few decades have brought almost every point on the globe into close contact with every other point. On the other hand, it is also plausible that the more the firm is integrated with and dependent on only one or a few firms, the more likely it is to locate in proximity to that or those firms to facilitate cooperation and synchronization for higher performances. The same trends have not undermined the region as the basis of dense and many-sided interactions, but in many aspects, have actually reinforced it. Many kinds of social and economic transactions remain extremely problematic, in the sense that significant failures occur when attempts are made to execute them over extended distances. In these cases, the mutual proximity of all relevant parties is required for effective inter-linkages to be established (Scott 1998).

Above all, and in spite of the great spatial extension of markets occasioned by globalization, the locational structure of production and work still by and large resist any universal tendency to geographic entropy. On the contrary, because production and work depend upon a myriad of detailed exchanges, dealings, flows, and webs of association that cannot be sustained effectively over long distances, the impacts of distance have been magnified (Scott 1998).

3.8 Agglomeration

Despite globalization, infrastructural improvements always have had a double effect, permitting dispersion of certain routine activities but also increasing the complexity and time-dependence of some other activities, and thus making agglomeration more important (Leamer and Storper 2001). Selected groups of firms and individuals persistently coalesce out on the landscape to form dense regional complexes of economic and social activity. The very existence of a dense and expanding global tissue of urban areas, together with the fact that the same area now account for much of the world's economic activities and population, are affirmations of the continued stubborn gyration of daily life around the orbit of the local. This is in spite the fact that the world is now simultaneously connected in multiple ways to a vastly wider field of geographic eventuation (Scott 1998).

The paradox of global links and the apparently diminished meaning of distance and location on the one hand, and the obvious agglomeration of industries and firms in specific regions on the other, emphasizes the availability of specific strategically important resources which are typically generated in a local or regional context where physical encounters and informal flows of information occur as a simple consequence of geographical proximity. The features that had made location an important factor in competitive advantage in the past have now been replaced by more complex features. Today, the firm achieve "more productive use of inputs" – the core of company performance by being more innovative. This requires efficient management of internal resources and external relationships. Geographical concentrations of interconnected companies, specialized suppliers, service providers, firms in related industries, associated institutions all make up the fabric of a firm's external relationships. Porter (1990) thus concluded that a cluster approach provides a new way of thinking about the meaning of location.

The term "agglomeration" was postulated by Alfred Weber to describe the concentration or clustering of economic activities in a location. Weber (1929), in this seminal work on locational economics, distinguished between three different categories of determinants in the location of manufacturing production, namely – transport costs, labor, and "agglomeration". He postulated three points. Firstly, he suggested that firms can accrue economies of scale related to the firm's production. He also propounded that clustering may occur because of proximity to suppliers, pooled labor market, or localized diffusion of knowledge. Lastly, he proposed that the concentration of production may give rise to external advantages or urbanization economies such as highly developed infrastructure, low costs of energy etc. The reasons for "agglomeration" were, in Weber's (1929) view, based on cost-minimization decisions by the firms. Hence, firms would agglomerate at one spot only if savings exceed the costs. In other words, "agglomeration" was conceived as trade-off between "agglomeration economies" and transport costs. Overall, however, locational economies became over-shadowed by the overwhelming impact of the general equilibrium paradigm, which was based on markets characterized by perfect competition and a lack of or negligible transport costs.

Krugman and Venables (1995) postulated that the Weber's "agglomeration" was actually describing "localization", and thus, they incorporated locational issues into a general equilibrium framework allowing for imperfect competition to revolutionize the paradigm on agglomeration to resemble core-peripheral models. They postulated that agglomeration of economic activities is created due to the interplay between the mobility of firms and labour, focused on the effects of differences in market size of countries, and propounded that firms benefit from economies of scale and network effects when they are located in close proximity to one another. Similarly, they noted that when firms cluster, firms have improved complementarities, linkages and accesses to multiple suppliers, greater specialization and division of labour, transaction-cost economies, customers, shared infrastructure, and higher chances to exploit knowledge spill-over or diffusion of ideas through competition and cooperation, to prevail over negative externalities or diseconomies which include crowding, congestion and price competition.

Agglomeration synergies can make a city become a growth pole which can be observed via the population count and the amount of economic activities in a city. NASA's satellite photographs of the earth's nightlights show agglomeration at the global, country and city levels – the northern hemisphere is brighter than the southern hemisphere; there are more bright nodes in the eastern and western coasts of USA (the whereabouts of New York, Chicago and Los Angeles), Western Europe and East Asia. These bright nodes represent the concentration of economic activities in particular spaces. Firms are also found to tend to agglomerate at cross-junctions or in the middle of a city-centre. Indicators such as population, number of skyscrapers, airport passenger numbers and nominal Gross Domestic Product

(GDP) per capita respectively reflect how a city has agglomerated economic activities – agglomeration tend to draw in workers and residents, skyscrapers to accommodate commercial offices, business travellers and passenger numbers, and increase a country's GDP. These indicators should be considered together, in relation to one another, and not in isolation, in order to better appreciate agglomeration and which cities are the most agglomerated – we may be misled if we are to only consider population, the number of skyscrapers, airport's passenger numbers, or GDP per capita individually.

3.9 Centrality

The central place theory is a geographical theory, created by Walter Christaller (1933), to explain the number, size and location of human settlements in an urban system. However, the validity of the central place theory may change due to local factors such as climate, topography, accessibility, history of development, land use, technological level and competition.

The core-periphery model is centrality at the world stage (refer to Fig. 3.2). The roots of the idea though go back to Hirschman (1958), who seek to explain the characteristics of a growth pole. Hirschman (1958) invoked two main sets of notions. The first is the polarization of a location to grow by means of their own magnet-like ability to draw in people and resources from distant location. The second is the spread or "trickle-down", signifying the countervailing flow of growth effects from more developed to less developed regions via increased spending in core regions on the products of the periphery, and governmental efforts to raise incomes and opportunity levels in the periphery. True to the model, it has been observed that the bulk of the population in the USA resides in a few clusters, around New York, Chicago and Los Angeles. It has also been noted that night-time satellite

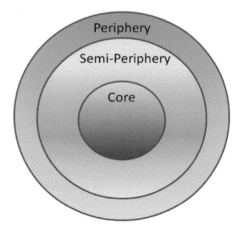

Fig. 3.2 Core, semi-core and periphery

photographs of Europe revealed little of political boundaries but clearly suggested several center-periphery patterns in the continent that highlights cities like London, Paris, Amsterdam and Milan.

3.10 Complementarities of Services

Globalization homogenizes standards and management models, but it needs diverse specialized economic capabilities (Sassen 2001). Countries have their own unique factors of endowments which give them absolute or comparative advantages to produce goods or services. Economic efficiency requires that countries collaborate with one another. Asia-Pacific is experiencing a renaissance because China is the low-cost producer; Japan provides high-tech innovation; Korea provides medium-heavy industries; Taiwan provides materials; some developing countries in the region acts as the hinterlands; Australia provides the natural resources; while Hong Kong and Singapore serve as business hubs while also housing research and development facilities and business-services infrastructures and networks to integrate all these players.

A country has to strike strategic alliances with its neighbours and other key partners in security, trade and cultural exchanges. Without such architecture of networks, a country would have to operate in solitude and would find it hard to succeed. An example of country-to-country partnering would be a trade pact. Ultimately, a transnational firm has to take into consideration the specificities and particularities of national economies and markets (Sassen 2001).

3.11 System of Cities

According to the Central Place Theory (Christaller 1933), a central place is an agglomerated area or location that provides higher-level services to its surrounding areas. Christaller (1933) observed that there are functional hierarchies of places with regards to spacing, size and function, and that:

1. The number of large cities is few, but the number of small towns are many;
2. The larger the settlements, the greater the distance between them;
3. The larger the settlement, the more function it holds; and
4. The larger the settlement, the more higher-ordered services are provided

Christaller (1933) henceforth advocated that there is a system of cities which determines the spatial distribution and complex pattern of movement, flow and linkages that bind them in space. The cities can be categorized by the role they play: central places, transportation cities and specialized function cities. These cities differ in their economic makeup, social and demographic traits, etc.

Table 3.2 shows the ranking of cities based on business activity, human capital, information exchange, cultural experience and political engagement while Table 3.3 shows the leading world cities in the world compiled by The Globalization and World Cities Study Group (GaWC 2008) based at Loughborough University. At the

3.11 System of Cities

Table 3.2 Ranking of global cities (Foreign Policy 2008)

1	New York
2	London
3	Paris
4	Tokyo
5	Hong Kong
6	Los Angeles
7	Singapore
8	Chicago
9	Seoul
10	Toronto
11	Washington
12	Beijing
20	Shanghai

Table 3.3 Leading world cities and their hierarchies (GaWC 2008)

Alpha World Cities ++	London, New York
Alpha World Cities +	Singapore, Hong Kong, Paris, Sydney, Tokyo, Shanghai, Beijing
Alpha World Cities	Milan, Madrid, Seoul, Moscow, Brussels, Toronto, Mumbai, Buenos Aires, Kuala Lumpur
Alpha World Cities −	Warsaw, Jakarta, Sao Paolo, Zurich, Mexico City, Dublin, Amsterdam, Taipei, Rome, Istanbul, Lisbon, Chicago, Frankfurt, Stockholm, Budapest, Vienna, Athens, Prague, Caracas, Auckland, Santiago
Beta World Cities +	Melbourne, Barcelona, Los Angeles, Johannesburg, Manila, Bogota, New Delhi, Atlanta, Washington D.C, Tel Aviv, Bucharest, San Francisco, Helsinki, Berlin, Dubai, Oslo, Geneva, Riyadh, Copenhagen, Hamburg, Cairo
Beta World Cities	Bangalore, Jeddah, Kuwait, Luxembourg, Munich, Kiev, Dallas, Lima Boston, Miami
Beta World Cities −	Sofia, Dusseldorf, Houston, Beirut, Guangzhou, Nicosia, Karachi, Montevideo, Rio de Janerio, Nairobi, Bratislava, Montreal, Ho Chi Minh City
Gamma World Cities	Guadalajara, Antwerp, Rotterdam, Lagos, Philadelphia, Perth, Amnan, Manchester, Riga, Detroit, Guayaquil, Wellington, Portland
Gamma World Cities −	Edinburgh, Porto, Tallinn, San Salvador, St. Petersburg, Louis, San Diego, Calgary, Almaty, Birmingham, Islamabad, Doha, Vilnius, Colombo

top of the hierarchy in the system of cities is the Primate city. The Primate city is the leading city in its country or region, and it is often disproportionately larger than any other cities in the urban hierarchy around it (Jefferson 1939). Among the best known examples of the Primate city are the Alpha World Cities++ or Super-cities of New York and London, followed by Alpha World Cities + that include Singapore, Hong Kong, Paris, Sydney, Tokyo, Shanghai and Beijing. The prerequisites of a truly global city include factors such as international prominence, active influence and participation in international events, a major international airport that serves as an established hub for several airlines, a fairly large population, mixed ethnic and cultures, international financial institutions, law firms, corporate headquarters, stock exchanges, international conglomerates, advanced communications infrastructure, a lively cultural scene, variety of media and sporting community, etc. A global city could on one hand, due to cumulative causation and spiral of self-reinforcing advantage, attract all the economic or commercial potential and activities in the region and create backwashes or adverse effects on other regions (Myrdal 1963); on the other hand, the global city could also create spillages to its neighbors. This phenomenon was also discussed in the Core and Periphery theory which strongly suggests that the industrialization of one new world region depresses the prospects for others (Redding and Venables 2004).

3.12 Firm's Behavior

Derruder et al. (2003), Taylor (2004) and Alderson and Beckfield (2004) studied city ranking in terms of the number of top business companies or service producer firms and found that indeed, core cities like New York, London, Paris, Tokyo, Hong Kong and Singapore house the most top enterprises around the world, such as the Forbes 500 companies. These scholars postulated that the world is structured in a certain way and world cities are formed into a complex spatial hierarchy (Sassen 2001; Taylor and Walker 2001; Derruder et al. 2003). The situation is slightly different for the architectural and engineering firms as Rimmer (1991) and Ren (2005) found that the three blocks of cities are competing for the leading position in the world – the Chinese city block, London and the American city block, and the South East Asian city block. This is probably because many architectural firms have been expanding their branch-office network to reach potential multinational clients in fast-growing locations instead of venturing into already developed economies. Tables 3.4 and 3.5 compare the traits of the world's global cities, and in particular, the degree-scores of the cities which host the most number of the world's top firms and the world's top 100 architectural firms respectively. "Degree" in the table measures the number and presence of top A/E firms present in the city; "Far-ness" or "closeness" refers to the total distances to other cities, which also reflects the city's connectedness in the global design network; "between-ness" of cities refers to how cities are likely to stand in the paths between other pairs of cities; and "power" refers to the number of ties a city has with other cities. Architectural firms are susceptible to rely heavily on the property development market. It was observed that the concentration of architectural firms tends to occur around production sites such as London and New York or consumption sites such as Shanghai and Beijing (Ren 2005).

The global air network also exhibits varying degrees of centrality and peripherality. Air-transportation hubs such as New York, London, Tokyo, Singapore, Amsterdam, Frankfurt and Paris are the key aviation nodes, creating a network of interdependent cities with hierarchy and ordering (Smith and Timberlake 2001; Derruder et al. 2003). Bel and Fageda (2008) also found that there is a significant relationship between the location of firm's headquarters, the supply of direct intercontinental flights and the forces of agglomeration. This infers

3.12 Firm's Behavior

Table 3.4 Comparative ratings of global cities

Taylor's connectivity	Degree	Closeness	Eigenvector centrality	Betweenness
London	London	London	London	London
New York	New York	New_York	New York	New_York
Hong Kong	Paris	Paris	Hong Kong	Paris
Paris	Tokyo	Tokyo	Tokyo	Tokyo
Tokyo	Hong Kong	Hong Kong	Paris	Hong Kong
Singapore	Toronto	Toronto	Singapore	Toronto
Chicago	Singapore	Singapore	Chicago	Singapore
Milan	Amsterdam	Amsterdam	Milan	Amsterdam
Los Angeles	Milan	Milan	Los Angeles	Los Angeles
Toronto	Los Angeles	Los Angeles	Madrid	Madrid
Madrid	Madrid	Madrid	Sydney	Frankfurt
Amsterdam	Chicago	Chicago	Amsterdam	Milan
Sydney	Sydney	Sydney	Frankfurt	Chicago
Frankfurt	Frankfurt	Frankfurt	Toronto	Sydney

Table 3.5 Degree-scores for the cities which host the most number of the world's top 100 architectural firms

Rank	City	Degree	Far-ness	Between-ness	Power
1	London	227	229	2,604	105
2	Shanghai	194	330	1,880	88
3	Washington, D.C	171	340	556	74
4	New York	168	334	567	73
5	Los Angeles	164	352	774	62
8	Hong Kong	131	359	781	65
9	Beijing	125	348	1,184	73
13	Singapore	113	358	824	61
40	Kuala Lumpur	49	394	235	38
Unranked	Ho Chi Minh	–	–	–	–

Source: Ren (2005)

that the headquarters would coordinate and command activities across geographically and functionally dispersed establishments within the organization after considering each city's flight-accessibility and agglomeration effects.

In this age of electronic information systems and internet-based search engines, information may be easily obtainable via the internet. However, sometimes, the vast amount of information available can lead to an increase in search and selection costs which in turn may be reduced by using personal information sources available in clusters. Clusters provide privileged access to both codified and tacit information, showing that spatial proximity and informal encounters still hold comparative advantages (Preissl and Solimene 2003). Therefore, a firm would choose to be proximate to the market and complementary services because proximity to clients increases personal touch, "good-will", reciprocity and trust (Morgan 2004). Proximity to other services enables firms to monitor the activities of local rivals, provide access to codified and tacit information, and make possible frequent personalized encounters between many different individuals occupying many different kinds of socio-economic niches, much like the Japanese Kanban system, whereby mutual proximity of participant firms aids the system to work effectively. The degree of benefit due to locational proximity of firms would be reliant on the rough corollary of scale and nature of the products or services provided. It is most probable that firms whose transactions with one another are small in scale, irregular and unpredictable, and dependent on intensive face-to-face intervention will probably find it to their advantage to be located in some sort of mutual proximity, whereas firms whose transactions with one another have the opposite characteristics are likely to be more free in their choices of location (Scott 1998).

3.13 Summary

Although the economic interconnections between different locations across the globe are expanding at a rapid pace, it has been observed that the state of the world remains far from approaching spatial liquefaction. Instead, major cities around the world continue to expand at a remarkable rate, contrary to a commonly held view that new transportation and communication technologies are beginning to subvert urbanization processes. This is very much due to the mobility of labor against the relative immobility of resources. Firms are embedded in their original locations because of organization inertia and the worry of resource sapping (Mackinnon and Cumbers 2007).

When a core city becomes very successful in attracting much of economic activities around the region, it acts like a black-hole that draws up increasingly amount of economic activities, and create back-wash effects for the periphery areas (Myrdal 1963). Therefore, the global mosaic now comprises of regional nuclei, regional semi-cores and surrounding dependent hinterlands, indicating that the geography of industrial and service development displays a widespread proclivity to locational clustering in the form of dense polarized complexes of producers on the landscape (Scott 1998).

Markusen's (1996) "Sticky Places in Slippery Spaces" gives a good explanation of the phenomena of why certain places manage to anchor productive activities while others cannot. This is because the centripetal forces of agglomeration outweigh its centrifugal forces. The polarization of "sticky" places attracts clusters, benefits from complementarities, localization and agglomeration effects to evolve to become growth poles of economic activities. Firms would be inclined to position their higher-value organizational activities such as leadership, finance, marketing, research and development in central and core cities but arrange lower-value or routine activities such as manufacturing in periphery locations. Figure 3.3 shows how flight-time affects agglomeration and location of firms, which in turn influences the internationalization, choice of business strategies and organization structures of transnational A/E firms.

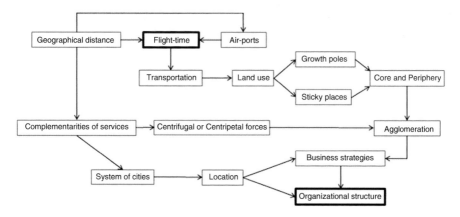

Fig. 3.3 Dynamic model of flight-time, agglomeration and organization structure's relationship

References

Alderson AS, Beckfield J (2004) Power and position in the world city system. Am J Sociol 109:811–851
Asad L, Lee PO (2008) Introduction. In: Asad L, Lee PO (eds) Regional outlook – Southeast Asia 2007–2008. Institute of Southeast Asian Studies, Singapore
Bel G, Fageda X (2008) Getting there fast: globalization, intercontinental flights and location of headquarters. J Econ Geogr 8(4):471–495
Bergman E, Feser E (1999) National industry cluster templates: a framework for applied regional cluster analysis. Reg Stud 34(1):1–19
Bergman M, Feser E (1999) Industrial and regional clusters: concepts and comparative applications. WVU Regional Research Institute Web Book, Morgantown
Braunerhjelm P, Svensson R (1998) Agglomeration in the geographical location of Swedish MNFs. In: Braunerhjelm P, Ekholm K (eds) The geography of multinational firms. Kluwer, Boston, pp 99–112
Braybrooke D, Lindblom CE (1963) A strategy of decision. The Free Press, New York
Christaller W (1933) The central places of southern Germany. Prentice Hall, Englewood Cliffs
Clark C (1951) Urban population densities. J R Stat Soc 114(4):490–496
Colby CC (1933) Centripetal and centrifugal forces in urban geography. Ann Assoc Am Geogr 23:1–20
Cole S (1998) Applied transport economics: policy, management and decision-making, 2nd edn. Kogan Page, London
Converse PD (1949) New laws of retail gravitation. J Mark 14(January):379–384
Coyle JJ, Bardi EJ, Novack RA (2000) Transportation, 5th edn. South-Western College, Cincinnati
Derruder B, Taylor PJ, Witlox F, Catalano G (2003) Hierarchical tendencies and regional patterns in the world city network: a global urban analysis of 234 cities. Reg Stud 37(9):875–886
Devletoglou N (1965) A dissenting view of duopoly and spatial competition. Economics 32:14–160
Dewey D (1969) A geometry of multiplant operations. Columbia University Press, New York
Friedman T (2005) The world is flat. Straus and Giroux, New York

Fujita M, Krugman P, Venables AJ (1999) The spatial economy: cities, regions, and international trade. MIT Press, Cambridge

Fujita M, Mori T (1996) The role of ports in the making of major cities: self-agglomeration and hub-effect. J Dev Econ, Elsevier 49(1):93–120

Globalization and World Cities Research Network (2008) The world according to GaWC. GaWC

Hakimi S (1964) Optimum locations of switching centers and the absolute centers and medians of a graph. Oper Res 12(3):450–459

Harris CD, Ullman EL (1945) The nature of cities. Ann Am Acad Polit Soc Sci 242:7–17

Hartshorn TA, Alexander JW (1988) Economic geography. Prentice Hall, Englewood

Henrikson AK (2002) Distance and foreign policy: a political geography approach. Int Polit Sci Rev 23(4):437–466

Hirschman AO (1958) The strategy of economic development. Yale University Press, New Haven

Hoover EM (1937) Spatial price discrimination. Rev Econ Stud 4:182–191

Hotelling H (1929) Stability in competition. Econ J 39(153):41–57

Huff DL (1963) A probabilistic analysis of shopping center trade areas. Land Econ 39:81–90

Hurd RM (1911) Principles of city land values. Record and Guide, New York

Isard W (1956) A general location principal of an optimum space-economy. Econometrica 20:406–430

Jefferson M (1939) The law of the primate city. Geogr Rev 29:226–232

Kohno H, Nijkamp P, Poot J (2000) Regional cohesion and competition in the age of globalization. Edward Elgar, Northampton

Krugman P (1991) Geography and trade. MIT Press, Leuven

Krugman P (1996) Confronting the mystery of urban hierarchy. J Jpn Int Econ 10:399–418

Krugman P, Obstfeld M (2000) International economics: theory and policy, 5th edn. Addison-Wesley, Boston

Krugman P, Venables AJ (1995) The seamless world: a Spatial model of international specialization. NBER Working papers 5220. National Bureau of Economic Research, Cambridge

Launhardt CFW (1885) Mathematische Begriindung der Volkswirtschafts-lehre. Engelmann, Leipzig

Leamer EE, Storper M (2001) The economic geography of the internet age. NBER Working paper No. 8450, Cambridge

Mackinder HJ (1904) The geographical pivot of history. Geogr J 23:421–437

Mackinnon D, Cumbers A (2007) An introduction to economic geography – globalization, uneven development and place. Pearson Education, Harlow

Markusen A (1996) Sticky places in slippery space: a typology of industrial districts. Econ Geogr 72(3):293–313

Marshall A (1890) Principles of economics. Macmillan and Co., New York

Morgan K (2004) The exaggerated death of geography: learning, proximity and territorial innovation systems. J Econ Geogr 4:3–21

Moses L (1958) Location and the theory of production. Q J Econ 72:259–272

Mydral G (1957) Economic theory and underdeveloped regions. Gerald Duckworth, London

Myrdal G (1963) Economic theory and underdeveloped regions. Methuen & Co., London

Passiante G, Secundo G (2002) From geographical innovation clusters towards virtual innovation clusters: the innovation virtual system. In: Proceedings of 42th ERSA congress "From industry to advanced services – perspectives of European metropolitan regions" University of Dortmund, Germany, 27–31 Aug

Perroux F (1955) Note sur la notion de pole de croissance. Economique Appliquée 1–2:307–322

Porter ME (1990) The competitive advantage of nations. Free Press, New York

Pred AR (1966) The spatial dynamics of US. Urban-industrial growth. MIT Press, Cambridge

Predoehl A (1928) The theory of location in its relation to general economics. J Polit Econs. 36:371–390

Preissl B, Solimene L (2003) The dynamics of clusters and innovation: beyond systems and networks. Springer, Heidelberg/New York

References

Rawstron EM (1958) Three principles of industrial location. Trans Inst Br Geogr 25:132–142

Redding S, Venables AJ (2004) Economic geography and international inequality. J Int Econ 62(1):53–82

Reilly WJ (1931) The law of retail gravitation. Knickerbocker Press, New York

Ren XF (2005) World cities and global architectural firms: a network approach. Paper presented at the social organization of urban space workshop, University of Chicago, 3 Nov

Rimmer P (1991) The global intelligence corps and world cities: engineering consultancies on the move. In: Daniels P (ed) Services and metropolitan development: international perspectives. Routledge, London, pp 66–106

Samuelson PA (1954) The pure theory of public expenditure. Rev Econ Stat 36(4):387–389

Sassen S (2001) The global city: New York, London, Tokyo. Princeton University Press, Princeton

Scott AJ (1998) Regions and the world economy – the coming shape of global production, competition, and political order. Oxford University Press, Oxford

Smith D (1981) Industrial location. Wiley, New York

Smith D, Timberlake M (2001) World city networks and hierarchies, 1977–1997: an empirical analysis of global air travel links. Am Behav Sci 44:1656–1678

Taylor PJ (2004) World city network: a global urban analysis. Routledge, London

Taylor PJ, Walker DR (2001) World cities: a first multivariate analysis of their service complexes. Urban Stud 39(2):367–376

Ullman EL (1956) The role of transportation and the bases for interaction. In: Blunden J, Brook C, Edge O, Hay A (eds) Regional analysis and development. Harper & Row, London, pp 52–65

Von Thünen JH (1826) Isolated state (trans: Wartenberg CM, 1966). Pergamon Press, New York

Weber A (1899) Information theory and urban spatial structure. Croom Helm, London

Weber A (1929) Theory of the location of industries (trans: Friedrich CJ). The University of Chicago Press, Chicago

Zipf GK (1946) The P_1P_2/D hypothesis: on the intercity movement of persons. Am Sociol Rev 2:677–686

Chapter 4
Internationalization of Singaporean A/E Firms

4.1 Introduction

This chapter discusses the paradox between the repelling forces of depletion and discontinuities due to distance apart and the pulling forces of global-interconnectivity, as well as how the consequent clashes and its residue profoundly impinge on the interpretation of the international environment. The chapter aims to provide a succinct description of the fundamentals of internationalization models of trade and business, and explain how firms act when they venture overseas into markets abroad.

4.2 Discontinuities or Inter-connectivity

"The Tyranny of Distance" by Geoffrey Blainey (1977) pointed out the inconveniences and costs required in bridging distance. The aphorism suggests that a firm's access to home-based resources would sap with distances, discontinuities or dislocations at countries and city borders. Concentrating on proximate markets minimize such disjointedness and reduce disconnectedness. The dictum also suggested that being nearer to the home environment allows access to and knowledge of resources, networks and markets, whilst being farther would erode the firm's comparative and competitive advantages.

Contrariwise, in 1997, Frances Cairncross suggested in "The Death of Distance" that the world is becoming an interconnected global village and that distance is already irrelevant. Friedman (2005) named ten forces that might have flattened the world. The forces are namely: market liberation, the proliferation of work-flow software to improve work processes and interoperability between engines, computer and man to enhance productivity, the advent of the World Wide Web and informing search engines such as Google to share or dig out information, in-sourcing of core competencies to internal units, out-sourcing, off-shoring and supply-chaining. These forces compress geographical and physical spaces so much so that the world is becoming a "global village", a term coined by Marshall McLuhan in 1962 to suggest the proliferation of communications with the rapid growth of contemporary information technology. These pervasive influences of new informational technologies have profoundly affected the spatial dimensions of economic activities. Globalization has amazingly, made collocation a possible reality.

Even though the transaction costs of many economic activities such as coordination and communication have fallen sharply indeed, claims of the "death of distance" are very much exaggerated, since the costs of transportation or logistics of resource and communications between people have by no means been reduced to zero (Cairncross 1997; Olson and Olson 2000). Proponents of "The Tyranny of Distance" had suggested that distance is "immortal" and would not fade away with globalization and the advancement of technology. There is an old Chinese proverb that says "the suitor who is near to the pavilion gets the moon and wins the damsel's heart". Similarly, some situations hand proximity a critical advantage or access to a treasured opportunity.

Furthermore, Root (1998) suggested that knowledge regarding high-context messages can be lost via email or phone-calls. Bradner and Mark (2001) also found that the perception of distance affects collaboration in terms of cooperation, persuasion and deception using computer-mediated communication technology. Being completely reliant on information and communication technology, without face-to-face communication, may result in a higher propensity to misunderstandings, miscommunications and problems in coordination and cooperation. Allen (1977) also found that there is consistency in this relationship ranging from short distances in few metres to long distances in thousands of kilometres. Studies have also shown a decline in frequency of telecommunication or electronic mail with increasing distance (Mayer 1993; Biksen and Eveland 1986). The explanation is that people communicate via telecommunication or electronic mail most frequently with those who are in their vicinity and those whom they meet up with regularly. Conversely, communications with peers in other foreign offices are less frequent because of the lack of personal relationships.

Distance has thus far proven to be as enduring in the business world despite the proliferation of technology, information and communication technology and globalization because logistics and communication is the life-blood of any organization and no matter how globalization and technology have bridged the tyranny of distance, there would still remain facets of organization logistics and communication that could get hindered, impaired and distorted by distance.

4.3 Economics and Internationalization

The neoclassical synthesis comprises Neoclassical economics and Keynesian economics which dominate mainstream economics today. Neoclassical economics is much founded on the equilibrium of supply and demand, rationality of preference and utility and full information which describes a "utopia" in which pareto optimality applies. It assumes rational expectations and an endogenous environment. It is therefore "ignorance-squared" and does not explain the exogenous factors that affect the system and is thus inadequate to interpret contemporary businesses environments (Ravetz 1993; Thompson 1997). Therefore, as our awareness of economic criteria changes, new paradigms of economic theories and models evolve and emerge.

International trade is essentially the exchange of goods and services across international boundaries or territories. Notably, with the passage of time, industrialization, advanced transportation, information technology, globalization and the internationalization of firms, new theories have evolved and accorded more deserved emphasis on transnational firms and the recognition of their roles.

Macroeconomics focuses on international or country-level economic growth, fiscal and monetary policies, inflation, unemployment, taxation etc. (Friedman 1953). The figure suggests that there is a circulation of influences in macroeconomics, and that a firm interacts dynamically with the government, financial markets, workforce market, commodity markets, the country's openness to foreign influences (e.g. FDIs), households, etc. Arising from the literature review undertaken in this study, a summary of the theoretical underpinnings of internationalization or Multinational Enterprise (MNE) theories from economic theories is shown in Table 4.1.

An internationalizing firm would have to internalize home and host macroeconomic and microeconomic systems to have an improved chance at success. Microeconomics focuses on the general equilibrium of prices due to supply and demand in the market, markets under asymmetry of information, choice under uncertainty, market failure etc. An internationalizing firm has to check out whether there is a real demand in the overseas markets, and whether the firm is able to provide products or services to cater to these markets.

4.4 MNE and FDI

Hymer (1976) defined a multi-national enterprise (MNE) as a firm involved in foreign direct investment (FDI) which implies transfer or formation overseas of all or some of the necessary factors of production and some element of control over their use abroad. Rather similarly, Seymour (1987) defined an enterprise as one that undertakes direct foreign investment to engage in production in countries other than the country in which the firm is registered.

Hymer (1976) suggested that firms internationalize due to variables related to the company's dimension and ownership of specific assets such as scale economies, diversification and knowledge accumulation and variables derived from the existence of market failures. According to Hymer (1976), there must be imperfections in the host markets for international firms to exploit for FDIs to occur.

Table 4.1 Evolution of theories on internationalization

Theory	Description	Authors
Early economic thought		
Wealth acquisition	Describes how personal or public wealth can be acquired, especially in the acquisition of goods and accumulation of wealth.	Aristotle (third century BC)
Mercantilist		
Mercantilism	Mercantilism is an economic theory that a country's prosperity is dependent upon its supply of capital. It is suggested that nations should accumulate financial wealth by increasing exports and discouraging imports.	Mun (1664)
Physiocrats		
Laissez faire	Refers to how the industry functions by self-interests and market forces and free of governmental restrictions and interventions.	Smith (1776)
Classical		
Classical economics	Primarily concerned with the dynamics of economic growth, it also discusses economic freedom and promoted ideas such as laissez-faire and free competition.	Smith (1776), Ricardo (1817), and Mill (1871)
Absolute advantage	Refers to the ability of a country to produce more of a good or service than competitors in absolute terms.	Smith (1776)
Comparative advantage	Countries should specialize in producing what they produce best and trade for other commodities.	Ricardo (1817)
Nationalism		
Imperialism	Imperial states acquire colonies to use them as sources of materials and markets. Most countries which used to be colonies have since gained independences.	Marx (1867)
Neoclassical synthesis		
Microeconomics	The branch of economics that analyzes the behaviour of individual consumers and firms in an attempt to understand the decision-making process of firms and households.	Smith (1776)
Neoclassical economics	An approach to economics that relates supply and demand to an individual's rationality and his or her ability to maximize utility or profit.	Veblen (1900)

(continued)

4.4 MNE and FDI

Table 4.1 (continued)

Theory	Description	Authors
Keynesian economics	It suggests private sector's decisions sometimes lead to inefficient macroeconomic outcomes and thus advocates active intervention by the state	Keynes (1936)
Macroeconomics	The field of economics that studies the phenomena and behavior of the economy such as changes in unemployment, national income, rate of growth, gross domestic product, inflation and price levels.	Keynes (1936)
New basic concepts		
Gravity	The Gravity model predicts trade based on the distance between countries and its interactions with the countries' economic sizes.	Isard (1956)
Non-availability approach	Countries imports goods or services that are not available at home. Similarly, MNEs tend to venture into markets where there are shortages of the products/services that they can provide.	Kravis (1956)
Leontief Paradox	Describes the paradox whereby a country with high capital-per worker has a lower capital: labour ratio in exports than in imports.	Leontief (1958)
Technology gap theory of trade	Innovating country enjoys a monopoly until the importing country learn to produce the goods.	Posner (1961)
Linder hypothesis	A conjecture that countries with a more similar demand structure would trade more with one another.	Linder (1961)
Diffusion of innovations	It explains how, why and at what rate innovations are spread. Innovations tend to diffuse from advanced countries to developing countries.	Rogers (1962)
Factor endowments	The Heckscher-Ohlin (H-O) model takes into account factor endowments, and predicts countries would export goods that make intensive use of locally abundant factors and import goods that make use of factors that are locally scarce	Leamer (1995)
Specific factors	A "short-run" version of the H-O model, it considers the point that specific factors may not be easily transferable in the short run.	Jones (1971)
Spatial economics	The study of how space or distance affects economic behaviour. Spatial economics cover location theory, spatial competition, and region and urban economics.	Kasper (1994)

(continued)

Table 4.1 (continued)

Theory	Description	Authors
New trade	Economic critique of international free trade from the perspective of increasing returns to scale and network effects.	Krugman (1996)
MNE		
Location theory	The Localization theory seeks to explain what MNE activities are located where and why.	Von Thünen (1826)
Industrial organization	The theory studies the strategic behaviour of firms and suggests that local firms understand local consumer taste, business customs, legal system etc.	Chamberlin (1933)
Institutionalism	Institutional economics focuses on the bounded rationality, learning and evolution of the firm.	Commons (1934)
Transaction costs	The Transaction-Cost Theory explains how costs incurred in search and information, contract, policing and enforcing affect the firm's choice of market and entry mode.	Coase (1937), Gatignon and Anderson (1988)
Diversification theory	Rational investors diversify their portfolio to spread out risks. Firms can diversify into other geographical or product/service markets.	Markowitz (1952)
Contingency	There could not be "one best way" for business strategies and management. Business strategies have to suit the situation.	Woodward (1958)
Growth of firm	The growth process of a firm is dynamically constrained. A firm can either grow organically by expanding its business activities or inorganically through mergers and acquisitions.	Penrose (1959)
Resource-based	The Resource-Based View argues that firms possess resources which enable them to achieve competitive advantage and superior long-term performance	Penrose (1959)
Monopolistic advantage	Explains why firms can compete in foreign settings against indigenous competitors. Transnational firms tend to benefit from economies of scale and are superior in capabilities.	Hymer (1960)
International product cycle	The theory describes the diffusion process of an innovative product from advanced to developing countries over time	Posner (1961)

(continued)

4.4 MNE and FDI

Table 4.1 (continued)

Theory	Description	Authors
Behavioural	The decision to internationalise may not be based on profit maximization but is instead motivated by internal management interests and external factors like client demands	Aharoni (1966)
International entrepreneurship model	entrepreneurship model It highlights the role of the entrepreneur or the management team on the firm's internationalization decisions	Perlmutter (1969)
Uppsala or Stage Growth Theory	The model states that firms initially choose to enter nearby markets with low market commitments.	Johanson and Wiedersheim (1975)
Market imperfection	MNEs owe their existence to market imperfections. Market imperfections allow MNEs to break into foreign markets.	Kindleberger (1984)
Networks	The theory suggests the interdependency of firms and how a firm can leverage on the strengths of its partners when it goes overseas	Johanson and Mattson (1988)
Integrated models		
Eclectic paradigm and internalization	The eclectic paradigm merges several isolated theories of international economics in one approach to suggest that ownership, locational and internalization advantages are crucial to an internationalizing firm	Dunning (1988)
National competitive advantage	A country's basis for competitive advantage in an industry can be measured by its factor conditions, demand conditions, related and supporting industries, firms' strategies due to structure and rivalry, government intervention and chances	Porter (1990)
Blue Ocean Strategy	The firm creates innovates to make competition irrelevant by creating a leap in value for buyers and the firm, thereby opening up new and uncontested market space	Kim and Mauborgne (2005)

Tejima (1994) expanded on this observation and suggested the motivation for FDIs include: preservation or expansion of market share, development of new market, reverse exports, exports, response to voluntary export restraints, promotion of specialization with the firm, diversification of facilities, securing inexpensive labour forces, vertical integration for controlled supply, request from host country, avoiding foreign exchange risk and development of products adapted to the local market. These factors also include push factors at home, the firm's response to external factors and the business and investment climate of the host country. Another motive for locating abroad could be to gain access to knowledge in foreign "centers of excellence" and to benefit from localized spillovers. The motives for FDI was later simplified by Brooke and Buckley (1998), to include cost reduction, market presence, market access, control of distribution, access to technology, access to resources and brand acquisition.

4.4.1 FDI

Foreign direct investment is defined as the movement of long-term capital to finance business activities abroad, whereby investors control at least 10% of the enterprise. It was suggested by the department that anything less than 10% is considered portfolio investment. Therefore, FDI is distinguished from other types of foreign market penetration by an MNE's intent to control. The decision to undertake a FDI can be regarded as a strategic decision whereby the firm attempts to achieve the best possible fit between the capabilities of the firm and opportunities. Countries worldwide try to attract FDI-inflows from global MNEs and at the same time, try to facilitate FDI-outflows for home-grown MNEs.

4.4.2 Trade-Agreements

Countries seek free-trade agreements (FTA) with partners so that there would be trade benefits for all involved parties. A firm can tap into these benefits due to their home-country's trade agreements with the host country to access market opportunities, key resources and distribution channels etc. firms can harness the infrastructures of these FTA to their benefits. These advantages will equip firms with strong competitive edges over other foreign firms which do not enjoy such privileges. Therefore, Singaporean firms, including construction-related firms would benefit from Singapore's FTAs with other countries.

4.4.3 Borne Global

A firm faced with a small local market, possesses good corporate networks, and exhibits organizational flexibility and learning is a naturally born global firm if equipped with financial and human resources, and information technology and systems (McKinsey et al. 1993). A/E services firms can be borne global firms (McKinsey et al. 1993). The export of A/E consultancy services can be done right from the birth of the firm, to very distant markets, and to enter multiple countries all at once, instead of having to develop in the traditional manner of getting through incremental stages with respect to their international activities. These firms may "leapfrog" over such stages during internationalization into foreign markets due to more and more homogeneous export markets (Hedlund and Kverneland 1985), the adaptability of the firm's products or services (Ganitsky 1989), the firm's high potential for growth (Bloodgood et al. 1996) and the international experience and network of the entrepreneur (Jones 1999).

4.4.4 Embeddedness

Organizational embeddedness is the totality of forces of fit, links, and sacrifices that keep people in their current organizations; while occupational embeddedness is the totality of forces that keep people in their current occupations (Ng and Feldman 2010). Embeddedness describes how home-bias and inertia causes a firm or person to be spatially rooted in a location to complicate relocation or internationalization efforts.

The internationalization of the firm has been described as a process consisting of a series of small steps, whereby firms gradually increase their international involvement (Johanson and Wiedersheim 1975; Johanson and Vahlne 1977; Welch and Luostarinen 1988). Firms tend to internationalize incrementally in terms of control of the overseas operations and from proximate to distant locations. Notably, accumulated time in the host market and the firms' resources have a tendency to increase control and distance of market for an internationalizing firm.

4.4.5 Barriers to Entry

Firms already in a market can create barriers to entries to deter other firms from getting into the industry or market-place. Examples of entry barriers are advertising, control of resource, cost advantages independent of scale such as proprietary technology and know-how, access to materials, favourable geographic position, learning curve cost advantages, customer loyalty, distributor agreement, economies of scale, globalization, government regulations, inelastic demand, intellectual property, investments, network effects, predatory pricing, restrictive practices, research and development, supplier agreements, sunk cost which increase risk to deter entry and vertical integration (Porter 1990).

4.5 International Construction

There are many reasons why international work for construction-related firms is attractive: new markets for specialized expertise, professionally challenging assignments, profit, building credibility overseas for future domestic opportunities, et cetera. However, the pull-backs against these motivations include: drain on senior resources, financial risk, impact on domestic projects, physical and financial risks, limited control, ethical problems and lack of legal recourse.

Construction covers a wide range of products, services and activities. Official statisticians tend to classify construction into four sectors, namely, contracting, consulting, building material production and construction plant (Williams 1997).

Dulaimi and Hwa (2001) highlighted that the lack of access to reliable information about the international construction markets and the potential of construction companies are impeding the internationalization process. It was also suggested that "the service nature of construction is evident when its export potential is considered. The immobility of construction items means that only managerial and technical skills, and some materials and equipment can be transferred from one country to another. The considerations of the construction enterprises wishing to operate overseas... would be similar to those relating to organizations in the service industry".

In 2009, the global construction value was US$4.6 trillion. According to another survey done by the World Trade Organization (WTO), the total value of construction exports in the world in 2007 was US$70 billion. The major exporters, in terms of value, are the European Union, Japan, China, Russia Federation and USA. The major importers are the European Union, Japan, Russia Federation, Saudi Arabia, Kazakhstan, China, Angola, Malaysia and Azerbaijan. Faster growth is however expected in Asia and other emerging economies such as Russia, Brazil.

4.6 Singapore-Domiciled Service Firms

The size of the service sector is increasing in almost all parts of the world (Lovelock 2009) due to changes in government policies, social changes, business trends, advances in information technology and globalization. The service sector tends to be more prevalent in developed economies. According to Singapore's Ministry of Trade and Industry, the service sector contributes to 68.8% of Singapore's Gross Domestic Product in 2008 (refer to Table 4.2).

Table 4.2 Indicators of the Singapore Economy

Structure of economy	Nominal value added (% share)	Real growth (%)
Total	100.0	1.1
Goods producing industries	26.0	−1.0
Manufacturing	19.4	−4.1
Construction	5.1	20.3
Utilities	1.4	2.1
Other goods industries	0.1	−4.0
Service producing industries	68.8	4.7
Wholesale and retail trade	17.1	2.6
Transport and storage	9.0	3.1
Hotels and restaurants	2.1	1.2
Information and communications	3.7	7.2
Financial services	13.1	5.5
Business services	**14.0**	**7.4**
Other services industries	9.8	5.3
Ownership of Dwellings	5.2	0.6
Business services		
Total	100.0	7.4
Real estate	45.6	7.2
Legal	4.0	4.2
Accounting	3.1	3.8
Business representative and Head/Regional offices	9.1	6.4
Business and management consultancy activities	8.1	6.1
Architectural and engineering activities	**9.3**	**8.5**
Others	20.8	8.9

Source: MTI (2008)

4.6.1 Singapore's Construction Industry

Singapore's construction industry actual demand in 2009 was S$18.88 billion and the forecast for 2010 is S$21–27 billion. It is an important sector of Singapore's economy. However, the country's construction industry has have had a poor reputation. To improve the construction industry in Singapore, the Construction 21 Report identified 6 strategic thrusts, namely, (i) enhancing the professionalism of the construction industry; (ii) raising the skills level; (iii) improving industry practices and techniques; (iv) an integrated approach to construction; (v) developing a external wing; and (vi) a collective championing effort for the industry.

In order to develop an external wing, the Construction 21 Report recommended (i) to encourage the formation of multidisciplinary firms to groom a core of internationally competitive firms; (ii) the Building and Construction Authority to assist Singapore's construction companies and consultancy firms in venturing overseas; and (iii) the Construction Industry Joint Committee to encourage companies to take proactive efforts, such as to form a consortia, to venture overseas.

4.6.2 Singapore's Construction Exports

According to a survey by the Building and Construction Authority (BCA) of Singapore, the value of construction exports by Singapore firms in recent years had grown from S$0.3 billion in 2000 to its peak of S$2.6 billion in 2004. However, the exports have dropped since then. In 2007, Singapore's construction exports were recorded as US$698 million. Its most important markets are ASEAN (44%), China (10.6%) and USA (8%). The value exports by these firms shows that international construction exports are also susceptible to cyclical demands and supply. The value of construction exports dropped from 1997 to 1998 because of the ASEAN financial crisis which inevitably affected other parts of the world. It then increased from 1999 to 2004, mainly because of (i) recovery of the economy from the ASEAN financial crisis in 1997; (ii) increase in sophistication and costs of construction projects; (iii) increase in demand for infrastructure and environmental-related construction projects. However, from 2005 to 2008, the value of construction exports by Singapore firms dwindled because of increased demand in the home-market instead.

The survey found that from 2002 to 2003, the number of Singapore construction exporting firms increased from 22 to 51, and from 2003 to 2006, it hovered at 51–53. This reflected that Singapore has about 51–53 construction firms with capabilities to export. The figure also showed that the markets accessed increased from 27 in 2002, to 31 in 2003, 35 in 2004 and 38 in 2005, but then dropped to 31 in 2006. This could be because Singapore construction firms had been trying to venture into new markets from 2002 to 2005 but would later (i) experienced difficulties to break into some overseas markets and were forced to retreat from those markets; and (ii) decided to be more involved in the bustling home-market instead.

The survey also showed that most of Singapore's construction exports in 2005 went to countries such as Vietnam and Malaysia in Southeast Asia, China in North Asia, India in South Asia, and United Arab Emirates and Saudi Arabia in the Middle East. These markets took up 76% of all construction exports by Singapore firms.

Similar to that of Singapore construction export firm, Singapore construction consultancy firms were increasing their participation in overseas markets, until they reached a state of overdrive in 2005, and had to decrease their involvement in 2006. The survey showed that Singapore construction consultancy firms' involvement dropped in China from 2004, as well as India and some other markets from 2005. On the other hand, Singapore construction consultancy firms' involvement has been increasing in Southeast Asia.

4.6.3 Architectural and Engineering Services

Among the types of consultancy services, the most sought after services from Singapore firms in 2007 were architectural and master-planning services which constituted more than half of the total number of consultancy contracts. Mixed consultancy services made up another 20% of the contracts.

Architectural and engineering (A/E) services, like master planning, landscaping, facilities management etc. belong to the construction-service sector. Construction design is always carried out by a diverse group of design professionals, including the architects, structural, mechanical, electrical and services engineers and other specialists. For a construction project, no discipline can work in isolation. A/E services are also like all services – non-storable and non-standard, and involve more complicated contacts, negotiations, and monitoring. Communications is therefore of significant importance for A/E consultancy services.

4.6.4 A/E Communications

Communication is the life-blood of most organizations. Work of different nature would probably be influenced by physical and virtual distances to a different extent (Lojeski 2007). This was supported by Allen (1997) who suggested that there are three types of technical communication. According to Allen (1997), Type 1 communication is "the right hand has to know what the left is doing" type of communication which exists in all organizations to coordinate work. Type 2 communication is necessary when the knowledge, upon which the organization draws, is dynamic. Type 3 communication is required where creativity is needed for such communications. Thus, an engineering firm would be deemed to require more Type 1 and 2 communications to coordinate their work and to keep abreast of technological developments whereas an architectural firm would require more Type 1 and Type 3 communications because of the creativity and abstractness involved in their works (architectural designs).

4.6.5 Supply-Chain of A/E Consultancy Services

A/E firms work together with their counterparts of other expertise as part of a supply chain or strategic alliance. For instance, a Singaporean developer may invite Singaporean contractors, architectural, engineering, quantity surveying, and legal firms to collaborate for an overseas project. This form of cooperative network has the potential to give organizations competitive and winning advantages over competitors as each firm strengthens each another with complementary capabilities. In Table 4.3, Ofori et al. (2001) highlighted the strengths of Singapore's construction-related firms. The construction industry is a complex chain of participation by many

Table 4.3 Strengths of Singapore's A/E and related firms

Sources of strength	Areas of strength
Architectural design consultants	
Transparency in project development procedures	Planning and designing of public infrastructure and institutional projects
Strong track record in producing effective design solutions	Production of designs sensitive to local cultural considerations and ability to blend western designs and concepts to suit local cultural contexts.
Singapore is a hub with foreign and local professional talents	
	Production of comprehensive designs that consider safety and buildability etc.
Engineering design consultants	
Ability to produce technically advanced and high quality work	Design and implementation of M&E installations
Ability to produce work that meets world standards, servicing MNEs abroad	Value engineering
	Procurement expertise and logistics support to source materials and resources
Ability to produce tenders which score highly on evaluated basis due to compliance with contractual conditions and specifications, and also innovative features	Project management
	Township planning, infrastructure and building design
Contractors	
Linkages with India and China	Experience in deep tunnels, building and demolitions works in congested areas
Government has helped to create a good brand name for Singapore	Facilities management
Successful use of management style: empowering the project manager with authority on site, while top management focuses on business development	Specific skills in precast construction, façade, cladding works, and work in complex soils
	Ability to apply latest M&E technology
Firms adopt systematic approaches and get things done fast	Design and construction of water- treatment projects
Quantity surveyors	
International outlook of the country, openness to foreign companies and the exposure to diverse business culture is an advantage	Time, quality and cost functions which quantity surveying firms do so well can be exportable
Technology advantage	

Source: Ofori et al. (2001)

different stakeholders. Architects and engineers are adjoined to the design and construction process by the clientele or developer, occupants, urban planners, authorities, other project consultants such as the quantity surveyor, contractor, specialists, suppliers, subcontractors, landscape architects, interior designers etc.

4.6.6 Role of the Government

To encourage and support the internationalization of Singapore's construction-related firms, Singapore's Economic Review Committee recommended that its construction industry (i) develop the culture to encourage and facilitate entrepreneurship; (ii) enhance its capabilities; (iii) foster the development of industry clusters when venturing overseas; (iv) enable conditions, such as regulations; (v) rationalize or divest GLCs or statutory boards; (vi) encourage a culture of partnership connections; (vii) provide capital such as support and facilitation, and catalysts such as incentives, waived or deferred taxation and encouragement; and (viii) establish a single dedicated agency to coordinate efforts to develop entrepreneurship and internationalization.

The government and its statutory boards play an important role in the internationalization of firms, mainly due to its (i) regulations; (ii) directives and (iii) facilitation. For instance, the Building and Construction Authority (BCA) regulates the construction industry; the Construction Industry Joint Committee (CIJC) acts as the think-tank to improve the industry; and International Enterprise Singapore and FTAs facilitate the internationalization of Singapore's construction-related firms.

4.7 Internationalization Risks

During the European renaissance around the sixteenth century, a few mathematicians such as Pascal, Fermat, Bernouilli, de Moivre, Laplace and Gauss, progressively built what became the theory of probability. This branch of mathematics created the toolbox to deal with the future in a rational and orderly manner. It was thought then that everything could be measured, either with a deterministic or with a probabilistic approach, that risk was thought to be under control. However, the unexpected destruction brought by the world wars and the sharp crises of several global depressions which followed speculative mania and financial euphoria showed that even the unthinkable can happen, altering the perception of risk. Often, these economical collapse passes contagion effects to neighboring countries. In our world today whereby there is much more integration due to globalization, there is also more accrued volatility as national economies are increasingly interlinked. At the same time, firms are more and more internationally exposed. The globalization of the world's trade, financial and technology markets has created a new world environment, full of opportunities, but fraught with uncertainty and spillover risks.

4.7.1 Risks and Uncertainty

Risk is the probability of an event occurring multiplied by the impact of the event. Risk is also defined as the threat or probability that an action or event will adversely or beneficially affect an organisation's ability to achieve its objectives (Holton 2004). Risks and uncertainty are different – Frank Knight (1921) established the distinction between risk and uncertainty, when he suggested that risk is a quantity susceptible of measurement whereas uncertainty is not. However, the measurement of risks is a tricky task because one measures well only what one perceives and defines clearly. The measurement of risk is closely related to its perception, which varies across space and time.

4.7.2 Country or City Risk

In 1986, Venezuela and Brazil were rated by the Economist to be in the "very low-risk" bracket like Taiwan and Singapore. The economies of Venezuela and Brazil however, collapsed not long after that. The global financial crisis of 2008 also occurred when investors lost confidence in the value of securitized mortgages in USA, and stock markets worldwide crashed due to contagion effects to enter a period of high volatility. Yet, just several months back before the crash, the economy and markets were all pink and rosy.

Country risk assessment requires timeliness, quality and standardization of information because country risks, which can take the form of political risks, institutional risks, economic risks, business risks, socio-cultural natural risks etc. have a major impact on the returns of cross-border financial investments. Country-Risk Analysis (CRA) therefore attempts to identify risks so that transnational firms can take effective measures to safe-guard their cross-border investments.

4.7.3 Forecasting

The Paradox of Tranquility (Minsky 1982) postulates that after a long period of relative tranquility, businesses and people tend to become complacent about economic prospects, when in fact, risks is never far away, just waiting to lull investors' awareness. In quantum mechanics, Heisenberg's principle (Heisenberg 1927) stipulates that the more precisely the position is determined, the less precisely the momentum is known in this instant, and vice versa. Businesses today must forecast and anticipate what the future will bring, make decisions based on their analysis, taking into consideration how today's choices are likely to affect their companies in the future.

4.7.4 Risk Management

According to Bernstein (1996), the change in attitudes towards risk management has channeled the human progression for games and wagering into economic growth, improved quality of life, and technological progress.

Risk management is the identification, assessment, and prioritization of risks followed by coordinated and economical application of resources to minimize, monitor, and control the probability and/or impact of unfortunate events (Hubbard 2009). Once risks have been assessed, the firm can choose to avoid, reduce, transfer or retain these risks (Dorfman 2007).

However, Bernstein (1996) suggested the science of risk management sometimes creates new risks even as it brings old risks under control. Bernstein (1996) noted that our faith in risk management encourages us to take risks we would not otherwise take. An example would be how seatbelts may encourage drivers to drive more aggressively, and consequently, the number of accidents increases even though the seriousness of injury in any one accident declines. The relative ease of access to information today has also given rise to an excess of information that requires careful scrutiny, discrimination and cross-checking. The wide availability and instant transmission of information can also combine to possibly trigger a herd instinct and self-fulfilling prophecy that result in spillover effects and crisis contamination.

Risk is a multi-faceted challenge. Clearly, the quantitative and qualitative approaches to country-risks are not exclusive from each other. As Rummel and Heenan (1978) conclude, the most effective risk analysis combines insight and wisdom with management science.

4.8 Market Entry

Internationalization into a foreign market can be fraught with dangers and barriers. Therefore, a good market entry strategy is required to spearhead and penetrate the foreign target country. Root (1998) pointed out that a firm would have to assess the products or services it offers, the markets available, its objectives and goals and its control systems to devise an entry mode and a marketing plan. Other than the push factors from the home country and the pull factors from the host country, these decisions could also be affected by the size of the firm and availability of resources (Welch and Luostarinen 1988) and the experience of the firm in managing foreign subsidiaries (Reid 1986).

4.8.1 Entry Mode

An entry mode is essentially an institutional arrangement for organizing and conducting international business transactions (Root 1998). The decision of how to enter a foreign market can have a significant bearing on the firm's internationalization. There are generally a few types of expansion, such as exporting, licensing, joint-venture and fully-owned subsidiary. The chosen entry mode would determine the extent to which the firm would get involved in developing and implementing marketing programs in the host market, and the amount of control of the expansion (Gatignon and Anderson 1988; Hill et al. 1990; Terpstra and Sarathy 1994).

A company's choice of entry mode for a given product and target country should be the net result of several, often conflicting forces. These forces can take the form of host country factors such as sales potential, competition, marketing infrastructure, production costs, import policies, geographical proximity, nature of economy, exchange controls, exchange rate depreciation, cultural distance, political risk; external factors from the home country which include FDI, size of market, competition, production costs, export promotion and restrictions on investments abroad; internal factors from the home country that include product differentiation, service intensity of product, technology intensity of product, product adaptability, resources and commitment; and the firm's resources, experiences, aversion to risk and costs of market access (Andersson and Svensson 1994; Root 1998; Ojala and Tyrväinen 2006).

4.8.2 Progression of Entry Modes

Erramilli and Rao (1993) postulated that internationalizing firms prefer to start with full-control modes. Notwithstanding that, the novice international firm would be cautious with the complexity and riskiness in international markets (March and Simon 1958; Cyert and March 1963). Thus, a typical establishment chain begins with occasional exports, then regular exports, set up of sales subsidiaries and fully-owned facilities abroad (Benito and Gripsrud 1992).

The "optimization of the imperfect situation" refers to the ability to undertake any form of international operations which is clearly limited by the means accessible to the firm to carry it out (Benito and Gripsrud 1992). Cyert and March (1963) contended that limited searches are an important characteristic of this process. When confronted with a problem, organizations tend to start their search for solutions among alternatives that are quite close to solutions that have been tried before. For medium and small firms, given their limitations in many areas, there is an obvious reason why less demanding directions of international development can be undertaken first, with major commitments only occurring well into the longer run when more international experience makes the firm's organizational belief and norm systems become less parochial (Welch and Luostarinen 1993). Then, as more knowledge and experience are acquired, firms consider more alternatives and venture further in terms of distance and also with more commitment (Carlson 1975). Contrariwise, larger firms with more resources are in better positions than smaller firms to make commitments (Caves 1974). Interestingly, Davidson (1983) also showed that the strong preference for close and similar markets weakens as firms acquire experience from operating abroad.

The learning-based sequential process model provides an important perspective on foreign expansion strategy (Johanson and Vahlne 1977). The model suggests that firms enter a foreign country initially with relatively small commitments such as exporting because of the high uncertainty due to a low level of knowledge of the operational environment of the host country. Then, as learning and experience are gained and accumulated over time, and when the uncertainty is reduced, firms gradually increase their levels of commitment in the country. The model also

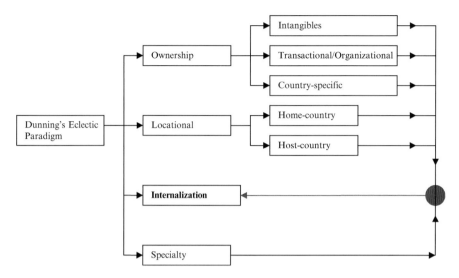

Fig. 4.1 Eclectic Paradigm

suggests that firms go through this sequential and incremental process of expansion not only within a foreign country but also when they stretch out from one foreign country to another; and that firms would move to geographically or socio-culturally distant countries only after having established a presence in more "proximate" countries (Erramilli and Rao 1993).

4.9 Eclectic-Diamond Framework

Firms incur significant extra costs of doing business abroad relative to domestic firms when they internationalize. Therefore, for a firm to become multinational, it must have offsetting advantages (Markusen 2004). Dunning's Eclectic Paradigm's (Dunning 1988) internalization component and Porter's Diamond Theory's (Porter 1990) strategy and structure due to rivalry component explain how firms internalize, strategize and organize themselves when they internationalize. Figures 4.1 and 4.2 show Dunning's Eclectic Paradigm and Porter's Diamond Theory respectively.

4.9.1 Eclectic Paradigm

Dunning's (1988) Eclectic Paradigm explains that there could be four motives for firms' internationalization. These motivations of international production are

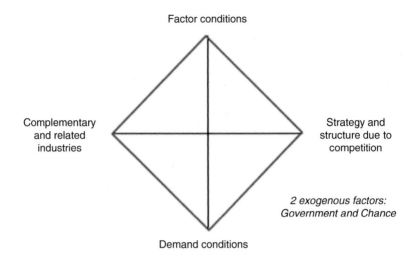

Fig. 4.2 Porter's Diamond Theory

namely: market seeking, resource seeking, efficiency seeking and strategic asset. Dunning (2000) also highlighted that the firm's competencies can be measured by its Ownership, Locational and Internationalization (OLI) capabilities.

Ownership advantages may be intangible asset advantages such as the firm's brand-name, business development capabilities and management competencies; transactional and organizational advantages such as flexible production and work systems, stakeholders' commitment, home government support and assistance; or country-specific ownership advantages such as ample supply of unskilled or skilled/productive workers, protection of legal and property rights, availability of cheap sources of funds and credit (Cuervo and Low 2003).

Location advantages may be host country's location advantages such as the size of market, cost of doing business, social-political and geographical factors; or home-host country induced advantages such as geographical proximity of home and host countries, similarity of language, relational affinity between home and host countries and real wage differentials etc. (Cuervo and Low 2003).

Firms internalize the external environment with the firm's organization which includes the need to avoid search and negotiating costs, to steer away from the costs of adverse selection in the choice of international subcontractors, to avoid or exploit government intervention to control materials, supplies and conditions of sale of inputs, to control markets and to be able to engage in practices as a business strategy. For Singapore's transnational construction-related companies, Cuervo and Low (2004) found that the major reasons for them to export their services overseas are: host governments' attitudes, policies and regulatory framework, the social, political, cultural and geographic factors, and the cost of doing business factors.

4.9.2 Diamond Theory

Porter's (1990) Diamond Theory suggests that the national home base of an organization plays an important role in shaping the extent to which it is likely to achieve or hold advantage on a global scale. Porter (1990) also postulated that there are four endogenous and two exogenous attributes that collectively and individually contribute to and determine national competitive advantage:

(i) Factor conditions: the situation in a country regarding production factors, like human and social capital, knowledge-base, infrastructure, accessibility, etc., which are relevant for competition in particular industries.
(ii) Home demand conditions: describes the state of home demand for products and services produced in a country, presence of sophisticated, demanding buyers that stimulates innovation, and emergence of new markets which can be introduced to the global market.
(iii) Related and supporting industries: the existence or non-existence of internationally competitive supplying industries and supporting industries.
(iv) Firm strategy, structure, and rivalry: these concern the corporate goals and quality of management within individual companies, and degree of competition existing that creates pressure on firms to improve costs structures, accelerates innovation, force firms to search for higher order competitive advantages and prepares them for international operations.
(v) Governmental intervention: the support or requirements which can facilitate or create barriers for businesses.
(vi) Chance: opportunities or threats.

4.9.3 Combining the Eclectic Paradigm with Diamond Theory

There are glaring short-comings in both the Eclectic Paradigm and the Diamond Theory. Table 4.4 shows the comparison between the Eclectic Paradigm and the Diamond Theory in terms of their strengths and weaknesses. Figure 4.3 and Table 4.5 show how the two paradigms can be fused together to complement each other. The combined model, named here as the "Eclectic Diamond Framework" provides a testable supra-national framework that considers the relationship between the variables, asset augmentation, cross-border alliances, importance of international businesses and FDIs and their interactions, and culture.

4.10 Distance and Internationalization

For most businesses, venturing abroad is both an exciting and daunting prospect. Exporting abroad would mean an opportunity to tap into much larger markets, potentially finding new markets for existing products and generating new demand

Table 4.4 Comparison of Eclectic Paradigm and Diamond Theory

	Dunning's (1988) Eclectic Paradigm	Porter's (1990) Diamond Theory
Strengths	An analytical framework that accommodates a variety of economic theories of the determinants of international businesses and foreign direct investments (Dunning 2000)	Has been widely researched and have proven to be useful to evaluate national competitiveness Perspectives from factor conditions, demand conditions, related and complementary industries, strategy due to competition, government's influence and chance (Porter 1990)
Weaknesses	Does not explain the causality between the variables described in it (Itaki 1991) Not possible to set up testable hypotheses (Williams 1997) Lacks the extension to consider asset augmentation (Dunning 2000) Does not amply cover cross-border alliances (Dunning 2000)	Underestimates the importance of international businesses and foreign direct investments and their interactions (Cartwright 1993; Dunning 1993) Does not amply discuss culture (Flanagan et al. 2007)

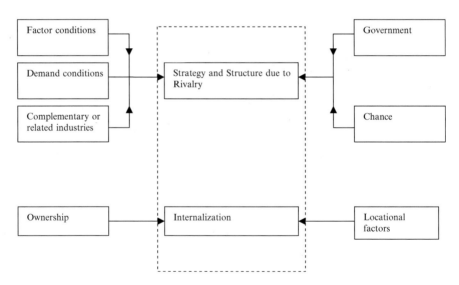

Fig. 4.3 Eclectic Diamond Framework

that was unavailable before. However, the risks of internationalization can deter market entry into the foreign market. It is suggested that "distance" plays a significant role in determining the understanding of risks in foreign markets and consequently, the internationalization of economic activities. Distance affects the level of interaction between the home and host country and the FDI between them. It also influences the level of international experience, the operation specific experience and the availability of resources of the internationalizing firm in the host

4.10 Distance and Internationalization

Table 4.5 Justification of the Eclectic Diamond framework

Dunning's (1988) Eclectic Paradigm	Complementing each other	Porter's (1990) Diamond Theory
Strengths An analytical framework that accommodates a variety of economic theories of the determinants of international businesses and foreign direct investments		Strengths Had been widely researched and have proven to be useful to evaluate national competitiveness Perspectives from factor conditions, demand conditions, related and complementary industries, strategy due to competition, government's influence and chance
Weaknesses It is not possible to set up testable hypotheses It lacked the extension to consider asset augmentation It did not amply cover cross-border alliances The model does not explain the causality between the variables described in it		Weaknesses Underestimated the importance of international businesses and foreign direct investments and their interactions It did not amply discuss culture

environment (Reid and OhUllachain 1997). Because of "distance", firms take calculated and calibrated responses in the international arena (Leong and Ku 2005).

Distance can be manifested in several ways such as geographic distance, economic distance, cultural distance etc. Which is near and what is distant can be manifested by many facets of distance. Distance can for instance, be measured in a physical sense (Luostarinen 1979; Kravis and Lipsey 1982; Terpstra and Yu 1988), the degree of differences such as cultural distance (Johanson and Vahlne 1977; Luostarinen 1979; Davidson 1983; Kravis and Lipsey 1982; Benito and Gripsrud 1992), and economic distance (Luostarinen 1979; Teece 1981).

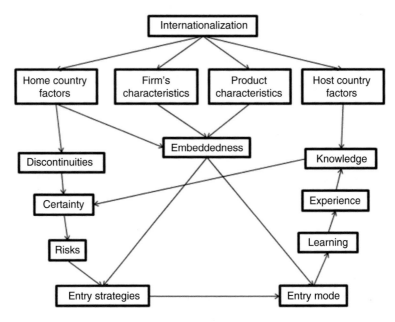

Fig. 4.4 Model of relationship between internationalization and entry modes

4.11 Conclusion

The chapter evaluates the existing theories on internationalization, discusses the paradox of the conflict between globalization and agglomeration, and discusses the risks incurred by an internationalizing firm. It is in this chapter that the study postulates that the flight-time between an A/E firm's home and host locations casts distance-rooted influences to the firm. Therefore, the study recommended that the internationalizing firm uses the Eclectic Diamond Framework, adapted from Dunning's (1988) Eclectic Paradigm and Porter's (1990) Diamond Theory, to consider all of the features shown in Fig. 4.4 to improve risk assessment and management for the internationalization of the transnational firm. The figure describes how a firm's success in internationalization is dependent on home and host country factors, the firm's traits and the characteristics of the product or services that the firm offers. When a firm ventures overseas, the firm's access to home-based resources is sapped, and the market conditions that the firm is familiar with is discontinued. When this happens, there is heightened uncertainty and risks incurred by the firm. A firm's understanding, or the lack of it, would influence the firm's entry strategies and entry mode into a market. However, as a firm learns and accumulate experiences and knowledge of international markets, it becomes less embedded and its understanding of international markets improves, and there is less uncertainty and risks.

References

Aharoni Y (1966) The foreign investment decision process. Division of Research, Graduate School of Business Administration, Harvard University, Boston

Allen TJ (1977) Managing the flow of technology. MIT Press, Cambridge, MA

Allen TJ (1997) Architecture and communication among product development engineers. The International Centre for Research on the Management of Technology, Sloan, MIT, WP 165–97

Andersson T, Svensson R (1994) Entry modes for direct investment by composition of firm-specific skills. Scand J Econ 96(4):551–560

Benito GRG, Gripsrud G (1992) The expansion of foreign direct investments: discreet rational location choices or a cultural learning process? J Int Bus Stud 23(3):461–476

Bernstein PL (1996) Against the gods: the remarkable story of risk. Wiley, New York

Biksen JD, Eveland TK (1986) New office technology: planning for people. Pergamon Press, New York

Blainey G (1977) Tyranny of distance: how distance shaped Australia's history. Sunbooks, Melbourne

Bloodgood JM, Sapienza HJ, Almeida JG (1996) The internationalisation of new high-potential US ventures: antecedents and outcomes. Entrep Theory Pract 20(4):61–76

Bradner E, Mark G (2001) Why distance matters: effects on cooperation, persuasion and deception, CSCW'02. New Orleans, Lousiana

Brooke MZ, Buckley PJ (1998) Handbook of international trade. Macmillan, London

Cairncross F (1997) The death of distance. Harvard Business School Press, Boston

Carlson S (1975) How foreign is foreign trade? Acta Universitatis Uppsaliensis, Studia Oeconomiae Negotiorum II, Uppsala, Sweden, Bulletin No. 15

Cartwright WR (1993) Multiple linked diamonds and the international competitiveness of export dependence industries: the New Zealand experience. Manag Int Rev 33:55–69

Caves RE (1974) Multinational firms, competition, and productivity in host-country markets. Econ Lond Sch Econ Political Sci 41(162):176–193

Chamberlin EH (1933) Theory of monopolistic competition. Harvard University Press, Cambridge

Coase RH (1937) The nature of the firm. Economica 4(16):386–405

Commons JR (1934) Institutional economics. Macmillan, New York

Cuervo JC, Low SP (2003) Significance of location factors for Singapore transnational construction corporations. Eng Constr Archit Manag 10(5):342–353

Cuervo JC, Low SP (2004) Global performance measures for transnational construction corporations. Constr Manag Econ 22(8):851–860

Cyert R, March J (1963) A behavioural theory of the firm. Prentice-Hall, Englewood Cliffs

Davidson WH (1983) Market similarity and market selection: implications for international marketing strategy. J Bus Res 11:439–456

Dorfman MS (2007) Introduction to risk management and insurance. Dorling Kindersley, Harlow

Dulaimi and Hwa (2001) Developing world class construction companies in Singapore. Constr Manag Econ 19(6):591–599

Dunning JH (1988) The Eclectic Paradigm of international production: a restatement and some possible extensions. J Int Bus Stud 19(1):1–31

Dunning JH (1993) Internationalizing Porter's diamond. Manag Int Rev 33(2):7–15

Dunning JH (2000) The Eclectic Paradigm as an envelope for economic and business theories of MNE activity. Int Bus Rev 9:163–190

Erramilli M, Rao CP (1993) Service firms' international entry-mode choice: a modified transaction-cost analysis approach. J Mark 57(3):19–38

Flanagan R et al (2007) Measuring construction competitiveness in selected countries – final report. The University of Reading, Reading

Friedman M (1953) Essays in positive economics. University of Chicago Press, Chicago

Friedman T (2005) The world is flat. Straus and Giroux, New York

Ganitsky J (1989) Strategies for innate and adoptive exporters: lessons from Israel's case. Int Mark Rev 6(5):50–65

Gatignon H, Anderson E (1988) The multinational corporation's degree of control over foreign subsidiaries: an empirical test of a transaction cost explanation. J Law Econ Organ 4(Fall):305–336

Hedlund G, Kverneland A (1985) Are strategies for foreign markets changing? The case of Swedish investment in Japan. Int Stud Manag Organ 15(2):41–59

Heisenberg W (1927) Ueber die Grundprincipien der Quantenmechanik. Forschungen und Fortschritte 3:83

Hill CWL, Hwang P, Kim WC (1990) An eclectic theory of the choice of international entry mode. Strateg Manag J 11(2):117–128

Holton GA (2004) Defining risk. Financ Anal J 60(6):19–25

Hubbard D (2009) The failure of risk management. Wiley, Hoboken

Hymer SH (1960) The international operations of national firms: a study of direct foreign investment. PhD dissertation, The MIT Press

Hymer SH (1976) The international operation of national firms: a study of direct foreign investment. MIT Press, Cambridge, MA

Isard W (1956) A general location principal of an optimum space-economy. Econometrica 20:406–430

Itaki M (1991) A critical assessment of the eclectic theory of the multinational enterprise. J Int Bus Stud 22(3):445–460

Johanson J, Mattson LG (1988) Internationalization in industrial systems – a network approach. In: Hood N et al (eds) Strategies in global competition. Croom Helm, London, pp 287–314

Johanson J, Vahlne JE (1977) The internationalization process of the firm: a model of knowledge development and increasing foreign market commitments. J Int Bus Stud 8(1):23–32

Johanson J, Wiedersheim PF (1975) The internationalisation of the firm – four Swedish cases. J Manag Stud 12:305–322

Jones RW (1971) The specific-factors model. University of Rochester, Rochester

Jones MV (1999) The internationalization of small high-technology firms. J Int Mark 7(4):15–41

Kasper W (1994) Spatial economics. ICS Press, San Francisco

Keynes JM (1936) The general theory of employment, interest and money. Macmillan/Cambridge University, London/Cambridge

Kim WC, Mauborgne R (2005) Blue ocean strategy – how to create uncontested market space and make the competition irrelevant. Harvard Business School Press, Boston

Kindleberger CP (1984) Multinational excursions. MIT Press, Cambridge, MA

Knight F (1921) Risks, uncertainty and profit. Houghton Mifflin, Boston

Kravis IB (1956) Availability and other influences on the commodity composition of trade. J Political Econ 64(2):143–155, Columbia University Press

Kravis IB, Lipsey RE (1982) The location of overseas production and production for export by U.S. multinational firms, NBER working papers 0482, National Bureau of Economic Research, Inc

Krugman P (1996) Confronting the mystery of urban hierarchy. J Jpn Int Econ 10:399–418

Leamer EE (1995) The Heckscher-Ohlin model in theory and practice. Princeton University Press, Princeton

Leong HK, Ku SCY (2005) China and South-east Asia – global changes and regional challenges. ISEAS Publications, Singapore

Leontief WW (1958) Factor proportions and the structure of American trade: further theoretical and empirical analysis: comment. Rev Econ Stat 40(1):111–116, Part 2. Problems in international economics

Linder SB (1961) An essay on trade and transformation. Almqvist & Wicksell, Stockholm

References

Lojeski KS (2007) The collapsing corporation and the rise of virtual distance: the challenges of driving innovation in a world without leaders. In: Conference on managing virtual distance, Anaheim, CA, 14–16 Nov 2007

Lovelock CH (2009) Services marketing, 9th edn. Prentice Hall, Englewood Cliffs

Luostarinen R (1979) Internationalization of the firm. Published dissertation, International Business, Helsinki School of Economics, Helsinki

March JG, Simon HA (1958) Organizations. Wiley, New York

Markowitz HM (1952) Portfolio selection. J Financ 7(1):77–91

Markusen JR (2004) Multinational firms and the theory of international trade. MIT Press, Cambridge, MA

Marx K (1867) Capital: a critique of political economy (1992) (trans: Fernbach D). Penguin, London

Mayer WG (1993) Trends in media usage. Public Opin Quart 57(4):593–611

McKinsey and Co. (1993) Emerging exporters: Australia's high value-added manufacturing exporters. McKinsey & Company and the Australian Manufacturing Council, Melbourne

Mill JS (1871) Principles of political economy. Longmans, Green, Reader and Dyer, London

Minsky HM (1982) Inflation, recession and economic policy. Wheatsheaf, Sussex

MTI (2008) Economic Survey of Singapore

Mun T (1664) English treasure by foreign trade. BiblioBazaar, NA

Ng TWH, Feldman DC (2010) The effects of organizational embeddedness on development of social capital and human capital. J Appl Psychol 95(4):696–712

Ofori G et al (2001) The potential of developing world-class Singapore construction and construction-related firms with strong export capability, Final Report on Research Project RP292 000-037-112. Department of Building, National University of Singapore

Olson GM, Olson JS (2000) Distance matters. Hum Comput Interact 15:139–179

Penrose ET (1959) The theory of the growth of the firm. Blackwell, Oxford

Perlmutter HV (1969) The multinational firm and the future. Ann Am Polit Soc Sci 403(9):139–152

Porter ME (1990) The competitive advantage of nations. Free Press, New York

Posner MV (1961) International trade and technical change. Oxf Econ Pap 13(3):323–341

Ravetz JR (1993) The sin of science. Knowl Creat Diffus Util 15(2):157–165

Reid S (1986) Migration, cultural distance and international market expansion. In: Turnbull PW, Paliwoda SJ (eds) Research in international marketing. Croom Helm, London, pp 22–34

Reid NO, OhUllaChain B (1997) Acquisition versus greenfield investment: the location and the growth of Japanese manufacturers in the United States. J Reg Stud Assoc 31:403–416

Ricardo D (1817) On the principles of political economy and taxation. J.M. Dent & Sons, London

Rogers EM (1962) The diffusion of innovations. Free Press of Glencoe, New York

Root FR (1998) Entry strategies for international markets (Revised edition). Jossey-Bass, San Francisco

Rummel RJ, Heenan DA (1978) How multinationals analyze political risk. Harv Bus Rev 56:67–76

Seymour H (1987) The multinational construction industry. Croom Helm, London

Smith A (1776) An inquiry into the nature of the wealth of nations. Methuen and Co., London

Teece DJ (1981) The market for know-how and the efficient international transfer of technology. Ann Am Acad Political Soc Sci 458(11):81–96. doi:10.1177/000271628145800107

Tejima S (1994) The recent trends of Japanese Foreign Direct Investment (FDI) and Prospects in the 1990s based on Japan EXIM Banks Survey Implemented in FY 1993. EXIM Review, Research Institute for International Investment and Development, Tokyo

Terpstra V, Sarathy R (1994) International marketing, 6th edn. Dryden Press, Fort Worth

Terpstra V, Yu CM (1988) Determinants of foreign investment of US advertising agencies. J Int Bus Stud 19(1):33–46. doi:10.1057/palgrave.jibs.8490373

Thompson H (1997) Ignorance and ideological hegemony: a critique of neoclassical economics. J Interdiscip Econ 8(4):291–305

Veblen TB (1900) The preconceptions of economic science pt III. Q J Econ 14:240–269

Von Thünen JH (1826) Isolated state (1966) (trans: Wartenberg CM). Pergamon Press, New York

Welch LS, Luostarinen R (1988) Internationalisation: evolution of a concept. J Gen Manag 14(2):34–55

Welch L, Luostarinen R (1993) Inward-outward connections in internationalization. J Int Mark 1(1):44–56

Williams B (1997) Positive theories of multinational banking: eclectic theory versus internalization theory. J Econ Surv 11(1):71–100

Woodward J (1958) The contingency theory of organizations. Sage Publications, Thousand Oaks

Chapter 5
Business Strategies and Organization Design

5.1 Introduction

Business strategies enable a firm to accentuate its strengths and attenuate its weaknesses. Without which, there is no focus and the firm may get lost in the business labyrinth. This chapter explains the linkages between internationalization, business strategies and organization structures. It also traces the roots, tracks the evolution and introduces the contemporary issues in business strategies and organization designs. In addition, it compares the different strategies and organization structures appropriate for different types of firms and suggests how these strategies and organization structures complement each other.

5.2 Military Strategies and Formations

There had been many exponents of military strategies from both the Eastern and the Western worlds. For instance, from the East, Sun-tzu's (sixth century BC) *Art of War* has had a profound influence on military and business thinking. Sun-tzu's teachings taught about the development of troops, detailed assessment and planning of waging a war, understanding and making use of terrain and battlegrounds, appreciation of weaknesses and strengths of forces, positioning of the army, military manoeuvres, the use of intelligence and espionage, strategic attack, variation and adaptability (Sawyer 1993). Miyamoto Musashi's (1645) *Book of Five Rings* focused on the art of fighting in a duel or a massive battle. In the manual, he emphasized on the importance of seizing the opportunity and initiative to win. From the West, Machiavelli's (1521) *The Art of War* wrote about the importance of instilling esteem into the modes and orders of military discipline, and detailed about how an army should be raised, trained and organized. In his even more famous book *The Prince* (Machiavelli 1532), Machiavelli wrote about how to defend a city, the use of aides, and how to conduct or portray one-self for his own benefit. Carl von Clausewitz's (1832) *On War* espoused the notion of a *total war*, whereby a belligerent engages in a mobilization of all available resources at its disposal.

In his book, Von Clausewitz famously highlighted the trinity of emotion, chance, and rationality in war-fare. The Prussian's book is still regarded as one of the most important treatises on strategy ever written to this day. Despite the passage of time, contemporary military strategies are still very much alike to these precursors. For example, the United States Army's Field Manual of Military Operations contains these sections which have marked resemblances to the art of warfare taught or used by military experts such as Sun-tzu, Musashi, Genghis Khan, Alexander, Hannibal, Machiavelli, Napoleon and von Clausewitz:

(i) Objective – to direct the military operation towards a clearly defined, decisive, and attainable objective;
(ii) Offensive – to seize, retain, and exploit the initiative;
(iii) Mass – to concentrate combat power at the decisive place and time;
(iv) Economy of force – to allocate minimum essential combat power to secondary efforts;
(v) Manoeuvre – to place the enemy in a disadvantageous position through the flexible application of combat power;
(vi) Unity of command – one responsible commander to unite efforts;
(vii) Security – to prevent enemies from acquiring unexpected advantage;
(viii) Surprise – to strike the enemy at a place, time, or manner for which he is unprepared; and
(ix) Simplicity – to hand out concise orders.

Greene (2007) put forward that there are many levels and types of military strategies, such as the grand strategy, polarity strategy, counterbalance strategy, command-and-control strategy, controlled chaos strategy, morale strategy, perfect economy strategy, counter-attack strategy, deterrence strategy, non-engagement strategy, intelligence strategy, misperception strategy, blitzkrieg strategy, centre-of-gravity strategy, diplomatic strategy, alliance strategy, fait accompli strategy, communications strategy et cetera. The grand strategy is the top-levelled master-plan and it encompasses the management of the resources of an entire nation in the conduct of warfare. This is very much like the concept of "Total Defence" in Switzerland, Sweden and Singapore, whereby military defence, civil defence, social defence, economic defence, psychological defence and diplomacy with allies are summoned together to create a comprehensive defence strategy.

It is suggested that part of these military strategies and formations of war-fare which had dealt with the planning and conduct of campaigns, the movement and deployment of forces have evolved into business strategies and organization structures (Krause 1995).

5.3 Theory of the Firm

The theory of the firm consists of a number of economic and management ideas which describe the nature of the firm, its existence, behaviour and relationship with the market (Holmstrom and Tirole 1989; Conner 1991). These concepts explain the emergence, boundaries and organization of the firm (Coase 1937). Arising from the literature review undertaken in this study, a summary of the theoretical underpinnings of the firm and international management concepts is shown chronologically in Table 5.1.

5.3.1 Resource-Based Theory

The Resource-Based Theory argues that firms have to possess resources which enable them to achieve competitive advantage and superior long-term performance. According to the theory, firms protect against resource imitation, transfer or substitution to sustain their competitive advantage (Penrose 1959). Hence, non-critical or non-core competencies which are not valuable, rare, in-imitable and non-substitutable can be outsourced and offshore-centres can tap into new or cheaper resources. Barney (1991) suggested that a firm's resources include all assets, firm attributes, capabilities, organizational processes, information, knowledge, et cetera. controlled by a firm that enable the firm to conceive of and implement strategies that improve its efficiency and effectiveness. Notably, Montgomery (1995) regarded the unique resources that give the firm its competitive advantage as the crown jewels of the firm.

It is postulated in this study that when firms venture into overseas markets, firms' accesses to home-based or location-specific resources get sapped, especially so with geographical distance and at country-borders.

5.3.2 Transaction-Costs Theory

The Transaction-costs Theory explains how the costs incurred in search and information costs, contract costs, policing costs and enforcement costs affect the firm's decisions such as establishment, choice of market and entry mode (Coase 1937; Williamson 1975). Therefore, a firm expands its operations by growing internally, until the point that the cost of internalization is the same as a transaction in the open market, after which it may organize the internationalization through an external intermediary.

Hu and Chen (1993) highlighted that there are three factors which may affect the transaction costs of services: (i) geographical distance; (ii) difference in culture, business customs and economic systems and; (iii) government policies and possible political risks. Transnational firms internalize their operations to reduce transaction costs due to the transfer of firm-specific assets (Williamson 1975; Caves and Bradburd 1988; Krugman 1991; Fujita and Thisse 1996).

This trait is exacerbated for construction-related firms because the immobility of construction items means that only managerial and technical skills, and some materials and equipment can be transferred from one country to another. Asset specificity refers to the extent to which the investments made to support a particular

Table 5.1 Firm and international management concepts

Concept	Description	Authors
Least cost location theory	Hierarchy of activities take the shape of concentric rings around urban centres. Industries tend to be located in a location so that transportation and land costs are minimized.	Von Thünen (1826) Weber (1929)
Demand theory	The analysis of the relationship between the demand for goods or services and prices or incomes.	Marshall (1890)
Traditional theory	Profit maximization or sales maximization is the goal of the firm. This is contrary to later theories such as the Behavioral Theory.	Marshall (1890)
Substitution analysis	Firms seek the optimal input-output combinations via the analysis, so that costs can be reduced and revenue/profits can be increased.	Marshall (1890) Isard (1956)
Heckscher-Ohlin trade theory	Explains the existence and pattern of international trade based on comparative cost advantages between countries producing different goods.	Ohlin (1933)
Transaction costs theory	The costs incurred in search and information costs, contract costs, policing costs and enforcement costs.	Coase (1937) Williamson (1975)
Cost-benefit analysis	The determination of the total value of a proposed investment's inputs and outputs. It is useful as an informal approach to make an economic decision.	Hicks (1939)
Game-theoretical strategies	Mathematically capture behaviour in strategic situations, in which an individual's success in making choices depends on the choices of others.	Von Neumann and Morgenstern (1944)
Nash equilibrium	Refers to a situation in which individuals participating in a game pursue the best possible strategy while possessing the knowledge of the strategies of other players	Nash (1950)
Behavioural settings	Explains how an entity would act according to its environment or external forces. It suggests that a firm has to be flexible and adapt to changes.	Lewin (1951)
Satisficing and bounded rationality	Firms do not have full knowledge and can only act within their best knowledge.	Katona (1951)
Informational costs	The costs of transmitting, collecting, processing of information for decision-making in centralized or decentralized systems.	Marschak (1954)
Second best theory	The 'second best' position can only be reached by departing from all the other Paretian conditions.	Lipsey and Lancaster (1956)
		Baumol (1959)

(continued)

5.3 Theory of the Firm

Table 5.1 (continued)

Concept	Description	Authors
Managerial theories of the firm	New goals may, for example, focus on sales or asset growth maximization instead of profit maximization	
Resource-based theory	The competitive advantage of a firm lies primarily in the application of the bundle of valuable resources at the firm's disposal.	Penrose (1959); Porter (1980)
Growth of the firm	Managers try to reach their optimal rates of power and prestige by following a path towards product excellence and maximum growth.	Penrose (1959)
Rational expectations	Individuals and companies, acting with complete access to relevant information, forecast events in the future without bias	Muth (1960)
Search theory	The analysis of how buyers and sellers acquire information about market conditions and how potential market participants are brought together.	Stigler (1961)
Synoptic ideal vs. incremental strategy	Firms often choose to gradually increase their commitments instead of taking a huge risk, even if their decisions go against their ideals.	Braybrooke and Lindblom (1963)
Optimally imperfect decisions	Firms seeks to make the best decision under the circumstances or with the information it has.	Baumol and Quandt (1964)
Product life-cycle	Product life cycle management is the succession of strategies used by management as a product goes through its product life cycle.	Levitt (1965)
Corporate networks	Intra-organizational relations between hierarchies, functions and departments; and inter-organizational relations with business partners.	Emery and Trist (1965)
Behavioral matrix	It describes the availability of information and the ability of the firm to use the information to its benefit.	Pred (1967)
Strategic information	Firms seek to scan, monitor and elicit strategic information so as to formulate appropriate strategies.	Aguilar (1967)
Theory of the multinational	Explains why multinational firms internationalize. It suggests that firms internationalize to seek for markets, resources, efficiency and strategic assets.	Lipsey and Weiss (1984); Markusen (1999)
Small is beautiful	The principle challenged the tradition of large organizations, which Schumacher claimed were inefficient and a danger to the environment.	Schumacher (1973)
Organizational theory	Goals and activities of a firm are the results of its organization structure. It stresses the importance of a firm's organization structure.	Willliamson (1975)
		Hymer (1976)

(continued)

Table 5.1 (continued)

Concept	Description	Authors
Industrial Organization Theory	Local firms know indigenous consumer taste, business customs, legal system et cetera better than foreign firms.	
Internalization theory	Suggests that by investing in a foreign subsidiary rather than licensing, the company is able to send the knowledge across borders while maintaining it within the firm, where it presumably yields a better return on the investment.	
Learning organizations	Suggests that an organization keeps transforming itself as it learns and acquires knowledge.	Argyris and Schön (1978) Senge (1990)
Contract theory	Labour and capital agree on the parameters of production, and the amount of risk and rewards each side will bear.	Okun (1981)
Contestable markets theory	Defines contestability as the effectiveness of barriers to entry and exit in a market.	Baumol et al. (1982)
Strategic flexibility and adaptability	Describes how firms adapt themselves or adopt new strategies in a new environment.	Aaker and Mascarenhas (1984)
Decision theory	In determining a course of action, an individual must evaluate rationally conditions of uncertainty and risk.	Sen (1985)
Agency theory	Essentially involves the costs of resolving conflicts between the principals and agents and aligning interests of the two groups.	Eisnehardt (1989)
Knowledge-based theory	The knowledge-based theory of the firm considers knowledge as the most strategically significant resource of a firm.	Kogut and Zander (1992) and Nonaka and Takeuchi (1995)
Value-based model of firm	The creation of customer value must be the reason for the firm's existence and certainly for its success.	Slater (1997)

transaction have a higher value to that transaction than they would have if they were redeployed for any other purpose (McGuinness 1994). The dimensions of asset specificity are:

(i) Site specificity, e.g. a natural resource available at a certain location and movable only at great cost;
(ii) Physical asset specificity, e.g. a specialized machine tool or complex computer system designed for a single purpose;
(iii) Human asset specificity, i.e., highly specialized human skills;
(iv) Dedicated assets, i.e. a discrete investment in a plant that cannot readily be put to work for other purposes; and
(v) Time specificity, an asset is time specific if its value is highly dependent on its reaching the user within a specified, relatively limited period of time (Williamson 1986).

It is postulated in this study that the costs of facilitating access to home-based or location-specific resources increase with geographical distance and at country-borders. A/E firms would then have to adjust its business strategies and organization design to be more cost-efficient and effective.

5.3.3 Behavioural Theory

Bernoulli's hypothesis suggests that the acceptance of a risk depends not only on the nominal value of what may be lost but also on the intrinsic value, or utility, of it to the person accepting the risk. Similarly, the Behavioural Model was derived by Aharoni (1966) to suggest that the decision to internationalise need not be based on profit maximization but is instead motivated by internal management interest, and external factors like client demands, stricter import controls and higher tariffs. The behavioural approach explains how decisions are taken within the firm (Cyert and March 1963) and puts forth the idea that people possess limited cognitive ability and so can exercise only bounded rationality when making decisions in complex, uncertain situations. It appears that different individuals or groups tend to make only satisfactory and sequential decisions (Simons 1997).

It is postulated in this study that geographical distance and at country-borders dissipates a firm's understanding of a foreign market. As a result, the firm does not make or is incapable of making an informed or best decision, but has to be contented with a cautious but satisfactory decision.

5.3.4 International Product Life-Cycle Theory

The International Product Life-cycle Theory describes the diffusion process of an innovative product from advanced to developing countries over time (Posner 1961). It suggests that when a commodity is invented, it commands a premium. Gradually, the price of the product would have to drop due to heightened competition and discerned demand in the original market, but demand increases in some less developed economies. The firms may then decide to shift the production centre to such a lower-cost location to reduce production costs. At the end of the diffusion process, developed countries have costs and production advantages and start to export (Hill 2007). The Product Life Cycle Theory also explains FDI as a stage in foreign market penetration and how technological innovation determines the structure of world trade and geographical distribution of products.

It is postulated in this study that firms tend to internationalize into markets which are less technologically developed than their home-markets. Firms that try to do the reverse usually face more difficulties.

5.3.5 Uppsala Model

The Uppsala Model is a dynamic and predictive model that incorporates the Behavioural Theory onto internationalization with psychic distance and the establishment chain. It explains the phenomenon that firms initially choose to enter nearby markets with low market commitment. Then, the firms begin to take incremental steps through extended commitment in a specific foreign market over time, or the progressive ventures into new markets with successively greater psychic and geographical distance (Johanson and Wiedersheim 1975). The model considers FDI as a subsequent step to exporting and attributes this incremental process to the difficulties in obtaining information about operations in further foreign markets. Such difficulties are derived from, for example, cultural, linguistic and institutional differences between countries. This evolutionary view of the internationalization process therefore argues that companies acquire more control and put in more commitment to foreign markets insofar as they accumulate experience and knowledge and reduce the asymmetry in knowledge, resources, networks and markets. However, whether firm performance is best served by incremental or radical change has been much debated (Miller and Friesen 1980; Tushman and Romanelli 1985).

It is postulated in this study that in the beginning of a firm's internationalization process, the firm tends to take up business strategies and organization designs that require less risk exposure. Then as the firm acquires experiences and knowledge of the foreign market, it increases its investments and commitments in the overseas market.

5.3.6 Networks Theory

Future competition will pit supply chains against supply chains and not merely company against company (Handfield and Nichols 2002). The Network Theory suggests how a firm can leverage on the strengths of its partners. Firms are interdependent and interact with one another for information, resources and opportunities. Johanson and Mattson (1988) argued that when a firm enters foreign markets, it establishes relationships and networks in those markets. This is also illustrated by the client-following strategy used by service firms to internationalize (Majkgard and Sharma 1998), usually achieved by means of international extension, penetration and connecting existing networks (Björkman and Forsgren 2000). Notably, on the other hand, risk increases and the growth of the firm may be impeded when a firm becomes over-reliant on its partners. Firms must discern whether to cooperate with other players or develop their own unique web of capabilities (Collins 2001).

It is postulated in this study that a firm's network and relationships with its business partners can be impeded by geographical distance or national borders. This

Table 5.2 Analysis of the environment, planning, matching and implementation

Analysis of the environment
Diversity of the new economy; Complexity of the environment, Business intelligence; Psychoanalyzing the organization;

Planning and Matching
Competency; Leadership; Human resources; Partnering; Strategies and Systems; Organization structures

Implementation
Internationalization; Entry strategies; Communications; Value creation; Learning and knowledge management; Cultural management

could in turn, result to loss of opportunities, communication and coordination problems and inefficiency of work.

5.4 Issues on Strategic Management

Markides (1999) considered that defining the business, in terms of its values, mission, capabilities, activities and customers is the starting point of any strategy. Strategic management integrates and expands key existing theories of the firm, and is defined as the art and science of formulating, implementing and evaluating cross-functional decisions that would enable an organization to achieve its objectives (David 1989). Strategic management essentially comprises a few key processes, namely, to assess environment for threats and opportunities, to assess internal strengths and weaknesses, and to consider suitable strategies using competitive analysis (Deresky 2000). Table 5.2 shows the key issues on the strategic management of a transnational firm. These issues are essentially divided into (i) analysis of the environment; (ii) planning and matching; and (iii) implementation.

5.4.1 New Economy

The firm would need to understand the new economy to manage stakeholders' expectations and devise business strategies at the different decision levels. Technology, communication and market advances are fundamentally altering the perspectives of time, distance and spatial boundaries (Yisa and Edwards 2002). Opening markets and digitization are pulling large corporations and SMEs beyond their national borders (Barkema et al. 2002). Professionals are shaping the boundaries of the industry. Firms are seeking to protect their positions, enter new markets, or find new ways or venues to leverage on their capabilities.

5.4.2 Complexity and Flexibility

The new economy is so unpredictable and complex today because of the increase in the rate of change, increase in the number of variables, the increasing interdependence of these elements, and the lack of knowledge of the causes and effects of these factors. These accelerating economic changes and the compounding complexities of business have stimulated the rapid emergence and transcendence of new management ideas (Clarke and Clegg 2000). Managing diversity and being flexible is increasingly important for organizations.

5.4.3 Intelligence

Business intelligence is required to manage the complexities the firm has to come to face. Business intelligence was first defined by Luhn (1958) as the ability to apprehend the interrelationships of presented facts in such a way as to guide action towards a desired goal. Now, it generally refers to the skills, technologies, applications and practices used by a firm to acquire a better knowledge of its commercial context, so as to facilitate better decision-making for the informed steering of the enterprise.

5.4.4 Psychoanalyzing the Organization

Psychoanalyzing the organization is as important as getting business intelligence. Chandler (1962) believed that business history can provide insights into the processes of business decisions such as the development of competitive strategy and the restructuring of organizational forms. Therefore, psychoanalyzing the organization is important.

5.4.5 Competency

A firm should be clear about its core competencies because these make up the competitive strengths of a firm. Core competency is a specific factor that a business sees as being central to the way it works (Hamel and Prahalad 1994). It can take various forms, including technical or knowledge know-how, a reliable process, or close relationships with customers and suppliers (Mascarenhas et al. 1998). Competitive strengths are the assets which give the firm an advantage over other competitors.

5.4.6 Internationalization

Internationalization is essentially, the phenomenon of increasing involvement of transnational enterprises in international markets (Dunning 1993). Many firms have ventured overseas in seek of resources, costs advantages or markets. However, firms may also incur internationalization risks such as cultural risks, business risks and institutional risks when they do so.

5.4.7 Strategies and Systems

When firms venture into international markets, they seek to implement strategies and systems to accentuate their competitive strengths and attenuate their weaknesses. According to the McKinsey 7S model, strategy is defined as the plans for the allocations of a firm's scarce resource, over time, to reach identified goals. Systems, on the other hand, is defined as the procedures, processes and routines, such as financial systems, hiring and promotion practices, and information systems that characterize how important work is to be done.

5.4.8 Entry Strategy

"A good start is half the battle won." Entry strategies are crucial for transnational firms to spear-head through the hard and resistant wall of the foreign market. Lasserre (1996) recommended different entry modes and entry strategies in Asia and noted that a firm tend to integrate into global or regional operations over time.

5.4.9 Organization Structure

Organization structure follows business strategies (Chandler 1962). Organization design involves the creation of roles, processes, and formal reporting relationships in an organization (Thompson 1967). Perlmutter (1969) suggested that there is a structural evolution of international operations. It is suggested in this model that firms tend to increase their complexity of international operations and commitment when time and experiences involved in international operations increase.

5.4.10 Leadership

Warren Bennis (1989) explained a dichotomy between managers and leaders when he drew distinctions between the two groups, such as "managers administer, but leaders innovate", "managers ask how and when but leaders ask what and why", "managers focus on systems but leaders focus on people" and "managers do things right but leaders do the right things" et cetera. In general, leadership has been described as the process of social influence in which one person can enlist the aid and support of others in the accomplishment of a common task (Chemers 2002).

5.4.11 Human Resource

Human resource management is the strategic and coherent approach to the management of people in an organization. Generally, this includes the employment, development, utilizing, maintaining and compensating their services in tune with the job and organizational requirements. The human touch is even more crucial in service industries, which consider three more "P"s – People, Process and Physical evidence on top of the 4 "P"s – Product, Price, Place and Promotion of marketing.

5.4.12 Partnering

Collaboration is a recursive process where two or more people or organizations work together in an intersection of common goals. On the other hand, business partnering is the development of successful, long term, strategic relationships between customers and suppliers, based on achieving best practice and sustainable competitive advantage.

5.4.13 Communications

Communication is the process of transferring information from one person to another. During the communication, there could be an exchange of thoughts, feelings or ideas. Communication is the life-blood of an organization, and it has to be conveyed properly to prevent miscommunications, and problems in coordination and inefficiencies in cooperation.

5.4.14 Marketing

Marketing is one of the most important functions of a firm because it helps to sell the firm's products or services. Marketing is defined as the activity, set of institutions, and processes for creating, communicating, delivering, and exchanging offerings that have value for customers, clients, partners, and society at large. There are several orientations of marketing, such as product, sales, production, marketing, customer and organizational orientation.

5.4.15 Value Creation

Porter (1985) suggested that a value chain is a chain of activities of the provision of a product or service, and that it is possible for the value chain to give the products more added value or synergy than the sum of the added values of each individual activity. Firms should always seek to improve or create extra value to stay competitive.

5.4.16 Learning and Knowledge Management

A firm should never be complacent. Knowledge management comprises a range of practices used by an organisation to identify, create, represent, distribute and enable adoption of insights and experiences (Nonaka and Takeuchi 1995). A learning organization is one that adopts knowledge management and evolves as it learns.

5.4.17 Cultural Management

People from different parts of the world exhibit different characteristic traits. They think, behave and act differently. A transnational firm ought to know how best to manage the cultural diversities and differences in different parts of the world.

5.5 Strategic Analysis, Planning, Matching and Implementation

A firm has to strategically analyse the diversity of the new economy and the complexity of the environment. Mintzberg (1998) put forward that strategic analysis is a critical part of strategic management. A firm needs to look at what is behind, above, below, beside, beyond, ahead and through to examine the important endogenous and exogenous elements of its business.

The psychoanalysis of the organization and business intelligences enable the firm to discern its plans in terms of Competency, Leadership, Human resources, Partnering, Strategies, Systems and Organization structures. In Corporate Strategy,

Table 5.3 Choice of entry modes

Product characteristics	Exporting	Licensing	Subsidiary	Equity	Contract
Differentiated	O		O		
Service-intensive			O	O	
Service products		O		O	O
Technology-intensive		O			
High-product adaptation		O	O	O	
Market factors					
Many players	O		O		
Few players				O	
Poor marketing infrastructure			O		
High production costs	O		O		
Restrictive import policies		O		O	O
Great geographical distance		O		O	O
Dynamic economy				O	
Stagnant economy	O	O			O
Restrictive exchange control	O	O			O
Exchange rate appreciation	O		O		
Great cultural difference	O	O			O
Low political risk			O	O	
High political risk	O	O			O

Source: Adapted from Root (1998)

Ansoff (1965) provided The Ansoff Model of Strategic Planning which is a cascade of decisions, whereby a set of objectives is first established, then the gap between the objectives and the current position is articulated, and finally, courses of actions are proposed and tested for their gap-reducing properties.

The McKinsey 7S (Peters and Waterman 1980) recommended that firms have to consider a fit between Strategy, Structure, Systems, leadership Style, Skills, Staff and Shared values. These strategic and organizational aspects should in turn match the opportunities and threats that the firm faces. The firm should implement a competitive strategy that responds to the environment and shape that environment to the firm's favour by amplifying its strengths and attenuating its weaknesses (Porter 1985). Porter (1985) also further recommended making improvements and integration along and at the adjoining interfaces of the value-chain to create a better end-product or to render better service-quality.

5.6 Entry Strategy and Entry Mode

An overseas venture can be like a business start-up which requires the entrepreneur to consider a whole array of things and preparations. It can range from the decision to take the plunge, to timing, targeting, naming, taking loans, site seeking, hiring, networking, setting up infrastructure, branding, marketing et cetera (Lesonsky 2007). A spearheading strategy concentrates its thrust into a new or foreign market by channelling all resources and efforts to jump over the barrier of entry or break

5.6 Entry Strategy and Entry Mode

Table 5.4 International entry strategies/modes: advantages and Critical Success Factors (CSFs)

Strategy	Advantages	Critical success factors
Exporting	Low risk;	Choice of distributor;
	No long-term assets;	Transportation costs;
	Easy market access and exits	Tariffs and quotas
Licensing	No asset ownership risk;	Quality and trustworthiness of licensee;
	Fast market access;	Appropriation of Intellectual Property;
	Avoids regulations and tariffs	Host-country royalty limits
Franchising	Little investment or risk;	Quality control of franchisee and franchise operations
	Fast market access;	
	Small business expansion	
Contract manufacturing	Limited cost and risk;	Reliability and quality of local contractor;
	Short-term commitment	Operational control and human rights issues
Turnkey operations	Revenue from skills and technology where FDI is restricted	Reliable infrastructure;
		Sufficient local supplies and labour;
		Repatriable profits;
		Reliability of any government partner
Management contracts	Low-risk access to further strategies;	Opportunity to gain longer-term position;
Joint ventures	Insider access to markets;	Strategic fit and complementarities of partner, markets and products;
	Share costs and risk;	Ability to protect technology;
	Leverage partner's skill, base technology and local contacts	Competitive advantage;
		Ability to share control;
		Cultural adaptability of partners
Wholly owned subsidiaries	Realise all revenues and control;	Ability to assess and control economic, political and currency risk;
	Global economies of scale;	
	Strategic coordination;	Ability to get local acceptance;
	Protect technology and skill base;	Repatriability of profits
	Acquisition provides rapid market entry into established market	

Source: adapted from Deresky (2000)

through the veneer of defence. Due to its lack of understanding, experience and networks in a new or foreign market, a firm should first seek to get a foot-hold with a spearheading campaign and only advance to diversify or expand after that.

The choice of entry mode into a new foreign market may have a major impact on the success of a firm's international operations (Ramaswami 1992). There is a continuum of non-equity to equity involvements/choices, like partnering, exporting, licensing, contracting, joint venture, asset floating and foreign direct investment in the transaction chain of internationalization when firms decide to supply their services in the international market (Low and Jiang 2004). There are many factors that can influence the choice of an entry mode. These integrated environmental and strategic factors include: country risk and environmental uncertainty, industry barriers, market size, cultural distance, firm's strategies and motivations, core competencies and core capabilities, firm size, top management's preferences (e.g. speed of entry, indirect and direct costs, flexibility, risks, investment payback period et cetera) international experience of management team, role of corporate culture, role of staffing, integration of production costs and uncertainty, network relationship, technology transfer et cetera (Kwon and Konopa 1993; Phatak 1997; Evans 2002; Zhao and Decker 2004).

These may be further complicated by corporate self-imposed constraints like time expectation of profits, product range limitations, functional limitations, geographical limitations, structural constraints (e.g. refusal to consider other than certain types of relationships), financial constraints, (e.g. refusal to seek external debt or equity financing). Table 5.3 shows Root's (1998) recommendations on how a firm may choose an appropriate entry mode given a set of conditions in a new market. In Table 5.4, Deresky (2000) outlined the advantages and Critical Success Factors (CSF) of the various entry modes.

Goodnow and Hansz (1972) found that a firm tend to pursue an entry strategy involving greater control and greater investment in marketing channel activities as the country's environment becomes "hotter" along an environmental "temperature gradient". For these firms, "hot countries" are politically stable, high in market opportunity, has good economic development and performance, has cultural unity, and low in legal barriers, physiographic barriers and geo-cultural distance. They also discovered that "warmer countries" tend to be geographically closer to the home-offices of the firms, and found that businessmen vary in the weight they give to variables when making decisions about specific countries.

In the context of the construction industry, Firat and Huovinen (2005) noted that a contractor, a supplier, or a designer, as an entrant, must face and penetrate an extremely "hard" wall surrounding the market consisting of local clients, architects, contractors, and other stakeholders that are glued together with local contracting rules, building regulations, traditions, and practices. Therefore, they proposed the "spearhead strategy" which is about choosing a competitive arena, identifying potential clients and influencers, adapting entrant's existing offering, differentiating company's approach towards potential clients, localizing entrant's capabilities, and tailoring entrant's sales arguments.

5.7 Organization Design

Markides (1999) described the organization as one made up of four elements: culture, structure, incentive systems and workforce; while Gabarro and Lorsch (1992) described the organization design as consisting of the structure, rewards, and measurement practices intended to direct members' behaviour towards the organization's goals. They also suggested that organization design needs to consider the environment, strategy and task, individual characteristics, top manager's style and experience and the company culture.

Organization structures must adapt to accommodate a firm's evolving internationalization in response to worldwide competition. Transnational organizations should be global but act local. To be "glocal", organizations must be more flexible and involves more inter-organizational networks and transnational design. The structural choices of these transnational companies depend on many factors – Dalton et al. (1980) put forward that organization design depends on organization development: the age, size, stages of evolution, stage of evolution and growth rate of the organization and industry; while Deresky (2000) advocated that the choice depends on geographical dispersion, difference in time, language, cultural attitudes and business attitudes.

In "The Age of Unreason", Handy (1989) provided insights on changing organization structures and developments such as knowledge working, outsourcing, and strategic alliances as the hallmarks of the new economy. Handy (1989) suggested that a number of organization forms would emerge: the sham-lock organization, federal organization, and the Triple I organization. The sham-lock organization bases itself around a core of essential executives and workers supported by outside contractors. The federal organization is a form of decentralised set-up in which the centre's powers to coordinate, advise, influence and suggest, rather than direct and control, are given to it by the outlying groups. On the other hand, the Triple I is based on Information, Intelligence, and Ideas.

There have been other authors who suggested different names for the organization structures. For example, Low (1990) posited that there are seven forms of organization structures: single marketing executive, the functional structure, divisional structure, products structure, geographical structure, matrix structure and complex structure; Miles and Snow (2003) suggested the cellular structure which comprises cells of self-managing teams, autonomous business units, operational partners et cetera that can operate alone and also interact with other cells to produce a more potent and competent business mechanism that allows the interdependence and independence of generation of knowledge and expertise. Quinn et al. (1996) agreed that different organizations are needed for different purposes and suggested that there are four intellectual dimensions most distinguished in each form: locus of intellect; locus of novelty; mode of linkage; and source of leverage.

Centralization is very costly to operate for transnational firms. As the overseas organizations grow in size and complexity, managers stationed in the headquarters are swamped with requests for information, guidance, support and decisions. To respond appropriately, they need to reinforce their resources, capabilities, and knowledge base, thereby increasing the size and bureaucracy of the central decision-making unit. The greater the diversity or more foreign the overseas environment, the more difficult it is for the headquarters. The global matrix was once thought to be the elixir to the management. But barriers of distance, time, language, culture and other differences have impeded the vital process of confronting and resolving differences. The Business International Corporation (1981) also pointed out some indicators of international organizational malaise (melancholy) such as failure to grow/go in accordance to plan, inefficiencies, clashes among divisions, subsidiaries, or individuals; divisive conflicts, flood of detailed data at the headquarters, duplication of administrative personnel and service, underutilization of overseas facilities, breakdowns in communications, unclear lines of reporting and ill-defined responsibilities. There is no one best way to organize. Therefore it was suggested that contingency theory applies to organization design as much as to any other aspect of management (Deresky 2000).

The best organization structure facilitates the firm's goals and is appropriate to its industry, size, technology and competitive environment, and it should be fluid and dynamic (Deresky 2000). The common problem underlying the search by companies for a structural fit was that it focused on only one organizational variable – the formal structure of a static set of roles, responsibilities and relationship that could not capture the complexity of the strategic task. Hence, Barlett and Ghoshal (1998) suggested building a matrix in the managers' minds instead of merely having a matrix organization structure. Barlett and Ghoshal (1998) also saw an organization in these terms: the anatomy – the organization structure that defines the distribution of assets and resources and the allocation of roles and responsibilities; the physiology – the flows of goods, resources, people and information around the organization and the processes and relationships such flows create; and the psychology – the culture, shared vision and values that give the organization a meaning and glue all things together.

5.8 Inter-dependence of Strategy and Organization Structure

Chandler (1962) was a strong advocate that organization design is intricately related to strategy. Chandler (1962) defined strategy as the determination of the basic long term goals and objectives, and the adoption of courses of action and the allocation of resources necessary for carrying out goals; and structure is the design of the organization through which the enterprise is administered – the lines of authority and communication between the different administrative offices and the officers, information and data that flow through these lines of communication and authority. Chandler (1962) saw environmental changes as the source of new opportunities and needs, and new strategies are adopted in response to such shifts in external conditions, which led to his proposition that "structure follows strategy" and to its corollary – that without structural adjustments, changes in growth strategy can lead to economic inefficiency. Porter (1980) also concurred with this string of thought, but added that the firm's strategy in turn follows the industry's structure and that in truth, strategy and organization structure takes their turns to lead each other. Hamel and Prahalad (1994) thought strategy and structure are inextricably intertwined. Li (1995) thought that strategy and organization structure are strongly related because the "optimal strategy" maximizes the organization's payoff, and the organization structure implements the optimal strategy and minimizes the cost of information processing. Hill and Jones (1995) also compared the relationships

Table 5.5 Strategy and the appropriate structural variations

	Multi-domestic strategy	International strategy	Globalization strategy	Transnational strategy
	Low ←─────────────→ Need for coordination ←─────→ High			
	Low ←─────────────→ Bureaucratic costs ←─────→ High			
Centralization of authority	Decentralized to national unit	Core competencies centralized; others decentralized to national units	Centralized at optimum global location	Simultaneously centralized and decentralized
Horizontal differentiation	Global area structure	International division structure	Global product group structure	Global matrix structure "Matrix in the mind"
Need for complex integrating mechanisms	Low	Medium	High	Very high
Organizational culture	Not important	Quite important	Important	Very important

Source: Hill and Jones (1995)

between the choice of strategy (internationalization) and the appropriate structural variations necessary to implement each strategic choice as shown in Table 5.5.

5.9 McKinsey 7S

The McKinsey 7S Strategic Framework (Peters and Waterman 1980) considers a firm's Strategy, Structure, Systems, Style of leadership, Skills of firm, Staff characteristics and Shared Values and proposes that these strategic and organizational aspects are inter-related and should be integrated by the firm.

D'Aveni (1994) provided the major critique of McKinsey's 7S framework. He opined that the quickening pace in many industries makes competitive advantage no longer sustainable using traditional paradigms. As each firm attempts to copy the best practices of other industry players, the firms become more efficient, but no more profitable. His critique suggested that the McKinsey 7S framework is too rigid and would be dysfunctional to handle the dynamic changes to a firm's competitive environment. He put forward that organizations need more speed, agility, and capacity for coping with uncertainty to prosper. D'Aveni's (1994) "New 7S Framework" identified (i) Stakeholder Satisfaction, (ii) Strategic Soothsaying (good sense of where the world is going), (iii) Speed, (iv) capability to Surprise rivals, (v) ability to Shift the Rules of competition, (vi) capable Signalling, and (vii) Simultaneous and Sequential Strategic Thrusts that create momentum and follow-on to contend with today's more competitive environments. D'Aveni's (1994) also suggested that strategic competition is war, and like it, strategic alliances are important.

Therefore, the study seeks to incorporate (i) dynamism to take into consideration stakeholder satisfaction, strategic acumen, speed, surprise, rules shift, signalling, simultaneous and sequential thrusts and (ii) the consideration of Supply-chain and Strategic Alliances to the existing McKinsey 7S toolkit. The new framework, named Dynamic 8S toolkit, will be discussed in the Chap. 6.

5.10 A/E Firm's Business Strategies

Kotler (1999) suggested different strategies for different industries. For instance, Kotler (1999) suggested technical expertise, speed of solution and reporting, competitive prices, and relationship marketing for professional services. On the other hand, Kotler (1999) suggested relationship building to get trust, fast response time, top management's involvement in selling, the need to do consultation, solution selling to demonstrate how these can help clientele, understand the clientele's business for project selling, service reliability and accuracy, and meeting price and time demands for industrial services.

A study on the profiles of some of the top A/E practices from USA and the United Kingdom, such as Skidmore, Owings and Merrill (SOM), Kohn Pederson Fox (KPF) and Hellmuth, Obata and Kassabaum (HOK), shows that world-class A/E firms implement business strategies such as:

(i) attracting the best talents by being the best employers;
(ii) providing multidisciplinary services;
(iii) to be technology or market leaders in niche areas;
(iv) diversification into different geographical markets;
(v) establishing a global network to facilitate the integration and enable synergy amongst offices;
(vi) strategic alliances;
(vii) mergers and acquisitions;
(viii) marketing and promoting corporate faces instead of individuals;
(ix) involvement in high-profile projects;
(x) iconic designs;
(xi) sustainable designs;
(xii) be an innovator;
(xiii) be the authority or benchmark for A/E services and practices;
(xiv) community involvement; and
(xv) winning prestigious awards.

The business strategies of these top A/E consultancy firms reflect the emphasis on resources, transaction-costs, behaviour and networks. This is in agreement with the Resource-based Theory, Transaction-costs Theory, Behavioural Theory and

Networks Theory, which altogether suggest that in general, internationalizing A/E firms tend to (i) build up their competitive resources; (ii) manage their transaction-costs by sharing information and resources between offices; (iii) behave in a way that need not be based on profit maximization; (iv) leverage on strategic alliances and networks.

5.11 Summary

This chapter brings together the synthesis of literature on a spectrum of strategic management topics such as coping with diversity in the new economy, managing complexity, psychoanalysing the company, gathering intelligence, building competencies, improvements and value-creation, management of human resource, leadership, collaboration with partners, marketing, organizational learning, organization design, communications, entry strategies, internationalization, culture and management, and privatization et cetera. It is suggested in this chapter that in general, business strategies and organization design have to consider (i) the transferability of resources; (ii) transaction-costs of products or services due to asset specificity (which includes site specificity, physical asset specificity, human asset specificity, dedicated assets and time specificity); (iii) the product or service's lifecycle; (iv) motivations and objectives of the firm; (v) the firm's tendency to make incremental decisions due to bounded knowledge and rationality; and (vi) networks.

References

Aaker D, Mascarenhas B (1984) The need for strategic flexibility. J Bus Strateg 5(2):74–82
Aguilar FJ (1967) Scanning the business environment. MacGraw-Hill, New York
Aharoni Y (1966) The foreign investment decision process. Division of Research, Graduate School of Business Administration, Harvard University, Boston
Ansoff I (1965) Corporate strategy. McGraw-Hill, New York
Argyris C, Schön D (1978) Organizational learning. Addison-Wesley, Reading
Barkema HG, Baum JA, Mannix EA (2002) Management challenges in a new time. Acad Manag J 45(5):916–930
Barlett CA, Ghoshal S (1998) Managing across borders: the transnational solution, 2nd edn. Harvard Business School Press, Boston
Barney JB (1991) Firm resources and sustained competitive advantages. J Manag 17:99–120
Baumol WJ (1959) Business behavior, value and growth. Macmillan, New York
Baumol WJ, Quandt RE (1964) Rules of thumb and optimally imperfect decisions. Am Econ Rev 54:23–46
Baumol WJ, Panzar JC, Willig RD (1982) Contestable markets and the theory of industry structure. Harcourt Brace Jovanovich, New York
Bennis W (1989) On becoming a leader. Business Books, Reading
Björkman I, Forsgren M (2000) Nordic international business research. Int Stud Manag Organ 30(1):6–25
Braybrooke D, Lindblom CE (1963) A strategy of decision. The Free Press, New York

Business International Corporation (1981) New directions in multinational corporate organization. Business International Corporation, New York
Caves RE, Bradburd RM (1988) The empirical determinants of vertical integration. J Econ Behav Organ 9:265–279
Chandler A (1962) Strategy and structure. MIT Press, Cambridge, MA
Chemers MM (2002) An integrative theory of leadership. Psychology Press, New York
Clarke T, Clegg S (2000) Changing paradigms. HarperCollins, London
Coase RH (1937) The nature of the firm. Economica 4(16):386–405
Collins J (2001) Good to great. Collins, New York
Conner KR (1991) A historical comparison of resource-based view and five schools of thought within industrial organization economics: do we have a new theory of the firm? J Manag 17(1):121–154
David F (1989) Strategic management. Merill Publishing Company, Columbus
Dalton DR, Todor WD, Spendolini MJ, Fielding GJ, Porter LW (1980) Organization structure and performance: a critical review. Acad Manag Rev 5(1):49–64
D'Aveni R (1994) Hypercompetition: managing the dynamics of strategic maneuvering. Free Press, New York
Deresky H (2000) International management – managing across borders and cultures, 3rd edn. Prentice Hall, Upper Saddle River
Dunning JH (1993) Internationalizing Porter's diamond. Manag Int Rev 33(2):7–15
Eisnehardt KM (1989) Agency theory: an assessment and review. Acad Manag Rev 14(1):57–74
Emery F, Trist E (1965) The causal texture of organizational environments. Hum Relat 18:21–32
Evans J (2002) Internal determinants of foreign market entry strategy. Manchester Metropolitan University Business School, NA. http://130.195.95.71:8081/WWW/ANZMAC2001/anzmac/AUTHORS/pdfs/Evans1.pdf
Firat CE, Huovinen P (2005) Entering regional construction markets in Russia. In: Porkka J, Kahkonen K (eds) Global perspectives on management and economics in the AEC sector. Technical Research Centre of Finland and Association of Finnish Civil Engineers, Helsinki, pp 57–68
Fujita M, Thisse JF (1996) Economics of agglomeration. J Jpn Int Econ 10(4):339–378
Gabarro JJ, Lorsch JW (1992) Handbook of organizational behaviour. Prentice Hall, Englewood Cliffs
Goodnow JD, Hansz JE (1972) Environmental determinants of overseas market entry strategies. J Int Bus Stud 3(Spring):33–50
Greene R (2007) The 33 strategies of war. Profile Books, London
Hamel G, Prahalad CK (1994) Competing for the future. Harvard Business School Press, Boston
Handfield RB, Nichols EL Jr (2002) Supply chain redesign – transforming supply chains into integrated value systems. Prentice Hall, Upper Saddle River
Handy C (1989) The age of unreason. Harvard Business School Press, Boston
Hicks J (1939) The foundations of welfare economics. Econ J 196:696–712
Hill C (2007) International business competing in the global marketplace, 6th edn. McGraw-Hill, Boston
Hill CWL, Jones ER (1995) Strategic management, 3rd edn. Mifflin, Boston
Holmstrom BR, Tirole J (1989) The theory of the firm. In: Schmalensee R, Willig R (eds) Handbook of industrial organization, vol 1. North-Holland, Amsterdam, pp 61–133
Hu MY, Chen H (1993) Foreign ownership in Chinese joint ventures: a transaction cost analysis. J Bus Res 28(2):149–160
Hymer SH (1976) The international operation of national firms: a study of direct foreign investment. MIT Press, Cambridge, MA
Isard W (1956) A general location principal of an optimum space-economy. Econometrica 20:406–430
Johanson J, Mattson LG (1988) Internationalization in industrial systems – a network approach. In: Hood N et al (eds) Strategies in global competition. Croom Helm, New York, pp 287–314

References

Johanson J, Wiedersheim PF (1975) The internationalisation of the firm – four Swedish cases. J Manag Stud 12:305–322

Katona G (1951) Psychological analysis of economic behavior. McGraw-Hill, New York

Kogut B, Zander U (1992) Knowledge of the firm, combinative capabilities, and the replication of technology. Organ Sci 3(3):383–397

Krause DG (1995) The art of war for executives: ancient knowledge for today's business professional. Berkley Publishing Group, New York

Krugman P (1991) Geography and trade. MIT Press, Cambridge, MA

Kwon YC, Konopa LJ (1993) Impact of host country market characteristics on the choice of foreign market entry mode. Int Mark Rev 10(2):60–76

Lasserre P (1996) Managing large groups in the east and west. In: Mintzberg H, Quinn JB (eds) The strategy process – concepts, contexts, cases, 3rd edn. Prentice Hall, Englewood Cliffs, pp 721–726

Lesonsky R (2007) Start your own business, 4th edn. Entrepreneur Press, Irvine

Levitt T (1965) Exploit the product life cycle. Harv Bus Rev 43:81–94

Lewin K (1951) Field theory in social science. Harper and Row, New York

Li H (1996) The organization structure of strategy. Discussion paper series, no. 185. School of Economics and Finance, The University of Hong Kong

Lipsey RG, Lancaster K (1956) The general theory of second best. Rev Econ Stud 24(1):11–32

Lipsey RE, Weiss MY (1984) Foreign production and exports of individual firms. MIT Press

Low SP (1990) The organization of construction export marketing. Avebury Press, Wiltshire

Low SP, Jiang HB (2004) Domestic issues, international construction and lessons in international project delivery systems for Singapore. In: Shuzo F (ed) Proceedings of the 20th symposium of building construction and management of projects, perspective: construction markets and construction management for East Asian countries. Architectural Institute of Japan and Kyoto University, Kyoto Science Park, Kyoto, 22–24 July, pp 65–74

Luhn HP (1958) A business intelligence system. IBM J Res Dev 2(4):314

Machiavelli N (1521) The art of war. Da Capo

Machiavelli N (1532) The prince (2008) (trans: Marriott WK). Red and Black Publishers, St Petersburg

Majkgard A, Sharma DD (1998) Client-following and market-seeking strategies in the internationalization of service firms. J Bus Bus Mark 4(3):1–41

Markides C (1999) All the right moves: a guide to crafting breakthrough strategy. Harvard Business School Press, Boston

Markusen JR (1999) Multinational enterprises, and the theories of trade and location. In: Braunerhjelm P, Ekholm K (eds) The geography of multinational firms. Kluwer, Boston, pp 9–32

Marschak J (1954) Economic information, decision, and prediction. Springer, Berlin

Marshall A (1890) Principles of economics. Macmillan and Co., London

Mascarenhas B, Baveja A, Jamil M (1998) Dynamics of core competencies in leading multinational companies. Calif Manag Rev 40(4):117–132

McGuinness T (1994) Markets and managerial hierarchies. In: Thompson G et al (eds) Markets hierarchies and networks. Sage, London, pp 66–81

Miles RE, Snow CC (2003) Organizational strategy, structure, and process. Stanford University Press, Stanford

Miller D, Friesen P (1980) Archetypes of organization transition. Adm Sci Q 25(2):268–299

Mintzberg H (1999) Managing quietly. Leader to Leader. Spring

Montgomery CA (1995) Of diamond and dust: a new look at resources. In: Montgomery CA (ed) Resource-based and evolutionary theories of the firm. Kluwer Academic Publishers, Boston, pp 251–268

Musashi M (1645) The book of the five rings (2005) (trans: Cleary T). Shambhala Publications, Boston

Muth JF (1961) Rational expectations and the theory of price movements. Econometrica 39:315–335
Nash J (1950) Equilibrium points in n-person games. Proc Natl Acad Sci USA 36(1):48–49
Nonaka I, Takeuchi H (1995) The knowledge-creating company: how Japanese companies create the dynamics of innovation. Oxford University Press, New York
Ohlin B (1933) Interregional and international trade. Harvard University Press, Cambridge, MA
Okun AM (1981) Prices and quantities. Brookings Institution, Washington, DC
Perlmutter HV (1969) The multinational firm and the future. Ann Am Polit Soc Sci 403(9):139–152
Penrose ET (1959) The theory of the growth of the firm. Blackwell, Oxford
Peters T, Waterman R (1980) In search of excellence. Harper & Row, New York
Phatak AV (1997) International management – concepts and cases. International Thomson Publishing, Cincinnati
Porter ME (1980) Competitive strategy: techniques for analyzing industries and competitors. Free Press, New York
Porter ME (1985) Competitive advantage: creating and sustaining superior performance (Revised edition). Free Press, New York
Posner MV (1961) International trade and technical change. Oxf Econ Pap 10(3):323–341
Pred AR (1967) Behaviour and location. Lund University Press, Lund
Quinn JB, Anderson P, Finkelstein S (1996) New forms of organizing. In: Mintzberg H, Quinn JB (eds) The strategy process – concepts, contexts, cases, 3rd edn. Prentice Hall, Englewood Cliffs, pp 350–361
Ramaswami SN (1992) Choice of foreign market entry mode: impact of ownership, location and internalization factors. J Int Bus Stud 23(1):1–27
Root FR (1998) Entry strategies for international markets (Revised edition). Jossey-Bass, San Francisco
Sawyer RD (1993) The seven military classics of ancient China. Basic Books, New York
Schumacher EF (1973) Small is beautiful: economics as if people mattered. Hartley & Marks Publishers, New York
Sen A (1985) Rationality and uncertainty. Theory Decis 18(2):109–127
Senge P (1990) The fifth discipline: the art and practice of the learning organization. Doubleday, New York
Simons H (1997) Administrative behaviour: a study of decision-making processes in administrative organization, 4th edn. Free Press, New York
Slater SF (1997) Developing a customer value-based theory of the firm. J Acad Mark Sci 25(2):162–167
Stigler GJ (1961) The economics of information. J Polit Econ 69(3):213–225
Thompson JD (1967) Organizations in action. Transaction Publishers, New Brunswick
Tushman ML, Romanelli E (1985) Organization evolution: a metamorphic model of inertia and reorientation. Res Organ Behav 7:171–222
Von Clausewitz K (1832) On war (1984) (trans: Howard M, Paret P). Princeton University Press, Princeton
Von Neumann J, Morgenstern O (1944) Theory of games and economic behaviour. Princeton University Press, Princeton
Von Thünen JH (1826) Isolated state (1966) (trans: Wartenberg CM). Pergamon Press, New York
Weber A (1929) Theory of the location of industries. The University of Chicago Press, Chicago
Williamson OE (1975) Markets and hierarchies: analysis and antitrust implications. The Free Press, New York
Williamson OE (1986) Economic organization: firms, markets, and policy control. New York University Press, New York
Yisa S, Edwards D (2002) Evaluation of business strategies in the UK construction engineering consultancy. Meas Bus Excell 6(1):23–31, Bradford
Zhao X, Decker R (2004) Choice of foreign market entry mode: cognitions from empirical and theoretical studies. Int J Bus Econ 3(3):181–200

Chapter 6
Theoretical and Conceptual Framework

6.1 Introduction

Transnational Architectural and Engineering (A/E) firms have increasingly been getting involved in international markets because of liberalization of markets, proliferation in the demand for complex projects, generalized demands due to globalization and the firms' own interests to venture abroad et cetera. However, there may be discontinuities at national and geographical boundaries, or there may be graduated differences that may sap the firm's access to home-based resources and erode the competitive advantages of firms which attempt to venture overseas. Therefore, it has been suggested that domestic A/E firms have substantial or unique advantages over foreign A/E firms because they have better reach and knowledge of resources, channels, networks and markets in their home-market. Hence, according to many internationalization models, international firms often make use of their geographical and cultural proximities to venture into potential countries or cities near to their home market because these foreign markets are operationally more similar to their home market. On the other hand, the mosaic of the world is such that a disproportionate amount of economic activities are agglomerated in a few key cities on the globe. Transnational firms tend to venture into these core locations in search for markets. The size of the overseas subsidiary, both in terms of investment and staff-size, would normally be subjected to the perceived market potential. Likewise, the formulated business strategies should fit with the characteristics of the host environment. This chapter seeks to identify the strategic interplay between flight-distance, gravitational distance, agglomeration, core and peripheries of cities, internationalization, strategy and organization design.

6.2 Theoretical Framework

The theoretical framework suggests how the literature reviews from different knowledge areas, namely: the gravity model, agglomeration, core and periphery system of cities, internationalization, risks management, business strategies and

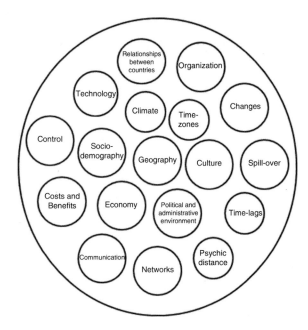

Fig. 6.1 Clustering on a common denominator

organization design, can synthesize with one another. Figure 6.1 shows how several seemingly separate elements may be commonly denominated by flight-distance/ flight-time. It is postulated in this study that flight-distance/flight-time is a causal factor that affects factors such as climate, time-zones, culture, administrative conditions, geographical distance, topological features, spatial interaction between two locations, economical distances, technological spillages, socio-demographical spill-over, affinities and organizational distance. It is espoused in this study that these factors are often inter-related.

6.2.1 Flight

Flight-distance is postulated to be the causal factor that affects cultural distance, administrative distance, topological distance, gravitational distance, geographical distance, economical distance, technological distance, socio-demographical distance, relational or affinity distance and organizational distance. Organizational distance, in turn, comprises of changes, spillages, time-lag, psychic distance, networks, communications, net costs-benefits, control, and friction with advances in general technologies, informational/communication technologies and globalization (refer to Fig. 6.2). It is further propounded in this study that a firm needs to internalize these changes in the different dimensions of distance and spatial economics with business strategies and organization design.

6.2 Theoretical Framework

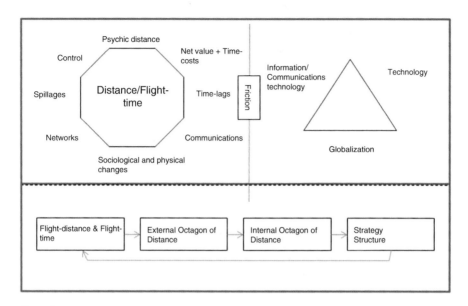

Fig. 6.2 Distance and its implications on business strategy and organization structure

6.2.2 Gravity Model

The model explains the extent of trade between countries due to their economical sizes and distances apart. The model mimics the Newtonian law of gravity which considers physical sizes of and distance between objects. The model have been extended to test and prove many spatial interactions since Reilly's (1931) application of the gravity model on retail trade between two locations, and Zipf's (1946) findings that migration is inversely proportional to the intervening distance. The model has also proven to be empirically strong through econometric analysis, and was further developed by Huff (1963), Linnemann (1966), Caffrey and Issac (1971), Wolf and Weinschrott (1973), Polak (1996), Rosenberg (2004) etc. to include analysis on diplomatic ties, membership of preferential trade areas, trade and trade policies, comparative advantage, Gross National Product (GDP), income level, employment rates, migration, transportation costs, information flow and social-psychic distance, etc. The model suggests that the more populated and proximate cities tend to have a higher intensity of mutual attraction of people, ideas and commodities. The model helps to anticipate traffic, telephone calls, transportation of goods and mails and other types of movement between places. It can be used to compare the gravitational attraction between continents, countries, states and even to neighbourhoods (Rosenberg 2004). Figure 6.3 shows the concepts (distance and size) behind a Gravity model.

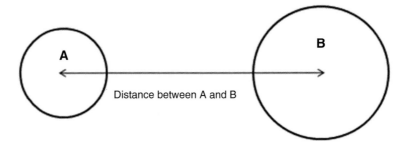

Fig. 6.3 Gravitational and spatial relationship

6.2.3 Agglomeration in Core Locations and Back-Washes in Periphery Locations

According to Christaller's (1933) Central Place Hierarchy, main marketing, administrative and transportation functions tend to be housed in central places because of their accessibility and centrality. Human and economic activities have always liked to localize and agglomerate together in core places to tap into the benefits of economies of scale and spillages. It is therefore common to find these marketing, administrative and transportation centres or hubs co-located in a city. However, while growth poles enjoy a concentration of commercial activities, other periphery locations incur "back-washes" – the deprivation of economic bustle due to the "black-hole effects" of the central places. It is postulated that alpha cities such as New York, London, Tokyo or Singapore act like a black-hole that sucks away all matter or economic potential around it. Christaller's (1933) Central Place Hierarchy also suggested that the larger the settlement, the more function it holds, the more number of higher-ordered services are provided, the fewer they are, and the greater distance between them.

6.2.4 Venturing Overseas

There are four main reasons why firms venture overseas: market seeking, resource seeking, efficiency seeking and strategic asset seeking (Dunning 1988). Yet, when firms internationalize, they have to confront uncertainty, and the depletion or sapping of proximity or access to resources, due to physical discontinuities or graduated changes. Furthermore, firms tend to be embedded in their home environment due to organizational and personnel immobility. Therefore, firms often take calculated, calibrated and incremental steps when they internationalize.

6.2 Theoretical Framework

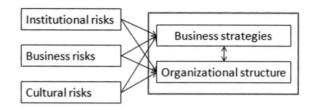

Fig. 6.4 Risks, business strategies and organization structures

6.2.5 Embeddedness

In the Principia, Newton's first law of motions suggests that in the absence of a net external force, a body stays fixated in a location. Newton's second and third laws also suggested that a force is needed to push the stationary object for it to be dislodged and move. Similarly, embeddedness is the forces of inertia to keep organizations and people in their current state. Organizational inertia prevents firms from venturing out of their home-markets. The embeddedness of firms is akin to celestial objects such as stars and planets creating a dent into time-space dimensions due to gravity. As a result, firms often stay stagnated in a fixed location, instead of being mobile and agile, until there is an external force to create an action and stir a reaction. The level of embeddedness of a firm often depends on the nature of its strategic resources.

6.2.6 Risks, Business Strategies and Organization Structures

Risk management is the identification, assessment and prioritization of risks followed by the firm's decision to minimize, monitor or control the probability of the occurrence of an event (Hubbard 2009). Basically, the organization can choose to avoid, reduce, transfer or retain those risks (Dorfman 2007). International construction firms are likely to encounter different risks in different markets due to different social and economic systems, as well as historical and cultural backgrounds. There are many types of risks that an international firm faces, such as political risk, economical risk, strategic risk, compliance risk, financial risk, operational risk etc., which can in turn be summed up by institutional, business, and cultural risks (refer to Fig. 6.4). It is postulated in this study that firms would have to internalize these risks with appropriate business strategies and organization design.

6.2.7 Dynamic 8S Framework

The study would be applying a modified McKinsey 7S model to take institutional, business and cultural risks into consideration. The McKinsey 7S model is a widely

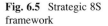
Fig. 6.5 Strategic 8S framework

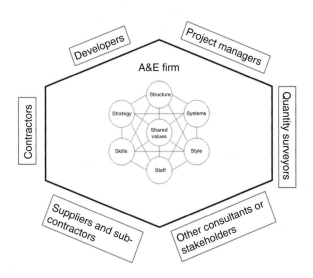

used framework that encompasses strategy, structure, system, staff, shared values, skills, style in its framework to analyze the organization and its activities. The McKinsey 7S is a comprehensive framework to assess the strategic capabilities of an organization. The 3S-es on the top are the "Hard S-es" or the hardware whereas the 3S-es at the bottom are the "Soft S-es" or the software of the firm. Strategy refers to the plans and policies to direct the firm to attain its identified goals; Structure refers to the organization of the firm, its departments, reporting lines, area of expertise and responsibilities; Systems refer to the formal and informal procedures that govern everyday activities; Skills refer to the capabilities and competencies of personnel or the organization as a whole; Shared values are the interconnecting centre of the model and represent the Super-ordinate Goals of what the organization stands for and believes in that guide employees to "valued" behaviour; Staff refers to the people resources and how they are developed, trained and motivated in terms of the numbers and types of personnel within the organization; and Style which refers to the cultural style or leadership approach of top management and the company's overall operating approach. The study adds "Supply-chain" to the existing toolkit to make a Dynamic 8S Framework as shown in Fig. 6.5. It is suggested that the 8S-es should be integrated and optimized to give the best strategic fit with the prevalent conditions.

6.2.8 Organization Design of an A/E Firm

An organization structure sets out responsibilities, functions and processes within a firm. There are many schools with different ways to categorize the various forms of organization structures. These organization structures differ from each other by its number of hierarchical levels, span of control, cross-management and reporting etc. Generally, the organization design of an internationalizing firm would need to consider the firm's own traits (e.g. firm size at home-office and in the overseas office, embeddedness of firm, risk averseness, business objective, business strategies, international experience, entry mode etc.) and the market's characteristics (e.g. restrictions and requirements, market uncertainty, market size etc.).

6.2.9 Isomorphism

The concept of isomorphism emphasizes the role of conformity and convention as a response to environmental pressures exerted on organizations (DiMaggio and Powell 1983). There are essentially three forms of isomorphism, namely: mimetic isomorphism, institutional isomorphism and coercive isomorphism. Mimetic isomorphism is the tendency for organizations to imitate other successful organizations, especially when they are faced with uncertainty and ambiguity. Institutional isomorphism, or normative isomorphism, occurs due to standards, rules and values imposed by universities, accreditation agencies, professional certification boards and training institutions etc. Coercive isomorphism is the result of formal or informal pressures in the form of force, persuasion or invitation to join a group or a plan, or to conform to the norms. Isomorphism explains the parent-subsidiary relationship, that overseas' branch offices often imitate the business strategies, organization design and other management methods of the home-office.

It is useful for Singapore's A/E firms to "listen to those who have been there before" and learn from world class or top firms because "they survived some of the toughest times the industry can face and emerged better than before. There are lessons to be learned from those times and the people who successfully managed their companies through them."

6.2.9.1 Eclectic Diamond Framework

Dunning (1988) suggested that the extent and composition of a company's foreign production is based on three sets of interdependent variables – the ownership, locational and internalization attributes. On the other hand, Porter (1990) suggested that there are four-plus-two attributes which are mutually reinforcing and interdependent in an internationalization system for a transnational firm – factor conditions, demand conditions, complementary and supporting industries, strategy due to competition, government intervention and chances. Dunning's (1988) Eclectic Paradigm is a model that starts from the within (the firm's ownership and locational qualities) to look out (to internalize the external environment), whereas Porter's (1990) Diamond Theory is a model that starts from the external (factor conditions, demand conditions, complementary and supporting industries, government intervention and chances) to look into

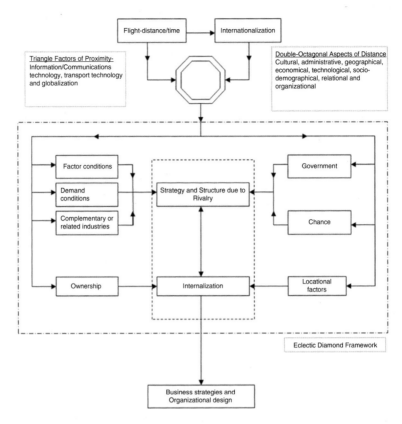

Fig. 6.6 The synergy of the eclectic diamond framework

the firm (strategies due to competition). The Eclectic Diamond Framework, as shown in Fig. 6.6, combines the strengths of both the Eclectic Paradigm (Dunning 1988) and the Diamond Theory (Porter 1990), while eliminating their individual weaknesses, to derive a holistic framework for firms to analyze their businesses. The figure illustrates how the internationalization of a firm, triangle factors of proximity and the double-octagonal aspects of distance can be denominated by flight-distance/time. The Eclectic Diamond Framework considers the factor conditions, demand conditions, complementary or related industries, government, chance, ownership and locational qualities when a firm internationalize, so that fitting business strategies and organization design can be devised.

6.3 Relationship Between Key Elements

When a transnational firm venture overseas, flight-time, postulated to be a causal factor to several aspects of distance, such as cultural, administrative, geographical, economical, technological, socio-demographical, relational and organizational

6.4 Conceptual Model of Study

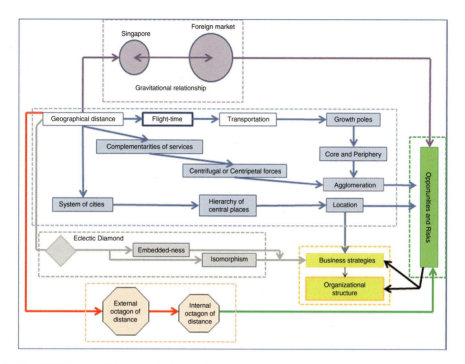

Fig. 6.7 Theoretical framework of research

distance, affects the magnitude and range of risks to be encountered by the firm, which sequentially influences how a firm should strategize and organize itself. Geographical distance, in turn, can be manifested in physical, topological and gravitational distance. The choice of markets, entry modes, business strategies and organization structures are very much inter-related and determined by the availability of market prospects and risks. It has been suggested that there are core locations in the hierarchy of cities around the world, whereby economic activities agglomerate, to present business opportunities. Figure 6.7 shows the theoretical framework of the study, and how these factors interact with one another.

6.4 Conceptual Model of Study

The 2009 Bloomberg Global Poll by international business leaders rated the world's top global cities in terms of attractiveness of location for businesses in 2011 as: (i) New York; (ii) Singapore; (iii) London; (iv) Shanghai; and (v) Dubai.

Figure 6.8 shows the conceptual framework of the study. The diagram uses the case of Singaporean firms venturing outwards into foreign markets, and illustrates how access to home-based resources sap with increasing distance from the point of origin. The figure shows how market opportunities in Singapore are undermined by

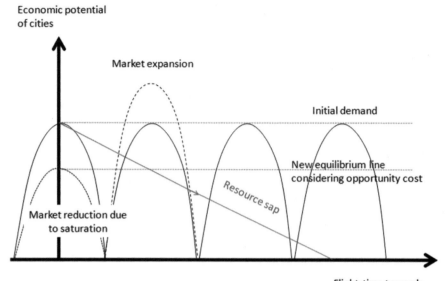

Fig. 6.8 Conceptual model

market saturation, while market potential in other places like Shanghai and Beijing expand due to economic and growth booms.

More importantly, the core and peripheral pattern of A/E markets can also be influenced by (i) power of the core city in the region; (ii) between-ness of the city; (iii) far-ness of the city; (iv) complementarities of cities in the region; and (v) industry's prospects in the city.

The illustration also shows, in a simplified manner of how the agglomeration of economic activities in core locations around the world behaves like a cosine-sine curve.

6.5 Parameters for Measurement

The study postulates that the Organization Design Matrix (as shown in Table 6.1) is shaped by:

- Porter's Diamond Theory = function {factor, demand, complementary services, strategy due to competition, chance, government}
- Dunning's Eclectic Paradigm = function {ownership, locational, internalization}
- Risks = function {factor, demand, complementary services, chance, government, ownership, locational}
- Organization Design Matrix = function {risks}

6.5 Parameters for Measurement

Table 6.1 Classifications of organization design

Hard design	Soft design		
Business strategies and Policies			
Structure (as in organizational chart)	Systems	Workforce	Culture
Organization structure	**Control from HQ**	**HRM – staff employment**	**Leadership style**
Single marketing executive	Centralized	Ethnocentric	Transactional
Functional structure	Decentralized	Polycentric	Transformational
Divisional structure	**Reward/incentive system**	Region-centric	**Delegation**
Products structure	Seniority	Geocentric	Autocratic
Geographical structure	Meritocracy		Democratic
Matrix structure		**HRM – staff advancement**	**Empowerment**
Complex structure	Fixed value	Promote from within	Empowered
Authority and responsibility	Variable component	External employment	Not empowered
Authority in line with responsibility	**Communications**		**Shared values**
Authority not in line with responsibility	Top-down	**Staff**	Ethnocentric
Reporting	Bottom-up	Number (break-down of permanent, contractual and temporary staff)	Polycentric
Hierarchical	Concurrent and integrated		Region-centric
Direct	**Networks**	Composition (ethnic, gender, education, experience etc.)	Geocentric
Simultaneous	Ethnocentric		
Flexible	Polycentric	**Skills and Training**	
	Region-centric	Generalized	
	Geocentric	Specialized	

Table 6.1 summarizes the key characteristics of the Organization Design Matrix adopted in this study. The key components of the matrix are business strategies and policies, organization structure, systems, workforce and culture. Under structure, there are organization structure, authority and responsibility, and reporting. Under systems, there are control from the headquarters, remunerations, communications and networks. Under workforce, there are staff employment, advancement, staff type, and skills. Under culture, there are leadership style, delegation and empowerment, and shared values. Table 6.2 shows the inter-relationship between the elements of the internal octagon of distance and the Eclectic Diamond Framework, and the constructs of these relations (refer to Appendix A for other ways of looking at the classifications of data).

6.6 Implications of Study

Table 6.3 shows the probable factors that affect key business strategies and organization structures when firms internationalize. The research field-work seeks to understand the extent of the impact of each of the listed factors, such as distance, control, psychic distance, net value-costs, time-lag, communications, changes, networks and spillages, on business strategies and organization design.

6.6.1 Interpolation and Extrapolation of Organization Design

Figure 6.9 postulates that business strategies and organization structures for a firm's new overseas venture may be interpolated or extrapolated according to flight-distances. It is also posited that firms which intend to venture overseas may also emulate the business strategies and organization design of their precursors. By following the predecessors' footsteps, fellow Singaporean firms would be able to take note of the critical success factors and avoid the pitfalls of internationalization.

6.6.2 Location Theory and Research Design

Von Thünen's (1826) Sectoral model, Axial model, and Concentric model explain land-use and development of land (refer to Fig. 6.10). According to the Location theory (Von Thünen 1826), sectoral development divides a land so that different segments have a dissimilar form of economic activity, i.e. agricultural, industrial and commercial. On the other hand, an axial development puts high-value economic activities in the city-centre, such that the lower the value of the economic activity, the farther away from the centre it would be. Lastly, the concentric model arranges economic activities in concentric rings.

Table 6.2 Table of constructs

Flight distance affects:	Porter's (1990) diamond theory					Dunning's (1988) eclectic paradigm		
	Factor	Demand	Complementary and related industries	Government	Chance	Ownership factors	Locational factors
Control	Number of staff		Procurement assessment criteria and options	**Intellectual property protection**		Authority	Management
	Skills of staff			**Legal impediments, e.g. hiring practices**		Delegation and empowerment	Access to resources
	Access to information			**Power of the state**		Reasons for entry	**Unionisation rate of the workforce**
	Reward systems			Type of law		Reputation	**Monitoring costs**
	Power			Flexibility of wage determination		Diversity of portfolio	
	Style						
	Nature of product/service						
	Contract type/nature						
	Code of ethics						
	Market share						
	Employee quality						
Psychic distance	Experience of top leaders	Understanding of markets	Industry and company's time horizons	Familiarity of regulations		Internationalization experience of firm	Experience of top leaders
	Experience of organization	Tacit know-how		*Information block (information symmetry)*			Experience of organization
		Commonality of markets					
							Attitude
							Time horizons
							Information uncertainty
							Managerial uncertainty
							Psychic distance
							Power distance
							Uncertainty avoidance

(continued)

Table 6.2 (continued)

Flight distance affects:	Porter's (1990) diamond theory					Dunning's (1988) eclectic paradigm		
	Factor	Demand	Complementary and related industries	Government	Chance	Ownership factors	Locational factors
							Individualism
							Masculinity
							Cultural affinity
							Historical affinity
							Linguistic affinity
Network			Extensiveness of networks	Government championing	Number of associations joined		*Degree of economical integration to the world*
			Percentage of Insourcing/ outsourcing	*Type of trade relations/ level of preferential trade agreement*	*Associations available*		
			Technology, finance and physical infrastructure				
			Agglomeration effects/ complementarity of indutries		*Business environment*		
Communications	Distortion		Coordination				Frequency of contact
	Difficulty of integrating or making sense		Access to partners				Difficulty of coding and messaging
	Extra efforts						Cost of transaction
	Deception						
Time-lag	Time lag due to medium (with sub-types)			*Approvals*		Investment payback period	*Work-days*
							Time-zones
Changes	Socio-cultural differences		Borrowing costs	Engagement in improving the performance of the industry	*Geography*	Objectives (non-profit and profit)	Corporate culture

	Commitment to R&D	Recent crisis	Local/foreign participation ratio	Latitude/climate
	Investment incentives	Proximity to low-cost countries		Time-zones
		Performance of domestic "competiting" industries		Inward and outward FDI and domestic/foreign investment ratio
				Geographical distance/ flight-time

Competition
Completeness of supporting industries
Direct and indirect costs

Skills of workforce
Work conditions
Conflict resolution
Investment in training
Adaptability to market changes
Customer focus
Profitability
Ability to assess and manage risk
Transaction processes
Implementation of contractual relationship
Geographical condition
Labour productivity
Technology level
Education quality
Codes and standards
Implementation policies
Role of professional associations
Role of government
Work-days
ICountry/political risks
Exchange rate
State of the economy
Infrastructure

(continued)

Table 6.2 (continued)

Flight distance affects:	Porter's (1990) diamond theory					Dunning's (1988) eclectic paradigm		
	Factor	Demand	Complementary and related industries	Government	Chance	Ownership factors	Locational factors
Spillages	**Cultural index**	**Construction volume**		**Government type**	**GDP per capita**		**Business conduciveness**
	Education	*A/E value/ market size*		*Corporate and personal tax rate*	*PPP*		*Set-up of infrastructure*
	Factor of productivity	*A/E/*					*construction growth prospect*
Reputation	**Market openness**	**Client's requirements**					
Value-costs	Growth rate of company	Market share	Financing costs	Tariff	Revenue and profit potential	Investing costs	Transactional costs
	Satisfaction/motivation	*Growth rate of demands*		Restrictions/regulatory burden and corruption	EVA	ROI	Operational costs
	Costs of production	**Demand**		Corporate tax	Speed of entry required	ROA	Barrier-entry costs
	Wages level	*Failure rate of companie*		***Difficulty of business in the city/country***		Debt-equity ratio	Transportation costs
	Inflation Exchange rate			*Personal tax*		Staff training	***Rental costs/commercial property prices***

Comments: Bolded italic depicts secondary data that should be available already; normal font depicts require to conduct field-work

6.6 Implications of Study

Table 6.3 Inter-relationship between internal octagon factors of distance, business strategies and organization design

	The McKinsey 7S (Strategy, Structure, Systems, Style, Staff, Skills and Shared values)							
	Entry mode	Organization structure	Control	Leadership	HRM	Network	Marketing	Technology
Distance	O	O	O		O	O	O	
Control	O	O	O	O	O	O	O	
Psychic distance	O	O	O	O	O	O	O	
Net value/costs	O	O	O	O	O	O	O	O
Time-lag	O	O	O		O	O	O	
Communications	O	O	O	O	O	O	O	
Changes	O	O	O		O	O	O	
Networks	O	O	O		O	O	O	
Spillages	O	O	O				O	

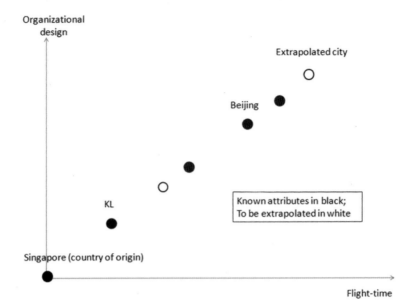

Fig. 6.9 Interpolation and extrapolation of organization design

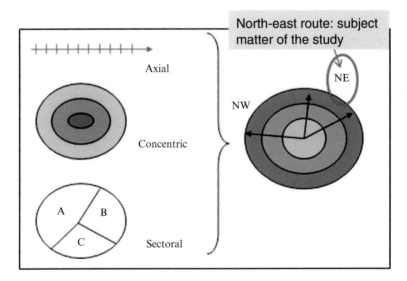

Fig. 6.10 Axial, sectoral and concentric land-use patterns (von Thunen 1826)

Singapore is strategically located near Malaysia, Vietnam and China to the North-east, Middle-east and India to the North-west, and Indonesia and Australia in the South. The study takes Singapore as the reference point, and Kuala Lumpur, Penang, Ho Chi Minh, Hanoi, Shanghai and Beijing which falls in or along the

North-eastern sector, for the research. These cities are also selected for the study because (i) they are located progressively away from Singapore; and (ii) they are Singapore A/E firms' preferred host locations. In this context, based on the theoretical and conceptual frameworks presented in this chapter, the study examines the most appropriate organization design for A/E firms domiciled in Singapore as they export their services to these cities.

6.7 Summary

Frances Cairncross (1997) famously suggested in "The Death of Distance" that the advances of modern communication technologies have caused geography, borders and time-zones to rapidly become irrelevant to the way people conduct their businesses and personal lives. Glaesar and Kohlhase (2003) also concurred with the notion that distance is no longer critical as the costs of transporting goods have decreased substantially. On the other hand, Anderson and van Wincoop (2004) counter-argued that trade costs are still large and the death of distance has been exaggerated. Overman et al. (2003) opined that distance is still the most important determinant of trade costs, and further added that the elasticity of trade volume with respect to distance is usually significant. This suggests that when distance increases, bilateral trade decreases. The Gravity model also explains that trade between countries, cities or regions are inversely proportional to their distance apart. Olson and Olson (2000) explained that wireless technology has not completely eliminated the impact of distance, and that even though the advancement of technology has given hope to "virtual collocation" and remote work, there are socio-technical conditions required for distance work – there must be common ground, coupling of work (integrating work), collaboration readiness, and collaboration technology readiness. They believed that distance is alive and in several essential aspects immortal as it affects local physical context, time zones, culture and language despite the use of distance technologies.

Disdier and Head (2004) researched on the persistence of distance effect on bilateral trade and discovered that the negative impact of distance in trade is not shrinking, but increasing over time, which suggested that technological changes have failed to end the effects of spatial separation. "The Tyranny of Distance" remains – firms still incur inconveniences and extra costs due to geographical distance and when they seek to bridge the impacts brought about by geographical distances.

This chapter explains how the conceptual framework seeks to link up and integrate flight-distance or flight-time, agglomeration effects, central and periphery places, embeddedness, isomorphism, internationalization, business strategies and organization structures. The conceptual framework suggests that distance is an important factor that influences spatial economics, control, spillages, psychic distances, networks, communications and benefit-costs considerations, and these in turn affect how organizations should best deploy certain strategies and organization design in an overseas market. Figure 6.7 shows how flight-time (a proxy for

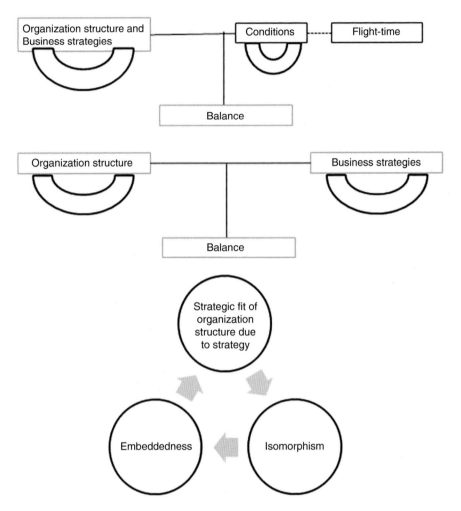

Fig. 6.11 Balancing business environment, business strategies and organization structures

geographical distance) causes changes in a business environment and a firm's spatial interaction with a market. That in turn has a profound implication on the firm's choice of business strategies and organization design. Nevertheless, it is acknowledged that a firm would have to balance (i) strategic fit of organization structure with business strategies; (ii) embeddedness of the firm; and (iii) isomorphism of the firm. Problems and difficulties would arise if there is a misfit or imbalance between the environment, business strategies and organization designs. Figure 6.11 provides a mind-map of the study's theoretical and conceptual frameworks and models to provide a better appreciation of how developments in the study have evolved.

References

Anderson JE, van Wincoop E (2004) Trade costs, Working paper No. 10480. NBER, Boston
Caffrey J, Issac HH (1971) Estimating the impact of college or university on the local economy. American Council on Education, Washington, D.C
Cairncross F (1997) The death of distance. Harvard Business School Press, Boston
Christaller W (1933) The central places of southern Germany. Prentice Hall, Englewood Cliffs
DiMaggio PJ, Powell WW (1983) The iron cage revisited: institutional isomorphism and collective rationality in organizational fields. Am Sociol Rev 48:147–160
Disdier AC, Head K (2004) The puzzling persistence of the distance effect on bilateral trade. MIT Press, Torino
Dorfman MS (2007) Introduction to risk management and insurance. Dorling Kindersley
Dunning JH (1988) The eclectic paradigm of international production: a restatement and some possible extensions. J Int Bus Stud 19(1):1–31
Glaeser EL, Kohlhase JE (2003) Cities, regions, and the decline of transport costs, Working paper No. 9886. NBER, Cambridge, MA
Hubbard D (2009) The failure of risk management. Wiley, Hoboken
Huff DL (1963) A probabilistic analysis of shopping center trade areas. Land Econ 39:81–90
Linnemann H (1966) An econometric study of international trade flows. North Holland Publishing Company, Amsterdam
Olson GM, Olson JS (2000) Distance matters. Hum Comput Interact 15:139–179
Overman HG, Redding SJ, Venables AJ (2003) The economic geography of trade production and income: a survey of empirics. CEPR discussion paper No. 2978
Polak J (1996) Is APEC a natural regional trading bloc? A critique of the 'gravity model' of international trade. World Econ 19:533–543
Porter ME (1990) The competitive advantage of nations. Free Press, New York
Reilly WJ (1931) The law of retail gravitation. Knickerbocker Press, New York
Rosenberg MT (2004) Gravity model: predict the movement of people and ideas between two places. http://geography.about.com/library/weekly/aa031601a.htm
Von Thünen JH (1826) Isolated state (trans: Wartenberg CM, 1966). Pergamon Press, New York
Wolf C Jr, Weinschrott D (1973) International transactions and regionalism: distinguishing "insiders" from "outsiders". Am Econ Rev 63(2):52–60
Zipf GK (1946) The P_1P_2/D hypothesis: on the intercity movement of persons. Am Sociol Rev 2(December):677–686

Chapter 7
Research Design and Methodology

7.1 Introduction

Research may be defined as a careful and systematic process of inquiry to find answers to problems of interest. There are six common types of research designs, namely case studies, surveys, experiments, correlational research, causal-comparative research and historical research. Each has its unique strengths and weaknesses in the ability to describe, predict, explain, interpret or demystify phenomena while some are more qualitative or quantitative than others (Tan 2004). This chapter presents the research design and methodology selected for the research, given the constraints and nature of the study.

The research had three main stages – the exploratory phase, the descriptive phase, and the validation phase. The exploratory phase was used to uncover the key issues when exporting A/E consultancy services. The descriptive phase was used to decipher and comprehend the complex web of internationalization, organization design and strategic management. Finally, the validation stage tested whether the relationship between flight-time, business strategies and organization designs can be authenticated and extrapolated.

7.2 Research Framework

The research framework sets the boundary of the study. The framework would streamline the scope and remove distractions to the study, and set up the relationship between the variables of the research. The research framework of this study covers:

(i) Singapore-owned Architectural and Engineering (A/E) consultancy firms;
(ii) Cities along the North-eastern flight-route from Singapore; and
(iii) Organization design

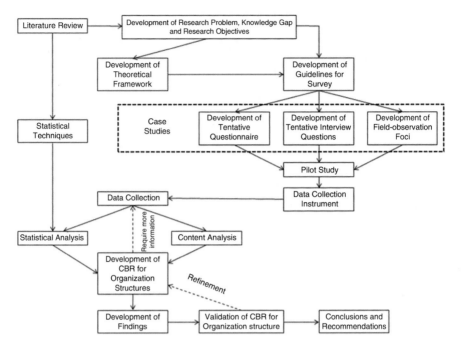

Fig. 7.1 Research design

Figure 7.1 shows the research design of the study. To start with, the research problem and knowledge gap were identified. Next, theoretical underpinnings established from literature reviews aided to develop the research objectives, research hypotheses, theoretical framework and guidelines for interviews and questionnaire surveys. Subsequently, a pilot study was conducted to review the interview and survey questions. The data collection instruments were finally formed, and ready to be used for data collection after some amendments and improvements. The collected data was analyzed by Content Analysis and Statistical Analysis. The findings were then inputted into a Case-based Reasoning Decision Support System (CBR-DSS) for internationalizing A/E firms. Last of all, the CBR-DSS was validated.

7.3 Pilot Study

An exploratory data analysis (EDA) was performed using a pilot study to discover possible new features, and to sieve out prominent and strategic issues and factors that firms stress about from the myriad and labyrinth of topics and considerations pertaining to the causes and effects of internationalization, business strategies and organization designs.

The pilot study was conducted with an academic, an architect and an engineer in March 2008. The pilot study was administered in the same way as it would be for the main study. In the pilot study, subjects were asked to identify ambiguities and difficult questions. The researcher would assess from the reviews whether (i) each question gave an adequate range of response; and (ii) replies could be interpreted. Unnecessary, difficult or ambiguous questions were then discarded revised or rescaled where needed.

7.4 Population and Sampling

The study sets to investigate the organization designs of architectural firms with multi-disciplinary or integrated architectural and engineering consultancy services. The population includes 524 architectural firms registered with the Board of Architects and 148 engineering firms registered with the Association of Consulting Engineers Singapore.

Table 7.1 shows the advantages and disadvantages of the different sampling methods. This study adopted judgment sampling which is also called purposive sampling, whereby cases can be selected according to their characteristics or contextual location. Judgment sampling has been chosen for the study to uncover the best practices of top Singaporean A/E firms. Other Singaporean A/E firms may wish to emulate them or benchmark themselves against them.

Six firms were chosen as samples to represent the population. The choices of firms are namely, private firms Firm A, Firm B and Firm D, and government-linked firms Firm C, Firm E and Firm F. The firms were selected because (i) they are market-leaders who have forayed successfully into regional A/E markets; and (ii) of availability and willingness to participate in the research. The two categories of firms would allow a comparison of managerial attitudes, internationalization strategies and organization structures between private and government-linked firms.

Table 7.2 shows the basis for the cities chosen for the study. The cities chosen are namely, Johor Bahru, Kuala Lumpur, Penang, Ho Chi Minh, Hanoi, Shanghai, Beijing and Tianjin. The cities were chosen because of (i) their progressive flight-time and therefore, their geographical distance away from Singapore; and (ii) Singapore A/E firms' preferred host locations.

7.5 Data Collection Instruments

The research involves the study of six case studies. The case study approach allows a purposive and penetrative probe into the case's natural field setting and the use of multiple sources of evidence to examine a complex issue. Multiple case studies allow a flexible and contextual research strategy that can achieve replication of the same study in different contexts, compare and contrast different cases, or aggregate information from different cases studied at different times (Tan 2004).

Table 7.1 Choice of sampling method

Sampling type	Description	Examples
Probability sampling	Each element has a known chance of being selected (Tan 2004)	Simple random sampling, systematic sampling, stratified sampling, cluster sampling
Non-probability sampling	Chance selection procedures are not used (Tan 2004)	Convenience sampling, purposive sampling, quota sampling, snowball sampling

Sampling method	Description	Advantage	Disadvantage
Judgment sampling	Sample is chosen based on the judgment of the researcher	Convenient	Unlikely to be representative
	Suits survey that requires respondents who are particularly knowledgeable about the subject matter (Tan 2004)	Expert opinion	

Table 7.2 Rationale for choice of cities

Country	City	Characteristics/reason for choice of country	Characteristics/reason for choice of city
Singapore	Singapore	Origin	To compare local and overseas markets
Malaysia	Johor Bahru	Nearest country to Singapore; Malaysia has a multi-ethnic and multi-cultural make-up	Nearest major city to Singapore
	Kuala Lumpur		Nearest capital city to Singapore
	Penang		A port-city, similar to Singapore
Vietnam	HCM City	Does not have a significant Chinese population (as compared to Malaysia or China)	Commercial centre of Vietnam
	Hanoi		Political centre of Vietnam
China	Shanghai	China is regarded as one of the world's most important destinations/markets for transnational firms	Commercial centre of China
	Beijing		Political centre of China
	Tianjin		A fast and growing Chinese city that does not have direct flights from Singapore

Data from these six case studies were collected from interviews, questionnaire surveys and detailed profiles of firms and cities. This allowed the solicitation of both qualitative and quantitative data to give a triangulated source of information. Figure 7.2 shows how different permutations of case studies were obtained – for example, the study of Firm 1 which has operations in its home country and also cities A, B, C, D and E, when bundled together (1-A, 1-B, 1-C, 1-D and 1-E), would provide a case study of a firm across different cities; while the study of Firms 1, 2, 3, 4, 5 and 6 in city E, when bundled together, would provide a case study of different firms in a particular city.

7.6 Data Collection

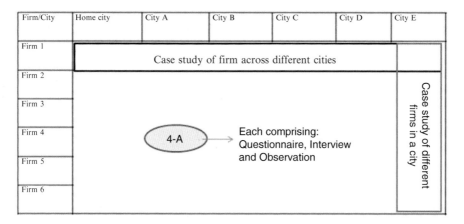

Fig. 7.2 Design of case studies

7.5.1 Questionnaire Surveys and Interviews

The case studies for this study were investigated through the elicitation of data and information from interviews and questionnaire surveys. The interviews were semi-structured so that the researcher can ask in different ways for different participants. A semi-structured interview is flexible, as it allows new questions to be brought up during the interviews as a result of what the interviewee says. Henceforth, the researcher would have the freedom to ask questions tailored to the interview situation or in the interviewees' context (Tan 2004). A questionnaire is a research instrument consisting of a series of questions, with the aim of capturing quantitative information of general characteristics, such as attitudes, values, beliefs and past behaviour of the population.

The study's interview and questionnaire survey are shown in Tables 7.3 and 7.4 respectively. The tables indicate the subjects, areas of focus and theoretical underpinnings of the semi-structured interview questions and questionnaire survey. The central themes are: distance, agglomeration, internationalization, risks, core competencies, business strategy and organization design.

7.6 Data Collection

Table 7.5 shows the data collection method for the study, from the exploratory stage, to the descriptive and validation stage. The source of information came from interviews, questionnaire surveys and observation of the firms. This is a triangulation technique, to synthesize data from multiple sources before its analysis. The

Table 7.3 Interview questions

Type	Section	Subject	Area of focus	Theoretical underpinning
Interview	A	Interviewee and firm	Designation, Role in organization, Experience, Basic firm information, Contact	Background information
	B	Internalization and Strategic models	Organization model; Strategic management model; Isomorphism; Ownership qualities, Locational qualities and Internalization factors; Factor conditions, Demand conditions, Supporting and related industries, Government intervention, Chances and Strategies and structures due to rivalry; Embeddedness	McKinsey 7S (Peters and Waterman 1980); Isomorphism (DiMaggio and Powell 1983); Eclectic Paradigm (Dunning 1988); Diamond Framework (Porter 1990); Embeddedness and Asset specificity (McGuinness 1994)
		Internationalization	Localization and Agglomeration; Distance and Internationalization; Transnational firm	Agglomeration (Krugman 1991), Transnational organization (Ghoshal and Barlett 1999)
		Organization designs and business strategies	Risks; Organization design; Entry strategy; Business strategy; Competitive strength; Critical Success Factors and Pitfalls; Pre-requisites; Learning and evolution of firm	Core competency (Hamel and Prahalad 1996), Strategic management and Organization (Mintzberg 1996a, b, c, d, e, f, g, h), Entry strategy (Root 1998)

quantitative data was interpreted using a Predictive Analytics SoftWare (PASW) whereas the qualitative part would be construed with a Content Analysis software. The findings were then transferred onto a CBR-DSS software.

7.6.1 Fieldwork

The researcher spent a week each, in China (November 2008), Malaysia (December 2008) and Vietnam (January 2009) for the study's fieldwork. During this period of time, the researcher interviewed A/E professionals as well as other construction-related professionals in Beijing, Tianjin, Shanghai, Hanoi, HCM City, Johor Bahru, Kuala Lumpur and Penang.

7.6 Data Collection

Table 7.4 Questionnaire survey

Type	Section	Subject	Focus	Reference
Questionnaire	1	Interviewee and firm	Designation, Role in organization, Experience, Basic firm information, Contact	Background information
	2	Internationalization	Proximity and access to resources, networks and markets	Embeddedness and Asset specificity (McGuinness 1994)
			Discontinuities	
			Compression of time-space dimensions, Virtual collocation and Global-connectivity	Globalization and Virtual collocation (Lojeski and Reilly 2007)
	3	Location of overseas offices or operations	Flight-time/geographical distance, Agglomeration and Location	Distance, Transportation and Central Places (Krugman 1991; Fujita and Mori 1996; Taylor 2004)
			Cost-value evaluation	CAGE framework (Ghemawat 2001)
			Communication	
			Psychic distances	
			Spill-over and the Core to the Periphery	
			Time-zones and time-lags	
			Sociological and physical changes	
			Control	
			Networks	
			Friction	
	4	Eclectic Diamond Framework	Factor	Diamond Framework (Porter 1990)
			Demand	
			Related and supporting industries	
			Government	
			Chance	
			Ownership	Eclectic Paradigm (Dunning 1988)
			Locational	
	5	Risk management	Risks	Risks (Bernstein 1996)
	6	Organization design and Business strategies	The relationship between organization design and business strategy	McKinsey (Peters and Waterman 1980)
			Organization design	

Table 7.5 Research design and methodology

Classification	Approach	A/E consultancy firms	Purpose
Exploratory stage	Survey	1. One academic to evaluate the survey questions	1. Pilot study to help sieve from a myriad of topics and considerations
		2. One architect and one engineer from a firm – non-probability judgement-sampling to understand the concerns of a successful government-linked A/E firm when venturing overseas	2. Evaluation to build better constructs
Descriptive stage	Historical research; surveys; and case studies (documentation, archival records, interviews and observation)	Case studies – questionnaire and interview to elicit information + Observations	1. Triangulation
		1. Approximately three personnel (senior management, middle management and executive level × 6 firms each × 8 cities	2. Content analysis
		2. Non-probability judgement-sampling –Singapore-domiciled A/E firms and their respective overseas subsidiaries or offices in Kuala Lumpur, Penang, HCM City, Hanoi, Shanghai, Beijing and Tianjin	3. Statistical analysis
			4. Creation of the CBR-DSS database
Validation stage	Induction, deduction and abduction	1. Two firms – non-probability purposive- sampling – one firm among the three government-linked A/E firms, and another from among the three private A/E firms, approached during the descriptive stage, that intends to evaluate its strategy and organization structure or intends to make further advancements in another overseas market	1. Knowledge transfer to "second-movers"
		2. Two firms – non-probability purposive-sampling: a government-linked A/E and another private A/E firm that had not been approached at descriptive stage	2. To understand at first-hand the predictability and applicability of the CBR-DSS

7.7 Statistical Analysis 141

In Beijing, the researcher interviewed a Vice-President and an administrative manager from Firm C, as well as two architects and an accountant from Firm D. In Tianjin, the researcher interviewed a Project Director from Firm C and a Vice-President (Business development) from Firm F. In Shanghai, the researcher interviewed a senior architect from Firm A; the Managing Director, a senior Vice-President and an architect from Firm C; a senior associate and an associate from Firm D; a senior manager, an urban planner and an account manager from Firm E; a Director of an A/E firm from USA; and the Managing Director of a quantity surveying firm.

In Hanoi, the researcher interviewed an administrative associate from Firm F and a Director of a quantity surveying firm. In HCM City, the researcher interviewed the Managing Director, a senior architectural associate and a business development manager from Firm C; the General Director and a senior architectural associate from Firm F; a project manager of an engineering firm; the General Director of a quantity surveying firm; a quantity surveying manager of a Japanese contractor; and a residential sales and marketing manager of a developer.

In Johor Bahru, the researcher interviewed the Principal of an architectural firm and the Managing Director of an engineering firm. In Kuala Lumpur, the researcher interviewed a Director, an associate and an architect from Firm A; two Directors and an associate from Firm D; a Deputy General Manager, a design manager and a business development manager from Firm F. In Penang, the researcher interviewed a Director from Firm A and a manager from a quantity surveying firm.

In Singapore, the researcher interviewed a Director, an associate and an architectural assistant from Firm A; two senior technical managers and an architect from Firm B; a Vice-President, a Principal Architectural Associate and an architect from Firm C; the Chairman, a General Manager and an architectural assistant from Firm D; a Vice-President, a senior project manager and a Principal quantity surveyor from Firm E; a Vice-President, a senior engineer and an engineer from Firm F; an architect from an A/E firm not amongst Firm A to Firm F; and an assistant manager of a quantity surveying firm.

7.7 Statistical Analysis

Table 7.6 shows how different statistical tests should be chosen for different data types, and highlights the reason for choosing the tests for the study.

The one sample t-test and Pearson correlation test were the two main inferential statistical tests conducted. These tests were selected due to the characteristics of samples and scale of measurements. The one sample t-test is able to test whether the mean of a normally distributed population has a value specified in a null hypothesis. The Pearson correlation coefficient measures the strength and direction of a linear relationship between two random variables. The main purpose of the statistical analysis is to investigate the correlation between independent and dependent variables in the survey. It should be noted that correlation can be prone to erroneous

Table 7.6 Table of statistical tools

Scale of measurement	One sample Independent sample	Single treatment; repeat measures	Multiple treatments; repeat measures	Two independent sample	K independent sample	Measures of association
Nominal	Binomial test; contingency table (one-way)	McNemar test	Cochrane Q test	Contingency table (two-way)	Contingency table	Contingency-coefficients
Ordinal	Runs test	Wilcoxon signed rank test	Friedman test	Mann-Whitney test	Kruskal-Wallis test	Spearman rank correlation
Interval or ratio	**Z or t-test; test of variance**	Paired t-test	Repeat-measures ANOVA	Unpaired t-test; test of variance	ANOVA	**Regression, Pearson correlation or time series**

Source: Tan (2004)

relationship due to lurking variables or confounding variables, and correlation does not imply causation (Tan 2004).

In this research, the one sample t-test was conducted to test the mean of a single variable against a specified constant. Then, the test statistic and the proposed population parameter were compared to accept or reject the null hypothesis based on the concept of the level of significance ($\alpha = 0.05$). The test hypothesis was set out as follows:

$H_0: \mu \leq 4$
$H_1: \mu > 4$

The software used for the statistical analysis was Predictive Analytics Software (PASW). The test value of 4 is used because it denotes mean/neutrality on the 1 to 7 Likert scale used in the questionnaires. To accept H_0 with values 1, 2, 3 and 4 is to say that the attribute being tested is insignificant or not a factor of significant concern; whereas to accept H_1 with values 5, 6 or 7 denotes that the attribute is significant.

The Pearson correlation measures the strength of the linear relationship between the quantitative variables. The correlation coefficients range from a value of -1 which depicts a perfectly negative relationship, to $+1$ which represent a perfectly positively relationship, whereas a value of 0 indicates absence of a linear relationship.

7.8 Content Analysis

Holsti (1969) defined Content Analysis as a technique for making inferences by objectively and systematically identifying specified characteristics of messages. Holsti (1969) suggested that Content Analysis can be used to (i) make inferences about the antecedents of a communication; (ii) describe and make inferences about characteristics of a communication; and (iii) make inferences about the effects of a communication, and is suitable for the analysis of subjects in social sciences and humanities; while Morris (1996) suggested that Content Analysis is a research technique used to systematically make inferences about the intentions, attitudes, and values of individuals by identifying specific characteristics in textual messages. Content analysis is commonly used to analyze recorded transcripts of interviews with participants, especially with conceptual analysis and relational analysis (Berelson 1971).

According to Morris (1996), the advantages of computerized content analysis over human coded content analysis include:

(i) Stability and reliability of the computerized coding scheme and coder (Weber 1990);
(ii) Explicit coding rules yielding formally comparable results (Weber 1990);
(iii) Easy manipulation of text to create word-frequency counts, key-word-in-context listings and concordances; and
(iv) Ability to process larger volumes of qualitative data at lower costs (Gephart and Wolfe 1989).

On the other hand, Morris (1996) also highlighted the limitations of content analysis. The weaknesses include:

(i) Lack of perfect natural language processing capabilities in the software;
(ii) Inability of the software to recognize the communicative intent (e.g. negation and irony) of word usage (Krippendorff 1980);
(iii) Inability of the researcher or programmer to provide an exhaustive list of every related word to an element;
(iv) Inability of the software to resolve references to words appearing elsewhere in the text, e.g. "it", "that", "them" etc. (D'Aveni and MacMillan 1990);
(v) Different unit of retrieval may give different results (Pfaffenberger 1988); and
(vi) Human judgement is still required to reduce the risks of abstracted empiricism (Gephart and Wolfe 1989) and to establish reliability and validity of the computerized content analysis.

The unobtrusive nature of content analysis makes it well suited for research studies in strategic management (Morris 1996). The content analysis software chosen for the research is Qualitative Data Analysis (QDA) Miner, a mixed-model qualitative data analysis software package capable of coding, annotating, retrieving and analyzing collections of documents or images. The software was chosen by the study because it is has lauded by users as "One of, if not the best multi-use text application, and "In sum, QDA Miner possesses outstanding mixed-model analytical tools, all of which work well. We are impressed not only by the range of functionality represented in this software, but also by the good design evident in how the program's user interface presents the various components of each tool to the user."

7.9 Case-Based Reasoning (CBR)

Application of Information Technology (IT) has been encouraged and becoming common in the construction industry. For instance, it has been used for computer aided design, management information systems, information exchange, construction project management, database systems, education and training, informatics and strategic management, professional marketing et cetera.

Artificial intelligence has also been promoted in the Architectural, Engineering and Construction (AEC) and Facilities Management industries to improve the speed, quantity and quality of work (Filos 2009). Specifically, artificial intelligence can also be used to facilitate decision-making (Yu and Skibniewski 1999). CBR is essentially a branch of Artificial Intelligence, and is broadly construed as the process of solving new problems based on the solutions of known facts in similar past problems, instead of relying on a generic logic.

CBR can trace its roots to Roger Schank's (1982) model of dynamic memory. Through the years, CBR has grown to be able to do legal precedents and references, medical diagnosis and medicine prescription, human resources, product recommendation, real estate, customs, travel etc. It is a four-step process which retrieves, reuses, revises and retains cases for future references and support (Leake 1996). New case studies would reconcile with the knowledge-base and adapt themselves to fill up cavities of the database for storage and future use.

Mintzberg and Quinn (1991) suggested that there are few modes of strategic decision making: the entrepreneurial mode, adaptive mode, planning mode, and logical incrementalism which is the synthesis of the other three, as interactive processes in which the organization probes the future, experiments, and learns from a series of partial commitments. The CBR possesses the virtues of these few modes of strategic decision making, to support the firm to make an informed decision.

The research would be using the CBR: Support Management Automated Reasoning Technology (SMART) software, with inputs from the Statistical Analysis and Content Analysis. The CBR product would enable users to define multiple case studies, questions and solutions, and to define the structure and behaviour of each case base.

The rationale of a CBR is that if relevant episodes can be quickly identified by an automated system, they would provide a rich source of potentially useful information as it is unlikely that any person can memorize the large volume of information and lessons they contain. However, CBR is less effective with complex tasks (Leake 1996), and can be misled by common or coincidental similarities between cases, and thus fail to recognize important matches that may make the difference between case-selection and case-rejection (Wagman 2003). Therefore, human judgement is still required to alleviate the risks of installing structural errors in the CBR build-up.

The CBR-Decision-Support System (CBR-DSS) can be used by firms to make rational decisions and help human judgment on appropriate business strategies that would function more efficiently and effectively if firms plan to foray into previously unchartered territories and markets of overseas cities. The study seeks to provide useful information on the appropriate business strategies and organizational structures that may be adopted as part of the organizational-learning based model. This is coherent with Cyert and March's (1963) suggestion that when confronted with a problem, organizations tend to start their search for solutions among alternatives that are close to solutions that have been tried before.

7.10 Validation, Reconciliation and Adaptation

Logical reasoning has three main types – namely deduction, induction and abduction. Inductive reasoning is the process of inferring probable antecedents as a result of observing multiple consequents; deductive reasoning is the process of deriving the consequences of what is assumed; and abductive reasoning is the process of inference that produces a hypothesis, beginning when an inquirer considers a set of seemingly unrelated facts to be somehow connected.

There are many ways of establishing the credibility or dependability of a finding, including: member check, interviewer corroboration, peer debriefing, prolonged engagement, negative case analysis, auditability, confirmability, bracketing and balance (Lincoln and Guba 1985). The findings from the case studies would be validated against knowledge bases, new subjects, or extension of the case studies.

7.11 Summary

The chapter highlights the nature of the research, presents the research framework, explains the choice of the firms and cities selected as the focal points of the research, and justifies the choice of research design and methodology. This chapter streamlines the scope and removes distractions to the study, sets up the boundary of the study, expounds the process of achieving the research objectives, sets up the relationship between the variables of the research, and elucidates the methods to attain data, interprets the data, for the testing of the research's hypotheses.

It was stated in this chapter that 30 completed questionnaire surveys were collected and 50 interviews were conducted with employees of six Singaporean A/E firms, across the cities of Singapore, Johor Bahru, Kuala Lumpur, Ho Chi Minh City, Hanoi, Shanghai, Beijing and Tianjin. The quantitative data and the qualitative data were then interpreted using a statistical software and content analysis software respectively, so that the relationships between variables could be assessed. These findings are then inputted into a CBR-DSS. It is suggested that the CBR-DSS would be a an useful toolkit and/or checklist by an internationalizing A/E firm to obtain preliminary guidance, advices and recommendations on business strategies and organization designs.

References

Berelson B (1971) Content analysis in communication research. Free Press, New York
Bernstein PL (1996) Against the Gods: the remarkable story of risk. Wiley, New York
Cyert R, March J (1963) A behavioural theory of the firm. Prentice-Hall, Englewood Cliffs
D'Aveni RA, MacMillan IC (1990) Crisis and content of managerial communications: a study of the focus of attention of top managers in surviving and failing firms. Adm Sci Q 35:634–657
DiMaggio PJ, Powell WW (1983) The iron cage revisited: institutional isomorphism and collective rationality in organizational fields. Am Sociol Rev 48:147–160
Dunning JH (1988) The eclectic paradigm of international production: a restatement and some possible extensions. J Int Bus Stud 19(1):1–31
Filos E (2009) Advanced ICT under the 7th EU R&D framework programme: opportunities for the AEC/FM industry. In: Zarli A, Scherer R (eds) eWork and eBusiness in architecture, engineering and construction. CRC Press, Boca Raton/London, pp 3–11
Fujita M, Mori T (1996) The role of ports in the making of major cities: self-agglomeration and hub-effect. J Dev Econ, Elsevier 49(1):93–120

References

Gephart RP, Wolfe RA (1989) Qualitative data analysis: three microcomputer-supported approaches. In: Hoy F (ed) Academy of management best paper proceedings. Academy of Management, Ada, pp 382–386

Ghemawat P (2001) Distance still matters: the hard reality of global expansion. Harv Bus Rev 2001:137–147

Ghoshal S, Barlett C (1999) Managing across borders. Harvard Business School, Boston

Hamel G, Prahalad CK (1996) Strategic intent. In: Mintzberg H, Quinn JB (eds) The strategy process: concepts, contexts, cases, 3rd edn. Prentice Hall, Englewood Cliffs, pp 41–45

Holsti OR (1969) Content analysis for the social sciences and humanities. Addison-Wesley, Reading

Krippendorff K (1980) Content analysis: an introduction to its methodology. Sage, Beverly Hills

Krugman P (1991) Geography and trade. MIT Press, Cambridge, MA

Leake DB (1996) CBR in context: the present and future. In: Leake DB (ed) Case-based reasoning: experiences, lessons and future directions. AAAI Press/MIT Press, Menlo Park, pp 3–30

Lincoln YS, Guba E (1985) Naturalistic inquiry. Sage, Newbury Park

Lojeski KS, Reilly RR (2007) Multitasking and innovation in virtual teams. In: Proceedings from the 40th annual Hawaii international conference, Big Island, 3–6 Jan 2007

McGuinness T (1994) Markets and managerial hierarchies. In: Thompson G et al (eds) Markets, hierarchies and networks. Sage, London, pp 66–81

Mintzberg H (1996a) Beyond configuration. In: Mintzberg H, Quinn JB (eds) The strategy process: concepts, contexts, cases, 3rd edn. Prentice Hall, Englewood Cliffs, pp 757–763

Mintzberg H (1996b) Crafting strategy. In: Mintzberg H, Quinn JB (eds) The strategy process: concepts, contexts, cases, 3rd edn. Prentice Hall, Englewood Cliffs, pp 101–109

Mintzberg H (1996c) Five Ps for strategy. In: Mintzberg H, Quinn JB (eds) The strategy process: concepts, contexts, cases, 3rd edn. Prentice Hall, Englewood Cliffs, pp 10–17

Mintzberg H (1996d) Generic business strategies. In: Mintzberg H, Quinn JB (eds) The strategy process: concepts, contexts, cases, 3rd edn. Prentice Hall, Englewood Cliffs, pp 83–92

Mintzberg H (1996e) Generic corporate strategies. In: Mintzberg H, Quinn JB (eds) The strategy process: concepts, contexts, cases, 3rd edn. Prentice Hall, Englewood Cliffs, pp 717–720

Mintzberg H (1996f) The manager's job. In: Mintzberg H, Quinn JB (eds) The strategy process: concepts, contexts, cases, 3rd edn. Prentice Hall, Englewood Cliffs, pp 19–34

Mintzberg H (1996g) The professional organization. In: Mintzberg H, Quinn JB (eds) The strategy process: concepts, contexts, cases, 3rd edn. Prentice Hall, Englewood Cliffs, pp 658–668

Mintzberg H (1996h) The structuring of organizations. In: Mintzberg H, Quinn JB (eds) The strategy process: concepts, contexts, cases, 3rd edn. Prentice Hall, Englewood Cliffs, pp 331–349

Mintzberg H, Quinn JB (1991) The strategy process: concepts, contexts, cases. Prentice Hall, Englewood Cliffs

Morris E (1996) Computerized content analysis in management research: a demonstration of advantages and limitations. J Manag 20:903–931

Peters T, Waterman R (1980) In search of excellence. Harper & Row, New York

Pfaffenberger B (1988) Microcomputer applications in qualitative research. Sage, Newbury Park

Porter ME (1990) The competitive advantage of nations. Free Press, New York

Root FR (1998) Entry strategies for international markets, Revised edn. Jossey-Bass, San Francisco

Schank R (1982) Dynamic memory: a theory of learning in computers and people. Cambridge University Press, New York

Tan W (2004) Practical research methods, 2nd edn. Prentice Hall, Singapore

Taylor PJ (2004) World city network: a global urban analysis. Routledge, London

Wagman M (2003) Reasoning processes in humans and computers: theory and research in psychology and artificial intelligence. Praeger, Westport

Weber, RP (1990) Basic content analysis. Newbury Park

Yu WD, Skibniewski M (1999) Quantitative constructability analysis with a neuro fuzzy knowledge-based multi-criterion decision support system. Autom Constr 8(5):539–558

Chapter 8
Data Collation and Results

8.1 Introduction

This chapter collates information collected from Singapore's private and government-linked A/E consultancy firms' business strategies and organization in their home market and their regional markets, namely: Kuala Lumpur, Penang, Ho Chi Minh (HCM) City, Hanoi, Shanghai, Beijing and Tianjin. Primary and secondary sources of data were sourced from questionnaire surveys, interviews and observations. The data was then processed by Content Analysis using the Qualitative Data Analysis Miner (QDA Miner), and Statistical Analysis using the Predictive Analytics Software (PASW) to generate information in the form of key contents and statistics.

8.2 Profile of Questionnaire Replies and Interviewees

Table 8.1 profiles the respondents in terms of designation. Senior managers ranged from General Managers, Vice-Presidents, Senior Vice-Presidents, Directors, General Directors, Managing Directors, Chief-Executive Officers (CEO) and Chairman; middle-managers included as Associates or Managers, whilst entry-level professionals ranged from senior architects or engineers, to assistant architects or engineers. Even though the study seeks to approach a top manager, a middle manager and an entry-level professional for every office, middle-managers comprised 50% of respondents in both the questionnaire surveys and interviews. This was primarily because middle-managers are generally the regular persons-in-charge of several overseas offices.

Tables 8.2 and 8.3 show the profile of the questionnaire respondents and interviewees. Thirty completed questionnaires were collected and 62 interviews were conducted with architectural and engineering professionals in Singapore and several overseas cities, including Johor Bahru, Kuala Lumpur, Penang, Ho Chi

Table 8.1 Profile of questionnaire and interview respondents in terms of designations

Designations of respondents	Number	Percentage (%)
Questionnaire (of targeted firms only)		
Senior	7	23.3
Middle-management	15	50.0
Entry-level professionals	8	26.6
Total from questionnaires	30	100
Interviews (of targeted firms only)		
Senior	15	30.0
Middle-management	25	50.0
Entry-level professionals	10	20.0
Total from interviews	50	100

Table 8.2 Profile of questionnaire respondents in terms of firms and cities

	Government-linked firms			Private firms				
Cities/firms	C	E	F	A	B	D	Total
Singapore	1	1	3	4	3	2	14
Kuala Lumpur	0	0	3	0	0	1	4
Penang	0	0	0	0	0	0	0
HCM City	1	0	1	0	0	0	2
Hanoi	0	0	1	0	0	0	1
Shanghai	3	1	1	0	0	2	7
Beijing	1	0	0	0	0	1	2
Tianjin	0	0	0	0	0	0	0
Sub-total of firms	6	2	9	4	3	6	–
Sub-total	17			13			–
Total	30						30

Table 8.3 Profile of interviewees in terms of firms and cities

	Government-linked firms			Private firms					
Cities/firms	C	E	F	A	B	D	Others	Total
Singapore	3	3	2[a]	3	3	3	2	19
Johor Bahru	0	0	0	0	0	0	2	2
Kuala Lumpur	0	0	3	3	0	3	0	9
Penang	0	0	0	1	0	0	1	2
HCM City	3	0	2	0	0	0	4	9
Hanoi	0	0	1	0	0	0	1	2
Shanghai	3	3	1	1	0	2	2	12
Beijing	2	0	0	0	0	3	0	5
Tianjin	1	0	1	0	0	0	0	2
Sub-total of firms	12	6	10	8	3	11	–	–
Sub-total	28			22			–	–
Total	50						12	62

[a]Firm F's interviewee in Tianjin was also interviewed in the capacity of an employee stationed in Singapore

8.3 Content Analysis

Table 8.4 Methods of Content Analysis

Method of Content Analysis	Premise/basis of measurement
Frequency	Frequency
Sequence matrix	Sequence
Co-occurrences	Co-occurrence
Proximity	Jaccard's coefficient $J(A,B) = \frac{|A \cap B|}{|A \cup B|}$.
Similarity	Similarity of a code's co-occurrence patterns with all the other codes
Similarity dendrogram	Similarity of a code's co-occurrence patterns with all the other codes
Strength of links between codes	Proximity

Minh City, Hanoi, Shanghai, Tianjin and Beijing. 61 interviews were conducted face-to-face while one was completed using the telephone. Out of the 62 interviews, 50 were conducted with staff from the six Singaporean A/E firms, namely Firm A, Firm B, Firm C, Firm D, Firm E and Firm F, whereas 12 were completed with either A/E professionals from other firms such as fellow Singaporean A/E firm Firm G in Singapore, or local A/E firms that included Firm H and Firm I in Johor Bahru, foreign A/E firm with a regional head-quarter in Singapore that included Firm J in Shanghai, fellow Singaporean A/E firm Firm K in Ho Chi Minh City, Singaporean developer that included Firm L in Ho Chi Minh City, Japanese contractor with its international head-quarter in Singapore such as Firm M in Ho Chi Minh City, and quantity surveyor with its head-quarter in Singapore such as Firm N in Singapore, Penang, Ho Chi Minh City, Hanoi and Shanghai. These 12 interviews were not included in the Content Analysis, but can help to provide a fuller picture of Singapore's A/E firms' endeavours at home and in the region; and also highlight the business climates of the various cities.

8.3 Content Analysis

Table 8.4 shows several Content Analysis techniques or methods to extract and interpret information. These are selected methods that would be applied in the study's collection of interview transcripts, so that (i) comparisons can be made; and (ii) analyses can be done from a few perspectives. This section also includes the use of graphs generated by the Content Analysis software to compare (i) private and government-linked A/E firms; and (ii) A/E offices' in different cities.

8.3.1 Content Analysis Methods

Coding

Figure 8.1 illustrates how coding was done in the Content Analysis program. It shows that when a related word or phrase of a code is used in a sentence (or paragraph), the sentence (or paragraph) would be tagged with that particular code.

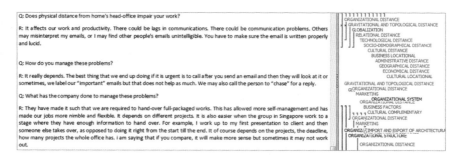

Fig. 8.1 Coding of documents in Content Analysis

Table 8.5 Frequently cited categories and codes

Rank	Code	Examples of related words	Frequency	Percentage (%)
1	Organizational distance	Virtual collocation, Communications	843	7.60
2	Business strategies	Entry mode, Marketing	768	6.90
3	Chance	Business, Client	699	6.30
4	Factor conditions	Human resource, Infrastructure	664	6.00
5	Service Provided	Multidisciplinary, Niche	617	5.60
6	Demand conditions	Expectations, Requirements	520	4.70
7	Marketing	Branding,	511	4.60
8	Locational factors	Distance,	389	3.50
9	Geographical distance	Physical distance, Flight-time	331	3.00
10	Government intervention	Restrictions, Requirements	319	2.90

Frequency

The Content Analysis software (i.e. the QDA Miner) was able to identify the most commonly cited phrases or words used by the pool of interviewees, out of the 42 codes set up in the program. These codes pertain to (i) international trade (exports and imports); (ii) forms of distance; (iii) different types of risks; (iv) organization designs; and (v) business/entry strategies. The top ten codes in terms of frequency of use of related phrases or words in the recorded conversations/transcripts of the 50 interviews conducted with the staff of the six targeted Singaporean A/E firms are shown in Table 8.5.

Sequences

Tables 8.6 and 8.7 shows the sequence matrix of all the factors inputted into the Content Analysis database with one another (A follows B and B follows A respectively). There is a sequence when a factor follows another factor (in a

8.3 Content Analysis

Table 8.6 Sequence matrix (A follows B)

Table 8.7 Sequence matrix (B follows A)

sequence). For example, if the saying "Structure follows Strategy" is true, then it should be reflected in the table that the factor "Organization structure" frequently follows "Business strategies" because interviewees would in most cases, discussed their firm's organization structures after discussing their business strategies. It is presented in a heat-map such that dark-colored boxes indicate higher sequence-frequencies between two factors. Conversely, lighter-colored boxes point to lower sequence-frequencies between two factors. It is shown in the sequence matrix, highlighted in red rings, that:

1. "Organization structure" mostly follows "Organization distance", "Business strategies" and "Business factors";
2. "Organization structure" mostly precedes "Organization distance", "Business strategies" and "Service provided";
3. "Geographical distance" mostly follows "Organization distance", "Business strategies" and "Business factors"; and
4. "Geographical distance" mostly precedes "Organization distance", "Business strategies" and "Business factors".

Co-occurrences

Table 8.8 shows the co-occurrences between factors in the same segments. It illustrates how often cases and codes are followed by one another. For example, if the saying "Structure follows Strategy" is true, then it should be reflected in the table that the factor "Organization structure" frequently follows "Business strategies" because interviewees would in most cases, discussed their firm's organization structures together with, or in the context of the firm's business strategies, reporting system, corporate culture, staff-size, staff skills, leadership style etc. It has been observed and highlighted in red, that "Geographical distance" co-occurs most frequently with "Organization distance", "Gravitational and topological distance" and "Globalization". It has also been observed and highlighted in blue that "Organization structure" co-occurs most frequently with "Organizational distance", "Service provided" and "Organization systems". These will be discussed later in Chap. 9.

Proximity

Using Jaccard's Coefficient to measure the proximity index of the numerous components included in the Content Analysis, the software was able to gauge the levels of proximities between factors. The Jaccard's Coefficient was chosen because Hubalek (1982) and Lugwig and Reynolds (1988) experimented with the Coefficient and agreed with its admissibility to compare proximity and diversity of sample sets. The maximum possible value of a Jaccard's Coefficient between two factors is 1, and the higher the value between the two factors is to 1 indicates that these two factors are more proximate.

8.3 Content Analysis

Table 8.8 Co-occurrences between factors

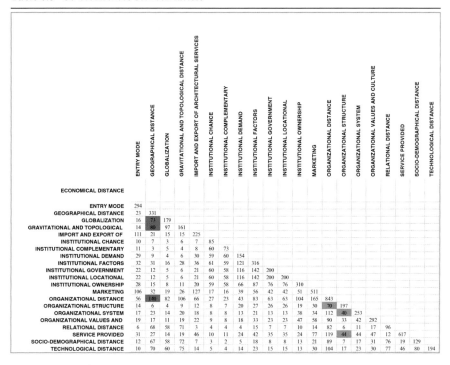

Table 8.9 ranks the level of propinquity or remoteness between geographical distance and other factors. According to the measurement of Jaccard's Coefficients, "Geographical distance" is more proximate graphically to "Globalization", "Organizational distance", "Business locational factors", "Marketing", "Gravitational and topological distances" etc., but is less proximate to the "Complementary role of countries or cities", "Cultural-ownership factors", "Institutional-complementary conditions", "Cultural-factor conditions" and "Cultural-chance factors". These co-occurrences will be further discussed in Chap. 9.

Table 8.10 ranks the top ten factors in terms of the level of proximity between organization structure and other factors. The table shows that the design of organization structures is more proximate with "Organizational system", "Organizational distance", and "Organizational values and culture" than "Complementary role of countries or cities", "Cultural-ownership factors" and "Institutional-complementary conditions. This information would be useful for constructing the CBR-logic later. These co-occurrences will be further discussed in Chap. 9.

Links Between Codes

Figure 8.2 demonstrates the web and strength of the relationships or links between the 42 codes set up, using classical scaling (instead of randomized positioning).

Table 8.9 Geographical distance and its proximity to other factors

Code	Co-occurs	Do not	Is absent	Jaccard	
Economical Distance	73	40	258	0.197	●●●●●●●●●●
Gravitational and Topological Distance	80	81	251	0.194	●●●●●●●●●●
Relational Distance	68	28	263	0.189	●●●●●●●●●
Socio-Demographical Distance	67	62	264	0.17	●●●●●●●●●
Cultural Distance	73	100	258	0.169	●●●●●●●●
Globalization	73	106	258	0.167	●●●●●●●●
Technological Distance	70	124	261	0.154	●●●●●●●●
Organizational Distance	140	703	191	0.135	●●●●●●●
Cultural Locational	66	175	265	0.13	●●●●●●●
Administrative distance	41	91	290	0.097	●●●●●
Business Locational	59	330	272	0.089	●●●●
Institutional Factors	31	285	300	0.05	●●●
Cultural Complementary	22	150	309	0.046	●●
Organizational System	23	230	308	0.041	●●
Marketing	32	479	299	0.04	●●
Import and Export of Architectural Services	21	204	310	0.039	●●
Entry Mode	23	271	308	0.038	●●
Business Strategies	33	735	298	0.031	●●
Cultural Factors	12	75	319	0.03	●
Service Provided	27	590	304	0.028	●
Organizational Values and Culture	17	275	314	0.028	●
Institutional Ownership	15	295	316	0.024	●
Cultural Demand	10	105	321	0.023	●
Institutional Locational	12	188	319	0.023	●
Institutional Government	12	188	319	0.023	●
Business Factors	22	642	309	0.023	●
Cultural Government	10	144	321	0.021	●
Business Demand	16	504	315	0.019	●
Institutional Demand	9	145	322	0.019	●
Cultural Ownership	7	62	324	0.018	●
Cultural Chance	7	83	324	0.017	●
Institutional Chance	7	78	324	0.017	●
Business Ownership	10	279	321	0.016	●
Agglomerationa and Localization	6	132	325	0.013	●
Business Chance	12	687	319	0.012	●
Business Government	8	311	323	0.012	●
Organizational Structure	6	191	325	0.011	●
Business Complementary	5	240	326	0.009	
Institutional Complementary	3	70	328	0.007	

"Do not" refers to the number of times when the factors do not appear along with each other; "Absent: refers to number of times when the factors do not appear with each other

8.3 Content Analysis

Table 8.10 Organization structure and its proximity to other factors

Code	Co-occurs	Do not	Is absent	Jaccard	
Organizational System	40	213	157	0.098	•••••
Organizational Distance	70	773	127	0.072	••••
Organizational Values and Culture	33	259	164	0.072	••••
Institutional Government	26	174	171	0.07	••••
Institutional Locational	26	174	171	0.07	••••
Institutional Demand	20	134	177	0.06	•••
Service Provided	44	573	153	0.057	•••
Institutional Factors	27	289	170	0.056	•••
Cultural Government	16	138	181	0.048	••
Technological Distance	17	177	180	0.045	••
Marketing	30	481	167	0.044	••
Business Ownership	20	269	177	0.043	••
Business Government	21	298	176	0.042	••
Institutional Ownership	19	291	178	0.039	••
Business Locational	19	370	178	0.034	••
Business Strategies	30	738	167	0.032	••
Cultural Complementary	11	161	186	0.031	••
Institutional Chance	8	77	189	0.029	•
Entry Mode	14	280	183	0.029	•
Import and Export of Architectural Services	12	213	185	0.029	•
Institutional Complementary	7	66	190	0.027	•
Gravitational and Topological Distance	9	152	188	0.026	•
Cultural Chance	7	83	190	0.025	•
Cultural Factors	7	80	190	0.025	•
Business Complementary	10	235	187	0.023	•
Cultural Demand	7	108	190	0.023	•
Socio-Demographical Distance	7	122	190	0.021	•
Business Demand	15	505	182	0.021	•
Relational Distance	6	90	191	0.021	•
Cultural Locational	9	232	188	0.021	•
Economical Distance	5	108	192	0.016	•
Geographical Distance	6	325	191	0.011	•
Globalization	4	175	193	0.011	•
Agglomeration and Localization	3	135	194	0.009	
Cultural Ownership	2	67	195	0.008	
Cultural Distance	3	170	194	0.008	
Business Chance	6	693	191	0.007	

The strengths of the links are determined by the proximity measures between the codes, and are indicative of the co-occurrences between the codes. A component with its node in a central position has a more complicated and denser web of inter-relationships with other components compared with one located in an outlying position. Thicker lines between nodes also represent stronger linkages between the factors. "Geographical distance" is situated near the bottom of the 3-D illustration, and does not have thick lines that connect it to other nodes. Instead, it is only linked lightly to globalization and organization distance. Therefore, it can be inferred that

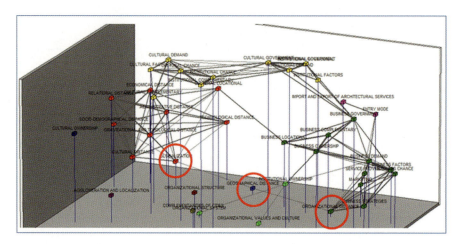

Fig. 8.2 Strength of relationship or link between factors perceived by Singaporean A/E firms

geographical distance does not have a direct link to business strategies and organization structures, but it may be linked indirectly to business strategies and organization structures. The relationships between these factors will be further discussed in Chap. 9.

Similarity

Table 8.11 shows the similarities between factors, using classical scaling. For example, the similarity index between "Gravitational and Topological Distance" and "Geographical Distance" is 0.19, while the similarity index between "Import and Export of Architectural Services" and "Geographical Distance" is 0.04. This implies that "Gravitational and Topological Distance" is a more similar factor to "Geographical Distance". The similarity test shows that "Geographical distance" is most similar to "Organizational distance", "Globalization" and "Marketing"; and "Organization structure" is most similar to "Organization systems", "Organization values and culture" and "Organizational distance". These will be further discussed in Chap. 9.

Figure 8.3 presents a dendrogram, which shows that geographical distance is first and foremost, similar to the various forms of distance, before being similar to risks, then business strategies and organization designs. This suggests that geographical distance, as an independent variable, affects the various forms of distance, as mediating factors, which in turn influences other factors such as risks, business strategies and organization designs et cetera. It is therefore posited that flight-time has a ripple effect on other forms of distances, which then spreads out to influence perceived risks, followed by business strategies and organization structures. The dendrogram also shows that organization structure is first and foremost, similar to institutional ownership, organization systems and organization values and culture, before being similar to e.g. business strategies. These will be further discussed in Chap. 9.

Table 8.11 Similarity between factors

	CULTURAL OWNERSHIP	ECONOMICAL DISTANCE	ENTRY MODE	GEOGRAPHICAL DISTANCE	GLOBALIZATION	GRAVITATIONAL AND TOPOLOGICAL DISTANCE	IMPORT AND EXPORT OF ARCHITECTURAL SERVICES	INSTITUTIONAL CHANCE	INSTITUTIONAL COMPLEMENTARY	INSTITUTIONAL DEMAND	INSTITUTIONAL FACTORS	INSTITUTIONAL GOVERNMENT	INSTITUTIONAL LOCATIONAL	INSTITUTIONAL OWNERSHIP	MARKETING	ORGANIZATIONAL DISTANCE	ORGANIZATIONAL STRUCTURE	ORGANIZATIONAL SYSTEM	ORGANIZATIONAL VALUES AND CULTURE	RELATIONAL DISTANCE	SERVICE PROVIDED	SOCIO-DEMOGRAPHICAL DISTANCE	TECHNOLOGICAL DISTANCE
ENTRY MODE	0.01	0.06	1																				
GEOGRAPHICAL DISTANCE	0.02	0.2	0.04	1																			
GLOBALIZATION	0.01	0.28	0.04	0.17	1																		
GRAVITATIONAL AND TOPOLOGICAL DISTANCE	0.01	0.34	0.03	0.19	0.4	1																	
IMPORT AND EXPORT OF ARCHITECTURAL SERVICES	0.02	0.06	0.27	0.04	0.04	0.04	1																
INSTITUTIONAL CHANCE	0.06	0.02	0.03	0.01	0.04	0.02	0.02	1															
INSTITUTIONAL COMPLEMENTARY	0.06	0.01	0.03	0.02	0.04	0.02	0.03	0.61	1														
INSTITUTIONAL DEMAND	0.06	0.02	0.07	0.02	0.02	0.02	0.09	0.33	0.36	1													
INSTITUTIONAL FACTORS	0.05	0.03	0.06	0.05	0.01	0.02	0.02	0.18	0.18	0.35	1												
INSTITUTIONAL GOVERNMENT	0.05	0.02	0.05	0.02	0.02	0.06	0.05	0.27	0.27	0.49	0.38	1											
INSTITUTIONAL LOCATIONAL	0.05	0.02	0.05	0.02	0.01	0.02	0.04	0.27	0.27	0.49	0.38	0.18	1										
INSTITUTIONAL OWNERSHIP	0.08	0.08	0.05	0.14	0.03	0.02	0.21	0.18	0.18	0.17	0.16	0.18	0.18	1									
MARKETING	0.02	0.02	0.15	0.01	0.09	0.12	0.03	0.03	0.03	0.06	0.07	0.06	0.06	0.07	1								
ORGANIZATIONAL DISTANCE	0.02	0.02	0.03	0.03	0.01	0.07	0.03	0.03	0.03	0.05	0.08	0.06	0.06	0.1	0.14	1							
ORGANIZATIONAL STRUCTURE	0.01	0.02	0.03	0.04	0.03	0.03	0.04	0.02	0.03	0.03	0.04	0.03	0.03	0.04	0.04	0.09	1						
ORGANIZATIONAL SYSTEM	0.02	0.03	0.03	0.01	0.02	0.38	0.05	0.02	0.03	0.04	0.06	0.05	0.05	0.07	0.05	0.08	0.07	1					
ORGANIZATIONAL VALUES AND CULTURE	0.1	0.46	0.02	0.19	0.27	0.03	0.01	0.02	0.02	0.02	0.04	0.02	0.02	0.03	0.02	0.09	0.02	0.03	1				
RELATIONAL DISTANCE	0.09	0.01	0.04	0.03	0.23	0.33	0.06	0.02	0.03	0.03	0.04	0.05	0.05	0.07	0.07	0.1	0.06	0.05	0.05	1			
SERVICE PROVIDED	0.01	0.01	0.03	0.17	0.19	0.04	0.04	0.01	0.01	0.02	0.05	0.03	0.03	0.04	0.03	0.09	0.02	0.05	0.06	0.02	1		
SOCIO-DEMOGRAPHICAL DISTANCE	0.02	0.38	0.02	0.17	0.23	0.38	0.04	0.01	0.01	0.02	0.04	0.03	0.03	0.03	0.03	0.1	0.02	0.05	0.08	0.51	0.03	1	
TECHNOLOGICAL DISTANCE	0.01	0.28	0.02	0.15	0.19	0.27	0.04	0.02	0.02	0.04	0.05	0.04	0.04	0.04	0.04	0.11	0.05	0.05	0.07	0.36	0.06	0.33	1

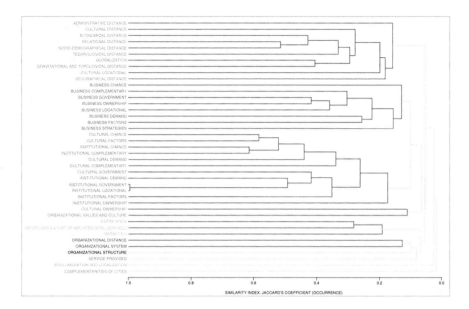

Fig. 8.3 Dendrogram using Jaccard's coefficient to measure similarity index

Figure 8.4 illustrates the similarities of the factors with one another in 2-D space, using classical scaling. A node tends to co-occur more with nodes located near its locus than nodes farther away. For instance, the figure shows that "geographical distance" co-occurs more with "organization systems", "organization values and culture", and "globalization" instead of "organization structure". In addition, nodes which are more similar with one another are indicates similar colors, and they tend to cluster near to one another in the map. These imply that geographical distance has a stronger relationship with organization systems, organization values and culture, and globalization. The proximities between these factors will be further discussed in Chap. 9.

8.3.2 Differences in Perceptions Between Private Firms and Government-Linked Firms

Figures 8.5 and 8.6 show the similarities of factors perceived by private and government-linked Singaporean A/E firms respectively, using classical scaling. It can be observed from these figures that private and government-linked firms may perceive different similarities between factors – private firms perceived "Geographical distance" as more similar to "Organization structure" than government-linked firms. This may be due to the differences in objectives, business approaches and structural qualities etc. of government-linked firms compared to private firms. Issues pertaining to the differences in such perceptions will be discussed in Chap. 9.

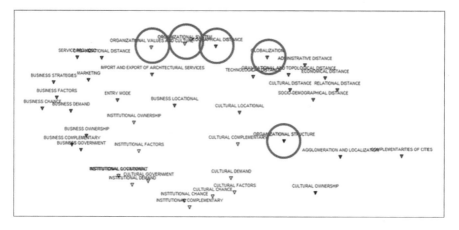

Fig. 8.4 Similarity between factors perceived by Singaporean A/E firms

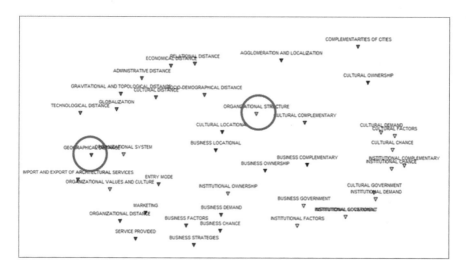

Fig. 8.5 Similarity of factors perceived by private A/E firms

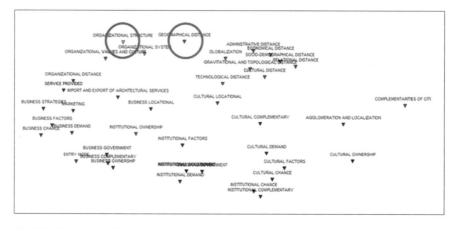

Fig. 8.6 Similarity of factors perceived by government-linked A/E firms

8.4 Statistical Analysis

All datasets from the questionnaires were first subjected to the student t-test for their modes, median, means, standard deviations and significances. The modes and medians would be used to interpret a dataset if the mean of the dataset could not attain a confidence level of 95%. Subsequently, the remaining datasets were subjected to factor analysis and reliability analysis. Factor analysis takes into consideration the best fit and values that are greater than or equal to 0.45 (Comrey 1973). It is useful as a method for reducing the number of variables, by grouping two or more variables into a single factor so that the statistical analysis and its interpretation can be made more meaningful. Tables 8.12, 8.13, 8.14, 8.15 and 8.16 show the questionnaire survey's findings, which will be further discussed in greater details in Chap. 9. The findings are presented in five sections – (i) Internationalization; (ii) Location of overseas offices and operations; (iii) Factor, demand, complementary and related industries, government, chance, ownership and locational factors; (iv) Risk management; and (v) Organization design. In general, the means of the responses were used. In cases whereby the means of responses were rejected due to unsatisfactory confidences, the modes and medians of those inquiries were applied instead.

8.4.1 Factor and Reliability

A reliability analysis checks the consistency of a set of measurements or measuring instruments. The most common internal consistency measure is the Cronbach's alpha coefficient (Nunnally 1978). Normally, for exploratory studies, a dataset can be accepted in terms of reliability as long as the Cronbach's alpha coefficient is greater than 0.7. Based on these two analyses, the datasets were either rejected or grouped. The means of the groups were then obtained. Table 8.17 explains how the datasets were rejected or grouped. These groups of datasets were then ranked according to their means.

8.5 Integration of Content Analysis and Statistical Analysis

Table 8.18 shows the key factors extracted from 42 codes in the Content Analysis. The extraction was based on terms of the frequency of emergence of key factors (and their related key phrases and words) during the recorded interviews. Table 8.19 shows the key factors extracted from the Statistical Analysis. The extraction was based on terms of the means of groups. These extracted factors are thus deemed to be most relevant to the research's central theme – flight-time and its influences on organization structures.

Table 8.12 Questionnaire survey's findings on internationalization

Finding	Mode	Median	Mean	Standard deviation	Confidence (2-tailed)
Branch-offices have accesses to resources from the Singapore head-quarter	4	4	4.533	1.479	0.016
Branch-offices have access to networks from Singapore	4	4	4.766	1.406	0.016
Branch-offices are not patronized by Singaporean business partners	4	4	3.566	1.813	0.020
Singapore head-quarter has access to branch-offices' resources	4	4	4.333	1.372	0.015
Singapore head-quarter has access to branch-offices' networks	4	4	4.300	1.664	0.019
Singapore head-quarter has access to branch-offices' markets	4	4	4.233	1.454	0.016
There are no discontinuities of access to resources, networks and markets at city boundaries	3	3	2.733	1.436	0.016
There are no discontinuities of access to resources, networks and markets at country boundaries	2	3	2.866	1.502	0.017
Access to home-office's location-specific resources does not erode with cultural distance	4	3	2.933	1.436	0.016
Access to home-office's location-specific resources does not erode with administrative distance	3	3	3.066	1.507	0.017
Access to home-office's location-specific resources does not erode with geographical distance	3	3	3.166	1.683	0.019
Access to home-office's location-specific resources does not erode with economical distance	3	3	3.133	1.332	0.015
Offices are inter-connected – there is significant time-space compression and virtual collocation	4	4	4.766	1.612	0.018

Table 8.13 Questionnaire survey's findings on location of overseas offices or operations

Finding	Mode	Median	Mean	Standard deviation	Confidence (2-tailed)
Flight-time is not an important consideration to select location of offices overseas	4	4	3.566	2.176	0.024
Availability of direct flights is a consideration to select setting up of offices overseas	2	4	4.133	2.177	0.024
Shuttling between cities/countries (including preparations, transit/transfers and flight-time) is physically or mentally demanding and tiring; it takes up a considerable amount of employees' working time and is an inconvenient aspect of transnational work	6	4	4.433	1.794	0.020
Long term overseas posting (more than 1 year) will help to improve on work efficiency in the foreign office	6	6	5.200	1.423	0.016

(continued)

Table 8.13 (continued)

Finding	Mode	Median	Mean	Standard deviation	Confidence (2-tailed)
Geographical distance is a consideration to select location of overseas offices	4	4	4.600	1.886	0.021
Geographical distance is a consideration to select procurement and allocation of resources	6	4	4.466	2.080	0.023
Geographical distance is not a consideration to select networks abroad	4	4	3.966	1.956	0.022
Geographical distance is a consideration to select overseas markets	4	4	4.233	1.813	0.020
Geographical borders is a consideration to select setting up of offices	6	4	4.500	1.925	0.022
Geographical borders is a consideration to select procurement of resources, choice of networks and choice of markets overseas	6	6	4.866	1.736	0.019
Accessibility to clients and partners is an important determinant to the location of the overseas office	7	6	5.566	1.454	0.016
Accessibility to amenities is an important determinant to the location of the overseas office	4	4	4.800	1.562	0.017
The organization incur significant transportation and freight costs due to air-travel/air-mails and packages	6	5	4.800	1.494	0.017
The organization incur significant communications costs due to the need to set up infrastructural network	4	4	4.400	1.588	0.018
The organization incur significant training costs to inculcate values and assimilate to host environment	4	4	4.100	1.398	0.016
The organization incur training costs because of the need to inculcate local staff with the company's values and culture	4	4	4.700	1.600	0.018
Geographical distance increases operating costs	4	4	4.466	1.795	0.020
Geographical distance reduces potential value	4	4	4.000	1.597	0.018
Geographical distance affects net value-costs.	4	4	4.300	1.704	0.019
There are losses of information	4	4	4.233	1.695	0.019
There are miscommunications	4	4	4.766	1.568	0.017
There are problems of coordination with overseas counterparts/colleagues	6	4	4.466	1.907	0.021
There are no problems of cooperation with overseas counterparts or colleagues (sometimes, familiarity and trust are absent)	4	4	3.933	1.680	0.019
There are no problems of reporting	2	3	3.366	1.731	0.019
There are problems and undesirable time-lags in decision-making due to geographical separation of the offices	2	5	4.533	2.012	0.023
The cultures between the cities are different	6	6	5.766	1.356	0.015
The organizational cultures between the offices are different	4	4.5	4.866	1.775	0.020
The location of regional offices are determined by spill-over and influences from the headquarter/Singapore's resources, networks and markets	4	4	4.233	1.524	0.017
The political environment in the host and home markets are not similar	1	3	3.233	1.941	0.022

(continued)

8.5 Integration of Content Analysis and Statistical Analysis

Table 8.13 (continued)

Finding	Mode	Median	Mean	Standard deviation	Confidence (2-tailed)
The economical environment in the host and home markets are not similar	2	2	2.766	1.851	0.021
The socio-cultural environment in the host and home markets are not similar	4	4	3.866	1.960	0.022
The demographical environment in the host and home markets are not similar	4	4	3.333	1.768	0.020
The technological environment in the host and home markets are not similar	2	4	3.433	1.695	0.019
There are no commonalities in demand in the host and home markets	4	4	3.766	1.832	0.020
Employees do not contact and communicate with their overseas counterparts/colleagues during their working hours which do not coincide with their working hours	1	4	3.566	2.329	0.026
Employees contact and communicate with their overseas counterparts/colleagues during their working hours which do not coincide with their own working hours	6	4	4.166	2.275	0.026
The differences in time-zones do not affect employees' work	1	2	3.166	2.182	0.024
Employees do not often have to wait for longer to receive their overseas offices' counterparts/colleagues' replies to continue with employees' work	4	4	3.933	2.083	0.023
Training is required to assimilate and educate staff because of socio-cultural changes	4	4	4.400	1.693	0.019
There are climate differences between the host and home cities	6	5	4.566	2.176	0.024
Physical changes necessitates different technologies	4	4	4.633	1.828	0.020
Physical changes necessitates different designs	4	4.5	4.800	1.584	0.018
Training is required to re-educate and assimilate staff because of the difference in the physical environment	4	4	4.033	1.956	0.022
The overseas branch-office is controlled by the headquarters	4	5.5	4.900	1.881	0.021
There is a control and autonomy paradox: Control is desired by the headquarters while Autonomy is preferred by the branch-offices	4	4	4.533	1.833	0.020
Networks are important for businesses/operations overseas	7	6.5	6.100	1.124	0.012
Friction in the form of bounded knowledge and rationality, and sequential actions increases with geographical distances	4	4	4.633	1.607	0.018
Telecommunications, technology and globalization have deemed distance irrelevant	4	5.5	4.966	1.711	0.019
Physical/personal presence and contact is becoming more important in modern business	4	5	5.033	1.401	0.016

Table 8.14 Questionnaire survey's findings on factor, demand, complementary and related industries, government, chance, ownership and locational factors

Finding	Mode	Median	Mean	Standard deviation	Confidence (2-tailed)
Changes in environment are huge and require the firm to switch business strategies and organizational design	4	4	4.700	1.417	0.016
Changes in accessibility require the firm to switch business strategies and organizational design	4	4	4.066	1.484	0.016
Diminished knowledge of overseas market requires the firm to switch business strategies and organizational design	4	4	4.433	1.675	0.019
The firm adapts well to environmental changes	4	4	4.700	1.368	0.015
The host market is not more sophisticated than the home market	4	4	3.933	1.837	0.021
The firm is capable of meeting the expectations of the host market	6	6	5.433	1.430	0.016
Related and supporting industries in the host environment are critical to the success of the firm in the overseas market	4	6	5.233	1.654	0.018
The overseas branch-office relies on local business partners more than home business partners	4	4	4.833	1.641	0.018
The firm is not able to turn statutory restrictions by the home government into opportunities	4	4	3.966	1.564	0.017
The firm is not able to turn statutory restrictions by the host government into opportunities	4	4	3.933	1.837	0.021
The firm is able to make use of the benefits given by the home government	6	5.5	4.500	1.870	0.021
The firm is able to make use of the benefits given by the host government	6	4	4.266	1.928	0.022
The firm is aware of the opportunities available	6	6	5.866	1.041	0.011
Business intelligence are accurate and useful to inform us of the opportunities around	6	6	5.400	1.191	0.013
The firm is concerned about the long-term sustainability of the firm in the overseas market	7	6	5.366	1.790	0.020
The foreign office has autonomy and is not controlled excessively by the head-quarters	6	4	4.433	1.851	0.021
The managers delegate to and empower the subordinates	6	5.5	4.933	1.412	0.016
The organization is Singaporean	7	6	5.300	1.841	0.021
The city is conducive for business	6	6	6.000	0.946	0.010
There are commonalities in the home and host markets	4	4	4.466	1.569	0.017
It is not difficult to coordinate work with a distant colleague	4	4	3.966	1.711	0.019
It is difficult to integrate work with a distant client	4	4	4.100	1.787	0.020
It is difficult to integrate work with a distant business partner	4	4	4.100	1.604	0.018
It requires extra efforts to integrate work with more distance	4	4	4.933	1.460	0.016
Deception is not more common when distance increases	4	4	3.933	1.617	0.018
Physical distance changes the cultural, attributional/institutional, geographical and economical aspects of the business environment	4	4	4.433	1.546	0.017

8.5 Integration of Content Analysis and Statistical Analysis

Table 8.15 Questionnaire survey's findings on risk management

Finding	Mode	Median	Mean	Standard deviation	Confidence (2-tailed)
The firm has a structured and elaborate risk management plan	4	4.5	5.033	1.376	0.015
Risk is an important consideration for overseas ventures	6	6	5.700	1.235	0.014
The firm is risk adverse (low threshold towards risks)	4	4	4.333	1.625	0.018
The firm seeks to minimize uncertainty by gathering intelligence and conducting due diligence	6	6	5.366	1.129	0.012
The firm uses framing of possible scenario to manage risk	4	4	4.600	1.404	0.016
The firm makes decision based on anticipation of regret/opportunity costs	4	4	4.600	1.452	0.016
The firm seeks to minimize risks by avoidance	6	4	4.433	1.715	0.019
The firm seeks to minimize risks by reduction	4	4	4.766	1.406	0.016
The firm seeks to minimize risks by transference	4	4	4.433	1.501	0.017
The firm does not seeks to retains risks	4	4	3.733	1.855	0.021
Political risks are not significant in this particular country/city	4	4	3.833	1.821	0.020
Legal risks are significant in this particular country/city	6	6	4.700	1.664	0.019
Market and industry risks are significant in this particular country/city	6	6	5.000	1.640	0.018
Financial risks are significant in this particular country/city	6	4.5	4.433	1.941	0.022
Socio-cultural risks are significant in this particular country/city	4	4	4.000	1.722	0.019
Management risks are significant in this particular country/city	4	4	4.166	1.599	0.018
Technological/engineering and project risks are not significant in this particular country/city	4	4	3.700	1.896	0.021
Design risks are not significant in this particular country/city	4	4	3.733	1.760	0.020
Risk perception of foreign market is not influenced by cultural distance	4	4	3.800	1.648	0.018
Risk perception of foreign market is influenced by administrative and political distance	6	4	4.666	1.516	0.017
Risk perception of foreign market is not influenced by geographical/flight distance	4	4	3.833	1.683	0.019
Risk perception of foreign market is influenced by access due to transportation and communications infrastructure	4	4	4.200	1.323	0.015
Risk perception of foreign market is influenced by economic distance	4	4	4.200	1.648	0.018
Risk analysis is an important component of value-costs evaluation	6	6	5.233	1.135	0.012
The choice of business strategies and management is influenced by the perception of risks	6	5.5	4.966	1.129	0.012
The choice of organizational design is influenced by the perception of risks	6	4.5	4.800	1.399	0.016

Table 8.16 Questionnaire survey's findings on organization design

Finding	Mode	Median	Mean	Standard deviation	Confidence (2-tailed)
Organizational design does not follows business strategies	4	4	3.266	2.016	0.023
The relationship between organizational design and business strategies is dynamic	4	4	5.066	1.284	0.014
Business strategies are organic and dynamic; it evolves with time and situations. It is a contingency/situational model that is flexible to deal with complexity	6	6	5.000	1.640	0.018
The organizational structure is organic and dynamic; it evolves with time and situations. It is a contingency/situational model that is flexible to deal with complexity	4	4.5	4.733	1.659	0.018
Value-costs evaluation influences business strategies and organizational design	4	4	4.966	1.098	0.012
The structure (reporting, communication, coordination, cooperation, authority and responsibility) can be flexible	6	5.5	4.933	1.529	0.017
The organizational structure is efficient and effective	4	4.5	4.933	1.529	0.017
The firm is a learning organization	6	5.5	4.933	1.574	0.018
The lines and processes of reporting are efficient	4	6	5.200	1.186	0.013
The lines of communication are not only top-down	4	4	3.666	0.994	0.011
The lines of coordination and cooperation are efficient	4	4	4.966	1.129	0.012
The set-out of authorities and responsibilities are effective	6	6	5.200	1.242	0.014
Power distance (preferential treatment to senior management) is not large	6	4	3.966	1.711	0.019
Masculinity/manliness traits is not preferred over feminism and emotionality	4	4	3.500	1.852	0.021
Staff have a short term time orientation	4	4	4.333	1.347	0.015
There is uncertainty avoidance	4	4	4.366	1.098	0.012
The staff does not practices individualism	4	4	1.507	3.266	0.017
Decision making is not autocratic	4	4	1.790	3.966	0.020
The firm does not encourages employee movements across offices	4	4	1.681	4.000	0.019
The firm employ senior staffs from "outside"	7	5.5	1.884	4.966	0.021
Employees do not share common values	4	4	1.080	4.933	0.012
The overseas offices are not fully functional, equipped to handle, e.g. procurement, financial, technology, networking, human resource, service, marketing and other aspects of a normal organization in entirety	7	6	1.769	5.200	0.020

8.5 Integration of Content Analysis and Statistical Analysis 169

Table 8.17 Clustering of questions into groups

Subject	Grouped (questions)	Mean (3 significant figures)	Rank	Rejected
Profiles of respondents and firms	None	NA	–	Questions 1–10 were not considered because they pertained to the profiles of the respondents
Proximity	11–16	4.28	8	None
Discontinuities due to borders	17 and 18	2.87	–	None
Discontinuities due to various forms of distance	19–22	3.14	–	None
Compression of time-space dimensions	27	4.67	4	Questions 23–26 were not considered because they were Yes/No answers
Flight-time/geographical distance, agglomeration and location	28, 32–39	4.52	6	Question 29 failed significance test and factor analysis; Questions 30 and 31 failed reliability test
Cost-value evaluation	41–43, 46	4.46	7	Question 40 rejected because it is an isolated item and cannot be tested on reliability; Questions 44 and 45 failed reliability test
Communication	47–52	4.22	–	None
Psychic distance	53 and 54	5.35	1	None
Spill-over	56–61	3.43	–	Question 55 rejected because it is an isolated item and cannot be tested on reliability
Time-zones and time-lags	64 and 65	3.86	–	Questions 62 and 63 failed significance test
Changes	67–70	4.51	5	Question 66 rejected because it is an isolated item and cannot be tested on reliability
Control	None	NA	–	Questions 71 and 72 failed reliability test
Networks	None	NA	–	Question 73 rejected because it is an isolated item and cannot be tested on reliability
Friction	None	NA	–	Questions 74–76 failed reliability test
Factor	None	NA	–	Questions 77–79 failed reliability test; Question 80 failed factor analysis
Demand	None	NA	–	Questions 81 and 82 failed reliability test

(continued)

Table 8.17 (continued)

Subject	Grouped (questions)	Mean (3 significant figures)	Rank	Rejected
Related and supporting industries	None	NA	–	Questions 83 and 84 failed reliability test
Government	85–88	4.18	–	None
Chance	None	NA	–	Questions 89 to 91 failed reliability test
Ownership	None	NA	–	Question 92 rejected because it is an isolated item and cannot be tested on reliability; Questions 93 and 94 failed reliability test
Locational – Difficulty of integrating work	97–99	3.99	–	Questions 95 and 100 failed reliability test; Question 96 failed factor analysis
Locational – changes and deception	101 and 102	4.25	10	
Risks perception and attitude	105, 106, 109, 113–125	4.26	9	Questions 103, 108 and 126 failed reliability test; Question 112 rejected because it is an isolated item and cannot be tested on reliability
Risks and its influence on business strategies	104, 107, 110, 111, 127 and 128	4.84	3	
Organization structure	130–137, 139, 140, 148–150	4.99	2	Questions 129, 138, 141, 143, 145 and 147 failed reliability test; Questions 142 and 144 failed factor analysis; Question 146 rejected because it is an isolated item and cannot be tested on reliability

8.5 Integration of Content Analysis and Statistical Analysis

Table 8.18 Key factors observed from Content Analysis in terms of frequency

Rank	Top ten important factors from Content Analysis in descending order
1	Organizational distance
2	Business strategies
3	Business risks – chances
4	Business risks – factors
5	Service provided
6	Business risks – demand
7	Marketing
8	Business risks – locational factors
9	Geographical distance
10	Business risks – government

Table 8.19 Key factors observed from statistical analysis in terms of mean

Rank	Top ten important factors from Statistical Analysis in descending order
1	Psychic distance
2	Organization structure
3	Risks and its influence on business strategies
4	Compression of time-space dimensions
5	Changes
6	Flight-time/geographical distance, agglomeration and location
7	Cost-value evaluation
8	Proximity
9	Risks perception and attitude
10	Locational – changes and deception

Commonalities between the top factors derived from the Content Analysis and Statistical Analysis were considered. The research selected the top five important factors (highlighted in and selected from Tables 8.18 and 8.19) from each analysis for correlation analysis (using the Statistical Software) and a re-run of a co-occurrence analysis (using the Content Analysis software). These combined factors include: psychic distance, business strategies and organization structures, risks and its influences on business strategies, compression of time-space dimensions, changes and service provided. Selected questions and datasets from the questionnaire surveys were then chosen to reflect the various key factors (refer to Table 8.20). Another subject – "Flight-time and geographical distance", the central premise of the study was also included in the list even though it did not appear to be a top five important factor (it was the 9th and 6th most important factors in the Content Analysis and Statistical Analysis respectively).

Table 8.21 shows the correlation between psychic distance, business strategies and organization structures, risks and its influences on business strategies, compression of time-space dimensions, training due to changes, service provided, and flight-time and geographical distance.

Table 8.20 Selected questions and datasets to reflect various key factors

Subject	Questions
Psychic distance	(53) The organization incur training costs because of the need to inculcate local staff with the company's values and culture; and (54) Geographical distance increases operating costs
Business strategies and Organization structures	(133) Value-costs evaluation influences business strategies and organization design; and (135) The organization structure is efficient and effective
Risks and its influences on business strategies	(104) Risk is an important consideration for overseas ventures; (127) The choice of business strategies and management is influenced by the perception of risks; and (128) The choice of organization design is influenced by the perception of risks
Compression of time-space dimensions	(27) The offices are well-interconnected with one another – there is significant time-space compression and virtual collocation
Changes	(70) Training is required to re-educate and assimilate staff because of the difference in the physical environment
Service provided	(150) The office is fully functional, equipped to handle, e.g. procurement, financial, technology, networking, human resource, service, marketing and other aspects of a normal organization in entirety
Flight-time and geographical distance	(28) Flight-time/geographical distance is an important consideration to select location of offices overseas

Table 8.21 Correlation between key factors

		QN27	QN28	QN53	QN54	QN70	QN104	QN127	QN128	QN133	QN135	QN150
QN27	Pearson Correlation	1	.000	.006	-.168	.112	.085	-.099	.162	.190	-.062	-.068
	Sig. (2-tailed)		.999	.976	.375	.556	.656	.602	.392	.314	.743	.722
	N	30	30	30	30	30	30	30	30	30	30	30
QN28	Pearson Correlation	.000	1	-.058	.074	.093	-.294	-.034	.299	.152	.198	-.201
	Sig. (2-tailed)	.999		.761	.699	.626	.115	.858	.109	.421	.294	.288
	N	30	30	30	30	30	30	30	30	30	30	30
QN53	Pearson Correlation	.006	.058	1	.731**	.159	.101	.220	.338	.041	-.141	.236
	Sig. (2-tailed)	.976	.761		.000	.401	.596	.243	.068	.830	.458	.210
	N	30	30	30	30	30	30	30	30	30	30	30
QN54	Pearson Correlation	-.168	.074	.731**	1	.249	.248	.531**	.530**	.033	.022	.108
	Sig. (2-tailed)	.375	.699	.000		.184	.186	.003	.003	.863	.908	.572
	N	30	30	30	30	30	30	30	30	30	30	30
QN70	Pearson Correlation	.112	.093	.159	.249	1	-.124	-.109	.179	-.016	.220	.187
	Sig. (2-tailed)	.556	.626	.401	.184		.514	.567	.344	.935	.243	.322
	N	30	30	30	30	30	30	30	30	30	30	30
QN104	Pearson Correlation	.085	-.294	.101	.248	-.124	1	.437*	.323	.170	-.047	.218
	Sig. (2-tailed)	.656	.115	.596	.186	.514		.016	.082	.368	.803	.248
	N	30	30	30	30	30	30	30	30	30	30	30
QN127	Pearson Correlation	-.099	-.034	.220	.531**	-.109	.437*	1	.738**	.138	-.081	.072
	Sig. (2-tailed)	.602	.858	.243	.003	.567	.016		.000	.467	.670	.703
	N	30	30	30	30	30	30	30	30	30	30	30
QN128	Pearson Correlation	.162	.299	.338	.530**	.179	.323	.738**	1	.355	.074	.156
	Sig. (2-tailed)	.392	.109	.068	.003	.344	.082	.000		.055	.697	.411
	N	30	30	30	30	30	30	30	30	30	30	30
QN133	Pearson Correlation	.190	.152	.041	.033	-.016	.170	.138	.355	1	.163	.075
	Sig. (2-tailed)	.314	.421	.830	.863	.935	.368	.467	.055		.390	.695
	N	30	30	30	30	30	30	30	30	30	30	30
QN135	Pearson Correlation	-.062	.198	-.141	.022	.220	-.047	-.081	.074	.163	1	.069
	Sig. (2-tailed)	.743	.294	.458	.908	.243	.803	.670	.697	.390		.718
	N	30	30	30	30	30	30	30	30	30	30	30
QN150	Pearson Correlation	-.068	-.201	.236	.108	.187	.218	.072	.156	.075	.069	1
	Sig. (2-tailed)	.722	.288	.210	.572	.322	.248	.703	.411	.695	.718	
	N	30	30	30	30	30	30	30	30	30	30	30

The Pearson correlation coefficient (r) provides a measure of the linear association between two variables. The measure (r) can lie between 0 (no relation) and 1 (perfect correlation) (Tan 2004). When $r = -1$, it means that there is a perfectly negative association. Therefore, the Pearson correlation coefficient can be used to uncover the direction and strength of bivariate relationships among measurable variables. For significance set at $\alpha = 0.05$, Question 27 was found to be significantly correlated to Question 28 and Question 53. In other words, Compression of time-space dimensions was found to be significantly correlated with Psychic distance, Flight-time and Geographical distance.

The combined factors identified earlier were then broken down into (i) important organization designs; and (ii) determinants of organization designs. A Content Analysis was subsequently re-run to obtain co-occurrences between these components. These values would be used later to acquire weights for these components for developing the CBR-DSS. The procedure will be explained in the Chap. 11.

8.6 Summary

Chapter 8 presents the collation of data, stratified in terms of (i) aggregation; (ii) private and government-linked firms; and (iii) cities; with the aid of QDA Miner, a Content Analysis software and PASW, a Statistical Analysis software. The purpose of the analyses is to identify important factors, their correlations and co-occurrences with one another, pertaining to the research's central theme of flight-time and its influences on organization design of Singaporean A/E firms when they venture into regional overseas markets which are within 7-h flight-radii away from Singapore. Discussions of these findings will be carried out in Chap. 9.

References

Comrey AL (1973) A first course in factor analysis. Academic, New York
Hubalek Z (1982) Coefficients of association and similarity, based on binary (presence-absence) data: an evaluation. Biol Rev 57(4):669–689
Lugwig JA, Reynold JF (1988) Statistical ecology: a primer on methods and computing. Wiley, New York
Nunnally JC (1978) Psychometric theory, 2nd edn. McGraw-Hill, New York
Tan W (2004) Practical research methods, 2nd edn. Prentice Hall, Singapore

Chapter 9
Background of Internationalizing Construction Firms and Cities

9.1 Introduction

This chapter examines the characteristics of Singapore's A/E firms and their motivations and objectives, competitive advantages and competitiveness, choice of markets, difficulties and risks incurred, and the prerequisites and Critical Success Factors (CSFs) for internationalization.

For example, design-oriented A/E firms and commercial-oriented A/E firms have different motivations, and often exhibit different traits. A commercial-oriented A/E firm tends to be more business and service-oriented. A commercial-oriented A/E firm also tends to focus more on the efficiency of the A/E design, whereas a design-oriented A/E firm tends to be a lot more aesthetic-centric. It is therefore explicable that the two genres of firms have dissimilar proclivity to internationalize, dissimilar business strategies and disparate forms of organization. For instance, a design-oriented firm tends to keep the A/E firm small to retain control, whereas a commercial-oriented firm tends to be operated on a demand-and-supply and profit-maximization basis.

The work-scope of an architect in different parts of the world might be very different, in terms of the architect's participation in seeking building approvals from the authorities on behalf of the client, preparing feasibility studies and building audits, communicating with stakeholders to appreciate their objectives and interests, conceptualizing the aesthetic and functional designs of the buildings or structures and spaces between them, and liaising and coordinating work with other construction professionals such as the quantity surveyor, engineer, contractor, sub-contractor, supplier, specialist, landscape architect and interior designer (Burgess 1983).

9.2 Singapore's A/E firms' Traits and Characteristics

Architectural consultancy services in Singapore typically include: (i) understanding the building or structure's objectives and functional requirements; (ii) working out a conceptual design; (iii) panning out detailed designs; and (iv) determining specifications.

A/E services are consultation services that require the intellectual inputs of a highly educated workforce. It is therefore a tertiary/quaternary service. For marketing of such services, 3 more Ps – Processes, People and Physical evidences are added to the 4Ps – Product, Price, Place and Promotion of marketing a commodity. The marketing function should be one of the firm's most important considerations when it decides to venture overseas because it has to consider whether marketing efforts should be aligned or even similar to the head-quarter or other branch offices in other locations.

In this section, firms are given a brief introduction, before being described in words by their own staffs. These statements would inform us of these firms' vision, objectives, target segments et cetera. These firms are considered to be among Singapore's best or most established A/E firms, and have actively pursued overseas markets or projects.

9.2.1 Firm A

Firm A was founded in the 1970s. In the 1990s, Firm A was incorporated to succeed the original partnership, in hope to inject new blood and energy. To catch up with the ever-changing needs of more sophisticated and professional clients and construction industry, two new subsidiary companies were formed in the late 1990s to better cater to growing needs in interior design services and project management services. Overseas offices in Malaysia and China to provide a full spectrum of complementary services were also set up. In the early 2000s, the Board of Directors was reorganized under the leadership of the current CEO. Since then, the firm has managed to make a mark for itself in the niche of corporate boutique niche. In the region, Firm A specializes in providing architectural master planning and architectural design consultancy services, particularly from the concept design stage to schematic design and design development. Currently, Firm A has projects in China, India, Dubai, Vietnam, Cambodia, Indonesia and Malaysia.

A Director of Firm A in Singapore described Firm A:

> We are a corporate boutique architectural Firm...We are more concerned about quality and good work, not quantities. We are conscious of our branding. We want to be consistent in our designs. We prefer timeless, contemporary, modern, clean and crisp designs. We want to respect this design fabric.

9.2.2 Firm B

Firm B was incorporated in the 1980s by seven registered architects, who brought together their experiences, expertise and resources in the field of architecture, in order to qualify for a government project. During ordinary times, it is actually four separate design firms, making Firm B a namesake only. One of the four design firms, B2 is the largest in terms of employee size among the firms. A senior technical manager of Firm B in Singapore described Firm B *"B2 is a sole-proprietorship; Firm B is a partnership"*. Firm B is often ahead of other architectural firms, e.g. in terms of internationalization efforts, improving its corporate systems and innovation. For instance, it was one of the first Singapore's A/E firms to have moved into China and to be certified with ISO 9001. Firm B's niche is in Green and Sustainable Buildings, but it also endeavors to do a wide range of project types. Firm B presently employs over 100 professional staffs, and has expanded its market areas to include China, Malaysia, India, Vietnam and Indonesia.

An architect of Firm B in Singapore described Firm B:

> *In my time in Firm B, I have not seen a project that requires the pooling of the four firms' resources together... We gain clients' trust because we are conservative, reliable and professional.*

9.2.3 Firm C

Firm C was born out of the corporatisation of a governmental department in the late 1990s. It thus inherited substantial work experience, accumulated knowledge and project references. In 2002, it was renamed Firm C. Around the mid-2000s, it was bought over and privatized by an overseas Group. Firm C currently has offices in Singapore, Malaysia, Philippines, Vietnam, China, India and the United Arab Emirates (UAE), and has business presence in Australia, Indonesia, Brunei, Cambodia, Laos, South Korea, Myanmar, Sri Lanka, Pakistan, Oman, Qatar, Seychelles and Turkey. Firm C's full spectrum of services encompasses multi-disciplinary architecture and engineering consultancy, project management, facilities management, construction management and materials testing. Firm C's multi-disciplinary design consultancy realm of services enables the firm to provide a full range of one-stop professional solutions.

The Managing Director of Firm C in HCM City described Firm C:

> *We are a branded multi-disciplinary consultancy firm, with strong track records since our days as a public department. We have high recognition by overseas governments.*

9.2.4 Firm D

Firm D started as a partnership in the 1960s and was incorporated in the mid-1970s to become a private limited company. With the increase in activities, two subsidiary companies – Firm D Design and Firm D Consultants were formed to provide interior design and project management services respectively. Presently, Firm D is a full service architecture firm based in Singapore and with offices in Malaysia, Indonesia, India, China, Thailand and UAE, and has undertaken projects in Malaysia, the People's Republic of China, Hong Kong, Taiwan, Korea, Indonesia, Philippines, India, Thailand, Vietnam, Africa and the Middle East. Firm D is one of Singapore's biggest private architectural firms, with more than 500 staff in Singapore and more than 700 worldwide. Its core competence lies in its experience and confidence to handle large-scale work both in Singapore and overseas. The firm's portfolio also includes a wide spectrum of building types, from commercial to residential, mixed development, institutional, religious, industrial, hospitality and transportation.

An associate of Firm D in Shanghai described Firm D:

Firm D does different types of buildings, as well as different scales of project.

A senior associate of Firm D in Shanghai described Firm D:

Firm D goes for quality. I have never heard them saying that they want to be the biggest Singaporean firm but I think the bottom-line is to do good works.

9.2.5 Firm E

Since the 1960s, Firm E's parent company has been synonymous with Singapore's industrialization and growth as a country. Firm E was formed in the 1990s to be its parent-company's internationalization arm. Firm E already has offices in Suzhou, Shanghai, Beijing, Chengdu, Bangalore, Hyderabad, Dubai and Abu Dhabi, and has completed more than 300 projects across more than 60 cities abroad. It core strength lies in its ability to provide a range of multi-disciplinary services, including master planning, architecture, civil and structural engineering, mechanical and electrical, quantity surveying consultancy services, design and build and turnkey projects.

A principal quantity surveyor of Firm E in Singapore described Firm E:

We provide multi-disciplinary services, ranging from architectural and engineering services, to laboratory analysis, industrial, and reclamation projects.

A Vice-President of Firm E in Singapore, described Firm E:

We provide a whole chain of niche services.

9.2.6 Firm F

Firm F was originally a division of a governmental board. The governmental board was itself established in the 1960s as a governmental agency to solve the country's housing crisis by providing affordable and quality housing for its growing population. In the 2000s, the division was corporatized. In the following year, it was acquired by an investment vehicle of the Singapore Government. Since then, Firm F has grown internationally, powered by its core businesses of township development, building and infrastructure consultancy, and property management. Firm F currently has offices in Kuala Lumpur, Ho Chi Minh City, Hanoi, Jakarta, Shanghai, Chengdu, Shenyang, Wuhan, Tianjin, Wuxi, Xi'an, Hyderabad, Chennai, Kolkata, Doha, Dubai and Abu Dhabi.

A Vice-President of Firm F in Singapore described Firm F:

> We are still very much a government-linked company… We sell Singapore's success stories of providing public housing for the masses and master-planning consultancy services.

9.3 Corporatized or Privatized Firms

Corporatization refers to the transformation of state assets or agencies into state-owned corporations in order to introduce corporate management techniques to their administration. Privatization, on the other hand, refers to the transfer of any government function or ownership of a business, enterprise, agency or public service from the public sector, to the private sector or a private firm. When firms corporatize or privatize, their organization systems often alter to emulate those of private firms, in hope that the organizational processes would be streamlined and improved. However, organizations cannot be expected to carry out a major realignment of roles, responsibilities and relationships overnight. A complete make-over is almost impractical and impracticable. These firms often retain some of their heritage from their previous forms as government-linked firms. It was found that corporatized or privatized A/E still retain part of their organizational heritages after their corporatization or privatization.

A Vice-President of Firm C in Singapore shared on how Firm C continued to have advantaged access to public-sector projects, for 5 years after its corporatization. Even after that, Firm C carried on to receive and handle many public-sector jobs, probably because (i) it has built up strong competencies and competitive advantages over other firms for institutional projects; and (ii) it has developed a superior partnering relationship with public-sector clients. He said:

> Our main clients are still from the public sector, like the Ministry of Health, Ministry of Education, Public Utilities Board et cetera. We used to be the automatic choice for these government or statutory boards, with the exception of maybe some government boards or agencies which have their own in-house departments. This was partly because of the moratorium of our corporatization in the late 90s. It stated that for the next 5 years, we would have the benefit of getting public-sector projects.

The Managing Director of Firm C in HCM City shared that it is common for staffs of government-linked firms to "cross-over" to other government-linked firms. This could be because (i) these firms would be able to tap into the skill-sets of one another to complement their own core services; (ii) the work cultures are more similar, and staffs would be able to blend into the new work-place easily; and (iii) internal understanding. He said:

> *Staff shuffling between these firms is present because these firms want to tap into the rich experiences of one another to complement their own core services.*

The Managing Director of Firm C in Shanghai shared on the benefits of privatization:

> *Firm C has successfully transformed to become a private firm. We have become more flexible. We have strong corporate governance, robust accounts systems and management processes. We also enjoy good business growth.*

A Principal quantity surveyor of Firm E in Singapore shared "*red-tape has been reduced*", the firm has streamlined their processes, and have become less bureaucratic. He also noted that employees have been willing to shed their previous practices and that "*staffs were receptive to changes*". Nonetheless, it has been widely known that younger staffs tend to be less entrenched in old practices, and are more receptive and flexible to the firm's transition from a government-linked firm to become a fully private firm. On the other hand, experienced or elderly staffs in government-linked firms could be too ingrained and regimented with the bureaucratic mode of doing things, and are likely to demonstrate more inertia to adapt to changes. The privatizing firm would have to finely balance the management of these older staffs, to continue to tap into their wealth of experiences and knowledge, and yet become more vibrant and dynamic. He said that:

A Vice-President of Firm F in Singapore shared that a government-linked firm is more likely to be more risk-averse and prudent. A government-linked firm is also obliged to be more transparent and accountable, in terms of allocation of resources and transactions with other parties. The Vice-President said:

> *Being a Singapore state-owned company and a government-linked firm, we are very much a cautious company that checks out its prospective clients' background.*

> *We are flat. We are no longer bureaucratic like in the past.*

9.4 Motivations and Objectives

A company's motivations and objectives would determine how eager it is to venture overseas, its business strategies, organization structure, organization systems et cetera. It was found that in general, firms seek to upgrade themselves in terms of skills and capabilities to become market leaders in the industry, provide good value-for-money services in order to satisfy clients, and make profits when they venture overseas. The finding on skills and capabilities is consistent with Penrose's (1959) Resource-based Theory and the Knowledge-based Theory (Kogut and Zander 1992; Nonaka and Takeuchi 1995) which suggest that staff's knowledge, skills and capabilities are critical and core resources of the firm, and should be protected and developed. The finding on value-for-money services is consistent with Slater's (1997) suggestion that the creation of customer value must be the reason for the firm's existence and is crucial for its success. The finding on making profits is consistent with Hicks's (1939) Cost-Benefit Analysis, which suggests that a firm seeks to generate a sum of revenue that is more than the costs it incur in order to make a profit.

A Director of Firm A in Kuala Lumpur shared on Firm A's ambitions:

To be ahead of the rest. Be a bench-mark for good design and innovation, and delivery.

A senior technical manager of Firm B in Singapore shared:

We aim to be the firm that last for at least 100 years. That means continuity and this is our objective. We aimed to be the top 10 architecture firms and we had achieved that since 2005.
For us, profit is the main criteria.

A senior associate of Firm C in HCM City shared:

To provide client-oriented, customized and excellent services and solutions.

Sometimes, an overseas office may be disoriented about the organization's business strategies. An associate of Firm D, working in Shanghai shared:

There are no clear strategic directions or business strategies.

It could be due to: (i) A/E firms or staffs tend to be less savvy on business strategies; (ii) the firm does not have a clear or explicit strategic direction; (iii) only the top management are involved, and are aware of the firm's strategic directions; (iv) the strategic directions have not been well-communicated to the organization's overseas offices; and (v) the overseas office has been disconnected from the home-office.

A senior Vice-President of Firm C in Shanghai shared:

We want to position ourselves as an international foreign firm.

We intend to venture into 2nd and 3rd tier cities like Wuhan and Kunming to tap into their market potential.

A senior manager of Firm E in Shanghai shared:

It is important that our clients are satisfied with our work.

A/E work is primarily a service. Clients who are pleased with the services provided to them are more likely to become repeat clients, then regular clients and business partners. A/E firms which managed to satisfy their clients are also more likely to get referrals and word-of-mouth recommendations from their clients.

An assistant General Manager of Firm F in Kuala Lumpur shared:

We try to provide value-add services.

9.5 Competitiveness and Competitive Strengths of Singapore's A/E Firms

Singapore's A/E firms were found to be more competitive in South-east Asian markets like Kuala Lumpur, Hanoi and HCM City, than in Chinese markets. This is most likely because of (i) physical and cultural proximities of these markets from

Singapore; and (ii) relative inactivity of international A/E firms in South-east Asia. Chinese markets, especially Shanghai and Beijing, are much more competitive, with American, European, Australian and Japanese firms that aggressively vie for all the best projects available in the market. The finding on physical proximity is consistent with Johanson and Vahlne (1977) findings that a transnational firm's internationalization process often follows a proximate to distant pattern. The finding on the relative inactivity of international A/E firms in South-east Asia reflects Predoehl (1928) Core and Periphery model and Weber's (1929) concept of agglomeration, which suggest that there are agglomeration of economic activities and talents in core locations but backwashes in periphery locations.

A senior associate of Firm D in Shanghai shared:

> USA sells. Local clients can be quite country-brand conscious.

A master-planning manager of Firm E in Shanghai shared:

> Japanese and Australia-New Zealanders always manage to clinch the top-notch projects, whilst Singaporean A/E firms scrap the average, mediocre projects. Singapore A/E firms are only behind Japanese A/E firms if you are only comparing Asians with Asians. Singaporean firms are more competent than Taiwanese and Hong Kong firms. You can also trust the Singaporean firms to deliver on their promises, but not the Taiwanese and Hong Kong firms. On the other hand, the private Taiwanese and Hong Kong firms may have better networks in China, and that is important in China.

It was shared that local A/E firms in China are learning fast and catching up with international A/E firms, and Singapore's A/E firms are seemingly sandwiched in between. This finding is consistent with Chamberlin's (1933) Industrial Organization Theory, which suggests that foreign firms do not understand local consumer taste, business customs and legal systems as well as the local firms. Nonetheless, Singapore's firms are constantly improving and keeping themselves competitive, and they are sometimes perceived in better light than international consultants.

A Director of Firm A in Kuala Lumpur shared:

> Green building is the trend and future and we are a member of the United States Green Building Council.

A senior technical manager of Firm B in Singapore shared:

> We will keep ourselves updated on the latest technology and green movements. As a matter of fact, we are the top two architecture Firms in Singapore that has the most "Green" projects. You can say that it is becoming a competitive edge for us. Thus, strategy wise, design and green projects go hand in hand. In addition, we have a very strong arm in project management.

It used to be the case of "Customers first, and employees last". Nowadays, a new paradigm of business management has emerged – "Employees first". An A/E firm's main and most important asset is its staff. Firm C seems to place a lot of emphasis on its human resources. It has also conscientiously developed or acquired skilled talents in a range of complementary and multidisciplinary services (e.g. consultancy services in A/E, project management, quantity surveying, building audit et cetera). This finding is consistent with Revans' (1974), Belbin (1981) and Welch's

(2005) suggests that it is important for a firm to have cross-fertilization of collective abilities; imperfect people make perfect teams through complementary roles; and a company needs the right people to become successful.

The Managing Director of Firm C in HCM City shared:

> *We have high quality human resources. The quality of our staffs is important because clients expect to look at the CVs (curriculum vitae) of our designers.*
>
> *We are not jack of all trades but master of none. We are masters of all.*
>
> *We are a company of repute and history. Our core expertise and strengths have been built up over the years. We have expanded and strengthened not because of vanity, but because of true exposure and real growth. Our wide range of service provision creates synergy. We remain a nimble firm.*

A senior associate of Firm D in Shanghai shared:

> *We are better in marketing and understanding and sharing clients' perspectives and concerns.*
>
> *Like most other Singaporean firms, we offer cheaper services than the USA, UK, Australian and Japanese firms. We speak their language. We are also more accommodating than international brand-names. We get a lot of referrals for jobs well-done previously. Singaporean developers are also increasing their presence here, and they like to work with us.*
>
> *International brand-names are rather egoistic and very stubborn. They do not change their stance and do not give in to their clients or partners. Singaporean architectural practices care about relationship-management with our clients.*

A senior manager of Firm E in Shanghai shared:

> *Glocalization is the only way to go if you want to stay competitive because the Chinese firms are learning very fast and will be on par with us very soon. I would expect them to raise their fee or project price in the future and if so, their cost would be equivalent to ours. As such, how we can win them is basically by brand name and strong track records, as well as clients' commendations.*
>
> *We have a good track record.*
>
> *Other firms may do empty-talk, but we have shown that we can deliver on promises.*
>
> *Firm E is a government-linked firm and when clients know that our firm has backing from the Singapore government which is well-known for transparency, they have trust that Firm E is stable and will always deliver, like the Singapore government.*

9.6 Internationalization of Singapore's A/E firms

In this section, architects and engineers share on why their firms are venturing abroad, especially into nearby "hot-spots" markets in South-east Asia, China, India and the Middle-east. It was found that Singapore's A/E firms prefer to venture into cities with booming construction markets, such as HCM City, Shanghai and Beijing. These cities are approximately 3, 5 and 6 h away from Singapore respectively. This finding reflects Mr. Goh's (2001) suggestion that Singapore's transnational firms should make use of their geographical and cultural proximities to reach out to countries or cities that are within 7-h flight-time away from Singapore.

9.6.1 Reasons for Internationalizing

There are several reasons why firms venture overseas: market-seeking, resource-seeking, efficiency-seeking and strategic asset-seeking. It was found that Singapore's A/E firms are more likely to venture overseas to seek new markets. Some interviewees shared that venturing overseas would reduce their firms' exposure to the risks due to cyclical markets in Singapore. This finding is consistent with Markowitz's (1952) Diversification Theory, which suggests that rational investors or firms should diversify their portfolio to spread out their risks.

An architect from Firm B, when asked on reasons for Firm B to venture overseas, shared:

For better profits and more markets.

A Vice-President of Firm C in Singapore shared:

Singapore is so small. The workload also fluctuates a lot. For example, just some time back, we were having an economic and construction boom, but now, we are facing a crisis. Therefore, we need to balance our workload by going overseas, so that in time of recession, we still have projects to do.

We must already plan to go overseas in good times, and not only do it during a recession. We can spread our risks by going overseas.

The Managing Director of Firm C in HCM City shared:

Our base in still in Singapore. Most of our works, like conceptual designs are done in Singapore. We are here (in Vietnam) to follow up and coordinate work only.

9.6.2 "Hot-Spots" and "Cold-Spots"

There are "hotspots" and "cold-spots" in terms of A/E markets in the world. "Hotspots" are locations that attract FDIs and tend to agglomerate economic activities. "Cold-spots", on the contrary, are unattractive locations for FDIs. In general, the interviewees thought that developing cities in China and Southeast Asia such as Shanghai, Beijing and HCM City are "hotspots". This mirrors Lee's (2005) remark that China and Southeast Asia are going through a renaissance and would present Singapore's transnational firms with enormous and numerous opportunities. The tendency of Singapore's transnational firms to export their services to developing cities is also consistent with Posner's (1961) International Product Life-Cycle, which describes the diffusion process of products or services from advanced to developing countries.

A senior technical manager from Firm B shared his view on "hotspots" and "cold-spots":

Hotspots are places that can be sustained in the longer term. An example is Beijing as they have been good since the 90s. As for cooling spots, maybe Dubai is one of them as it had expanded too fast due to limited population.

A Vice-President of Firm C in Beijing predicted that Tianjin could be the next "hot-spot" in China:

> Tianjin is only about 100 kilometers away from Beijing. It will boom and prosper because commercial activities in the Beijing-Tianjin region will take place in Tianjin while Beijing remains as the political centre of China. Tianjin is also less costly and makes a good location for off-shoring activities for firms in Beijing.

An associate of Firm D in Shanghai shared his thoughts:

> Shanghai will become the next New York. The other cities have their own weaknesses. For example Beijing, being the political center of China, will have a lot of constraints, and will become like Washington. Shenzhen and Guangzhou lack history and culture to become a Chinese metropolitan city. The other cities like Chongqing and Chengdu are even further behind. They can only become potential areas to be developed and help bring chances of foreign direct investments to China.

A senior manager of Firm E in Shanghai shared his views:

> A top city must have an international airport. This leaves us with cities like Shanghai, Beijing and Guangzhou. These cities have positioned themselves differently. I think Guangzhou will lose out because the city has no focus. Shanghai and Beijing will win because Shanghai is the focal city for multinational companies in China while Beijing will remain as the political center of China. Beijing has benefited from 2008 Beijing Olympics. Shanghai will also benefit from 2010 World Expo Exhibition. China is much more attractive than other countries in the region because it offers enormous market potential. Chongqing may also become more prominent in the future due to good leadership from the mayor of Chongqing and the city's strategic location as a gate-way to the western region of China. Chongqing has also recently organized a CEO Conference that successfully marketed the city.

A master-planning manager of Firm E in Shanghai opined that "hot-spots" can be temporary, and that a "hot-spot" may cease to be "hot" one day. However, he believed that Beijing and Shanghai will continue to prosper:

> Currently, the first-tiered cities are Beijing, Shanghai, Shenzhen and Guangzhou. The second-tiered cities are Dalian, Chengdu, Chongqing, Nanjing et cetera. In our opinion, Beijing and Shanghai will stay on as first-tiered cities, but as market changes, some cities may accelerate their growth while others stagnate and fade away.

A senior associate of Firm D warned of the fallacy that there would always be more job opportunities in bigger cities:

> A city with a lot of potential does not guarantee more jobs for the firm, thus, a firm should not deploy more staffs merely on the basis of the city's potential.

When asked on which cities in China are deemed to be "hot-spots" or "cold-spots", a Vice-President of Firm F for Tianjin shared:

> The hot-spots are 2nd-tier cities for those who have come in late. Shanghai is still hot, but there are little windows left to compete in. Shanghai is becoming too competitive for new entries. It would have been fine if you had moved in ten years ago.
>
> The cold spots are places like Xinjiang, because of its socio-political problems. However, some other people might see opportunities in crises.

9.6.3 Preferred Locations to Venture Overseas

Not every firm would like to internationalize. For example, some A/E firms may (i) lack the resources to venture abroad; (ii) prefer to stay focused on their home-market; (iii) are content with the opportunities present in Singapore; or (iv) are risk-averse and choose to export only et cetera. The findings agrees with Aharoni's (1966) Behavioral model, which suggests that a firm's decision to internationalize need not be based on profit maximization, but instead can be motivated or discouraged by other interests. The finding on the firm being risk-averse is also consistent with Cyert and March's (1963) idea that people and firms make satisfactory and sequential decisions instead of optimal decisions when they face complex and uncertain situations.

A Director of Firm A shared on why Firm A has not set up more offices in China:

We would like to control our quality of work. We would be squeezed if we are to locate there.

An architect from Firm B, when asked for reasons why he thought there are some Singapore's A/E firms that only export but do not take up other entry modes shared:

They may not have enough resources. They want to ensure consistency in their quality. They would rather collaborate with local design institutes (LDIs), and not take up jobs entirely by themselves when they are not very familiar with the environments of overseas markets.

An architect from Firm B opined that (i) Singapore's A/E firms would not be able to compete with American, European or Australian firms in their own markets; and (ii) different construction methods and technologies in these markets would make it even more difficult for Singapore's A/E firms to penetrate these markets:

There are a few reasons: there are more market potentials in developing countries like Vietnam and China whereas Australia and Europe are developed economies facing stagnation or little growth. It is less costly to set up offices in developing countries. There is less competition in developing countries; Singaporean A/E firms cannot compete with Australian and European A/E firms, moreover, in their own markets. And last but not least, temperate countries like Australia and European countries use dry-trades and have different construction methods and technologies, thus requiring different architectural considerations to what architects trained in Singapore are used to, whereas in China and South-east Asia, construction technology are more alike.

The Chairman of Firm D explained why Firm D has not ventured into several other locations, or why Firm D had not moved into several markets earlier:

Hong Kong is full of architects. We happen to have a client who appreciates the work we did in Singapore and gave us the opportunity in Hong Kong but the resources that we need from Singapore is of no use as it is so far away.

We did not move into Thailand because of language barrier and protectionist policies. Hong Kong being full of bright, young architects, did not need us. We did not go to Manila as at that time, there was no development. We did not go to Vietnam at that time because it was not ready. We did not go to India because we were too busy in Singapore. If you look at India, it had began to open up in around 2000, the same with Middle-east. It was only the last 5–7 years, there was a market. Prior to that, there was no market.

9.6 Internationalization of Singapore's A/E firms

> *We are getting into Middle-east and India. We were contemplating to try out Africa and Europe before we are hit by this crisis. If there wasn't a crisis today, we might have been in Europe but the crisis has caused us to review our strategies again.*

The pilot study found that Singapore's A/E firms tend to internationalize into regional markets such as Malaysia, Vietnam, China, India and the Middle-east. In these countries, transnational firms like to locate themselves in Kuala Lumpur in Malaysia, HCM City and Hanoi in Vietnam, Shanghai and Beijing in China et cetera. In fact, Singapore's A/E firms rarely venture into other places. It is also common that when Singapore's A/E firms seek to internationalize, they would choose to locate themselves in big cities because (i) they would have access to a larger market (market correlation) and (ii) of agglomeration benefits. Table 9.1 shows Firm A, B, C, D, E and F's presences in regional markets.

An architect from Firm D in Beijing shared:

> *Firm D has offices in Beijing to take care of China's northern markets, Shanghai for central markets, and Shenzhen for southern markets.*

A senior technical manager from Firm B explained why Firm B had only entered into familiar markets:

> *Going overseas may pose as a form of discontinuity. We will try ways to replace the competitive edge as it is important that the base must be strong. We will first start with a few areas that we are more familiar with and that we can market in for example residential before we expand. We will first look at the potential of growth. That is our first criteria. After which, we will prefer somewhere where we have a local presence. It makes things easier when we go overseas.*

A firm's preferred location would also have to do with how its capabilities fit into the market demand abroad. A business manager from Firm C in HCM City shared:

> *The clients in Shanghai ask for brand-names from USA, UK and Japan, but the Vietnamese market is not as choosy yet.*

A senior associate of Firm D in Shanghai shared:

> *Shenzhen was where we set up our first office. It was one of the first Special Economic Zones (SEZ) in China to open up and be accessible to foreign firms. We have Shenzhen, Shanghai and Beijing so that the Southern, Middle and Northern regions can be taken care of.*

A master-planning manager of Firm E in Shanghai shared that most transnational firms in China would locate their regional HQs or offices in Shanghai or Beijing:

> *Some people may feel that Shanghai is a better place to live in because of its lifestyle amenities and infrastructure. They may also prefer Shanghai because of its economic potential and laissez-faire stance towards foreign direct investments. It used to be that firms choose between Beijing and Shanghai to set up their regional headquarters, but some firms are starting to have regional offices in Beijing, and also in Shanghai. Basically, if the firm's role is to do marketing or research, the office has to be in either Beijing or Shanghai because most of the talents in China have concentrated into these two cities. Moreover, firms would be able to get higher-quality information and reach out*

Table 9.1 Presence of Singaporean A/E firms in regional markets

Firms/cities	Singapore	JB	KL	Penang	HCM	Hanoi	Shanghai	Tianjin	Beijing
Firm A	O		O	O			O		
Firm B	O								
Firm D	O		O		O		O		O
Firm C	O				O		O	O	O
Firm E	O						O		
Firm F	O		O		O	O			

> to the biggest clients in these two cities. Both cities have developed transportation infrastructure. Sometimes it may depend on where the clients were located in.

Apart from Singaporean A/E firms, a Director for an American A/E Firm in Shanghai shared why his firm chose to locate its office in Shanghai instead of Beijing or other cities in China:

> Other than the fact that both are metropolitan cities, Shanghai has an environment that is more "international", has more expatriates. There are more international schools, including a Singapore International School, here in Shanghai. The climate is not as cold and dry like Beijing. There are also too many expert committees in Beijing that can threaten to negatively affect or cause complications to a business endeavor. Shanghai is more transparent and regulated, and better suited for business for multinational companies. Shanghai is also more central in terms of location. Beijing is too far North. Therefore, Shanghai is a more ideal office or regional-headquarters location.

> Shanghai and Beijing are still the top tier cities in China. They attract the best companies with the best technologies and best human resources. You may encounter quality issues if you locate elsewhere.

9.6.4 Countries and Cities

The high-tech infrastructure, highly competitive travel, transport and logistics solutions and the accessible, flexible resources of the knowledge-based economy have facilitated an increasing number of commercial organizations and individuals worldwide to look beyond their national borders into new markets and the opportunities they offer.

Asia is now going through a renaissance, especially with the resurgence of China, India and South-east Asia attracting a large amount of FDIs (Lee 2005). This section looks at the South-east Asian and Chinese cities chosen for the study, namely Singapore, Kuala Lumpur, Penang, Ho Chi Minh City, Hanoi, Shanghai, Beijing and Tianjin, and specifically discusses these cities' histories and heritage, economic and commercial potentials, communications and transportation infrastructures, and architectural fabrics.

9.6.4.1 Singapore

Singapore had been a destination for immigrants from China, Arabia and India from the 1820s to the 1950s, when it was a British colony, used as a trading entrepot. It achieved independence in 1963, as part of the Federation of Malaya, together with Malaya, Sabah and Sarawak. In 1965, it seceded from the Federation to become an independent republic.

Singapore is now an island-nation with a population of about 4.86 million people, with a composition of about 75% Chinese, 14% Malay, 9% Indian, 2% Caucasian and others. Despite its small size and apparent lack of natural resources, Singapore stands out with a combination of a highly educated, motivated and productive human resource, multi-ethnic and cosmopolitan make-up, vibrant cultural and arts scene, socio-political stability, and excellent transport and communication infrastructure according to an Employment Conditions Abroad (ECA) International's survey.

Singapore is also amongst a handful of countries with AAA credit rating. Today, Singapore is one of the global hubs in stocks exchange, foreign exchange, international banking, asset and wealth management, insurance, research and education, et cetera. The country also holds top spot as the best place in Asia for international companies to set up their regional headquarters and for expatriates to live in.

Singapore has one of the world's busiest airports in term of international passenger traffic. The Changi International Airport is connected to more than 180 cities in 58 countries, serves 84 airlines, and has on average 4,199 flights per week. The Port of Singapore Authority is the world's busiest transhipment port. The country is very well-interconnected by expressways, highways and roads. It has also been ranked as one of the most digitally interconnected countries or cities in the world.

The architecture of Singapore displays a wide spectrum of influences from different places and periods. Designs can be eclectic and hybrid, reflecting its ethnic and religious diversity. For example, there are the Vernacular Malay style, Palladian, European Neo-classical, Gothic, Renaissance, Art Deco, International, Post-modern styles et cetera. Modern tropical designs are also well represented in the country as the architectural trend in Singapore heads towards green buildings and sustainability.

Singapore can be considered as the core city of South-east Asia. Singapore houses most of the region's key functions. It is the financial, commercial, transportation, information technology, research and educational hub of the region. Singapore is not only considered as a powerful global city. It is also strategically located in the middle of the Asia-Pacific, between New Zealand, Australia and Indonesia to the South, and Malaysia, Thailand, Vietnam, China, India, Middle-east et cetera to the North. Furthermore, the Economic Development Board of Singapore has managed to (i) attract foreign investments; (ii) grow Singapore's industries; and (iii) enhance Singapore's business environment. As a result, many international firms, including international A/E firms, tend to set up their regional head-quarters in Singapore.

A Principal quantity surveyor of Firm E when asked on why international firms would want to locate their regional head-quarters in Singapore noted that:

> Singaporean's English proficiency. Majority of the population are Chinese, know the Chinese language and culture, and would be helpful to venture into China. Singapore is a non-Muslim country in the archipelago of Muslim states, and it offers a better and safer environment for business amongst South-east Asian countries.

A senior manager of Firm E in Shanghai commented on Singapore's A/E firms:

> Singapore is reputed to offer the combined advantages of the East and West. Some of the services they provide are also more competitive than international consultants. Another strength that Singaporean firms may possess is that they are quite good at codes and regulations. This is probably due to its own home environment, where codes and regulations have to be strictly followed. Singaporean Chinese sent here are also capable of reading and writing Chinese and speaking Mandarin. As a side-note, Taiwanese practice traditional Chinese characters whereas Singaporeans and Chinese practice simplified Chinese characters. Hence, Singaporean firms have less problems understanding the Chinese documents here. However, Singaporean A/E firms are less creative than the Americans, Europeans, Japanese and Australia-New Zealanders. That is one of the weaknesses that Singaporeans have and it is something that Singaporean firms have to overcome.

Singapore has managed to transform itself drastically since its independence in 1965, to become an advanced and developed country. Many developing countries in the region see Singapore as a role model, and aspire to emulate Singapore's accomplishments.

A Vice-President of Firm F shared:

> Firm F has been able to secure projects overseas successfully due to the Singapore's success stories which we made use extensively. We sell Singapore' success stories of providing public housing for the masses and master-planning consultancy services. The reason being that any foreigner who come to Singapore is attracted to our public housing social program. It speaks very much of our country – how a country organizes social program within short period of time with such a success.

9.6.4.2 Malaysia

Malaysia as a unified state did not exist until 1963, when Malaya (now Peninsula Malaysia), Singapore, Sarawak and Sabah received their independence from the United Kingdom to form the Federation of Malaya. After Singapore separated from the Federation, the country has been separated into two regions – Peninsula Malaysia and Malaysian Borneo. Presently, Malaysia is a federation consisting of 13 states, namely – Johor, Kedah, Kelantan, Melaka, Negeri Sembilan, Pahang, Penang, Perak, Perlis, Selangor, Terengganu, Sabah and Sarawak. The capital city is Kuala Lumpur, while Putrajaya is the seat of the federal government. The early years of independence were marred by the conflict with Indonesia over the formation of Malaysia, Singapore's eventual exit in 1965, and racial strife and riots in 1969. As a result, the controversial New Economic Policy was created with the intention to increase the share of the economic pie of the indigenous people, called the Bumiputras.

Malaysia now has a population of 27 million, made up of 62% Malays and Bumiputras, 25% Chinese, 8% Indians and the rest are Caucasians and others. The country benefits from its abundant endowment of natural resources in areas such as agriculture, forestry and minerals, and is also making steadfast progress in its secondary, tertiary and quaternary industries. Previously, it was composed of several separate kingdoms. Now, Malaysia is a constitutional monarchy. Its legal system is based upon English common law. The Civil Law Act (1956) incorporated principles of English common law as at 1957. Contracts are mainly written in English although government-related contracts may be written in both Malay as well as English.

Malaysia has extensive roads that connect all its major cities and towns. Seaports and airports can also be found around the country. The architecture in Malaysia is a mixture of Malay Islamic, Asian, Colonial, Modern and Post-modern influences. Most of the architecture has been modified to make use of locally available resources, and to acclimatize to the local climate.

As in other countries, different cities of Malaysia concentrate on, or endeavor to specialize in different activities. Most of Peninsula Malaysia's economic and commercial activities are carried out in Kuala Lumpur (KL), Penang and Johor Bahru (JB). Other than Singaporean A/E firms, a manager of a quantity surveying firm in Penang shared:

> Perlis is near the borders of Southern Thailand and has little development; Johor Bahru does not have a good port; Melaka was one of the British's port, is more for tourism now but is losing out in location in terms of attracting economic activities; economic activities are concentrated in KL; Penang was the British first port in the region long time ago, lost its prominence to Singapore, but is fast-growing again recently because of its strategic location as a sea and flight port, as one part of the Golden Triangle with Thailand and Indonesia for logistics in the region, promotion of the city and incentives given out to investors.

Kuala Lumpur

Kuala Lumpur is the economic and business centre of the country. The city is host to many multi-national companies' regional offices or support centres. Most of the country's largest indigenous companies have their headquarters based in the city. The population of Kuala Lumpur is about 1.5 million, but the Greater Kuala Lumpur, also known as the Klang Valley, is an urban agglomeration of about 7.2 million people. Kuala Lumpur is also the fastest growing metropolitan region in the country.

A Director of Firm D in Kuala Lumpur shared:

> We decided to locate in KL because it is a first-tiered city, the capital city, and center of commerce of Malaysia. We also chose KL after considering its potential and the amount of competition we might face.

Penang

The State of Penang is the third-largest economy amongst the states of Malaysia with a prominence that trails only Kuala Lumpur and Johor Bahru. It has a population of about 1.5 million. Analogous to Malacca, its entrepot trade has greatly declined due in part to the loss of its free-port status, and also due to the active development of Port Klang near Kuala Lumpur. It has a manufacturing base, but is gradually losing its attractiveness due to the cheaper labour costs in India, China and Vietnam. It is also the only place in Malaysia where the Chinese ethnic group forms a majority.

A Director of Firm A in Penang described Penang:

> *Penang is pro-tourism, pro-preservation of heritage and pro-business. Thus, policies in Penang may be different compared to other cities or states.*

Johor Bahru

Johor Bahru benefits from its proximity to Singapore, and often acts as a hinterland for Singapore. There is a significant presence of Singapore-owned companies in Johor Bahru. Moreover, it has been estimated that currently, 300,000 Malaysians work in Singapore, and as many as 150,000 Malaysians from Johor commute daily to work in Singapore, even though Johor's population is only about 890,000. The Iskandar Development Region project, the country's southern development corridor, is expected to stimulate much economic growth in the region.

Other than Singaporean A/E firms, a Principal of an engineering firm in Johor Bahru shared:

> *Competition between local consultants here is cut-throat. There are not many foreigners here. Foreigners are mostly in KL. There has been over-building in the past few years. There have been many Johor Bahru's Malaysians working in Singapore, but many of them are getting retrenched due to the economic crisis. These can make things worse from now to the near future.*

> *Johor Bahru is coming up with lots of opportunities, such as the Iskandar Project, but would need to tackle problems in security, political bickering and rivalry, and federal versus state differences.*

He then shared his views on why Singapore's A/E firms have reduced their offshoring activities in Johor Bahru:

> *There could be a few deterrents: traffic jams and inconveniences at the customs which incur time, costs and fuss. Johor Bahru is a location for shopping for Singaporeans, not for A/E services. Kuala Lumpur is a better location because KL has more and better talents, yet a cheaper cost of living and operating a business, bigger market, and is also easily accessible from Singapore; Singaporean firms may prefer to offshore to China or India. Johor is not as cost-efficient.*

9.6.4.3 Vietnam

Vietnam was ruled by the Chinese until its independence in AD 938. During the mid nineteenth century, it was colonized by the French. The resistance against the French led to a nation divided politically into the North and South. The civil war continued during the Vietnam War. The country was war-ravaged and there was much resentment after the wars. The central government's planned economic decisions also hindered the reconstruction of the country until 1986, when economic and political reforms allowed the country to reintegrate itself into the world economy.

Vietnam has a population now of about 84 million, made up of about 86% Vietnamese Kinh. It is very much motivated by the market economy, even though the state remains officially committed to socialism as its defining creed. The country has been posting 7% economic growth since 1990, making it the world's second fastest growing economy, behind China. Vietnam is divided into 58 provinces and also five centrally-controlled municipalities, which exist at the same level as provinces. The provinces are further subdivided into provincial municipalities, townships, counties, towns and communes, whereas the centrally-controlled municipalities are subdivided into districts, counties and wards.

In the big cities such as Hanoi and Ho Chi Minh City, road and transportation systems are still in abysmal conditions. The main means of transport within cities are still motorbikes, buses, taxis and bicycles. Traffic congestion and air pollution are pressing problems that the cities must tackle so that they do not stifle FDIs and economic growth. Architecture in Vietnam has to consider the differences in latitude and the marked variety of topographical relief that makes the climate of different provinces vary considerably.

HCM City

HCM City is the economic centre of Vietnam. It is populated by about 9 million people. Even though the city only makes up about 0.6% of the total land area of the country, and 7.5% of the Vietnamese population, it attracts about 35% of all FDIs and is responsible for 27.9% of the country's industrial output. The Chinese makes up about 8% of the city's population. About 80% of the city's population practices Buddhism, Taoism or Confucianism.

As in every developing market, HCM City is disorganized and sporadic. Add to the fact that the country had only recently re-opened itself to FDIs and freed up to market economy, HCM City is becoming one of the most challenging but rewarding locations in the region for transnational firms.

An associate of Firm C in HCM City compared his work experiences in Xiamen of China and HCM City:

Xiamen was more manageable (than Ho Chi Minh). It is really quite chaotic here.

Other than Singaporean A/E firms, the General Director of a quantity surveying firm in HCM City described HCM City:

It is a unique place with a unique history and a unique period of growth. There is no other country in the world that is like it and that could be due to its history. It was colonized by the French, then United States, followed by the invasion of Cambodia and China. Then it turned towards communism. It was the Pearl of the Orient before it got embroiled into these conflicts for 40–50 years.

Other than Singaporean A/E firms, a Director of a quantity surveying firm compared HCM City with Hanoi:

HCM has more opportunities and better prospects. The business environment of HCM and its business community is one factor. There would be more chances for developers and it is the largest city anyway. HCM attracts more foreign direct investments, is more commercially astute, and has more private construction.

Hanoi

Hanoi is the capital and political centre of Vietnam. It has a population of about 6.2 million, and is the second-largest city in the country. Similar to HCM, Hanoi is also enjoying a rapidly-developing economy and real estate market. However, businesses and people in Hanoi are still very much instilled with the conventions of the command-economy. Therefore, most foreign-owned companies prefer to locate themselves in HCM City than Hanoi.

An associate of Firm F in HCM City described:

Hanoi, and all the north, is still a central command-and-control city.

9.6.4.4 China

China has one of the world's oldest and continuous civilizations. Its ambit of influence extended across the entire East Asia, including Mongolia, Japan, Korea, Vietnam and Taiwan, and also the rest of South-east Asia. The Republic of China was established in 1912 when the monarchy system was overthrown by Sun Yat-Sen's Kuomintang. However, the Chinese Civil War between the Nationalists and the Communists ensued after World War 2. It was later won by the Communists led by Mao Zedong. Mainland China underwent a series of disruptive socioeconomic movements in the late 1950s with the Great Leap Forward and in the 1960s with the Cultural Revolution. It was only with the economic reforms initiated by Deng Xiaoping in 1978 that the country's smothering economic policies were emancipated, and re-opened the country to the world's economy.

China's accession to the World Trade Organization in 2001 further accelerated the country's growth and provided greater opportunities for international contractors and construction-related firms to enter the Chinese market. By 2008, it was already the world's second largest market economy, only behind the US, with a GDP of US$7.8 trillion and had the largest construction volume in the world. The market-oriented reforms that were implemented have spurred individual initiatives and entrepreneurship. However, there is much wealth and income disparity within the country. The eastern coastal areas are much more developed than the central and western regions. The market economy has gained rapidly in scale every year as it subsumes more and more sectors, and the government's role in the economy has been lessened to a great degree.

The Chinese population is estimated to be about 1.3 billion. China's transportation infrastructure is still not fully developed in many aspects, especially in the central and western regions. Communications infrastructure and systems are also not as comprehensive, and may be subjected to sanctions by the authorities. Today, architecture in China is influenced by ancient Chinese, Soviet neoclassical and Colonial architecture, as well as Feng-shui or geomancy.

Doing business in China is never easy. Firms are likely to encounter problems such as red tape, arbitrary rules, "guan-xi" and "special taxes" (Backman and Butler 2004). An associate of Firm D in Shanghai shared:

China is more complex than Singapore. The government regulations in China have a "tail" such that the government has the final say so it is not that you are able to memorize the regulations in China, you would succeed. You would need to rely on your actual experience from running projects in different states.

Other than Singaporean A/E firms, the Managing Director of a quantity surveying firm in Shanghai shared:

China is not as regulated as Singapore. There is a lot of unknown and uncertainty. There could be often changes in decrees and regulations. Planning and regulations in China can get haphazard. They "trial and error" because its economy and markets are still relatively inexperienced. Cost estimations may be inaccurate. Sometimes, clients' expectations are too optimistic, over-aggressive and over-ambitious.

As in other countries or regions, every city in China has its own premeditated function and purpose. The Managing Director of the quantity surveying firm in Shanghai shared:

Every city has its own function. They have different markets. For example, Guangzhou suits the smaller entrepreneurs more; Shanghai will attract big multinational firms; Tianjin will be the port and side-kick for Beijing, to form a greater Beijing-Tianjin cosmopolitan city. For example, Chongqing offers good opportunities and possible returns.

Beijing

Beijing is one of the world's great cities, being the capital of several ancient empires. Beijing is now China's second largest city, after Shanghai, with a population of 18 million, and is recognised as the political, educational, and cultural centre of the People's Republic of China. Beijing is also a major transportation hub, with dozens of railways, roads and motorways passing through the city. It is also the focal point of many international flights to China.

When an A/E firm internationalizes, it has to overcome challenges such as (i) different design requirements due to climatic changes from the home-market to the overseas market; and (ii) unfamiliarity with codes and regulations.

A senior associate of Firm C shared:

Beijing and Singapore is different – the orientation is different and the northern, winter. It became a standard practice as it became a regulation there.

Shanghai

Shanghai is the centre of finance and trade in mainland China. Modern developments in the city only began in 1992, a decade later than many of the Southern Chinese provinces which became Special Economic Zones (SEZs), but since then Shanghai has quickly overtaken those provinces. Shanghai is now the largest city in China in terms of population and one of the largest metropolitan areas in the world, with about 19 million people, and is administered as a municipality with province-level status. It has also the world's busiest cargo port.

Shanghai is ranked second in terms of hosting the most number of the world's top 100 architectural firms, only behind London (Rimmer 1991; Ren 2005). London is widely acknowledged to be the world's A/E production site, whereas Shanghai is regarded to be the most attractive A/E consumption site in the world today.

An associate of Firm D in Shanghai commented:

Shanghai will become the next New York.

Majority of firms choose Shanghai as a first choice as it attracts more talents and there is more contact with the clients. We have quite a lot of projects so this idiom works when we are closer to the clients.

A senior manager of Firm E in Shanghai shared:

We also conduct business development here because most of the multinational companies are agglomerated here.

Other than Singaporean A/E firms, the Managing Director of a quantity surveying firm in Shanghai shared:

China and Shanghai have made a come-back these few decades. Now, the city is a comfortable and well-organized place to live and do business. It is highly populated, attracts Chinese from many other provinces, has top schools and universities, and is a well-governed and safe city for expatriates and foreign firms. Shanghai is a municipality. This makes it the equivalent of a province. The central government manages the municipalities and provinces; the provinces manage the cities within their territories; the cities manage the counties, and so on. Being a municipality, Shanghai has more autonomy to self-rule.

Our office here in Shanghai is the center and coordinator of all our other Chinese offices. Shanghai is also at the forefront of building and management technologies. It is a more sophisticated market than the other cities. Market here is also enormous. Talents are also concentrated here.

Shanghai is also considered to be the least corrupted and most transparent city in China. Shanghai is the pioneer for international businesses in China. The disadvantage could be that the city suits the big firms more. Smaller entrepreneurial firms may be squeezed out. These firms may prefer to locate themselves in counties to seek higher returns.

It used to be that foreign direct investments would choose Shanghai because firms would be able to employ staffs and start work immediately in Shanghai. This is slowly changing due to growing costs in Shanghai and also opportunities in other cities.

Tianjin

Tianjin has a population of 11 million and is the sixth largest city of the People's Republic of China in terms of urban population. Administratively it is also one of the four municipalities that have provincial-level status that enables it to report directly to the central government. It benefits from its proximity to Beijing and the spillages from the capital city. It also serves as the hinterland and sea-port of Beijing.

9.7 Difficulties of Internationalization

Firms are already facing more competition than ever before. Furthermore, a firm's ability to build new strategic capabilities or explore new markets depends on its existing organizational attributes (configuration of assets and capabilities built over the years). However, the firm's heritage can be both an asset and impediment in the internationalization process. Some systems or work are so communications intensive and relationship dependent that they do not function well when the functional units are separated by substantial time and distance barriers (i.e. when firms internationalize). It was found that when firms internationalize, they would have to surmount even harder and more difficulties than when in their home-markets due to: (i) reduced access to location-specific resources; (ii) unfamiliarity of markets; (iii) restrictions in host-market; and (iv) problems with communications et cetera. These findings are consistent with Olson and Olson (2000) and Kitchin and Dodge's (2002) suggestion that Cairncross's (1997) submission of "boundary-less" is misleading and over-exaggerated. The finding on communications is also in line with Allen's (1977) findings that there still remain facets of organization communication that could be impaired and distorted by geographical distance.

An architect of Firm A in Beijing shared:

The main problem is the language in technical aspects so you have problems speaking those technical terms in Chinese, expressing what you want to say in architectural jargons.

A senior technical manager of Firm B shared:

In Singapore, we are much more organized as we abide by rules but things are flexible and not so rigid but when we go abroad, there are much more regulations to abide by and the boundaries between black and white is pretty clear. In addition, it is difficult to take action there as we are overseas and we lack resources.

I had set up an office in Beijing and the process was very complex. It is unlike in Singapore where everything is streamlined. There are a lot of procedures involved. In addition, there are a lot of departments we have to go to get the legislation settled but the distance between the departments are so far apart so one must allow time and resources to register a company overseas. This is unlike Singapore which has a one-stop place to register the company.

When we go overseas, we face with a lot of difficulties. There are certain factors like availability of overseas projects and special interests in politics which is beyond us.

The Managing Director of Firm C in Shanghai shared:

International firms have not been able to get a full license to practice in China. Likewise, our Singaporean engineers and architects are not licensed to practice here. We need a licensed firm and certified professionals to commission our work.

A senior Vice-President of Firm C in Shanghai shared:

A foreign architect will have to take as many as ten tests in Chinese to become a licensed architect. This is an almost impossible task because of limitations in our language proficiency. We may be able to converse, read and write, but taking professional tests in Chinese is easier said than done.

A senior associate of Firm D in Shanghai shared:

The foreigner has to take about ten examinations in Chinese. They test you on everything. It is extremely difficult for a foreigner to pick up all the Chinese technical jargons. It is probably not worth the effort, because the LDIs in collaboration with the foreign firms can do the rest of the jobs that are restricted from the foreign firms.

There were only a few enthusiasts. We had problems getting people to come over. We asked but they were not willing to come over.

What we have been trying to do is that we are trying to get good staff but it is difficult in China.

An associate of Firm D in Shanghai shared:

It is a hard market to break into by the fact that this is not Singapore where everyone knows us. I think you need some projects under your belt before you get better projects.

Other than Firms A to F, a project manager of an engineering firm, who has worked in Dubai before commented:

Dubai is a Muslim country so they have Fridays off and they worked Saturday to Thursday. Furthermore, Dubai also has a 4 hour time difference with Singapore. This to some extent affects our work coordination with the offices because of the reduced common work-days and work hours.

Government intervention, codes and regulations and labor laws. Language is also a problem even though local graduates are fine in English. We have to translate documents, and in doing so, incur costs.

Other than Singaporean A/E firms, the Managing Director of a quantity surveying firm in Shanghai shared:

There is still much protectionism despite claims of openness.

China is a big country and there are so many states around so it has always been a challenge for us to maintain the quality of all offices, communication, as well as the quality of all services.

Other than Singaporean A/E firms, a marketing manager for a developer in HCM City shared:

For our project, we found it difficult to get approvals. The authorities, from the top to bottom, apparently wanted bribery, but we, as a public-listed company, do not entertain such requests. There are also much red-tapes. We had to rely on our consultants to be our middle-men.

9.8 Management of Risks

A firm's stance on risk management impinges on its business strategies and organization designs. As mentioned before in the earlier chapters, risk management is the identification, assessment and prioritization of risks, followed by the firm's decision to minimize, monitor or control the probability of the occurrence of an event, by choosing to avoid, reduce, transfer or retain these risks. This section discusses Singaporean A/E firms' concerns and attitude towards risks and the firms' risk management policies. From the interviews, it was found that Singapore's A/E firms tend to start out small when they try to internationalize into markets overseas because they are unfamiliar with the new environment. Then, as time passes by, these firms gained experience and incrementally put in more investments and become more committed to the foreign market. This is coherent with the Uppsala model (Johanson and Wiedersheim 1975), which suggests that transnational firms acquire more control, put in more commitment, but expose themselves to more risks in foreign markets insofar as they accumulate experience and knowledge of the markets.

A Director of Firm A in Singapore shared on how Firm A avoids and reduces the risks incurred:

We overcome such risks by good leadership and sticking to our regular clients.

A senior technical manager of Firm B in Singapore commented on risk management:

It gives us more confidence. It is quite logical that once you minimize the risk, the more daring you are to venture. It is proportionate.

A senior associate of Firm C in Singapore shared of Firm C's attitude to risks:

We have training for risk management. We are becoming risk-takers in terms of the way we judge opportunities. We will try out and we will take some risks. After all, you have to take risks to earn profits. We will take up the project which might be more risky. Any Singapore firm has to do that or you will be left behind.

The Managing Director of Firm C in HCM City shared:

The lack of transparency of institutions creates a lot of unknown and uncertainty. Rules and regulations are always changing.

A Director of Firm D in Kuala Lumpur shared:

Every company must be able to handle this kind of market volatility to survive and prosper. We also incur delay risk. There are no re-course for fees when there are project delays.

Another Director of Firm D, working in Kuala Lumpur, shared on Firm D's risk strategies:

To make sure our clients pay, we ask that they fulfill 28 credit terms for proof of their liquidity and ask for collaterals in case of failure to pay up. We communicate to them the importance of having cash flow as we need to pay for materials and so if they don't pay, we can't maximize the human resources required to carry out the job. Thus, we may have to slow down but not stop the project as we emphasize to them timely payments are important. It is important for us to inform the Inland Revenue Department (IRD) on such defaults with related invoices so that our profit taxes can be reduced accordingly.

Currency risks due to exchange fluctuations. We have a clause in our contracts to enable us to revisit payment sums when exchange fluctuations escalate beyond 10%. However, this is an ambiguous clause, and good-will is required.

An architect from Firm D in Beijing warned of a business risk in China:

Firms may disguise themselves as sincere clients, but are actually trying to steal design ideas only, without genuine intentions to hire us. To counter such risks, we check our prospective clients' background before we commit ourselves.

A manager for Firm E in Shanghai cautioned that there are extra risks to be considered when firms venture overseas:

Singapore, comparably, is smaller in population so they may emphasize more on trust. However, in China, if you are dishonest in Beijing, you can move to another city where no one knows you. Thus, there is a higher default risk.

A Vice-President of Firm F shared on what risks Firm F is most concerned about, and how Firm F manages the risk:

Default on payment. Therefore, we have selective collaboration. We take an avoidance and absorption approach.

Other than Singaporean A/E firms, a business development manager of Firm F in Kuala Lumpur shared:

One note-worthy risk is nationalistic sentiments. Look at Shin Corp in Thailand, and how Singaporean firms like Singtel got implicated. We focus on corporate clients instead to minimize such risks. Another risk is default on payment. Default ratio is low, but always present. To minimize such risks, we carry out background checks on prospective clients, especially on their financial capability and reputation as a pay-master. We may also seek contras and collaterals from clients who default on payment. Other than these, we have professional and liability risks due to negligence. We mitigate such risks through due diligence and stringent checks on work-related matters. We also have established templates and frameworks as a guide.

Other than Singaporean A/E firms, the General Director of a quantity surveying firm in HCM City likewise shared:

Corruption and lubricant monies, default on payments, semantics and interpretation of law, codes and regulations.

Other than Singaporean A/E firms, a Director of a quantity surveying firm in Hanoi similarly shared:

There are risks like uncertainty, tax complexity, legislation favoring the locals, cash-flow, currency risks, interest rates, decisions made by government such as policies and risks of nationalization, free market initiatives, economy, piracy, market volatility et cetera.

9.8 Management of Risks

Other than Singaporean A/E firms, a contracts manager of a contractor firm in HCM City shared:

We are selective with clients. We work only with Japanese clients, whom have worked with us before in Japan. We develop relationships with our clients. We do international projects. We rather not entertain local clients because of their communist background and lack of financial stability. We try to be as cautious as we can.

A senior Vice-President of Firm C, stationed in Shanghai, shared on the firm's default on payment risks. A default on payment occurs when a firm does not get paid for the services and work it had provided. Firms worry about default on payments because it could represent a significant economic loss to the firm. Usually, firms minimize such risks by (i) checking on the prospective client; (ii) demanding for deposits or collaterals before work starts; and (iii) asking for interim payments et cetera. He shared:

If you are not stationed in China or other countries and try to do business there, there is always collection risk because you are not there physically so like when you fly, they are not in and when you try to chase for money, they will say you are not around or my subordinates are complaining you are not responding well enough so in this sense, you eliminate the excuse. We have teams checking on the delivery and project team progress. The technical people do the delivery and will report to us. The finance people will check it via contract so if there is any delays, they will raise the question on why it is not moving. This will help us to filter out quickly any projects that have not been moving so that we can move into it and investigate it or the finance people will say that you have an invoice that has not been fulfilled in one month and the project team could say "because the client has certain conditions for the payment so we are aware that they are paying just at later part". If the project team said things like they are not aware of it, then it will raise the alarm and we will go into investigation and understand what is happening.

A Director of Firm D in Kuala Lumpur shared:

It used to be much worse – about 40% earlier on, around 5, 6 years ago. There should be more researching on prospective clients' background. We arrested the problem by researching on prospective clients. We check with our fellow profession peers and check on their clients' returns and get feedbacks for their reputation as pay-masters, check on the companies' financial health et cetera. Thus, after the improvement, we get a rate of about 10–15% which in my personal opinion is quite low. The default rate means that you have invoiced and you can't collect so you have to show that you have done your best to collect as the income tax requires you to send lawyer letters or summons to your clients and you can't just show it to be "bad debt", without making your best effort. However, over here how many people are willing to do that as it may sabotage the relationship so they try their best to collect in a friendly manner and rather it to be late payment than bring it to litigation. This default rate does not happen in the middle of the project as we usually have staged payments and for unknown clients, we usually ask for a commitment fee and I practice that. For example, if I know the client and he will like to do an 8 week project, I will get him to pay me a commitment fee of 50 000 or 75 000 and then perhaps split it to 2-stages. We will work for 3 weeks probation for first stage. Occasionally, some of our clients would offer a one-sum payment so that would be a one-off thing.

An associate of Firm A stationed in Kuala Lumpur shared on how transnational firms could sustain investment-related risks due to currency risks, capital risks and liquidity risks. Firms incur currency risks mainly because (i) a depreciation of currency would translate to lower earnings; and (ii) there could be restrictions on the remittance of incomes. Firms incur capital risks mainly because there may be a shortfall to the projected returns-on-investments (ROI). Firms incur liquidity risks mainly when there is too much cash out-flow than cash in-flow. The associate shared:

> We incur financial risks because we are the first one in, but last one out of a project. There may be default of payments when things go wrong.

A senior technical manager of Firm B shared:

> We have a clause in our contracts to enable us to revisit payment sums when exchange fluctuations escalate beyond 10%. However, this is an ambiguous clause, and good-will is required.

Other than Singaporean A/E firms, a Director of a quantity surveying firm in Hanoi shared:

> The currency restrictions are a problem in terms of remittances. The issue is you have it in Vietnam duong, it is very hard to take it out of the country as there is a need to have the money inside the country.

Other than Singaporean A/E firms, a marketing manager working for a developer in HCM City shared:

> The duong was recently devalued and that caused a substantial problem to us because we have been selling our units in duong.
>
> Economic and fiscal risks include interest rates to borrow monies. We are considering whether or not to have sales and other contracts in US$; we try to pre-qualify contractors, then give the job to the lowest bidder or whoever promises the best value-for-money.

An architect of Firm C in Shanghai shared on how firms could incur business-related risks due to (i) economic crises that dampen demand of their services; (ii) stiff competition; and (iii) professional risks et cetera. In fact, the 2009 Ernst & Young risk report identified the top ten business risks as: the credit crunch, regulation and compliance, deepening recession, radical greening, non-traditional entrants, cost-cutting, managing talents, executing alliances and transactions, business model redundancy and reputation risks. The architect shared:

> We run the risks of obscurity if we do not produce some extraordinary works or make some great building as companies may seek local companies instead because local companies learn really fast. Thus, I think it is a risk for Firm C. I think for me, it is very important to get iconic or landmarks. It would also be easier for clients to recognize you and accept your ideas if you have a noticeable building around. It is very important for the shape and design to be different to be set apart.

A Project Director of Firm C stationed in Tianjin shared:

> China is not affected as much as other countries but the market is still slightly affected by economic and financial crisis. The current real estate problem is more of an internal problem as previously the real estate prices had rose far too quickly. This is because over here, China consumers form the bulk of the market and thus, foreign problems do not have that much impact.

9.8 Management of Risks

The Chairman of Firm D shared:

We have faced up with several crises before. This reflection is a good time for us to do some reflections again, and set up our company's new direction. Most importantly, the spirit of the firm must stay.

A Director of Firm D in Kuala Lumpur shared:

You try to comply with the other requirements. When things go wrong, it would be through professional integrity insurance.

Another Director of Firm D in Kuala Lumpur shared:

When I talked to the professionals, they said that they have weathered the storm better and they have been eating porridge, not spending exorbitantly. Demand of projects have dropped drastically now. Every company must be able to handle this kind of market volatility to survive and prosper.

A General Manager for Firm D in HCM City shared:

Currently, it is very buoyant and good. The economic crisis did not affect locals. It affects foreigners mainly. Despite the fact that there are some developers who pulled out, there are more jobs from people who are rich enough for us with for example projects with a thousand over residential units.

An associate of Firm D working in Shanghai shared:

Definitions of codes can be blurred. This leaves gaps for interpretations. One example is the fire-code. Government authorities and officials may have the final say in such interpretations. Every city in China is like a different country. Codes may be different or interpretation of codes may be different in these cities. Some regulations are also too rigid. China is more complex than Singapore. Singapore's regulations are very detailed and it is either a yes or no. The government regulations in China has a "tail" such that the government has the final say so it is not that you are able to memorize the regulations in China, you would succeed. You would need to rely on your actual experience from running projects in different states.

A master-planning manager for Firm E working in Shanghai opined:

The shrinkage of the economy may be a bad news. Nonetheless, it offers an opportunity to open up new markets. The crisis is important because the bubble has to burst. The economy has been over-heated for some time. There have been over-building and projects have been over-priced but the quality of projects has been compromised.

A design manager of Firm F in Kuala Lumpur shared:

Instead of downsizing, we will be re-distributing our work. We will also be outsourcing our non-core activities.

Other than Singaporean A/E firms, a Director of an American A/E firm in Shanghai shared:

With the pending economic crisis, it is a good time to think over, and re-posture our business model and business strategies. It is an employers' market now. The few things we can do are: to add interior design services, go into evergreen sustainable design, and to rope talents into the organization.

Other than Singaporean A/E firms, the Managing Director of a quantity surveying firm in Shanghai shared:

> *Professional and consultancy works run the risks of professional negligence when things go wrong. We minimize such risks by performing our work diligently. We may also include indemnity clauses in contracts. The firm is also insured.*

9.9 Prerequisites and CSF

"Prequisites" generally refer to the prior conditions, required in advance, of an organization or project to succeed. On the other hand, "critical success factors" (CSF) are generally regarded to be elements which are necessary for an organization or project to achieve its mission. Prerequisites and CSF can be used as a guide for companies to do the right things, at the right place, and at the right time. Most of the interviewees suggested that transnational A/E firms ought to be flexible and be able to adapt to manage cultural differences and the challenges of international work. The finding on adaptability is in line with Argyris and Schon's (1978) recommendation that a firm should have the capacity to manage change, and constantly learn. The finding on the importance of being able to manage cultural differences reflects Hofstede (1980) and Trompenaars and Hampden-Turner (1998)'s proposition that people of different gender, ethnics, religions and background may act, think and behave differently.

A Director of Firm A in Singapore shared his thoughts on the critical success factors of an A/E firm:

> *Value and integrity in design, relationships with institutions, winning awards and using them as marketing tools. The world is becoming universal, globalized and barrier-free. The firm must be able to be consistent in its design quality. It is dehabilitating for firms to pass design work to cheaper companies. Building rapport is important.*

A Director of Firm A in Kuala Lumpur shared:

> *Different places have different difficulties. As businessmen, we think of the positives. For example, I can view the current economic crisis as a threat, or as an opportunity to improve our staffs' skills levels and work attitude.*

A senior technical manager of Firm B pointed out that learning from mistakes and improving from these mistakes are important:

> *We will look at our success factors and what lead to our failures, learning from our mistakes so over the years, we have actually improved and this routine have become natural for us now.*

A Vice-President of Firm C in Beijing shared the importance of client management and communication between staffs:

> *Client management and service orientation by the team.*
>   *Staffs are important. Teamwork and communication are important. Integration between offices is important.*

A senior project manager of Firm E in Singapore shared:

Having clear directions, leadership, teamwork, being strong minded, independent and quick witted, knowing the ground well, understanding their culture, client management, balance between assertiveness and tolerance.

An account manager of Firm E in Shanghai shared:

The firm must be able to make money. It must offer good value-for-money. It must have a good brand-name and experience. Quality of leadership and human resource is important. Marketing-competence is important too because you need to tell your clients or prospective clients what you can do. Business people doing businesses in China should also know the history, traditions and culture of the Chinese. For example, a business-person must be able to comprehend and read "in-between the lines" when they have conversations with government officials, authorities and business partners. In addition, it is important to remain competitive. It is just like a restaurant. You must have good food and keep changing menu to remain interesting to have business.

A Vice-President of Firm F shared:

People going overseas must have a good track record to show-case. In Firm F's case, nobody can dispute our housing records.

Other than Singaporean A/E firms, a Director of an American A/E firm in Shanghai shared:

The firm must keep re-inventing itself. The firm is a team. We do not allow prima donnas and mavericks doing wild stuffs. We are a corporate-style company, and we do competent things. Values are important. Accumulated knowledge is critical too. Personally, social skills are important.

Other than Singaporean A/E firms, a marketing manager of a developer in HCM City shared:

Learning their language helps you to integrate into their environment better.

9.10 Summary

The chapter presents the background information and experiences of Singapore's A/E firms in regional markets in Johor Bahru, Kuala Lumpur, Penang, HCM City, Hanoi, Shanghai, Beijing and Tianjin. In general, it has been found that (i) not every firm aspires to internationalize; (ii) Singapore's more established A/E firms have the requisite competencies and are competitive to internationalize; (iii) Singapore's A/E firms prefer to set up overseas offices in big cities such as Kuala Lumpur, HCM City, Shanghai and Beijing; (iv) Singapore's A/E firms face more difficulties and incur more risks in overseas markets than in their home-market; and (v) Singapore's A/E firms should build up or improve their capabilities to diversify into or sustain themselves in the overseas markets.

References

Aharoni Y (1966) The foreign investment decision process. Division of Research, Graduate School of Business Administration, Harvard University, Cambridge, MA
Allen TJ (1977) Managing the flow of technology. MIT Press, Cambridge, MA
Backman M, Butler C (2004) Big in Asia – 25 strategies for business success. Palgrave Macmillan, Basingstoke
Belbin RM (1981) Management teams: why they succeed or fail, 2nd edn. Butterworth-Heinemann, Oxford/Boston
Burgess PG (1983) The role of the architect in society. Carnegie Mellon University, Department of Building, Pittsburgh
Cairncross F (1997) The death of distance. Harvard Business School Press, Boston
Chamberlin EH (1933) Theory of monopolistic competition. Harvard University Press, Cambridge, MA
Cyert R, March J (1963) A behavioural theory of the firm. Prentice-Hall, Englewood Cliffs
Goh CT (2001) New Singapore. Prime Minister Goh Chok Tong's National Day Rally speech at the University Cultural Centre, National University of Singapore on Sunday, 19 Aug 2001. Singapore Government Press Release, Media Division, Ministry of Information and the Arts
Hicks J (1939) The foundations of welfare economics. Econ J 196:696–712
Hofstede G (1980) Culture's consequences: international differences in work-related values. Sage, Beverly Hills
Johanson J, Vahlne JE (1977) The internationalization process of the firm: a model of knowledge development and increasing foreign market commitments. J Int Bus Stud 8(1):23–32
Johanson J, Wiedersheim PF (1975) The internationalisation of the firm – four Swedish cases. J Manag Stud 12:305–322
Kitchin R, Dodge M (2002) Virtual reality, space and geographic visualisation. In: Unwin D, Fisher P (eds) Virtual reality in geography. Taylor & Francis, London, pp 341–361
Kogut B, Zander U (1992) Knowledge of the firm, combinative capabilities, and the replication of technology. Organ Sci 3(3):383–397
Lim L (2005) Asia experiences new era of renaissance – Keynote speech by Lee Kuan Yew at the official opening of the Lee Kuan Yew School of Public Policy and conference on managing globalization: lessons from China and India. The Straits Times. 5 April 2005
Markowitz HM (1952) Portfolio selection. J Finance 7(1):77–91
Nonaka I, Takeuchi H (1995) The knowledge-creating company: how Japanese companies create the dynamics of innovation. Oxford University Press, New York
Olson GM, Olson JS (2000) Distance matters. Hum Comput Interact 15:139–179
Penrose ET (1959) The theory of the growth of the firm. Blackwell, Oxford
Posner MV (1961) International trade and technical change. Oxford Econ Pap 13:323–341
Predoehl A (1928) The theory of location in its relation to general economics. J Polit Econ 36:371–390
Ren XF (2005) World cities and global architectural firms: a network approach. In: Paper presented at the social organization of urban space workshop, University of Chicago, Chicago, 3 November
Revans R (1974) Action learning. Blond & Briggs, London
Rimmer P (1991) The global intelligence corps and world cities: engineering consultancies on the move. In: Daniels P (ed) Services and metropolitan development: international perspectives. Routledge, London, pp 66–106
Slater SF (1997) Developing a customer value-based theory of the firm. J Acad Mark Sci 25(2):162–167
Trompenaars F, Hampden-Turner C (1998) Riding the waves of culture, 2nd edn. McGraw-Hill, New York
Weber A (1929) Theory of the location of industries (trans: Friedrich CJ). The University of Chicago Press, Chicago
Welch J (2005) Winning. HarperCollins, New York

Chapter 10
Findings and Synthesis of Themes

10.1 Introduction

This chapter discusses the main findings of the study and seeks to synthesize the various themes brought together by the study. The study explains how flight-time, as an independent variable, could be a causal factor to total or partial mediators such as the market size of a city, attraction and spatial interaction between two locations, and the other dimensions of distance, which could in turn affect the dependent variable: organization design. Figure 10.1 shows a mediational model. Instead of hypothesizing a direct causal relationship between an independent variable and a dependent variable, a mediational model hypothesizes that the independent variable causes the mediator variable, which in turn causes the dependent variable. The mediator variable thus serves to clarify the nature of the relationship between independent and dependent variables.

10.2 7-h Flight-Radius

Since Mr. Goh Chok Tong (2001) exhorted Singapore-domiciled businesses to venture into regional markets which are within 7-h flight-radius away from Singapore, to make full use of Singapore's physical and cultural proximities to these markets, Singapore's A/E firms have been rapidly and actively exporting their services to, or setting up offices in these regional markets. The raison d'être makes a lot of sense because when an office is located further away from its home-office, the overseas office goes through a sap of access to home-based resources. According to the Resource-based Theory (Penrose 1959), the firm's key resources include assets, attributes, capabilities, organizational processes, information, knowledge et cetera. Very often, these home-based resources are critical resources which enable the firms to achieve competitive advantages and sustain superior long-term performance. When an overseas office is situated further

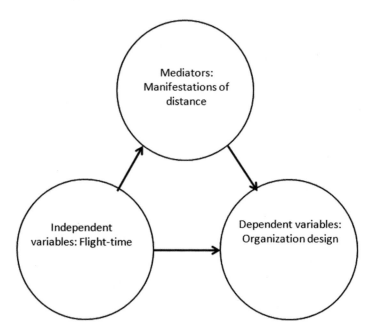

Fig. 10.1 Independent variables, mediators and dependent variables of the study

away from these resources, it becomes less able to tap into these home-based location-specific resources. Coincidentally, Mr. Goh's (2001) recommendation matches with Goodnow and Hansz's (1972) Litvag-Banting (temperature gradient) model of internationalization, which through an empirical study, found that firms preferred to venture into "warmer countries" that tend to be geographically closer, politically stable, low in legal barriers and high in market opportunity.

However, the 7-h flight-radius is actually a ballpark figure that has not been perfectly substantiated. Many other factors, such as (i) the mobility of the firm; (ii) relativity of distance; and (iii) appeal of market opportunities could affect the reach or sphere of influence of the firm, or how far the firm is willing to traverse.

For instance, A/E firms from countries that actively encourage and facilitate internationalization, such as Holland, Sweden, Korea, Japan and China would be more mobile than firms from countries that do not. This suggestion is consistent with Porter's (1990) Diamond Framework, which considers government intervention an important factor for a firm's internationalization efforts. An A/E firm is also more mobile than a builder because an A/E firm's main assets are its people, whereas a contractor's main assets are its heavy and bulky equipments, thereby causing the contractor to face more logistical constraints and embeddedness in its home-market or environment. This suggestion is consistent with McGuinness's (1994) concept of location-specificity of resources. Therefore, it is normally easier for an A/E firm than a contractor to venture further away from its home-market.

10.2 7-h Flight-Radius

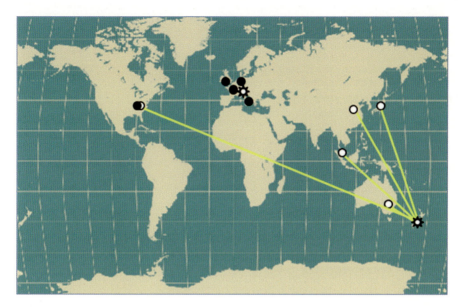

Fig. 10.2 A comparison between New Zealand and Germany and their top trading partners

Figure 10.2 compares New Zealand (denoted by a white star – ✪) and Germany (denoted by a black star – ✸) and their top five trading partners respectively (white circles for New Zealand's top trade partners; black circles for Germany's top trade partners). New Zealand's top five trading partners are Australia, USA, China, Japan and Singapore; Germany's top trading partners are France, Netherlands, USA, United Kingdom and Italy. It can be observed that New Zealand's trading partners are located significantly further away from the country. This suggests that distance is relative. Therefore, a firm from a country that is located far-away from other locations (e.g. New Zealand) is more likely to venture into a market that is geographically further away.

Nonetheless, it has been observed that generally, a country is more likely to trade more frequently with its neighbours or with countries that are proximately located. For instance, Germany's top trading partners are France, Netherlands, USA, United Kingdom and Italy; New Zealand's top trading partners are Australia, USA, China, Japan and Singapore; China's top trading partners are USA, Hong Kong, Japan, Korea and Germany; Malaysia's top trading partners are USA, Singapore, Japan, China and Thailand; Singapore's top trading partners are Malaysia, China, Indonesia, Hong Kong and USA et cetera. Apparently, countries tend to trade with counterparts which are located geographically nearer to themselves, with the exception of USA, which is the world's largest importer. This finding is consistent with Isard's (1956) Gravity model which suggests that trade between two countries is based on the countries' intervening distance.

Notwithstanding that, Singapore's A/E firms have mainly ventured into cities in South-east Asia, China and India, all markets within the 7-h flight radius away from Singapore. A few Singapore A/E firms have also ventured into cities in the Middle-east, such as Dubai, which is about 8-h flight-time away from Singapore. Notably, Singapore's A/E firms have not ventured into other continents such as North America, South America, Europe and South Africa, unlike some top international A/E firms, such as Skidmore, Owings and Merrill (SOM), Kohn Pederson Fox (KPF) and Hellmuth, Obata and Kassabaum (HOK), which have been able to set up their offices all over the globe. This is presumably because Singapore's A/E firms are not as competitive as these international A/E firms, and are thus limited to Asian markets which are nearer to Singapore. This finding is consistent with the Industrial Organization Theory (Hymer 1976) which suggests that indigenous firms understand local consumer taste, business customs, legal systems et cetera. In the same way, Singapore's A/E firms have more historical, cultural and language affinities with South-east Asian, Chinese and Indian markets, and understand these markets better than international A/E firms from e.g. USA and Europe. As Singapore's A/E firms acquire more international experiences and expertise from abroad, they would be able to venture further away, beyond 7-h flight-time away from Singapore.

It should also be considered that the appeal of a market affects the spatial interaction between the home and overseas cities. The gravitational relationship between two locations is taken to be a function of (i) appeal of the overseas market; (ii) size of the home-market; and (iii) intervening distance between the cities. Therefore, an appealing market (e.g. Shanghai and Beijing) is more likely to attract firms from all around the world. This is why there have been so many American firms crossing the oceans and lands to do business in China, but less so in Africa.

Furthermore, flight-time between two cities, by itself, is not a perfect gauge of physical distance between the two locations. Flight-time for a journey is dependent on the velocity of the flight and the geographical distance from the start-point to the destination, which would in turn be influenced by the aircraft's make, flight-route taken, jet-streams, head-wind and tail-wind et cetera. Another point to note is that one might need to have a stop-over and arrange for a transit flight to reach a destination if there are no direct flights to get there.

For these cases, flight-time would be a poor indicator of the distance between two cities, and should not be taken as a proxy for flight-distance. On the other hand, when a flight flies in the north–south direction, the climate of the destination changes; and when a flight flies in the east–west direction, the local time of the destination changes. Furthermore, it has been observed that nations further away from the equator are wealthier, and that there seem to be a global North–south divide that separates the wealthy and the poor (Diamond 1997; Masters and McMillan 2001). Longer flight-time also causes more severe disruption to a person's circadian rhythm. Therefore, flight-time is not without its merits, and can be used as a proxy for geographical distance as long as one does not stay oblivious to its limitations. Interviewees from Singapore, Johor Bahru, Kuala Lumpur, Penang, HCM City, Hanoi, Shanghai, Beijing and Tianjin shared their views below.

Some firms seem to take flight-time seriously into consideration for their overseas ventures. A senior technical manager of Firm B shared:

> For Malaysia, it is much easier. You can just fly down in 35 minutes and you can just come back on the day itself whereas for far-away markets it will need about many hours so geographical proximity plays an important part, especially when we need resources or help from the HQ. The higher travelling cost to further-away markets also means that we have to cut down on expenses.

An architect from Firm C in Shanghai shared his thoughts on business-travelling:

> I am a guy who likes travelling very much but the feeling for me when I fly to some cities is bad as I fly to airport, do my work and fly back. For example, I have been to Tianjin five times but I don't know how the city looks like. I only know how the airport looks like. Actually, I don't like this kind of feeling because beside job, you still have your life but sometimes they will allow you to stay there for one or two days to look around. However, sometimes after meeting, you have to fly back to meet your boss. Flying is great if you are on a holiday. It is tiring for work.

A senior Vice-President of Firm C in Shanghai opined:

> Flying in and out has its limitations. You may be rushed to complete your work. You cannot serve your clients well enough. Flying in and out was tiring. Worse still, when you have to shuttle between cities in China and Singapore, the sense of belonging to either places erode away from you. My personal preference is that if flight distance is less than two hours, then I am willing to commute regularly. If not, I would rather be stationed in the overseas city, like what I am doing now in Shanghai.

The Chairman of Firm D, when asked for comments on the suggestion that firms tend to venture into nearby markets initially, agreed:

> From our own experience, we started off with nearer markets like KL, then Jakarta, then Hong Kong.

A senior associate of Firm D in Shanghai shared:

> Shanghai is only five and a half hours away from Singapore. We can be in both offices on the same day, as if the two offices are in Changi and Jurong.

A Vice-President of Firm F in Singapore, when asked whether Singapore's firms have advantages when they venture into nearby markets agreed:

> We have physical and cultural proximity.

Flight-time or geographical distance does not have a simple linear relationship with market opportunities. A Vice-President of Firm F in Singapore, when asked whether distance from the firm's home-city affects a firm's choice of market, shared:

> If you look at our business model, we set up our Abu Dhabi office earlier than our Vietnam office though the latter is nearer to Singapore. Once again, it is dependent on the projects you are able to secure. The projects in Vietnam is not as fast and profitable as the one in Abu Dhabi thus for us, this theory (of a simple linear relationship) may not hold. If you are asking about the ease of doing business and getting projects, in a way they are not related. In terms of culture, this theory may hold some ground as the ease of working in Malaysia is much easier than Abu Dhabi.

A Vice-President of Firm F in Tianjin shared:

We have an operational model that we would set up offices which are about one and a half hour flight-time from each other, in a network of cities in China. But, we apply this model only for China, and to a certain extent, India and the Middle-east. We also look at the market prospects of these countries or regions. This model is also complicated by for example, the oceans.

Other than Singaporean A/E firms, a project manager of an engineering firm in HCM City shared:

Singapore is too small. Singapore's construction industry is too small and too competitive. Therefore, firms are venturing out into foreign markets. When you fly to places like Dubai, which is about 8 hours away, you are actually spending 8 x 2 = 16 hours on flight-time alone. When flight-time is less, you can afford more time for your work and family. However, I do not agree that Singapore is limited by 7 hours. 9 hours should be closer to the truth.

10.3 Core and Periphery Locations

There is a clear relationship between construction activity and economic growth and development (Bon and Crosthwaite 2000). Bon and Crosthwaite (2000) made these few observations:

1. The share of construction in total output first grows and then decline with economic development
2. The volume
3. In later stages of economic development, new construction volume declines and maintenance and repair volume grows
4. In later stages of economic growth construction inputs from manufacturing decline and those from services grow.

Economic and commercial activities tend to of construction output first grows and then declines with economic developmentconcentrate in several locations (refer to Tables 3.2–3.5 and Fig. 3.8). This can be reflected by the city's population (refer to Table 3.2), the number of skyscrapers in the city (refer to Table 3.3), number of passengers received by airports in the city (refer to Table 3.4), and Gross Domestic Product (nominal) per capita of the city (refer to Table 3.5). Night-lights photographs taken by NASA from outer-space have also shown how economic activities on earth were concentrated around several locations (refer to Fig. 3.8). These observations are consistent with the concepts of agglomeration and central places (Predoehl 1928; Christaller 1933; Krugman 1991).

Contrary to the impression of the proliferation of virtual clusters, these physical clusters or growth poles are the result of localization and agglomeration of commercial firms in the world's core locations, such as New York, London, Tokyo, Shanghai and Singapore. Generally, firms localize or agglomerate together when they perceive that the centripetal forces of the location prevail over the centrifugal

10.3 Core and Periphery Locations

forces. These locations then grow to be "sticky places" and attract more firms to localize and agglomerate, so much so that these places develop into central places, which act like black-holes, to suck up the economic potential in the area, causing back-wash effects on neighboring peripheral location, and make the core-periphery mosaic of regions even more distinct. The concept of Central Place Hierarchy suggests that the larger a settlement, the more functions it holds, the more higher-ordered services are provided, the fewer they are, and the greater distance between them (Christaller 1933). Therefore, Singapore as a central place or core location, is disposed to draw in much of the economic potential in the region around it, but its neighboring cities could suffer from the back-wash effects of Singapore's success, even though these nearby peripheral locations may benefit from lower-ordered spillages from the core locations. Hubs in transportation also enjoy a similar advantage to central places (Krugman 1991). The notion of friction suggests how optimum routes are obtained by adhering to the principle of minimization and the principle of traffic. Hence, cities which are strategically located in a region often become aviation or sea-port hubs of that region. The concept of Central Place Hierarchy (Christaller 1933) suggests that these central cities then evolve to become marketing, administration and transportation hubs and command-centers of transnational firms.

A senior Vice-President of Firm C in Shanghai shared her views on Chinese cities and how Firm C preferred to venture into key economic, transportation and communications hubs:

> *Chongqing as you know is dominated by Hong Kong developers so it is not easy for us to go into the market. In Chengdu and X'ian, there is the advantage of going further into the west.*
>
> *Chengdu is one of the key economic, transportation and communications hub of south-western China and it also acts as a gate-way to the west.*

A Director of Firm D in Kuala Lumpur opined:

> *Agglomeration allows vibrancy, availability and gentrification, even though it also allows competition.*

An associate of Firm D in Shanghai shared:

> *Economic, transportation and communications hubs will benefit. One possibility (of cities that could prosper in the future) could be Xi'an because of its rich history.*

Agglomeration can take place even within cities. An administrative associate of Firm F in Hanoi shared:

> *Hanoi's architectural firms are sporadically located. All offices are like that.*

A Vice-President of Firm F in Tianjin shared his views on agglomeration in core locations and the back-wash-effects on peripheral locations:

> *Not so much in China. The whole of China is booming. But I agree with the idea of concentrated development around several areas in a region or country. For example, in Singapore, we have other than the CBD, Jurong, Tampines and Woodlands. In China, we*

have Beijing and Tianjin, Shanghai and Nanjing, Guangzhou and Hong Kong, and Chengdu as the main areas of economic development.

Other than Singaporean A/E firms, the Managing Director of an engineering firm in Johor Bahru shared:

> Architectural firms like to be near to the authorities, administrative centre and town councils; engineering firms like to be, but not necessarily, near the authorities. Engineering firms are more sporadically located.

Internationalizing firms should understand the importance of "location, location, location". This statement is supported by Weber's (1929) Location Triangle and Hotelling's (1929) observation of firms' locations. The Weberian Location Triangle (Weber 1929) suggested that a firm locates itself in a place to have the best "middling" accessibility to key resources and markets. The Hotelling Phenomenon (Hotelling 1929) put forward that a firm locates itself in relation to its competitors and target-market. Therefore, it is common for A/E firms to locate themselves in central places to have access to human resources, as well as to tap into its larger market. For that reason, firms have the proclivity to locate themselves in production sites such as New York and London, and consumption sites such as Shanghai and Beijing. This inclination is shown in the trend that more Singapore's A/E firms are setting up offices abroad in order to be physically close to these overseas markets. Being located in a significant overseas market swarmed with many competitors is better than staying away from the market – at least the firm puts the consumer or client in a zone of indifference, whereby consumers or clients in the zone do not prefer any firm due to where the firm is located. However, if the Singapore's A/E firm chooses not to set up a branch-office overseas, it is likely to forfeit the market opportunities in the overseas market. This finding is consistent with Dunning's (1988) Eclectic Paradigm, which suggests that the transnational firm has to internalize its ownership and locational qualities to be successful in a foreign market.

A General Manager of Firm D in HCM City shared on why a firm's physical presence in an overseas market is important:

> We won the competition but we lost the contract. The first three winners supposed to negotiate with the investors but the problem why we lost was because we did not have chance to negotiate. We did not hear from them but we heard number 3 invited them over to Hong Kong and after a few drinks, they signed the contract. It is important being there and having a physical presence. The contract is much more valuable than winning the competition. You have to keep knocking on their door, bring them to Singapore and so on.

> They look at design plus they look at you and how they communicate. The whole feel of things determines if you will get the job. They will think that 'You are a good architectural firm so I expect you to do a good job and that the rest of the factors matters a lot too.' So having a physical presence is important.

A/E firms like to locate themselves in production sites such as New York and London, consumption sites such as Shanghai and Beijing, or middle-places like Singapore. These locations have a few similarities: (i) power – importance of the city in the world economy; (ii) centrality – how much the city is a hub of activities; (iii) near-ness – the physical proximity of the city to other cities; (iv) between-ness – how much the city is located along the trade routes between other cities;

(v) connectivity – how the city is connected to other cities; and (vi) role of the city in the complementary system of cities in the region. For example, New York and London are powerful cities; Silicon Valley in San Francisco is a hub for research; Paris is near to London, Amsterdam and Munich et cetera, but Auckland is far-away from other major cities other than Sydney; Singapore is in between Australia and China/India/Middle-east; New York and London are the most connected cities (to other cities) in the world; Hong Kong and Singapore are the financial centers of Asia et cetera.

In this context, the Managing Director of a quantity surveying firm in Shanghai shared on why his firm chose to locate its Regional HQ in Shanghai:

> *Like New York, London and Singapore, Shanghai is strategically located. It is a port-city located at the mouth of the Yang-tse river. The port is the busiest in the world and it gives Shanghai a very significant advantage over the other cities.*

10.4 Gravitational Distance

The Transaction Costs Theory (Coase 1937) suggests that distance between markets increases a firm's transaction costs, efforts and time. Many laws, such as Reilly's Law (Reilly 1931) and Huff's Law (Huff 1963), modeled after Isaac Newton's Gravity Law, have highlighted that spatial interaction is a function of the attraction between the two entities. Spatial interaction between two locations is dependent on the gravitational distance between them. Gravitational distance is understood as the product of the size of the A/E market (or an attribute) of Location A and the size of the A/E market (or an attribute) of Location B, divided by the square of the intervening distance between Location A and B.

A cross-section of the Central Place Hierarchy (as shown in Fig. 10.3) would tell us that the size of a market is very much influenced by the market's physical distance away from a core location. Distance, in this case, also takes into consideration cultural distance, administrative distance, geographical distance, topological distance, economical distance, socio-demographical distance, technological distance, relational distance and organizational distance. Gravitational distance is also encroached by the complementarities of services in different cities, intervening opportunities, and transferability of a spatial interaction.

Take East Asia for example: complementary products or services are provided by different countries or cities because each of these countries or cities enjoys either absolute or comparative advantages over other countries or cities in providing particular products or services. In East Asia, Hong Kong is the financial center in the region, Japan is the technological hub in the region, China provides the manufacturing base et cetera. Therefore, gravitational distance would have to take into account the complementarities of countries or cities.

Intervening opportunities are also considered. A firm's resources are limited. Thus, the firm is likely to allocate resources to where there would be maximum returns and least opportunity costs. For example, Auckland in New Zealand is

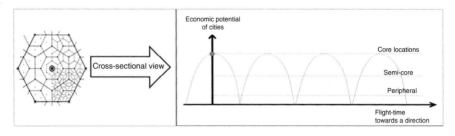

Fig. 10.3 Cross-sectional view of the central place hierarchy

far-away from most other major cities apart from Sydney. Firms from Auckland are thus more likely to venture into farther-away locations, such as Singapore, which is 12-h flight-time away. On the contrary, Singapore is more centrally located, has many more significant markets within 7-h flight-radius, and is thus less inclined to venture farther-away.

Transferability of the product or service to be exported is also an important consideration. Transferability distorts the time-space dimensions of the export. For example, an A/E firm is naturally a global firm, suitable for exports, because the main asset of an A/E firm is its staff. A/E professionals are able to easily communicate with their peers on the web, or commute between home and overseas markets. This way, the concept of time and space becomes less critical.

Furthermore, as Taleb (2007) pointed out with his observation of the Black Swan phenomenon, there are always high-impact, hard-to-predict, and rare outlier events beyond the realm of normal expectation, the landscape of the mosaic of the region and of the world is often distorted by topological features such as land-locked-ness, oceans or seas, lack of infrastructure (e.g. airports, sea-ports and network of roads). Relativity of distance should be considered. For example, topological distance suggests how two countries seem to be more remote from each other if there are other countries, seas or barriers located in the space between them.

A country or city's location in relation to other countries or cities is also a very important determinant of its role in the Core and Peripheral System of Cities. There are also cases whereby firms skip the intervening opportunities which are located nearby, to take up challenges further abroad. The reasons can be aplenty: decisions by top leaders, personal preferences, chances et cetera. Therefore, a firm may neglect proximate locations to venture into farther away places, even though there seem to be no lack of opportunities in the nearer markets. This finding is consistent with Baumol's (1959) Managerial Theory of the Perlmutter's (1969) International Entrepreneurship model, which suggest that factors such as new goals or the role of the entrepreneur may influence the transnational firm's internationalization decisions. Figure 10.4 shows how a normal relationship between flight-time (as a proxy for geographical distance) from a core location and economic potential in a city is distorted when there are market saturation, market expansion, inaccessible markets (e.g. seas or lack of appeal of markets), and irregularities of a core location's sphere of influence.

10.4 Gravitational Distance

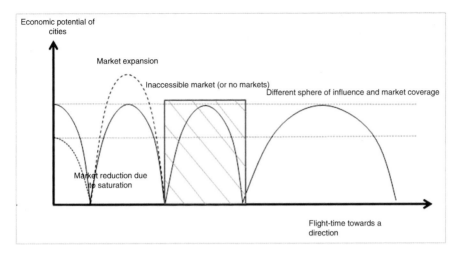

Fig. 10.4 Distorted pattern of agglomeration

Figure 10.5 shows how a bridge can be built between two locations so that distance between the two locations can be compressed. One example would be trade between USA and Singapore. Most of Singapore's top import and export partners are geographically proximate to the island-country, but USA is one of Singapore's top trade partners despite being very far away geographically. One major explanation is that the USA-Singapore FTA has constructed a "bridge" that has managed to shorten the distance between the two countries. It is thus suggested in this study that bridges can be created via means such as FTA, networks and relationships et cetera.

Figure 10.6 shows the compression of viable markets for the transnational firm. It is acknowledged that firms only have bounded rationality. Often, they make satisficing decisions instead of optimal ones, because of diminished knowledge of a foreign market. This suggestion is consistent with Katona's (1951) and Braybrooke and Lindblom's (1963) concepts of satisficing and bounded rationality, and synoptic ideal and incremental strategy. The attractiveness of overseas markets and the opportunities they present may be ebbed and compressed by such lack of understanding and the firm's tendency to take up choices that are satisficing. On the other hand, there could be special circumstances whereby viable opportunities increase or expand with increasing distances from the home market. Such examples can possibly be found in industries from places such as Singapore, New Zealand and the Scandinavian countries. These countries do not have an adequate volume of home-demand necessary for indigenous firms to grow. Hence, these firms tend to venture overseas to seek bigger markets. Figure 10.6 shows the expansion of viable markets for the transnational firm.

Large multinational firms can set up regional headquarters in different parts of the world. For example, a world-class firm from New York may have a regional headquarters in each continent or region, such as London or Paris in Europe, Tokyo

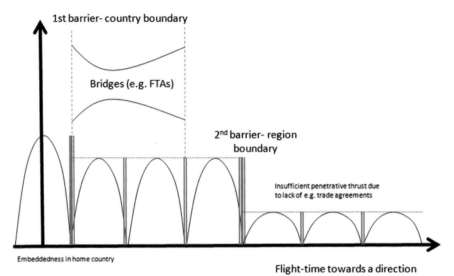

Fig. 10.5 Improved access to distant markets due to "bridges" such as FTA and networks

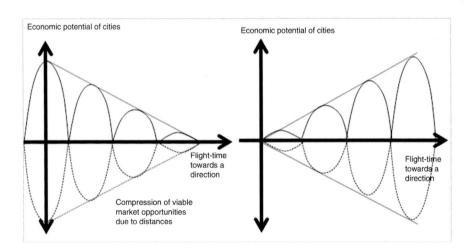

Fig. 10.6 Compression of viable markets (*left*) and expansion of viable markets (*right*)

or Singapore in Asia-Pacific, Shanghai or Hong Kong for the Chinese market et cetera. Figure 10.7 shows how regional offices may help to strut-up access to the firm's network of resources. When an A/E firm venture overseas, its access to home-based resources is sapped and reduced – the further the firm moves geographically away from its home market, the less it is able to draw on its home-based resources. The firm could start small, then incrementally grow in size and scope in

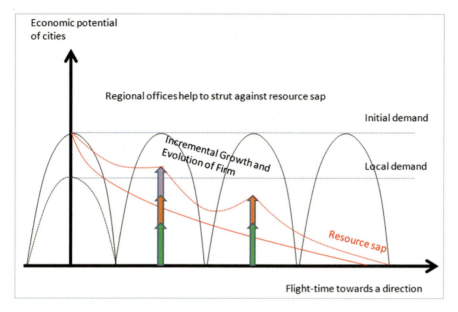

Fig. 10.7 Regional offices to strut against resource sap

the overseas market, and evolve to become a regional office. These various forms of offices, such as representative office, joint-venture and wholly-owned subsidiary, in the firm's overseas markets, together with its home's head-quarters, offer a network of resources to each of the organization's offices, and help to strut-up the firm's overseas office's access to the organization's resources.

10.4.1 Globalization and Virtual Collocation

Some interviewees seem to agree with Cairncross (1997) and Friedman's (2005) suggestion that globalization and the advances in communication technologies have made the world today highly inter-connected and virtual collocated. A/E firms, which are borne global because of the mobility of its strategic resources (McGuinness 1994), are set to benefit from such a shift, to be more proficient to internationalize into foreign markets.

A Project Director of Firm C in Tianjin opined:

> Most engineers have common training and should be able to understand the works of one another, despite physical separation. They are able to comprehend each other's ideas and conceptualized work. Modern communication technologies have also reduced the need for face-to-face interactions. Of course, sometimes there is a need for face-to-face communications. Currently, I did not face the need of having to fly to Shanghai to communicate certain ideas.

A senior manager of Firm E in Shanghai shared:

Distance should not be a problem

What matters more is communications skills. You are aided by emails and teleconferences to convey your messages to your counterparts situated physically away from you, in another city or country.

Other than Singapore A/E firms, an engineer from Firm F in Singapore shared:

In this HQ organization, there is IT service that will help us communicate with the overseas branches.

Other than Singaporean A/E firms, a Director of a quantity surveying firm in Hanoi shared:

Distance is not important in terms of deciding the location of a company.

Other than Singaporean A/E firms, a marketing manager of a developer in HCM City shared:

Technology has narrowed the distance between Vietnam and Singapore. One can always fly in or out. Time difference is not as much an issue to us than the Americans and Europeans.

10.4.2 Importance of Physical Presence

Architectural and engineering consultancy service is essentially a service, making People, Process and Physical evidence important, on top of the 4Ps, namely Product, Price, Place and Promotion in marketing (Kotler 2005). Moreover, interfaces between stakeholders and participants in a construction project are likely to require face-to-face round-table communications. In this section, the interviewees share their views on how physical presence is relevant to their businesses in overseas markets. In general, the interviewees believe that having a physical presence aids in (i) understanding the local market; (ii) improving business networks; (iii) facilitating firm's marketing efforts; (iv) identifying job requirements; (v) enhancing communications with clients, partners and colleagues; (vi) internalizing the firm's internationalization endeavour. These industry practitioners also shared on the significance of setting up a representative office or wholly owned office in the foreign market. The advantages are: (i) the firm demonstrates its commitment to stay in the market; (ii) the firm would be able to understand the market and its requirements; (iii) the firm is able to service its clients; (iv) the firm is able to improve its communications and coordination with other stakeholders in the project; and (v) the firm would be able to "glocalize" itself in the market. A firm would however, have to also strike a balance between "glocalization" and "localization" if it intends to market itself as a foreign firm in these regional markets. This could mean that the firm should not localize itself to the extent that its client feel that its value-added service are conducted locally, and deserve only local rated fees. Therefore, the firm has to contemplate potential risks and benefits of

10.4 Gravitational Distance

setting up a physical presence in its overseas market, and to devise and implement a degree of physical presence best suited for its internationalization efforts. A senior associate of Firm C in Singapore shared:

> We are looking for opportunities. We are not looking at distance so even if it is far side of China, we will go there. Distance is of course part of consideration as there is greater risk if it is further off so we assess to see if it is viable and feasible. Distance alone does not determine the outcome of the decision.

To start with, it should be noted that not all architects or engineers in an A/E firm would need to commute between cities even when their firms have projects abroad. An architect from Firm B in Singapore noted:

> The person-in-charge or a senior manager, or other decision-makers may need to fly down a few times for the project.

Some A/E firms still see the need for their staff to commute between home and overseas offices to communicate better with their clients, partners and colleagues and to coordinate work. An architect from Firm B in Singapore shared:

> Architects are all design-trained, so they can easily have common understanding between themselves. Architects may have a harder time trying to describe their designs to clients who do not have design-backgrounds.

A senior technical manager of Firm B in Singapore shared:

> You can have the first hand feel of the market and know where to target. The downside is that the risk is also higher.

An architect from Firm D in Beijing shared:

> Sometimes I will fly back to Singapore to have design meetings with the chairman and the board, and then fly back to China to convert the designs into drawings. The coordinating design work is still done in China but we are still conceptualizing in Singapore.

> There are many creative aspects of architecture that require face-to-face communication. There might be information losses but whether or not it is important, it is dependent on the communicator. Sometimes, it may be the real-time communication that may be more important. We are in a way, handicapped when we are away from the main team in Singapore. The main team in the home-office does most of the work, and we are supposed to coordinate their work with our partners and clients here. Sometimes, there could be informational loss. The creative aspects of design could be lost in translation. Other than that, access of other resources is okay. Video-conferencing has a limitation – it would not be able to detect moods or emotions that are occurring in your fellow consultants.

A senior manager of Firm E in Shanghai described an A/E firm's common interfaces with clients and partners who are located in overseas markets:

> When you have design and new projects, we will organize a team consisting of architects, engineers and project directors and managers. This team will fly to clients' office and get as much information as possible, interacting as much as possible with clients and their staff and relevant personnel. After which, they will come back to the office to start on the design. After which, we will have the review in clients' office. It will happen two to three times and this is taken into consideration into computing the project cost. Sensitivity is heightened for design as you have to fly the architect there to listen to the clients' wants. The project management will be stationed at site where the construction will be so clients will normally be nearby the site. Our project directors have to visit the clients once a month to provide with a review. He will visit the site once a while and he will have weekly meetings for the

project manager with all the manpower and et cetera. Then the project director will endorse the report and send it to the client. That is how the system works. The project management team does not need to visit the clients, only the project directors. It is client management that the project directors have to visit the clients, instead of just emailing.

The General Manager of Firm F in Kuala Lumpur shared on the benefits of physical presence:

Interaction between architects and engineers are often round-table exchanges, not linear moving. There can be teething problems.

Other than Singaporean A/E firms, the Managing Director of a quantity surveying firm in Shanghai shared on the benefits of having a permanent office in the overseas market:

I think for our services, first of all there is a need to service our clients if there is a project because the construction is going 24/7 so you have a lot of challenges everyday and you will need to handle these challenges.

Travelling costs can be reduced. Work can be transferred internally.

10.5 Double-Octagonal Perspective of Distance

Many scholars have debated on the relevance of distance in our world today (Blainey 1977; Cairncross 1997; Olson and Olson 2000) Some have claimed that virtual collocation has made the world a global village and has killed distance (Blainey 1977; Ohmae 1999), while others argued that the impact of distance has been exacerbated, citing how modern businesses stress the timely delivery and speed of doing things, and how distance requires efforts, money and time to overcome (Cairncross 1997; Olson and Olson 2000). To the latter group of people, the first law of Geography which suggests "Everything is related to everything else, but near things are more related than distant things" (Tobler 1970) still holds true – distance causes discontinuities, dislocations and disconnections.

Flight-time between two cities is suggested, in this study, to be a common denominator or a mediator between flight-time as an independent variable and other facets of distance as dependent factors. Distance can be manifested as Cultural distance, Administrative distance, Geographical distance, Economical distance, Technological distance, Socio-demographical distance, Relational and affinity distance and Organizational distance. Organizational distance can in turn, be manifested as changes, spillages, time-lags and time-differences, psychic distance, networks, communications, net cost-benefit and control. Dissimilar types of firms and different cities have dissimilar sensitivities to the different forms of distances. For instance, products with low value-of-weight or bulk ration are less mobile and more sensitive to physical distance, whereas consultancy services are less sensitive to distance, and have more opportunities for global arbitrage; while countries with more FTAs are less sensitive to physical distance (McGuinness 1994; Ng and Feldman 2010).

A senior manager of Firm E in Shanghai shared:

> *Different activities have different sensitivities to distance. For example, architects may have to fly to meet clients to get more information and understanding clients' interests. Project managers may need to station on-site and report to clients regularly. Proximity may be important for client management. Master planners also need to fly often to meet up with clients, collect information on-site to do research and feasibility studies, and doing presentations to clients. Distance matters to all consultants because consultancy work is very much person-to-person.*

From a cultural perspective, transnational firms find it easier to transfer their technologies, human resource practices, operating procedures and to achieve internal consistency through standardization when the home and host locations are more culturally similar. This observation is consistent with Barlett and Ghoshal (1998), Ghemawat (2001) and Tihanyi et al.'s (2005) findings that differences between countries and cities of different societal value systems add an additional burden for transnational firms to adapt to local cultural values.

An associate of Firm C in HCM City shared:

> *Networking with the locals requires you to navigate through a complicated web of approaches. Moreover, meeting times can be prolonged because of need of translation. Most often than not, I did not have sufficient time, and had to sacrifice a lot of rest time to get the work done. It is extremely draining on the body and mind.*

Other than Singaporean A/E firms, the Managing Director of a quantity surveying firm in Shanghai advised how Singapore's A/E firms should adapt to working in Shanghai:

> *You may have to make adjustments to the way people here work. Personal relationships are important here.*

From an administrative perspective, transnational firms are more comfortable doing businesses in a location which is administratively more proximate in terms of the level of capitalism, laissez faire, state intervention, laws et cetera. This observation agrees with Ghemawat's (2001) suggestion that transnational firms may encounter host government's restrictions and requirements, which can be made even more hostile when the internationalizing firm is unfamiliar with the administrative structures and practices of the location.

A senior architect of Firm B noted how overseas markets have different administrative set-ups:

> *There are different practices, contractual norms and by-laws. Furthermore, there may be lack of transparency.*

An associate of Firm C in HCM City shared:

> *In theory, the advent of technology might have dispensed with the need to fly around the globe to do coordination. But the truth is that business trips have been increasing, not decreasing. This should be because different cities or countries may have very different environments, with different institutions and procedures to do business.*

It is important for a firm to be attentive to how codes and regulations can be interpreted in overseas markets. A senior Vice-President of Firm C in Shanghai shared:

> It is common for experienced Chinese or international consultants to "Cha Bian Qiu (插边球)[1]" – to exploit loop-holes in the interpretations of codes and regulations.

From a geographical perspective, transnational firms are more attracted to locations which are closer and geographically nearer to where they come from. This observation is in sync with the Gravity model (Isard and Peck 1954) which states that "Any two bodies attract one another with a force that is proportional to the product of their masses and inversely proportional to the square of the distance between them". The observation also agrees with the Uppsala or Stage Growth Theory (Johanson and Wiedersheim 1975), which suggests that firms initially choose to enter nearby markets with low commitment so as to reduce risk their exposure to risks.

A Director of Firm D in Kuala Lumpur concurred:

> We need to be near to our clients. Or else, we can only do front-end jobs like marketing and liaison.

> For architecture services, you need a presence because from a day-to-day basis, the client will look at you to see how you handle.

A senior associate of Firm D in Shanghai suggested that physical proximity to the home-office and physical presence in markets is important:

> It is sometimes easier to go down and tell them the line is wrong, rather than draw it out and send it over and email them to tell them it is wrong. It takes longer and of course, you have to word your email properly or there will be miscommunications.

> It (physical distance) affects our work and productivity.

A senior project manager of Firm E in Singapore shared his thoughts on the inconveniences distance brings:

> It can also be inconvenient for a carrier to bring work-related samples overseas. Information may be distorted or misunderstood when people have to rely on emails. This is especially true in our field of work because detailed coordination is often required for architectural and engineering integration. There could be inconveniences due to time-zone differences, and sap of resources and decrease of familiarity.

From an economical perspective, it was shared that transnational firms benefit from improved economical ties between host and home countries when FTAs and better infrastructure are in place between the two locations to shorten the economical distance and facilitate trade between the two locations. This finding is consistent with Transaction-costs Theory, which suggests that transnational firms incur internationalization costs due to the transfer of firm-specific assets to their offices abroad (Coase 1937; Williamson 1975).

---

[1] To hit the ball such that it just tips over the net.

10.5 Double-Octagonal Perspective of Distance

A Director of Firm A in Singapore shared:

FTAs ease a firm's entry into a foreign market. However, the benefits are not so obvious for architectural firms.

From a technological perspective, it was observed that A/E firms from Singapore tend to export their services to developing countries in the region, such as Malaysia, Vietnam and China. This observation is consistent with the Theory of International Product Cycle (Posner 1961) which suggests that transnational firms with advanced technology or knowledge prefer to transfer their technologies or knowledge to intermediately technologically advanced locations because of similarities in demand and the higher prices they get to charge in these markets. The observation is also consistent with the Flying Geese Paradigm, which suggests that firms tend to transfer their technologies or knowledge to less advanced markets.

A senior project manager of Firm E commented on technological spill-overs:

Yes, technology has short-distance spillovers. This is why IT firms cluster themselves together in Silicon Valley.

Other than Singaporean A/E firms, the General Director of a quantity surveying firm in HCM City shared:

We have such a high expatriate ratio deliberately so that we can have better knowledge transfer to the staff and technology transfer.

Other than Singaporean A/E firms, a marketing manager of a developer in HCM City observed:

Technology has narrowed the distance between Vietnam and Singapore.

From a socio-demographical distance, it was observed that A/E professionals tend feel more comfortable with people who have the same professional training and cultural habits. This is consistent with the Bogardus Social Distance Scale (Bogardus 1926), which suggests that people are more willing to inter-mingle, inter-relate, communicate and cooperate with people who are socio-demographically more similar to themselves.

An associate of Firm A in Kuala Lumpur shared:

I have worked for Malay bosses before. They are not good managers – they are not organized and disciplined. They are not good financial planners. They adopt a "Que Sera Sera" attitude. They tend to rely on Bumiputra[2] projects which allow elastic budgets and times. They have a different ball-game. Connections are important for them. Chinese are more dog-eat-dog – competitive.

An architect of Firm B in Singapore noted:

We may have cultural differences from other cities – in Singapore, we want things fast, whereas pace of work may be slower abroad.

---

[2] Indigenous people of the Malay archipelago.

From an affinity perspective, transnational firms find it easier to venture into markets which are more relationally affiliated to where they come from. This is more so in Asia, where Sinic or Confucianism values permeate. Asians have the proclivity to collaborate with fellow Asians. A case-in-point is how firms from Taiwan, Hong Kong and Singapore are better equipped to tap into China's markets. This finding is consistent with the Network Theory (Johanson and Mattson 1988), which suggests that an organization tend to collaborate more often with other firms which share the same heritage and values.

An associate of Firm A in Kuala Lumpur shared:

> *They (Malays in Malaysia) tend to rely on Bumiputra projects which allow elastic budgets and times. They have a different ball-game. Connections are important for them.*

From an organizational perspective, it was observed that the internationalizing A/E faces distance-rooted changes when they venture overseas. Distance causes (i) changes in the landscape; (ii) spillovers from where they come from; (iii) time-lags in communications and time-differences between offices in different time-zones; (iv) level of psychic understanding of the host market; (v) level of ethnocentric, region-centric and polycentric networks; (vi) communications between offices which are physically separated; (vii) increase of transaction costs; and (viii) dissipated control.

Corporate geography represents the spatial viewpoint in business studies. Competition need not manifest itself through locations or distance – it can for example, be in price, quality and customer awareness et cetera. However, all these manifestations have geographic expressions. For instance, delivery becomes more expensive and tortuous with increasing distance; so does the possibility of monitoring the market with communications costs; the competitive clout declines with increasing distance from the base of operations and geographical bias emerges; customers nearer suppliers are less tolerant of long delivery times than more distant customers; learners tend to go to marginal markets whereby risks are lower et cetera.

Therefore, *ceteris paribus*, firms would prefer to venture into markets which are nearer to their home-markets in terms of cultural proximity, administrative proximity, geographical proximity, economical proximity, technological proximity, socio-demographical proximity, relational proximity and organizational proximity.

10.5.1 Changes

The A/E firm would have to adapt itself to a new landscape when it internationalizes overseas. This is consistent with Seeley's (1995) suggestion that there are very significant differences in the requirements for buildings located in different parts of the world. A senior Vice-President of Firm C in Shanghai shared why Firm C only offers consultancy services pertaining to architecture, master-planning, project management and building audit, but not mechanical and electrical engineering:

> *Singapore has been viewed to be a tropical country. Most clients feel that we are not experienced enough to do up the heating mechanisms for the cool weather they experience during winter. These are the reasons why we have not started any other office lines (in mechanical and electrical engineering.*

An architect from Firm D in Beijing shared:

> *We just adapt to the environment. Actually regulations-wise, you can get from the books. From my own opinion, acclimatizing the work style is something to be considered for example the design consultants here may work very differently from those in Singapore. We adjust as the projects go and adjust our perceptions of their working style and values.*

> *The climate is different. Architects here have to consider North–south solar orientation. For residential projects, architects have to place major rooms in the south. Architects also have to pay attention to building distances.*

A Vice-President of Firm F shared:

> *A tropical design and a temperate design differ a lot so that one (understanding the building requirements) will become a prerequisite to operate overseas.*

10.5.2 Spillages

Spillages can take the form of off-shoring of activities to nearby locations that offer cheaper resources. An interviewee shared that there had been cases of Singapore's A/E firms off-shoring their A/E activities in Malaysia. Similarly, it was observed that Tianjin and Suzhou are being used as off-shoring options for A/E work in Beijing and Shanghai respectively. This finding is consistent with Conley and Ligon's 2002) suggestion that there are spillages between neighbouring countries or cities.

A senior architect of Firm A in Shanghai shared:

> *Off-shoring is much cheaper. For example one may offshore to Tianjin which is much cheaper than Beijing.*

A Vice-President of Firm C in Beijing shared:

> *Tianjin is only about 100 kilometers away from Beijing. It will boom and prosper because commercial activities in the Beijing-Tianjin cosmopolitan will take place in Tianjin while Beijing remains as the political centre of China. Tianjin is also less costly and makes a good location for off-shoring activities for firms in Beijing.*

Other than Singaporean A/E firms, the Managing Director of a quantity surveying firm in Shanghai shared:

> *Tianjin will be the port and side-kick for Beijing, to form a greater Beijing-Tianjin cosmopolitan city. These cities will grow into different roles.*

10.5.3 Time-Lags and Differences

Most interviewees shared that they have to manage time-differences and time-lags in communications when they work with colleagues, clients and other work partners located in another country or city. Time-differences and time-lags in communications are likely to cause problems in communications, coordination and cooperation. This finding is consistent with Lojeski and Reilly's (2007) concept of Virtual Distance, which suggests that assignments involving team members located in different locations can be affected by time-differences and time-lags.

An architect from Firm B shared his views on how dissimilar work-days and local-times in different cities can create inconveniences to firms:

> *Time-differences between offices, cause a not-so-ideal situation whereby firms try to adjust or cramp everything into their common days and common hours.*

A Vice-President of Firm C in Beijing shared his view on real-time communication:

> *Undoubtedly, competitiveness drops when coordination of our work is not real-time.*

An associate of Firm D in Kuala Lumpur shared:

> *Distance may create friction in communication – email replies could be slow or have time-lags. This can prove problem-some when clients expect quick responses, and there must be agreement and understanding (for example, bottom-line considerations) between head-office and satellite-office's communication.*

An architect of Firm D in Beijing shared:

> *There could be no real-time input, thus not knowing and understanding the work done in the other office. People may also put off communication until the last minute, or when really necessary, thus causing miscommunications, and resulting to wastages of resources. Other than that, emails and telephones would be sufficient to communicate between offices.*

A senior project manager of Firm E who often commutes to Firm's E project office in Abu Dhabi shared:

> *There could be inconveniences due to time-zone differences.*

An account manager of Firm E in Shanghai shared:

> *We, at Shanghai, may have to report to our regional headquarters in Suzhou. They will have to contemplate before they report to our Singapore's headquarters. They will again have to contemplate. Then, they may ask for refinements in our proposals. All the dilly-dallying at the different stages of reporting and approvals may make us miss the boat to catch the opportunities.*

10.5.4 Psychic Distance

The interviewees shared that transnational firms have to understand their foreign markets in order to devise appropriate business strategies and organization designs. They also highlighted the importance of knowing what to do in some contexts.

This is because different countries or cities have different social norms. Therefore, firms would have to manage these asymmetries, in terms of how people think, behave and act differently. Transnational firms may be put off by their lack of psychic understanding or uncertainties of the foreign markets. This finding is consistent with Cyert and March (1963) suggestion that firms have limited knowledge of the environment around them, and bounded rationality of the optimal decisions in different situations.

Psychic distance measures the level of understanding of a market. An associate and a senior architect of Firm A shared:

> *We need to understand social, climate conditions and so on. One would have to meet the needs of the people and thus, context is very important to see if the building fits into the criterion.*

A senior Vice-President of Firm C in Shanghai shared:

> *There are slight differences among countries and places and you will need people in that locality to know these differences so you definitely need local people to tell you.*

10.5.5 Communications

The interviewees were divided whether distance impairs communications within the organization and with external parties. This finding is in agreement with the Paradox of Globalization and Localization. A possible reason for this observation is that globalization and the advances of information and communications technology have made virtual collocation possible, but there remain some aspects of A/E consultancy services that require physical presence or proximity.

Communications is the life-blood of all organizations. An assistant architect of Firm A shared:

> *Usually we communicate through emails and recently, our clients set up the web-base exchange services which are used to upload designs. The main problem if there is any, is that of our USA counterpart but it is not a big problem as you will still be able to find a common time for example, for us it will be 10 a.m.*

A Director of Firm A in Penang shared:

> *The communication system with our colleagues has been problem-free. We use telephones, sms or call cell-phones, emails, facsimile et cetera to communicate and solve the issue of distance so there are so many ways. If it is hard to explain over the phone, we will sketch it out and fax. You sometimes have to be creative to communicate.*

A General Manager of Firm D in HCM City shared:

> *(Communication is affected) Not so much of physical distance but more of by the lack of broadband. Physical distance is no problem if you have good network. They have Starbucks but the internet connection there is still very slow. It could be the building itself. Our office has slow broadband. Our office has a lot of problems with the internet. It could be that they did not do the connection properly. Down there, once it rains, the internet is gone so we communicate by telephone and so on.*

A senior associate for Firm D in Shanghai noted:

> There could be lags in communications. There could be communication problems. Others may misinterpret my emails, or I may find other people's emails unintelligible. You have to make sure the email is written properly and lucid.

An accountant for Firm D in Beijing commented on communications within the firm and with Firm D's home-office:

> I am not quite used to the Singaporean English. When I talked to them (home-office in Singapore), I was unable to converse well with them and I feel that the English is not perfect so I could not understand perfectly. It sounds like it has a mix with Malay language.

> Basically, there also may be some communication misunderstandings and interpretations as both counterparts may not fully understand the context of the conversation.

A Vice-President of Firm E shared:

> There is time-space compression as we can use emails to communicate with one another.

However, his colleague, a senior project manager, thought:

> Information may be distorted or misunderstood when people have to rely on emails.

A Vice-President of Firm F in-charge of Tianjin commented:

> There are bound to be teething problems. But on the whole, communication with the Chinese is still quite okay. We Singaporeans are bilingual, so after a while, we are able to get accustomed to the Chinese way of doing things or the way they communicate. It is a learning curve.

A senior engineer of Firm F in Singapore shared:

> If you are referring to communication, I don't think that it is a problem due to modern technologies such as email. All of these can shorten the distance. It is quite easy to exchange ideas and info between the HQ and overseas branches.

Other than Singaporean A/E firms, the Managing Director of a quantity surveying firm in Shanghai noted:

> I will not say that there are no problems. Of course, as I mentioned we can talk on the phone. We also do VC (Video-conferencing) and we travel but it is always not as perfect as when you talk face to face. It takes away a certain degree of efficiency. We can always email each other especially for designs and we talk on email, phone, VC but it is not as good as face to face so that is why we go over to HQ and vice versa. That will waste time and compromise on efficiency but it is a challenge that we have to face and minimize the problem with measures taken.

> Learning English is important for locals, for convenience of communications. This is very important for employees in international firms.

> We have exchange, we do have annual meeting and ops managers meet to exchange information. Of course, we have daily communications.

> I believe that if given a chance to talk for half a day, when we go back to communicating with each other via email, the feeling will be a lot better. We try to help each other out more and work more efficiently.

10.5.6 Networks

Most interviewees agreed that networks and relationships are important when an internationalizing firm seek to enter a foreign market. This is consistent with the

Network Theory, which suggests that firms can leverage on the strengths of its networks (Johanson and Mattson 1988). Networks can be local, regional, national, international and global. Localized networks appear to be more stable than international strategic alliances. To have a good localized network, Bergman ad Feser (1999) advocated that there must be tacit knowledge and trust between partners in a network, and physical encounters and thus spatial proximity plays a major role in enhancing these features.

A senior technical manager of Firm B shared:

Networking is very important. I do network with other companies in Beijing but it takes a longer time than if you are introduced via referrals. First, they don't know you and second, after a long courtship, they may only first give small jobs before they entrust you with a bigger project so this takes a long time.

A Project Director of Firm C in Tianjin commented:

The business development personnel in China should be good at networking and building social relationships.

An associate of Firm D in Shanghai noted:

It is not only important to have good designs, it is also important to have good networks.

Other than Singaporean A/E firms, the Managing Director of a quantity surveying firm in Shanghai noted:

Networks are important. You need to know people who can make things work for you or get you referrals. You may need government officials. You need to maintain these contacts.

10.5.7 Cost-Value

Transnational A/E firms consider the costs and value implications when they internationalize into markets abroad. These firms seek to create additional value or generate extra revenues to cover the costs of internationalization. This finding is consistent with the Transaction-Costs Theory (Coase 1937), which suggests that firms consider costs and value implications when they have to choose between expanding their operations by growing internally or organizing their internationalization through external intermediaries.

An associate of Firm A suggested that having an office in the overseas markets has its advantages:

It is always better to meet someone face-to-face as internet still causes some misunderstandings and miscommunications sometimes. Furthermore, design is subjective so it is always good to get direct and clear feedback to know which part of the design that ought to be changed.

However, there are also concerns about the extra costs incurred when setting up an office abroad. A Vice-President of Firm C in Beijing shared on why Firm C withdrew from Guangzhou and Chongqing, and is cutting back on Beijing because of costs:

The cost of the branch offices may not be covered by the revenues sometimes. The reason why it shrunk was due to the fact that expenditures exceed revenues. We have contradicting views on whether to expand our operations here. The home-office is overly concerned about costs, whereas we see more benefits and revenue-making opportunities. They prefer to look at 2nd or 3rd tiered cities like Xi'an. I beg to differ.

An architect of Firm D in Beijing shared his views on how distance may affect costs-benefits:

For example, you have 50 million in the project and you invested 20 million. The question is whether you will be able to get back 30 million in 20 years. Will you throw your money in? Yes, if you can control well. However, if you cannot, it may not be viable.

In my opinion, the profit margins and revenues are less when you invest in distance far away because you still have to invest in some technologies and so on.

A Vice-President of Firm E when asked whether distance would affect any dimension of the firm's internationalization:

It affects costs and productivity.

A senior manager of Firm E in Shanghai shared:

The expenses will be like lodgings, travel costs, air-tickets, insurances and visas, annual leave and salary. There isn't any per diem allowances.

When asked what would be the tilting factor for the firm to decide to set up an office abroad, a Vice-President from Firm F opined:

It depends on whether revenue exceeds costs.

An architect from an A/E firm in Singapore, not among Firms A to F, shared on how tender-prices were made-up:

We calculate director, associates and professional hours required for the project, plus external consultants' fees and costs to make models. For overseas trips which include flight-tickets, accommodations and daily allowances, either the clients would pay for them, or the company would have already included them in the costs structure.

Other than Singaporean A/E firms, the Managing Director of a quantity surveying firm in Shanghai noted how distance affects costs-benefits:

It takes away some work efficiency. Sometimes, we may have to travel and commute to meet up face-to-face.

Rental of office space, employment, expatriate terms and remuneration and office-infrastructure like computers and servers for work and communications. It used to be that faxes and IDD calls were so expensive that we had to pay about fifty thousand RMB for them every month. Now, we can simply use emails and video-conferencing via the internet.

10.5.8 Control

It was observed that the level of autonomy or control a head-quarter reins over its overseas office depends on a myriad of factors, such as the firm's characteristics and availability of resources, the firm's objectives, costs of exporting consultancy services to the foreign city et cetera. These findings can be explained with the Resource-based Theory (Penrose 1959), Behavioral Theory (Aharoni 1966) and

Transaction-costs Theory (Coase 1937) respectively. These theories suggest that a transnational firm seeks to protect its critical and core competences, acts according to its objectives and motivations, and tends to expand its operations by growing internally until the point that the cost of internalization gets to be the same as a transaction in the open market.

A Director of Firm D in Kuala Lumpur noted:

> *If there is a big project, we definitely have to go back to the HQ to communicate with the HQ though.*

An associate of Firm D in Shanghai commented:

> *Control is important for the office here to move in line with the plans decided by the headquarters. However, staff here may not get as much job satisfaction. Turnover of staff may thus increase.*

Other than Singaporean A/E firms, a marketing manager of a developer in HCM City shared:

> *People here are not conscious with time; they are very relaxed and would cause delays to project time-lines. We put time buffers, and give step-by-step instructions in A-B-C instead of A-C method, so make sure tasks can be completed on time, and done correctly. In a way, we need to micro-manage them. You must learn to do more things on-the-ground and on-the-go. Vietnamese cannot keep secrets, so we do not share trade-secrets with them.*

10.6 Eclectic Diamond Framework

The Eclectic Diamond Framework merges the strengths of the Eclectic Paradigm (Dunning 1988) and the Diamond Theory (Porter 1990) to encompass ownership, locational and internalization qualities from the Eclectic Paradigm; and factor conditions, demand, related and complementary industries, strategies due to competition, government interferences and chances from the Diamond Theory.

By merging Dunning's (1988) Eclectic Paradigm and Porter's (1990) Diamond Theory, the Eclectic Diamond Framework provides a supra-national and testable model to assess a firm's competitiveness in international markets. The Eclectic Diamond Framework helps to analyze the firm's competitiveness in international or regional markets in terms of the firm's factor conditions, demand conditions, complementary and supporting industries, strategy due to competition, government intervention, chance, ownership qualities, locational qualities and internalization. The framework condenses these factors to evaluate a business venture's exposure to uncertainties, risks and business opportunities so that the firm is able to come out with an appropriate risk management plan and set of business strategies and organization design to internalize these uncertainties, risks and business opportunities. It is also posited that when Singapore's A/E firms venture overseas, they acquire the strengths from the Eclectic Diamond Framework of conditions of other cities, which is the hall-mark of transnational firms.

10.6.1 Factor Conditions

Factor conditions can generally refer to the natural or man-made endowments of a location, such as the availability of locally-available materials, high-quality transportation and communication infrastructure, well educated and trained human resources et cetera. Generally, a more favorable factor condition allows the firm to operate with more ease and convenience, and is desirable to the firm. However, some constraints can stimulate specialization to confront the limitation, and in the process, form a critical competitive advantage for the firm. An example would be how Japanese firms turn to technology to assuage the problem of expensive manpower in their own country (Porter 1990).

Push and pull factors of markets can also be regarded amongst factor conditions. A push factor could be (i) assistance from the home-government to help firms to venture abroad; and (ii) shortage of home-market demand, which forces firms to seek markets overseas. A pull factor could be (i) need of a product or service due to a booming market and (ii) need of product or service to technology and knowledge-transfer.

A senior architect of Firm A in Shanghai shared on how firms are "pulled" into locations with more favorable conditions.

> *We wanted to locate in Shanghai because of the accessibility to supporting industries as well. In addition, the environment here is easier for Singaporeans to adapt.*

An associate from Firm D in Shanghai shared the characteristics of Singapore's A/E and developer firms:

> *Singapore's specialty is modern and more clean-cut designs.*

> *They (Singapore's developers) are good investors. They are very commercial and business-driven. They may not commission iconic or landmark projects but they always manage to maximize their returns from their buildings.*

Other than Singaporean A/E firms, a Principal quantity surveyor of Firm E shared why Firm E has been "pushing out":

> *Singapore is already very developed, to the point that it has limited opportunities.*

10.6.2 Demand Conditions

Porter (1990) thought that three attributes of the home demand are significant: the composition of home demand, the size and pattern of growth of home demand, and the mechanisms by which a nation's domestic preferences are transmitted to foreign markets. Porter (1990) suggested that the quality of the home demand shapes how firms perceive, interpret, and respond to buyers' needs, and how they devise strategies as well as innovate to beat the competition. A demanding home market is also useful to an internationalizing firm if it anticipates global or regional demand. Last but not least, home demand conditions may also include client-following or foreign-sales conditions – for example, a Singapore's developer is likely to invite a Singaporean A/E partner for an overseas project. Singapore's domestic demand for

10.6 Eclectic Diamond Framework

Fig. 10.8 Positive feed-back loop of internationalization

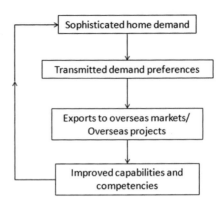

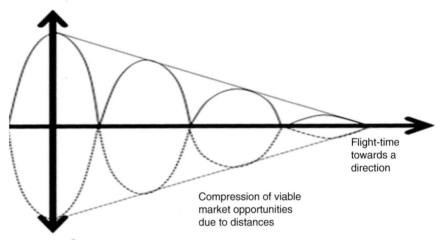

Fig. 10.9 The spatial model

A/E services is considerably and comparably sophisticated, and its domestic preferences are often transmitted to regional markets in South-east Asia, China, India and the Middle-east. Therefore, Singapore's A/E firms and their services are very welcomed in these markets. When Singapore's firms venture overseas, a positive feed-back loop of internationalization (refer to Fig. 10.8) is formed – Singapore's A/E firms acquire more experiences, knowledge and expertise, and these improved capabilities and competences will enable them to attract even more foreign clients and ever-more sophisticated projects.

A Director of Firm A shared on how A/E firms have to keep abreast of developments and trends in building designs:

> For the past one-and-a-half years, the trend has been towards sustainable and green designs. The signatories of the Sao Paolo and Kyoto Initiatives and Protocols will make

green buildings the trend. There has been much research on green buildings by Japanese and American firms. Firm A must also take the lead and embrace the idea of going green and doing green.

A Vice-President of Firm C in Beijing shared on why Firm C withdrew from a few Chinese cities:

I think it mainly boils down to the market demand. At that time, there was insufficient demand.

A senior Vice-President of Firm C in Shanghai shared on how despite the tendency for local clients to go for low-cost services, there are always some clients who are willing to pay more for premium services:

The locals are the one who are taking the lion share. They provide the service, just that there is always this up-market.

10.6.3 Related and Complementary Industries

Firms today operate in an open system (Sanchez 2003). Spillages from complementary or related industries provide forward and backward linkages that can benefit firms, and firms often leverage on the strengths of their partners to enhance themselves. These advantages could be in the form of preferential access to cost-effective inputs, efficiency of supply-chain, collaboration to innovate and upgrade, or the creation of new opportunities et cetera (Porter 1990).

A good example would be how Toyota and its network of suppliers and subcontractors put into practice Just-in-time (JIT) techniques and Supply-chain management (SCM) concepts to reduce inefficiencies and wastages, and save time, costs and effort. Johanson and Mattson (1988) and Björkman and Forsgren (2000) argued that when a firm ventures overseas, it would have to consider whether to search for and establish new local networks in the host environment, or alternatively, rely on its home-network by international extension, penetration and connecting existing networks.

Majkgard and Sharma (1998) also found that service firms often use client-following strategies to internationalize. Networks are probably more important in Asia than in other parts of the world. Akin to how physical distance between collaborators affects the efficiency of Just-in-time (JIT) techniques (e.g. co-manufacturing of automobiles and their parts by car manufacturer Toyota and its suppliers), distance affects a firm's networks, the fluidity and efficiency of its work processes, and how a firm can leverage on its partners' resources and strengths. Hence, Singapore's A/E firms would do well to collaborate with local or even regional clients or partners from related and complementary industries, as well as co-opetitors (cooperation and competition) to venture into markets in the region.

10.6 Eclectic Diamond Framework

An associate of Firm A in Kuala Lumpur shared on how complementary or supporting industries affect a firm's work:

> Engineers are not challenged enough in KL. The quantum of fees is low because of cutthroat competition, costs of living is high and staff costs is high. These compromises engineering consultancy's quality. This channels expectations on architects to coordinate with the engineers to make sure the goods are delivered.

A senior associate of Firm C in HCM City shared:

> If there are any dispute, Vietnamese will supercede English laws so it is good to have own legal help.

A Vice-President of Firm C in Beijing shared on how local complementary and supporting industries are important to an internationalizing firm.

> Singaporean developers who may not be very familiar with the host environment and conditions here may also prefer local consultants so that the local consultants can complement them with local advice – "Yi Chang Bu Duan (以长补短)[3]". Hong Kong Firms like to engage us for our trustworthiness and because of our business development with them.

An associate of Firm D in Shanghai shared:

> Foreign firms work with local design institutes (LDIs). Experience is also helpful. The engineers here are more passive and risk adverse. Sometimes you may wonder why in America, certain designs can work but not in China. It is not that in China, they don't have the capabilities. The regulations are not flexible enough.

> International contractors are expensive and would not be able to compete here. In my impression, there are no overseas contractors. Thus, there are less technology and knowledge spillovers. Shanghai is using twenty years to complete a hundred years of development. Projects were rushed. Detailing in designs and construction are compromised. When you look up-close, you would realize the faults and imperfections. Engineers here are more reactive than proactive. They like to "ding-dong" with you. They (Singapore's developers) are good investors. They are very commercial and business-driven. They may not commission iconic or landmark projects but they always manage to maximize their returns from their buildings.

Other than Singaporean A/E firms, the Managing Director of a quantity surveying firm in Shanghai shared:

> We make connections with universities. We may sponsor their events. Then, we give talks in these universities to promote our firm.

> The quantity surveying consultant will need to understand the designs to make good measurements. He/she may have to interact with the clients, architects and engineers. A quantity surveyor has to piece things together despite the gaps in information.

Other than Singaporean A/E firms, a marketing manager of a developer in HCM City shared on why her firm likes to collaborate with some Singapore's engineering and contractor firms:

> We like to work with an engineering firm from Singapore. That particular firm has offices in Singapore and HCM. We have a good understanding between us that makes it easier for us to work together.

> Singaporean contractors are flexible in terms of payment, open to suggestions, and willing to have constructive meetings.

---

[3] Using a strength to compensate for a weakness.

10.6.4 Strategies Due to Competition

Strategic assets are the source of advantage, and the strategy of a firm would contain a statement of the firm's strategic assets, the markets the firm intends to operate in, the assets required to compete in these markets, and how these assets are to be developed or acquired (Bowman 2003). Porter (1990) claimed that there were strong empirical findings to imply a significant association between vigorous domestic rivalry and the creation and sustenance of competitive advantages. This suggests that a firm grows to become efficient, innovative and competitive because of pressure from domestic rivals. Tallman (1992) also noted a growing phenomenon among multinational firms to make use of international markets to provide opportunities for discovering new resources or developing new organizational capabilities. The fittest survives the cut-throat competition in these overseas cities, but the safari of strong and mighty international competitors also serves to greatly elevate the capabilities and competitiveness of the firm.

Singapore, as a core location in the region, attracts many international A/E firms and houses even more local firms. These A/E firms benefit from the vibrancy of the market-place, with sophisticated demand, fierce competition and competent complementary and supporting services. Many of these Singapore A/E firms have grown to become firms offering multi-disciplinary services or niche services, and are very much sought after in the region.

The small market of Singapore has encouraged Singapore's A/E firms to venture abroad in search for larger markets. Additionally, A/E firms have good mobility and are borne global service providers. Singapore's A/E firms should succeed and excel in exporting their services or setting up branch offices abroad.

A senior technical manager of Firm B in Singapore shared how Firm B dealt with competition and co-opetition:

> *Sometimes we may come into competition with very renowned American firms when we take part in those competitions with several firms taking part in. In those competitions, we will see where our strengths are, improving ourselves. We can also reposition ourselves as we find out from clients what their needs are, tackling them, especially those that are more relevant. By and large, who wins is dependent on the quality of ideas. We also have cases where we work and go in together for competition. In the latter, it is a win-win situation as we tap into each other's expertise.*

A senior Vice-President of Firm C in Shanghai shared on why some clients prefer to engage international consultants instead of local ones even though their fees are much higher, and how Firm C strategizes due to competition from local and other foreign firms. She also highlighted how local firms in China have been improving themselves so quickly and becoming strong competitors to international consultants:

> *The locals may not have experience in certain concepts if they have not done certain designs before, not to say that Singapore knows a lot but we have been exposed to a lot of western influences so it is easier for us.*

> *Some local firms are very honest and they say they have not done before but they are very good in their submissions so the client is willing to let us team up together.*

10.6 Eclectic Diamond Framework

Foreign developers or clients prefer international brand-names like how some people may prefer Gucci and Prada. Local consultants lack exposure and experiences.

It is a threat whenever there are new comers and we believe that there may be a day the locals would be able to catch up and be as good as the foreigner

For us, it is important and also a long-term strategy for us to be localized because these local partners will improve in their services and very soon, we will reach the same level. Of course there are other architecture firms like SOM[4] but honestly we are not in direct competition because they are in upmarket market for tall buildings. There are our competitors like Zhong Jian International. They are very competitive. They even employ foreigners and export their services abroad.

The Managing Director of Firm C in HCM City shared on how Singapore's A/E firms provide relatively cheaper services to clients in Vietnam, and how this has enabled Singapore's firms to take up a bigger market-share than American and European firms:

The American and European firms are not big players because they have a different culture, and they charge expensive fees. For example, an American firm may charge ten times more than a local firm, whereas Singaporean firms may charge twice or thrice that of a local firm.

A senior associate of Firm D in Shanghai shared:

The top architectural firms are from USA, then UK, then Australia. We are somewhere in the middle, ahead of other Asian firms except Japan.

Other than Singaporean A/E firms, the Managing Director of a quantity surveying firm in Shanghai shared:

We do not compete head-to-head (with local quantity surveying firms). They work for local clients while we work for international clients.

10.6.5 Government Interference

Governments play an important role in the internationalization of firms as they are able to manipulate or influence the business and operating environments to become more conducive or difficult for in-coming and/or out-going firms. Singapore's government has been very active in dispatching delegates on trade missions to build rapport with foreign countries, and to find out more about available business opportunities overseas before disseminating the information to Singapore's firms. Singapore has also signed many valuable free-trade agreements (FTAs) with other countries. A FTA is a legally binding agreement between two or more countries to reduce or eliminate barriers to trade and facilitate cross border movement of goods and services between the territories of the signatories. Currently, Singapore has regional and bilateral FTAs with ASEAN (Brunei, Indonesia, Malaysia, Philippines, Thailand, Cambodia, Laos, Myanmar and Vietnam), ASEAN-Australia-New Zealand, ASEAN-China, ASEAN-India, ASEAN-Japan, ASEAN-Korea, Australia, China, Gulf Cooperation Council (Bahrain, Kuwait, Oman, Qatar, Saudi Arabia and the United Arab Emirates), Jordan,

---

[4] Skidmore, Owings & Merrill LLP, a world-class architectural firm based in Chicago, USA.

India, Japan, Korea, New Zealand, Panama, Peru, European Free Trade Association (Switzerland, Liechtenstein, Norway and Iceland), Trans-Pacific Strategic Economic Partnership (Brunei, New Zealand and Chile), and USA. These FTA super-highways connect Singapore to major economies and new economies, eradicate technical barriers such as double-taxation or unfair restrictions in the host countries, free up capital and human resource mobility for Singapore-based investors and firms in these markets, and allow Singapore' A/E firms to enjoy a myriad of benefits like tariff concessions, preferential access, faster entry into markets and Intellectual Property (IP) protection.

Nonetheless, Singapore's A/E firms inevitably still face veiled or oblique host markets' regulations and encumbrances that impede their internationalization efforts. For instance, in Malaysia, the Bumiputra Policy requires firms to be Bumiputra-owned if they are to submit tenders for public projects. In Vietnam, local firms and businesses are still very much entrenched in command-control and Vietnamese authorities are still cautious and wary of foreign investors even though the country has opened up to the global economy and has been inducted as a member of the WTO in 2007. In China, it is not infrequent that often changing or contradicting policies confuse foreign firms.

An associate of Firm D in Shanghai shared on how codes and regulations in China can be blur and changes frequently:

> *Definitions of codes can be blurred. This leaves gaps for interpretations. One example is the fire-code. Government authorities and officials may have the final say in such interpretations.*

A senior manager of Firm E in Shanghai shared on how government intervention can affect an overseas firm's operations in China:

> *Local people are protected by Chinese labor laws that govern employment.*
>
> *There could also be confusion or contradiction of policies from the different government authorities. The policies by central government will affect the raw materials for example oil and steel, which will in turn affect our project prices so I should say that Firm E in China have to look at excess quality risk, social risk and environment risk before we arrive at a decision and pull out an assessment before we embark onto a project.*
>
> *It is very common that the Chinese authorities of different departments don't communicate with each other, meaning that we can go to this department and tell them that we need their endorsement for this project. Different authorities may give different instructions. Sometimes, it is puzzling how things can be in the jurisdiction of different authorities, and how they expect things should be done differently. Higher levels of authorities may also overrule decisions made at the lower levels. Risk assessment can be very qualitative and subjective.*

Other than Singaporean A/E firms, a Director of a quantity surveying firm in Hanoi shared:

> *Legislation has yet to be fully developed and there will be preferences given to local companies… in the future, there will be legislation coming through and there will be changes to preferences given to local companies due to cost-efficiency.*

Other than Singaporean A/E firms, the Managing Director of a quantity surveying firm in Shanghai shared:

10.6 Eclectic Diamond Framework 241

Back then, the government intervened by instructing all local transnational firms and financial institutions to locate in Pudong. During the first few years, firms located there also enjoyed concessions and tax rebates.

10.6.6 *Chance*

Chance events are important to new market entrants because they create discontinuities that allow shifts in competitive positions (Porter 1990). Chance events help new market entrants to nullify the advantages of established competitors and even supplant them to achieve competitive advantage in response to new and different conditions. A pre-requisite for entry into an overseas market is the imperfection of the foreign market and an internationalizing firm that is capable of spear-heading through this imperfection to surmount the home-advantages conceded to the host competitors (Porter 1990).

Chances are closely associated with a firm's business networks and reputation. This is why firms join associations or partake in seminars so that they can get to network with one another to establish connections and get to be informed of business opportunities et cetera.

It is a matter of fact that Singapore's A/E firms seldom advertise. Most of their jobs come from repeat clients or referrals. This sets a limitation on chances and opportunities. On the other hand, this mode of operation has its advantages and reasons – (i) repeat or referred clients are less likely to default on payments; (ii) the industry is small, therefore advertising may not be necessary; and (iii) there are stringent regulations governing the marketing of professional services that influence the lives of others, such as doctors, architects and engineers.

A Director of Firm A in Singapore shared:

There is direct correlation between the foreign market's volume of work and whether a firm would want to set up a satellite office abroad. Before the A/E firm decides to cast its net overseas, it must consider its labor resources, brand and marketing.

A Vice-President of Firm C in Shanghai shared:

A firm need not have a sizeable organization to correspond with a sizeable market. It all depends on "possibilities" and "willingness". A bird in hand is better than three birds in the bush.

If you are big, you may consider more on whether to set up an office there but if you are handling a small project, there are fewer considerations and you may go where-ever. You may enter into a city because of the client relationship and the request that a client made. The client may ask you to go into a city and do up a project there for him. Under that circumstance, you can simply go anywhere requested.

An architectural assistant of Firm D in Singapore shared:

Every firm and every market is different. Internationalization strategy and entry mode would have to suit the characteristics of the firm and market.

Other than Singaporean A/E firms, a Director of a quantity surveying firm in Hanoi shared:

If the opportunity arises, we may consider moving into 2nd-tier cities, say in maybe 5 years.

10.6.7 Ownership Qualities

Singapore is a brand-name in the region that stands for reliability, efficiency and value-for-money. This is why many A/E firms from the country proudly market themselves as Singapore's A/E firms, to make good use of the nation's fine reputation. Many of Singapore's exporters of A/E consultancy services have been very successful in Singapore – they are likely to have contributed significantly to the country's accelerated development and beautiful skyline from its nascence. These experiences have placed these Singapore's A/E firms in an enviable position to market and sell their consultancy services to emerging markets in the region.

Organizational heritage is like the DNA of the organization. Overseas offices are like off-springs or descendants of the home-office. Overseas offices carry forward the genes of their home-offices, and the characteristics of the home-offices are reflected in the overseas offices' business policies, strategies and organization design et cetera. The level of similarity between the home-office and the overseas office is dependent on the firm's embeddedness and the firm's inclination to institutional, coercive and mimetic isomorphism. Some firms are more naturally embedded in their home-markets, while others may be born global. The behavior of a firm may take after common practices in the industry, or by previous decisions and experiences. Take a firm's entry strategy for example – a firm that is heavily embedded in its home-market is less likely to want to venture overseas via an entry mode that requires more commitment and home-based resources from the firm. Conversely, a firm which is less embedded and is more freely disposed to internationalization.

A senior architect of Firm A in Shanghai opined that Singapore's A/E firms often exhibit a limitation when they venture overseas:

> *In Singapore, it is famous for regulation. When you graduate, you have to learn how to supply services that fit into the regulations, as well as create regulations for office. Thus, a lot of times you will see architects who want to learn how to regulate. We have no choice but to familiarize ourselves with regulations such as fire hazards, so much so that our knowledge of such regulations is excellent, compromising on our time to gain technical knowledge. However, such regulation knowledge is not relevant when you go overseas.*

The Managing Director of Firm C in HCM City shared:

> *Vietnam sees Singapore as a role model, especially in terms of infrastructure and planning. It also depends on who are our clients and their preferences. Singaporeans offer the best value-for-money.*

A General Manager of Firm D in HCM City shared:

> *Singapore designs are more rational and they are overly concerned on the numbers. The foreign counterparts are more into philosophy and that is how we are all brought up – how much we get paid, how much are we maximizing and efficiency and so on. The foreign designs are more narrative in nature. I would say that if they are 5, we are 3 so we are still not close.*

An associate of Firm D in Shanghai, who has worked in Singapore before shared:

Singapore's regulations are very detailed and it is either a yes or no.

In Singapore or in other Southeast-Asia regions, I feel that the buildings are not of exceptional special nature that you will take note which firm did which buildings. However, they are very neatly done, just that they are not particularly outstanding. This sometimes has something to do with Singapore's culture. The designs are not bad but it is not the best. Singapore's developers have the problem. It is not that it cannot do 100 %. It is just that it seeks for a balance with the cost.

Singapore does not have a distinct and colorful culture. This may explain why they may not have a distinct design style in general. However, there are several firms that specialize in resort-theme designs. Some firms have its own in-house design team that produces artwork-like designs. Some firms from Singapore have also won numerous international design awards.

An architect of Firm D in Beijing shared:

We are ethnocentric in terms of work culture management because we want to retain Firm D (Singapore)'s consistency in quality and work ethics.

A senior manager of Firm E in Shanghai shared:

We have used Singapore standard and they are very satisfied with Singapore standard.

A business development manager of Firm F in Kuala Lumpur shared:

Asian clients do not like rigid business partners because they do not want to get litigation when things go wrong. Singaporean firms understand local culture well. In fact, Singapore and Malaysia are quite alike, only that Singapore is more advanced.

Other than Singaporean A/E firms, the Managing Director of a quantity surveying firm in Shanghai shared:

Firms from the USA and United Kingdom are flatter (in terms of organization structures). Hong Kong firms have more tiers. This could be because Asians are more status-oriented.

10.6.8 Locational Factors

Location advantages include host country's location advantages such as the size of market, cost of doing business, social-political and geographical factors; as well as home and host-country induced advantages such as geographical proximity between home and host countries, similarity of language, relational affinity and real wage differentials et cetera.

Locational factors of a city are geographically determined. For example, studies have shown that (i) soil is more fertile in temperate regions than equatorial areas; (ii) economies are more developed in the northern hemisphere; and (iii) GDP per capita increases as one move from the equator towards the north or south-poles et cetera. Tobler's (1970) first law of geography states that everything is related to everything else, but near things are more related than distant things. It is apparent that geographical distance has an intricate relationship with locational factors of a place.

The spatial interaction between two locations is also dependent on the gravitational distance between the two places. Therefore, Singapore's A/E firms are more likely to venture into markets which are less gravitationally distant away from Singapore.

Not only that, Niels and Harzing (2003) also found that intra company flows and control mechanisms applied by the headquarters or home-office reflect the geographical isolation of offices that are located far-away from other offices (e.g. offices in Australia and New Zealand are far away from offices in USA, Europe and Asia) and that the role of the subsidiary depends on the resource profile, local embeddedness, strategic considerations and geographical distance. Therefore, Ojala and Tyrvainen (2006) suggested that *ceteris paribus*, firms enter into markets which are geographically nearer.

A Project Director of Firm C in Tianjin opined how firms choose to locate their first offices or regional HQs in China:

> *The first city to enter should be Shanghai which is a global hub. That should be where the headquarters is.*

An associate of Firm D in Shanghai shared:

> *I personally feel that countries like Singapore, Japan and other countries, are aware of their landmark so when they design a building, they take care that it is special and at the same time, not spoil the feeling of the entire country.*

Other than Singaporean A/E firms, the Managing Director of a quantity surveying firm in Shanghai shared:

> *Different locations require different considerations. The quality of staff we can get in these cities may be a problem.*

10.6.9 Internalization

Globalization and technologies have changed how A/E firms work today. Through globalization, tastes of building designs have been assimilated. Improvements in information, communication and transportation technologies have also enabled firms to internationalize into markets which are geographically far-away, and yet stay well-connected to the home-office.

Firms internalize factor conditions, demand conditions, complementary and supporting industries, government intervention, chances, ownership qualities and locational qualities so that (i) resources are put to their best uses; (ii) opportunities are fully exploited; and (iii) limitations are circumvented. This suggestion is consistent with Lewin's (1951) and Aaker and Mascarenhas (1984) suggestion that firms act according to its environment or external forces by adapting themselves or adopting new strategies.

10.6 Eclectic Diamond Framework

On the functional front, an A/E firm's work requirements and performance needs, such as submitting construction drawings differ from those of sending inventory reports. The frequency of the former is less but the potential damage caused by an erroneous message is larger. Therefore, problem-free contact time is more important than immediate availability for an A/E firm. At corporate and business levels, the role of the parent company, web of or home-host offices' relationships, and the internalization and compatibility between the different levels and types of strategies are crucially vital for synergy of value-creation.

An architect from Firm B in Singapore shared:

In terms of technology, we used to have manual presentation. Now, we have Computer-aided designs (CAD) software to enhance our design works. This has been very useful for nice presentations and our final pitches.

We have benefitted IT-wise, from LCD screens, AUTOCAD, 3D Max for perspectives, Sketch Up for modeling, 3D make-up and Photoshop, and emails and teleconferencing.

An architect of Firm B in Singapore shared:

It is fulfilling when you can get recognition, but it is very bad when things go wrong, and you need to do reworks and reworks. You have a few jobs on hand every-time, so you are always kept busy. You will handle a wide variety of tasks. It is upsetting when you have to compromise on the quality of your work because you are over-stretched.

Our directors, associates and some senior architects are given Blackberry hand-phones so that we can remain contactable at all times, via emails, phone calls and video calls.

The Chairman of Firm D lamented about how Firm D missed out some good opportunities in overseas markets:

We were 10 years behind time but we began to realize then that China is a big market so one of our clients helped us out and gave us a job there. From the 1980s to mid 1990s, we used Hong Kong as a platform to get into China. After China relaxed its regulations and opened up to foreign investors, we decided to move our Hong Kong office straight to China. However, we did not make a grand entry into China, thus missing out the great opportunities there during its earlier boom, because we were swamped with projects in Singapore. It was the same with India – we missed out some good opportunities there too.

A Director of Firm D in Kuala Lumpur shared:

If you want to go for government-related or nation-building project, it is obviously an advantage if you have a Bumiputra director. However, in practice there are a lot of ways to circumvent this problem as people have actually partnered other companies. They could get a Bumiputra firm to do the submission for them.

A Vice-President of Firm F in Singapore shared:

Our work in Firm F, when we go overseas, is not to set up an office from day one or with just one or two jobs on hand. We set up overseas office only when we have enough jobs to be independent abroad, for our local office to be able to run on its own. In between, the time period to the set-up is the time when we plant business seeds in those overseas markets to look out for business opportunities as critical mass of jobs is important. These business development seeds are remotely controlled from distance. Firm F is a conservative company – we will want to make sure that the foreign office is capable of being independent, able to function properly by itself, and will not incur any losses.

Other than Singaporean A/E firms, a Director of an American A/E firm in Shanghai shared:

> It is an adaptation problem. The things that matter are: who you put here, how you get the talents, and the services the firm offers.

Other than Singaporean A/E firms, the Managing Director of a quantity surveying firm in Shanghai shared:

> We have a Standard Practice Manual. Communication can also be done via emails and video-conferences. Managers in the different office also have to attend annual meetings. Annual meetings are important because they enable the managers to get the bigger picture of what is going on around them.

10.7 The 8S Framework

The 8S Framework diagnoses the firm in terms of its strategy, structure, systems, leadership style, skills, staff, shared values and supply-chain, and recommends that there should be a strategic fit between these strategic and organizational elements so that a firm is efficient and effective. This study recommended a 8th "S" – supply-chain, to be added to the existing McKinsey 7S Strategic Toolkit because of the increasing importance of upstream and downstream partners and their activities to a firm.

Firms have to regularly review their business strategies and organization design so that the passages of time and the complex forces acting around the firm are not ignored. The Evolutionary Theory of Firms (Coase 1937) suggests that a firm grows organically and it is important for the firm to be stay flexible, be able to readjust itself strategically, structurally and systematically, and to realign its strategy, structure, system, leadership style, skills, staff, shared values and supply-chain to reduce inefficiency and loss of effectiveness through friction due to incompatibilities in these strategic and organizational parameters.

The 8S framework takes into account the macro, micro and task environment of the firm, to the on one hand, formulate business strategies and organization design to circumvent the firm's weaknesses, market limitations and other difficulties; and on the other hand, to accentuate the firm's strengths, and to maximize and tap into business opportunities.

10.7.1 Business Strategies

Planning strategies and implementing them are not always so straight-forward. For instance, the International Entrepreneurship Model (Perlmutter 1969) highlights the role of the entrepreneur or the management team for the firm's internationalization decisions. Another example in point is the Behavioral Theory (Aharoni 1966), which suggests that managerial decisions are not always fully rational, and that firms do not always seek to maximize their profits.

Lawrence and Lorsch (1967) suggested that different parts of the organization may be facing different types of environment. In this case, the firm would do best to subscribe to Ashby (1958)'s notion of "only variety can destroy variety". However, satisficing and bounded rationality suggests that the management team members do not always have full knowledge, and are only able to act within their best knowledge (Katona 1951; Baumol and Quandt 1964). Furthermore, firms would have to complement corporate-level, business-unit level and functional level business strategies and organization design. In this section, interviewees share their firms' entry strategies and some other strategies.

10.7.1.1 Entry Strategy

The interviewees agreed that the entry strategy is crucial to an internationalizing A/E firm. Firat and Huovinen's (2005) noted that "In the context of construction markets, a contractor, a supplier or a designer, as an entrant, must face and penetrate an extremely 'hard' wall surrounding the targeted competitive arena consisting of local clients, architects, contractors, and other stakeholders that are glued together with local contracting rules, building regulations, traditions, and practices (p. 58)'. They therefore proposed that a "spearheading strategy" is required.

A senior technical manager of Firm B shared:

> We will first look at the potential of growth. That is our first criteria. After which, we will prefer somewhere where we have a local presence. It makes things easier when we go overseas. We will get clients whom are attracted to how we are like and we will also look at what we are strong at. We will then repackage our strengths to target certain market... We will build up our base and bring in an expert whom very often than not, will go with us when we are overseas initially doing marketing. The expert will then assess the clients' needs and see ways in which we can solve that if we do not have the strengths needed.

> We will fly there, especially when we are not familiar with the country, so that we can feel the site. Very often, we will want to go to the most happening area to look at what is their best project over there to be used as a benchmark. Many a times, we start through social connections. The local context and the developers available are very important. We also get referents from consultants and our present clients so that is more effective.

A senior associate of Firm C in HCM City shared:

> Firstly, you consider who the clients are, secondly what is the opportunity cost and thirdly how long do you have to travel there, what is the frequency of travel, the cost and how do you scout for opportunities. Judging from my experience, when you set up a company overseas, you cannot simply go over there and impose your own country's style. You have to do some adjustments to suit the local climate. If you go over there to impose the Singapore routine, you may not get local staff to work for you unless you pay them so well that you can tell them "look we are foreign companies and you work for us.

> When we extend an arm to China and India and even to Vietnam, we position ourselves to be in a more Asia Pacific position.

> It is marketing seeking more than brand building. In any case, brand building does not come straight away. You have to build slowly, even in developing countries.

A business development manager of Firm C in HCM City shared:

Three years ago, we set up a business development team which comprises of 2 or 3 locals. They help us to spearhead the company, to get exposure, and to network with associations and possible clients. We offer a suite of service, at competitive prices. We are good at integrating all these services too.

A senior Vice-President of Firm C in Shanghai shared:

We started by marketing ourselves as a Singaporean brand that is trust-worthy and reliable. We also demonstrated our impressive track records. We even put up both Singapore's and China's flags at our office's entrance to tell people that we are a "glocal" company. In the long-term, we decided to localize ourselves and to get a license to be almost on par as a foreign service provider.

A General Manager of Firm D in Vietnam shared:

Ours is to really build up a name so the competition is very important to us. We want to complete the building project reference and want to demand for a higher fee but this strategy is diluted for the project earlier mentioned as the building is not completed.

A senior associate of Firm D in Shanghai shared on why Firm D decided to set up an office in Shanghai:

We were set up because of the project. The client requested that there will be someone here. Our then current model of drawing up projects and then flying to and fro was found to be too slow by our clients. They need an instant reaction and they needed us to be on-site. It was not because of size of that project. We did bigger projects without having to do that. It was just that for this project, we are supposed to be involved during the construction stage which is going to be difficult if you are only based in Singapore. I am sure that at the back of bosses' minds, they were also thinking that it would be easier to meet the clients.

Shenzhen was the first (of our offices in China) because we had projects at the South of China. Beijing we had a point but it was not a full-fledged office and Shanghai came, becoming the HQ with Beijing and Shenzhen becoming the branch office.

A senior project manager of Firm E shared on the factors that may influence a firm's decision to set up an overseas office, and how a firm usually evolves in a foreign market:

The commercial prospects of the city must be so attractive so that it is viable for us to set up a fuller office. Other factors of consideration are: set-up costs, security of the location in the longer run, whether it is sufficient for us to commute in and out of the location instead of having to commit a full office there, and whether it is necessary for us to do so to be able to build an effective network useful for us in the market.

First, there is an export opportunity, then the firm may need a project office, then possibly a joint venture as a way to maneuver around foreign-local equity regulations, and finally wholly-owned company. Firm E has a mixture of these different modes in different cities.

The General Director of Firm F in charge of Vietnam shared on how Firm F may decide to venture abroad:

They are three mainly: 1) business contacts by clients so clients who want to do projects overseas and have contacts, we will help them to go overseas and launch the projects; 2) local markets such as conducting a market research there or going down to investigate the site; 3) purposely set up an office there for presence and marketing purpose. It was then we assess the profitability of it. The third mode is very expensive so we decided to only set up an office if we have a project.

10.7 The 8S Framework

She then shared on the costs that a firm would have to incur to set up an overseas office:

> The cost of these entry modes depends on the main component of the cost which is rental and manpower. After which, the miscellaneous cost comes in. For example, in Vietnam, it takes about S$50,000, for a set-up. However, it is much higher if it is in Saudi Arabia which may take a potential S$80,000. Of course, if you are talking about China, it is cheaper. Thus, it is really dependent on the market. It is the cheapest without having an office there and you can still get projects as you fly in and out.

A Vice-President of Firm F in charge of China shared:

> I am basically in charge of marketing and business development for the whole of China. Right now, we have offices in Shanghai, Wuxi, Wuhan, Chengdu, Xi'an, Tianjin and Shenyang. We also have a representative office in Nanjing. By representative office, I mean we only have one to two staff there, in a Small-Office or Home-Office (SOHO), to do marketing and business development to get connections and get to know opportunities around; by offices, I mean offices that offer a full suite of services such as administration, technical work and business development.

Other than Singaporean A/E firms, the General Director of a quantity surveying firm in HCM City shared:

> First of all, you need to send in a license application which needs to be approved by the Ministry of Construction who is in-charge of construction in the whole of Ho Chi Minh City. What you need to write is around 3–5 years of account and you need to write a corporate CV. The foreign firm faces a barrier of entry – they must demonstrate that they have a proven track record. No Tom, Dick and Harry can just set up a project management or architecture firm. I am aware that it is the official time to get registered is around 45 days. When you are an architect engineer, you have to undergo the same procedure. There are two bodies that you have to go to. The investment license states your scope. As I mentioned earlier, you need to have an initial outlay of capital and you definitely need to identify the current market. In our days, we were allowed to get away with less amount of initial capital but now, it is about 200–280 thousand USD in Vietnam as operating capital.

It was observed that A/E firms understand the importance of human touch and the extra qualities that an A/E firms should possess and exhibit. This is consistent with Kotler's (2005) suggestion that service marketing needs to consider three additional "P"s – People, Process and Physical evidence, on top of Product, Price, Place and Promotion. These marketing strategies could mean providing technical expertise, speed of solution and reporting, competitive prices, relationship management with customers and other significant stakeholders et cetera.

A Director of Firm A in Singapore shared on the importance of marketing and branding:

> For an architectural firm, it is important to have value and integrity in design, relationships with institutions, winning awards and using them as marketing tools.

> Building rapport is important. For example, I just went down to Calcutta to make a presentation.

> Firms go abroad to market themselves. It is important today, to brand yourself, and to market yourself other than offering competitive prices and value. A firm should strive to be like Prada, to think and market itself out of the box.

> We target blue-chip projects that are high-profiled and high-valued. These projects will be useful as project references, to act as our marketing tools.

An architect of Firm B in Singapore shared on how A/E firms market themselves:

> We do not advertise ourselves. The industry is small, everybody knows one another. We do not see the need to spend money to advertise. Instead, we rely on project references, word-of-mouth, referrals, continued projects and return customers. Interested people can also check out our website.

The Managing Director of Firm C in Shanghai shared:

> We tell our clients that Singapore is a melting pot of talents from different culture and nationality. We are no longer marketing ourselves as a Singaporean firm, nor an Australian or Hong Kong firm. We are marketing ourselves as an Asia-Pacific and international firm.

A Vice-President of Firm C in Beijing shared on his business development responsibilities:

> I have to follow the progress of projects that are under my charge, until final payments. I am also required to establish and maintain business networks and contacts, look out for opportunities, and to update the home or regional offices of trends and changes.

An architectural assistant of Firm D in Singapore shared:

> We are very service-oriented and client-friendly. Based on this, providing customer service is the best word of mouth spread in the architecture field.

> We rely on project references and word-of-mouth recommendations. Our directors have their own clientele base too. We also publicize ourselves in publications like industry journals and magazines. Our web-site is also a useful medium to introduce to others what is Firm D about. We do not advertise ourselves. This is probably because the industry is so small – everyone knows which firm can provide what type of services. Clients give in more to international big names.

> Firm D is not as highly regarded as SOM, but I think we are comparable in terms of quality.

A Director of Firm D in Kuala Lumpur shared:

> We will do cold-calls to clients but very rarely I will woo a job, as we are fairly busy but if we are invited to participate, we will go all out if we are interested such as projects which have architecture significance, something that we have not done before and could add value to our portfolio; projects which have pay; projects that have very good profiles, and projects that pay well. Basically, we like to do projects that have very good profiles are iconic or land-mark projects that can be used as valuable project references in the future.

He added that branding can sometimes be a double-edged sword:

> We have a problem with perception as a lot of people perceive us to be a Singaporean firm. It is good because it is an international firm but over here, many Malaysians wonder if you are going to be around for long and want this to be able to last for 5–6 years. My challenge would be to convince them that our practices are locally incorporated that they will benefit. So being Singaporean office is a double-edged sword, internally and externally.

An associate of Firm D in Shanghai shared:

> Firm D however is more conservative and it is based on client' relationship plus word-of-mouth. It engages in a very systematic process of getting projects.

> The directors are the ones responsible to market the firm.

10.7 The 8S Framework

We are too conservative. We can expand faster. Now, we are reliant on referrals. We should do more market branding. We are also not offering top pays in the employment market. When this happens, we cannot get the best talents.

An architect of Firm D in Beijing shared:

The firm retains its globalized, cosmopolitan image for marketing purposes.

A master-planner of Firm E in Shanghai shared:

Singapore and Firm E are both brand-names. Marketing is Singaporean firms' core strength. Singapore is reputed to offer the combined advantages of the East and West. Marketing-competence is important too because you need to tell your clients or prospective clients what you can do. Business people doing businesses in China should also know the history, traditions and culture of the Chinese.

A design manager of Firm F in Kuala Lumpur shared:

We market ourselves as a Singaporean brand, ensuring quality, sincerity, security and stability. It helps that we are owned by a strong government-investment company. We also use project references as track records to market ourselves.

The General Director of Firm F in Vietnam shared:

We have a market intelligence marketing team which works with various branch offices. The HQ will gather information from branch offices. Over here, there is a team of people who will sit down and discuss business strategies, as well as gathered intelligences.

A Director of Firm A in Singapore shared:

We attract the better graduates because we pay better than average and because of our renown. We also give other incentives. However, like at other big firms, these fresh graduates may take Firm A as a training ground to get more exposure and mileage in their CV, then job-hop to other firms.

An architect of Firm B in Singapore shared:

We upgrade ourselves by attending courses and seminars; we have also gradually increased in staff-count.

A senior technical manager of Firm B in Singapore shared:

We have a buddy system in the company such that two architects can help each other and so far, it works very well. We will select buddies suitable for each other, based on their experience and project sizes and complexity of project. We also use the buddy system when we go overseas.

There is a system for new staff as we orient them in order to tell them of our system. We will align their vision to what we are looking for. In addition, we like to share our experience and introduce our juniors to the work that we do, freeing ourselves of certain work. When I first joined the company, there is a mentoring system. I was lucky to be mentored by the boss of the company.

The Managing Director of Firm C in HCM City shared on an expatriate's remuneration package:

You can earn two or three times more than back home. Package can be negotiated. The package includes posting allowances, housing allowances, home trips, medical benefits and insurances et cetera. Top executives receive better overseas allowances.

A senior Vice-President of Firm C in Shanghai shared that Firm C encourages internal shuffling of staff between different offices in different cities:

> Staff can apply to get some experiences in the ten different offices in different cities we have in China. Selected staff may even get an exchange experience in Singapore. An exchange lasts about three months.

The Chairman of Firm D highlighted the importance of injecting young professionals into the company to rejuvenate the firm every now and then:

> The renewal energy with the word "energy" being the key word as older people, already successful, do not need to work so hard but the young, still hungry with family to look after, seek to be successful. The Singapore government only selects the brightest, young and talented. Only with that, we are able to grow another lap.

An associate of Firm D in Kuala Lumpur shared on the importance of providing support to employees so that they are enabled to do their work productively and with less frustration:

> We give our staff good remunerations and relevant perks, and provide them with infrastructural support, for example, communication infrastructure, to reduce any helplessness in their work. We encourage them at work, give them motivations and conduct trainings.

A senior associate of Firm D in Shanghai shared:

> Interviews are done by either my boss or me. Of course, we have the 3-month probation period as I find that it is really difficult to find out what the person is like at interview stage so the probation period is a good period to learn what the person is like. We are not narrow-minded. We do not have pre-conceived notions on people. We grant them equal chances.

The General Director of Firm F in Vietnam, Thailand and Russia shared on how prospective employees are assessed:

> We track qualifications as a base. We will assess their previous experience such as being overseas in certain context. The other way is to headhunt, especially for senior positions and get agencies to look for relevant people.

Other than Singaporean A/E firms, the General Director of a quantity surveying firm in HCM City shared:

> The best method we have found was to post it on recruitment web-sites whereby candidates either post their CV or we post a certain amount of job openings every year. We get a huge response rate and we have a filtering rate internally. Our human resource department would filter them using several key performance indicators. I trust my HR to filter out and not to miss out the good ones.

Other than Singaporean A/E firms, a marketing manager of a developer in HCM City shared:

> We advertise online, or ask around people we know of good candidates. We trust referrals more because there is more credibility than a job resume. We have two rounds of interviews to check out suitable candidates. Vibes are very important.
> Staff are also taught to manage the business as if it is their own, and are told to spend only when necessary.

10.7 The 8S Framework

The Managing Director of Firm C in Shanghai shared:

We have very clear key performance indicators for business needs to meet in every financial year and we have very robust accounting system such that each unit operating out of Singapore is very well-monitored by the HQ.

A senior Vice-President of Firm C in Shanghai shared:

You have a budget and you just spend the budget but now we have all of these benchmarks and adjustments that we have to measure ourselves but we do carry the heritage of doing it in terms of having honesty and we do not over-promise.

The management has policy indicators that monitor to see if we are putting the company into a very slow process of suicidal as you deplete your cash flow and you have insufficient cash to operate, letting the senior management monitor us. Thus, because of this guidelines, we know what to do but at the same time, we do not always have to go back to get permission so that helped us to get clearances very fast and we can give quotations to clients within 24 hours, if you understand the project very well.

Other than Singaporean A/E firms, a marketing manager of a developer firm in HCM City shared:

We go with the flow, to borrow wherever there are lower interest rates, and arrange accounts wherever permissible. We always spend below budget, unlike some government-linked companies which make sure they spend all of the budget they are able to get.

A Director of Firm A in Kuala Lumpur shared:

We do all types of projects. The projects we handle are usually high-end, boutique, residential projects. We are at the top of the league in Malaysia. We are branded and we have received numerous awards.

Another Director of Firm A in Kuala Lumpur shared:

We stress a lot on good design that is also realistic and sustainable.

An architect of Firm B in Singapore described Firm B:

Firm B was registered as a firm in the earlier times, for government projects that required a minimum size and capital outlay. Firm B only works together when the need arises. In normal times, it operates as 4 different firms.

A senior technical manager from Firm B in Singapore shared:

Our corporate strategies include focus on a growing middle-income market and private developments, promoting sustainable designs, and building and maintaining governmental relations. We also try to provide value-add services. For example, we can provide design analysis.

We will get clients whom are attracted to how we are like and we will also look at what we are strong at. We will then repackage our strengths to target certain market. For example in China and Malaysia, we are not used to their architecture so we will put a lot of emphasis on it during training. We will build up our base and bring in an expert whom very often than not, will go with us when we are overseas initially doing marketing. The expert will then assess the clients' needs and see ways in which we can solve that if we do not have the strengths needed. This is the same for developers, I think. The main thing is that we can give something that they cannot have.

An architect from Firm B in Singapore shared:

We do not want to over-commit. Furthermore, we can only do design work in these cities because we do not have full practicing license in these locations. We still prefer, and need the locals to work together with us to complete the projects.

The Managing Director of Firm C in Shanghai shared:

They have processes in place to monitor the month-to-month system but we do have enough room for us to make certain adjustments to our business models in order to adapt to local environment, not compromising on our local governance and management controls.

A senior Vice-President of Firm C in Shanghai shared:

We do not have to go back to Singapore for clearance before we can secure our plans because we have enough checks and balance in the system.

The senior management, over the years, knows what the market rate is and because we have been very conscious of our stakeholders, we need to make profits. That itself is an in-built system to make sure we do not undercut.

In business, you can never be too comfortable with what you are today and must always be planning to become better, in case the partners today may one day become our competitors.

We sincerely work hard to deliver all that we promise. I think we have more flexibility and we have better adaptability.

An architect of Firm C in Shanghai shared:

I do not really have access to such information as I mainly communicate design information to clients. I am not really sure as I am still fresh here.

A Project Director of Firm C in Tianjin shared:

The regional head-quarter in Shanghai decides (on the strategies).

A Director of Firm D in Kuala Lumpur shared:

It could be due to the fact that they are handling the jobs in the beginning stage such as the front-end of conceptualizing of design. We also do that in Vietnam and Korea. We are only concept designers there.

A senior associate of Firm D in Shanghai shared:

We rely on our Singapore's home-office for strength and experience. We don't work very independently as we are still very much connected to Singapore, definitely in terms of design… The good thing about that is that you will be able to get the whole-range of support from Singapore. You get their experience and all the examples that you are looking for.

An architect of Firm D in Beijing shared:

May be in Singapore, there is (operational objectives communicated down to the employees) but over here since we are so far away, I think it is more difficult (for the top to communicate them down). I do know that we have a certain budget that we have to abide by.

The General Director of Firm F in Vietnam shared:

We feel that localization, equivalent to setting up an office there, is useful. It lowers the operating cost. When we have an office there, we give more attention to the clients' needs and our people can communicate and serve them better. We have an office there, so our

10.7 The 8S Framework

manpower will be tapped into local's income level so from the HQ's point of view, the manpower cost is low.

A Vice-President of Firm F in Singapore shared:

We have a Standard Practice Manual Communication can also be done via emails and video-conferences. Managers in the different office also have to attend annual meetings. Annual meetings are important because they enable the managers to get the bigger picture of what is going on around them.

Other than Singaporean A/E firms, the Managing Director of an architectural firm in Johor Bahru shared:

We try to have stable and good developers as our clients.

Other than Singaporean A/E firms, a Director of an American A/E firm in Shanghai shared:

We understand that it is difficult to carve market share in a rather saturated market. Furthermore, the SOMs and KPF[5]s already have their footholds here. Therefore, we are taking the niche approach – hospitality and mixed development.

Other than Singaporean A/E firms, a Director of a quantity surveying firm in Hanoi shared:

We intend to focus on traditional quantity surveying work here because project management here is troublesome and not profitable here. We will also publish knowledge papers and provide cost information.

Other than Singaporean A/E firms, the Managing Director of a quantity surveying firm in Shanghai shared:

We have standard procedures and procedural manuals. We get the manuals from the Singapore HQ so it is more or less standardized but of course, we do alter it a bit to suit the local clients. In general, we follow same procedures and rules.

Other than Singaporean A/E firms, a marketing manager of a developer in HCM City shared:

We plan to stay here, but in the shorter run, we are concentrating on our current project. Generally, we buy low and sell high.

We are known for our good value-for-money, quality and reasonable prices.

A senior technical manager of Firm B in Singapore shared:

We review quite regularly and we made adjustments accordingly.

We break down the office into different partners (during our sharing sessions) and we have two teams in a group. Our regular meetings are held every once a month, whereby we update the projects, look at the progress of each project and the current status. This serves as a good guide as each of the architects in the group will report the problem they encounter and share their experiences. If we feel that there is a necessity, we will share issues between the two groups.

---

[5] Kohn Pedersen Fox, a world-class architectural firm based in New York, USA.

An architect of Firm B in Singapore shared:

With the pending economic crisis, it is a good time to think over, and re-posture our business model and business strategies. It is an employers' market now. The few things we can do are: to add interior design services, go into evergreen sustainable design, and to rope talents into the organization.

A senior associate of Firm D in Shanghai shared:

The best thing that we end up doing if it is urgent is to call after you send an email and then they will look at it or sometimes, we label our "important" emails but that does not help as much. We may also call the person to "chase" for a reply.

A senior project manager of Firm E in Singapore shared on his experience:

The project was fraught with problems at one point. There were lapse in management between the higher-authorities; drastic delays to the project; the project manager resigned; and the owner was seeking litigation against Firm E. Firm E sent staff to communicate with each stakeholders, and individual staff to solve each individual problems. It was a period of crisis management and fire-fighting. The project was rushing for Temporary Occupational Permit (TOP). We removed two redundant, trouble-making staff and told everyone to pull together to make the project work. We did away with inefficient double-reporting, re-designed our organization structure for a newly-defined reporting line and detailing of responsibilities, so that more people can share the work-load. The crux is getting the right people with the right calibre, and not more people to do the job. It was critical for us to remove the ulcers of the organization, for the sake of morale and work momentum.

We gave an ultimatum to our staff, that they either quit or work doubly hard. We must work as a team. There may be side-effects and back-lash following such measures, but as long as we explain our rationale to the implicated. Reason travels more miles. We have to set good examples, convince people, and make them respect us.

A senior manager of Firm E in Shanghai shared:

We have annual surveys with our clients. These feed-backs help us to know more about ourselves and our performances. It is important that our clients are satisfied with our work. The feed-back system also provides a platform for us to reflect and improve our services.

A Vice-President of Firm F in Singapore shared:

We need not commit mistakes, and then learn to avoid such mistakes in the future. We can learn from other peoples' mistakes from a lot of case studies in the market. In a way, our management allows us to review other people's mistakes.

Other than Singaporean A/E firms, the Managing Director of a quantity surveying firm in Shanghai shared:

Our firm has witnessed and experienced several crises before and has been resilient against these crises. Fortunately, our firm is an international group and resources can be shared. We will continue to work well with our long-term clients who have strong finances but avoid "speculators". We are conservationist. We won't over-expand. We are also targeting bigger projects.

10.7.2 Organization Structure

An internationalizing firm normally designs its organization structure for an office in an overseas market according to (i) strategic fit (to business strategies, organization systems, leadership style, firm's skills, characteristics of staff, corporate values and supply-chain characteristics; (ii) embeddedness of the firm to its home conditions; and (iii) inclination to mimetic isomorphism, institutional isomorphism and coercive isomorphism of the firm.

The organization structure of a firm is an integral part of the Dynamic 8S framework. A misfit between organization design and other strategic and organizational parameters could short-circuit the firm. It is also important that the firm in search of structural fit should not be tied to a formal structure that cannot capture the complexity of the strategic tasks. In this case, Ghoshal and Barlett (1999) suggested that the firm should have the "matrix in the mind", and to always seek a balance between the psychology (soft values), physiology (organization systems) and anatomy (organization structure) of the firm.

A Director of Firm A in Kuala Lumpur shared:

In KL, we have one director, one associate, eight architects, eleven draftspersons, and three administrative staff. In Penang, we have one director, one architect, two draftspersons, and two administrative staff.

An architect of Firm A in Kuala Lumpur shared that there are no fixed teams in the firm, and commented on the strengths and weaknesses of such a structure:

The advantage of being so mobile is that we can save time because we are only roped in whenever our contribution is required. However, the disadvantages are silos because we may not be aware of the project developments, no accumulated experiences, and that we would have to learn indirectly.

As in every other firm, an architectural firm does not comprise only of architects – there would be architectural assistants, draftsmen, engineers, quantity surveyors, project managers, accountants, administrative staff et cetera in the firm as well.

An architect from Firm B in Singapore shared:

We have about 100 staff. About 30 % of our staff are architects or architecture-trained. The other 70 % are support professionals.

A senior technical manager from Firm B in Singapore shared:

We have one boss, an associate, few senior architects, then architects, architectural assistants and support staff.

Another senior technical manager of Firm B shared:

Our office comprises of 4 partners. We have about 100 staff which constitutes us to be somewhat middle size so in that sense, we are similar to other architecture firms. Our organizational structure is such that we have the boss, followed by 5 principals and then followed by senior architects.

The Managing Director of Firm C in HCM City shared:

Under the group, we have subsidiary firms that specialize in A/E consultancy, project management, facilities management, laboratory et cetera. The Managing Director is the head of Firm C Consultants, followed by the senior Vice Presidents (SVP) of Architecture, Civil and Structure (C&S) Engineering, Mechanical and Electrical (M&E) Engineering, Quantity Surveying, and the various Managing Directors of overseas offices. Under me, we have a technical group and a support group. My technical director manages the architectural team, C&S and M&E teams. In each of these teams, we have associates. We have managers in charge of business development, and finance, administrative, informational technology, and other junior staff in our support group.

A business development manager of Firm C in HCM City shared:

We have a technical group and a support group. Under the technical group, we have an architectural team, civil and structural engineering team, and mechanical and electrical engineering team; under the support group, we have a business development team and a finance/administrative/IT team. Basically, we have a managing director at the top of the hierarchy, then a technical director, technical associates, and the rest of the staff.

An architectural assistant from Firm D shared:

Firm D has a flat organizational structure. There is little specialization. Instead, we are trained to "do all". Our managers give us a lot of leeway to express ourselves creatively, yet realistically. The organizational structure and the management do not impede our work. The senior members share with us their experiences.

Every firm is unique. They can be different in size, expertise, resources et cetera. Every firm would have to organize themselves according to their needs.

A Director of Firm D in Kuala Lumpur shared:

Organizational design depends on geographical location, local conditions, and the intrinsic values of the firm.

A senior associate of Firm D in Shanghai, when asked to describe how organization structures are simpler in overseas offices shared:

They are compact, and suitable for multi-tasking. It depends on the project.

He then shared on Firm D's experience when it was starting out in Shanghai:

I was one of the expatriates, together with my boss and a fresh graduate student who wanted to work for a year here. That was the basic backbone. The three locals were a secretary, a young local senior architect and a young architect. There was six of us, but it fluctuates as we also had a few of us who fly in and out with temporary visas.

An associate of Firm D in Shanghai noted that the firm may become less efficient when the firm grows too fast and its organization structure cannot cope with the growth.

We were getting a little inefficient due to our growth and expansion. Our organizational structure had too many levels.

An architect from Firm D in Beijing shared:

Firm D worked like a big family. Like what the director always said, the door is always open. There is no close-door policy in Firm D. It is easy to approach the directors which are quite different from certain architectural firms whereby the star architect is not as approachable. Even though there is hierarchy, I feel that there are connections in between.

We have less hierarchies and we started as a very small office of about 4–5 people. Firm D (Beijing) is a young establishment. Everyone have to cover everything, overlapping each other. Most of the time, we communicate with the headquarters in Singapore and get the general direction. After which, we will do things by ourselves. We try to be self-sufficient but if we need assistance, we will get them from Singapore.

10.7 The 8S Framework

The General Director of Firm F in Vietnam shared that overseas offices tend to be less bureaucratic than their home-offices:

For me who handle overseas, it might not be so much bureaucratic.

An architect from an A/E firm in Singapore, not among Firms A to F, shared on how a larger-sized (more than 100 staff) A/E firm in Singapore would be structured:

We have the chairman at the top, then the MD, directors, associates or team leaders, senior architects, executive architects, architects, assistant architects and draftsmen. We have contract, design, engineering, administrative, finance, interior design, IT and technical departments.

10.7.3 Organization Systems

Organization systems include the processes, procedures, routines that characterize how work in an organization is to be done. It was found that the overseas offices of transnational A/E firms tend have less rigid and bureaucratic organization systems. These offices are likely to be more flexible in processes and procedures et cetera due to (i) the firms' smaller sizes in terms of employee numbers, and (ii) the need to be nimble in foreign markets.

A Director of Firm A in Kuala Lumpur shared:

We are using ISO 9000 to standardize and systemize our operations and to streamline our resources, and ISO 14000 to manage sustainable designs.

An associate of Firm B in Singapore shared:

There is a system for new staff as we orientate them in order to tell them of our system. We will align their vision to what we are looking for. In addition, we like to share our experience and introduce our juniors to the work that we do, freeing ourselves of certain work. When I first joined the company, there is a mentoring system. I was lucky to be mentored by the boss of the company. For the current staff, we hold regular office meetings to share with each other the challenges, as well as update them what the latest thing that happen in the office is, spearhead certain strategies and prioritise the different things to do.

The Managing Director of Firm C in HCM City shared:

Firm C replicates its strong systems across offices. These systems are modified slightly to suit the new environments though. We also have a team of dynamic design staff to coordinate work.

An associate of Firm D in Kuala Lumpur shared:

We have templates and standard letters or way of writing.

A senior project manager of Firm E in Singapore, who has worked in many other overseas offices before, shared:

Processes may change abroad. When you are abroad, you do not adhere to exact processes. The bottom-line is to get your work done. Work and life traditions and cultures may be different abroad.

An architect from an A/E firm in Singapore, not among Firms A to F, shared:

We have auditors who are also architecturally-trained to make sure our documents are of ISO standards to comply with the authorities' requirements.

A senior manager of Firm E in Shanghai shared:

Every year, we have a survey done with all of our past clients and the feedback is that our quality is always the best so we don't only mention it, we also do a real survey. We also welcome feedbacks from them and we improve on that so we are very much in control.

A Vice-President of Firm F in Singapore shared:

The person who voice these problems tend to be the people that the management feel is of high potential. It is typical that we will open this up to certain individuals so the feedbacks are all very genuine and good for the company.

A Planner of Firm E in Shanghai shared:

We do not have regular meetings. Our meetings are informal. We organize meetings whenever there is a need or we feel that we should update each other on events.

So there are no complicated relationships and conflicts. People are open to one another. Employees have their freedom and not strictly bound by the company's management or regulations.

A Director of Firm D in Kuala Lumpur shared:

When you do the evaluation, there are a few areas that you look at, namely: responsibility, initiative, how they function as a team, leadership, delivery, are they punctual. This is very basic and we also conduct Emotional Quotient (EQ) on-site. It all links back to the team and whether they are able to engage with the team, how they interact with clients. We get feedback from clients sometimes which is a good thing, I suppose. We also assess job capability which is a separate issue, depending on what they are being assigned to and see how well they perform. You won't use a boy to perform a man's job. You see their technical knowledge on industry, based on feedback and interaction so I will only evaluate people that I work closely with. We have 100 people and 4 directors in the space here. I may have a team of 40 and I may have worked very closely with these 40. Each director assesses his own employees. There are always cross-references with other directors, associates and project directors too. After which, we will talk to the employee himself and tell him that that is the evaluation, asking him if he agrees with it. Sometimes, you will get very interesting feedback. That period of time would be when you compare the evaluation.

A Vice-President of Firm C in Shanghai shared:

We also prefer to promote our own staff to senior positions rather than employing from outside.

The Chairman of Firm D shared:

We promote from within. We also try to have more young people because they can provide more energy to the firm. We constantly look out for young, bright and talented staff to bring us to the next lap. The older directors have given up their shares. This is a renewal process, much like how our Singapore's government rejuvenates its cabinet.

A Director of Firm A in Singapore shared:

We have a liberal remuneration system. We pay our staff above market rates. However, during poorer times, we also have bigger pay cuts.

10.7 The 8S Framework

A senior technical manager of Firm B in Singapore shared on how employees in Firm B are remunerated:

> *(Remuneration here in Singapore) is lower than in USA and Australia. Firm B offers average salaries. There is no per diem allowance when we are handling projects in third world countries which have low costs of living, and the management sees no need to give staff extra compensation. For these locations, we are only given air-fare and accommodation compensations. However, per diems may be given in Middle-east where costs are much higher.*

Bonuses and variable pay are not a significant part of the remuneration package of an architect or engineer. An architect of Firm B in Singapore shared:

> *We had it only once, for China Square project. It was an one-off, because of the project's size and value. Our boss wanted to make sure that we stay on for the duration of the project, and thus assured us that we would be given bonuses. For other projects, people can come in and fit in easily.*

An architect of Firm C in Shanghai shared on his remuneration as an expatriate in Shanghai:

> *We have housing allowances. Our remuneration system is such that foreigners or expatriates are expected to lead by example. We may have living allowances but we do not have over-time pay. The locals get what they are being assigned to, follow orders and enjoy over-time pay. The foreigners here have more responsibilities for our work.*

An associate of Firm D in Kuala Lumpur shared:

> *We have a variable pay scheme that rewards staff according to their performances.*

A Director of Firm D in Kuala Lumpur shared:

> *We pay 10 % more than the market rate to attract talents.*

> *We need to pay slightly more to attract.*

Top A/E firms in Singapore appreciate the importance of trainings and staff development. This is in line with Montgomery's (1995) suggestion that human resources are unique resources and should be regarded as crown jewels of the firm. Effective training or development is particularly vital in today's changing workplace as staff is exposed to new technologies and environments. Therefore, architects and engineers in Singapore are required by regulations in Continual Professional Development to attend courses or seminars to keep them abreast of the latest developments in the industry. In addition, trainings are also routinely held within organizations to develop and strengthen the skills of their employees.

The General Manager of Firm F in Kuala Lumpur shared:

> *We conduct trainings. Such a system creates consistency and expectations between colleagues, thus reducing miscommunications and teething problems.*

A senior engineer of Firm F in Singapore shared:

> *Our orientation is done together in a whole company, together with the sub-companies as well. The lower positioned staff may not receive as detailed training as middle-position staff and top management.*

10.7.4 Leadership Styles

The leader in a firm is like a captain of a ship. The leader sets the strategic directions of the company, and other staff in the firm, like the crew on the ship, would do their part to carry out the leader's instructions. Fiedler's (1967) Situational Contingency Theory suggested that leadership style is interactive with situational favourableness. A leader's traits may include: drive (in terms of achievement, motivation, ambition, energy, tenacity and initiative), leadership, honesty, integrity, self-confidence, cognitive ability and knowledge of the business or profession, and maybe charisma, creativity and flexibility (Kirkpatrick and Locke 1991). Some interviewees shared on the leadership styles of their firms in this section.

A Director of Firm A in Singapore shared:

We are very positive. We do not point out problems. We advise. Subordinates may present options to their bosses and challenge their bosses.

In the old days, it used to be that the conceptual designs are privy to senior partners only; now, the firm practices meritocracy, and gets the young and passionate designers to do the conceptual designs, while the senior managers supervise and advise.

A Director of Firm A in Kuala Lumpur, who is the sole person-in-charge of Firm A in Kuala Lumpur, shared:

I am a dictator. But, I am beginning to delegate more responsibilities to my employees.

His associate in the same office shared:

He is an autocratic leader. It is a pro when you need to drive an idea, and you need someone who is very driven. It becomes a con when you become over-reliant on one person. It is not a good way to go forward. Staff satisfaction may also be compromised.

An architect in the same office shared:

It is good when you know who you can approach or who can make the decisions. It is bad when he changes his mind, sometimes frequently. Moreover, you cannot foretell his mind. We need to consult him on many issues.

A senior technical manager of Firm B in Singapore shared:

There is still much central control, but there are also areas of work that is democratic. There is also leeway in reporting and empowerment in day-to-day operations.

Our leaders have shorter decision-making horizon. Our leaders are more reactive than proactive. Occasionally, probably once a year, we do forecasts. They are conservatives. They are simple and only undertake projects that are commercially viable.

An architect of Firm B in Singapore shared:

There is delegation and empowerment to staff, but things pertaining to reputation, costs, relationships and designs are still managed by the bosses. All others can be managed by the associates.

An associate of Firm B in Singapore shared:

Most of the time, decision making is top-down but we give a lot of leeway to prevent the jeopardizing of projects as we allow them to do decision making. We will set certain guidelines and give them room to move around, with certain major decisions being held quite tightly. I will make most of the decisions but if it affects the relationship and it is critical, I will consult my boss because he has a lot of experience that we can tap on.

A senior Vice-President of Firm C in Shanghai shared:

As opposed to a centralized system whom you need to go back to the office to get clearances or go-ahead before you can go into your plans, control is not over-centralized or rather, decentralized in our Singapore's head-office. We may not need clearances from our Singapore's head-office for most matters. This way, we can correspond much quicker with our clients or partners at work.

We have an open concept. We can call one another by names and discuss work openly. We also have shared leadership. We identify talents and empower them to train them to become future leaders.

Her colleague, an architect in the same office agreed:

We are very open. We call each other by names. We just follow and when they introduce themselves by their names, we call them by their names. We agree to disagree.

Two of my heads are very open and this could be because we are of an educated background for example masters and bachelor. We know what we want and they also have their own ideas so sometimes we have to fight with each other to keep your ideas in this project. However, we get very good communication with our boss.

A senior associate of Firm C in HCM City shared:

I treat the locals as friends but as an expatriate, we have to lead as a senior person and set a good example for them to follow.

An associate of Firm D in Kuala Lumpur shared:

Decisions are not unilaterally decided. Instead, we often make team-decisions. Only monetary issues are solely handled by the directors.

An architectural assistant of Firm D in Singapore shared:

Our managers give us a lot of leeway to express ourselves creatively, yet realistically. The organizational structure and the management do not impede our work. The senior members share with us their experiences.

A Vice-President of Firm F in Singapore shared on what are the qualities an international manager should demonstrate:

He must have the ability to manage cultural differences and get things done.

An engineer of Firm F in Singapore agreed with Fiedler's (1967) concept of Situational Contingency:

Leadership style is dependent on where the organization is located at.

10.7.5 Skills and Staff

An A/E firm may have a particular niche or competence. The firm's competences have a direct inference and implication on its staff and the skills they should possess. It was found that more common than not, the overseas office of a Singapore's A/E firm would be in charge of: (i) maintaining presence and doing business development in the overseas market; and (ii) coordinating design and other works with its home-office. Therefore, an expatriate or senior staff may even have to wear several hats and be involved in design coordination, business development, client management, marketing, management and administrative matters.

A Director of Firm A in Singapore shared that there is a limit to how big an A/E firm can grow. This finding matches with Dunbar's (1996) suggestion that the neocortex ratio for man is roughly 150. The director shared:

> *150 is the optimum size, with the amount of directors and managers we have.*

A senior architect of Firm A in Shanghai shared that the firm engages part-timers to help him:

> *They help me on the accounts, expenses, bank statements and so on. As for project side, we do not have much part-timers but we used to have a few to help us prepare documents.*

A Vice-President of Firm C in Singapore shared that being multi-disciplinary has its advantages as well as disadvantages:

> *It depends on the clients' belief. Some people may see it as a positive, but others may see it as a negative. For example, some may prefer better integration of work. However, some clients prefer to have more check and balance, and will prefer to have quantity surveyors and project managers from other firms.*

A senior Vice-President of Firm C in Shanghai shared:

> *We also practise job rotation so that our staff learn more skills.*

An architectural assistant of Firm D in Singapore opined:

> *The culture and skills requirements between countries are different. Singaporean architects are less exposed, experimental, adventurous and innovative.*

The General Manager of Firm D in HCM City shared:

> *The skills of local staff are poor. Very poor. It is not so much technical. It is more of mentality. The mentality there for first 5 years – I interviewed 20 over candidates and they do not know what they have done. You will ask them if they can draw and they say they do. But when you ask them "What is the drawing about?", they will answer "not so sure" so they have no idea what they are doing. In general, they are all like that. They also don't like and cannot be pressured. It is very difficult to get good candidates. It is simply the mentality and training of it.*

An associate of Firm D in Shanghai shared:

> *Skills set-wise, Firm D has the tendency to do hybrid projects and services are good as we are responsible and are focused in coordination. We do service and we emphasize on the value brought by the service.*
>
> *Firm D provides a whole range of services to give more value. So, we have a variety of skills. The directors are the ones responsible to market the firm.*
>
> *Our work is good rather than great, and not as creative as international firms like SOM and Foster. We are always able to get designs that can score 70 to 80 marks, but not more. We lack the skills to do perfect jobs.*

Staff here are simple and amicable and have no conflicts with one another.

Firm D has a group of people who specializes in certain category of buildings and to them, as long as they can do concept design, it won't really explore new aspects of what the employees can do but if you wish, there is a small group that the company would allow its talents to explore what they would like to do. However, we are a commercial firm and we have to do cost management but at the same time master designers can go about doing what they want.

A senior manager of Firm E shared on how Firm E recruits in Shanghai:

Normally, recruitment can be done using head-hunter companies, newspaper advertisements and on-line advertisements. Resumes will be assessed. Preliminary interviews with people from other provinces are done either through telephone or video calls so that they need not travel all the way down to Shanghai. A short-listed candidate may then have a face-to-face interview before his or her confirmation.

A planner of Firm E in Shanghai shared:

The American, European, Japanese and then the Singaporean firms offer the most prestige in terms of employment. It is extremely tough to get into internationally-renowned firms. Firm E also has its own screening processes. For example, it does not employ fresh graduates and seeks to hire people who can provide true value to the company.

Chinese government-linked firms have social responsibility to the society and community; while foreign private firms are more interested in revenues and profits. It is likely that different types of employees may strive and excel in different work conditions motivated in different ways. Employees search for suitable employers; and employers search for suitable employees.

A Vice-President of Firm F in Singapore shared on how government-turned privatized firms inherit skills and staff from their previous forms:

We have a critical mass of talents from our background as a governmental board but along the way, we still managed to grow to how we are today. It is our skills in executing a comprehensive consulting service that attracts them and what you can do at the end of the day – the know-how, thinking process and these are things that we are proud of.

An architect of an A/E firm in Singapore, not among Firms A to F shared:

We are integrated to benefit from the synergy of these different disciplines. It is also easier to coordinate work within the firm, because then, the people involved in the project would all be working for the company's interests. Other firms may not have as many specializations under one roof.

10.7.6 Shared Values

Peters and Waterman (1980) postulated that a set of shared values in a firm is important because it serves to bind all the other strategic and organizational parameters (i.e. business strategies, organization structure, systems, leadership style, skills of firm and staff' characteristics) together. It is important for transnational managers to cultivate shared values in subsidiary offices overseas so that

(i) staffs are kept congruent with the company's vision and goals; (ii) the values permeate to influence the staff's thoughts behavior and actions.

A Director of Firm A in Singapore shared:

> *The culture is good. We do not have bad practices like scape-goating. The top management ignores office-politics and hopes that by doing so, can reduce it. There is much trust within the firm and morale of the team is good. Management of expectations and human touch are very important – they can solve most problems. We are open and transparent. We are holistic in our sitting arrangement. Firm A is like a family-styled A/E firm. We have a democratic culture. We are not dismissive because we know it may dampen morale. We have a contrive approach in doing things.*
>
> *Firm A's philosophy is that we agree to disagree. If it is a case of "birds of the same feather flock together", there would no balance in the organization. I am vocal, while some of my colleagues are quiet, we complement one another.*

When asked on what are the most important values of Firm A as an architectural firm, he opined:

> *Integrity and professionalism. Credibility and corporate social responsibility.*

A Director of Firm A in Kuala Lumpur shared:

> *We make no enemies, do not play politics internally nor externally, cultivate networks, treat everyone well, and be good, serious, professional and credible in all our work and delivery.*

The Managing Director of Firm C in Shanghai shared:

> *Whatever deals we signed, we make sure that we have the capabilities to deliver and can collect the money. That itself is a culture system that is built in to the process so we do not go around telling people that we do free things for them or telling them that we have special deals but at the end of the day, we don't have sufficient revenue to sustain.*

An associate of Firm D in Shanghai shared:

> *We are ethnocentric in terms of work culture management because we want to retain Firm D (Singapore)'s consistency in quality and work ethics.*
>
> *Firm D's culture is quite family-like. In the 40 years that it has been set up, you could feel that even in times of difficulties, they will not fire people. They may resign but they will not fire or retrench people. We have a comfortable working ambience. People feel comfortable in the culture as we do look after the feelings of staff and we do not neglect their feelings, resolving contradictions if there are any. The working atmosphere is friendly.*

10.7.7 Supply-Chain

A supply chain includes the firm's internal departments, its clients, partners, suppliers and subcontractors. The supply chain is emerging as an important point of differentiation for companies which have hitherto relied on themselves. The A/E firm's supply-chain could include the developer, authorities, engineers, quantity surveyors, project managers, landscapers, interior designers et cetera. It was observed that supply chains are often highly regarded in other industries, but perhaps less so in the construction and A/E industry.

Architects are often regarded as the leaders of construction projects. A Director of Firm A in Singapore remarked:

> They (architects) are like Indian chiefs, to have to control other participants involved in the project. Architects must be able to discern and make judgments from mixed signals.

> Building rapport is important. For example, I just went down to Calcutta to make a presentation.

The aptitude of a firm's supply chain affects its proficiency. An associate of Firm A in Kuala Lumpur shared:

> Engineers are not challenged enough in KL. The quantum of fees is low because of cut-throat competition, costs of living is high and staff costs is high. These compromises engineering consultancy's quality. This channels expectations on architects to coordinate with the engineers to make sure the goods are delivered.

An architect has to communicate, cooperate and coordinate with many different stakeholders of a construction project. The relationships between an architect and other stakeholders can be determined or influenced by the nature of the contract for the construction project. An architect from Firm B in Singapore shared:

> Architects may have a harder time trying to describe their designs to clients who do not have design-backgrounds.

> We can only do design work in these cities because we do not have full practicing license in these locations. We still prefer, and need the locals to work together with us to complete the projects.

> It depends on the nature of the contract and the needs of the client. For traditional contracts, architects manage the project, and can get to choose partners for themselves. Often, architects can recommend to clients on choice of partners. Subcontractors also need to be endorsed by architects.

The Chairman of Firm D shared:

> Our work requires us to liaise with the developers, authorities, quantity surveyors et cetera. So, when we move abroad, we may have to find new partners to work with us. It is not necessary to have a local partner as local partners can always be found. What is important is whether there is a demand for our services.

A senior associate of Firm D in Shanghai shared:

> We have not joined any associations or affiliations here. We only loosely know some "who and who".

A planner from Firm E in Shanghai shared:

> Firm E has no practicing license. Therefore, Firm E has to rely on local design institutes for all jobs.

A Vice-President of Firm F shared:

> Contacts and networks are important.

Other than Singaporean A/E firm, an assistant manager from a quantity surveying firm in Singapore shared:

> The construction industry is a fragmented industry. There is in general, a low level of cooperation in the construction industry.

10.7.8 Dynamic Strategies

A firm has to change with the times to survive, or even to be ahead of its time to prosper (Aaker and Mascarenhas 1984). A firm's business strategies and organization design has to be dynamic. It is thus suggested that firms have contingency and flexible strategies. Dynamic strategies, according to contingency theories are flexible and are applied according to location, time and other situational conditions. It is also suggested that the best way to organize depends on the nature of the environment. Changes such as digitization, faster information transmission, lower costs of information storage and transmission, geographic dispersion of value chain, integration of states and opening of markets, and the globalization of markets are inducing new organizational forms and competitive dynamics. Lewin (1951) and Hunger and Wheelen (2007) hence advocated that firms must keep abreast of such developments and develop strategic flexibility and capabilities to tackle these management challenges.

A Director of Firm A in Singapore shared:

The young designers are also good catalyst to the senior managers because the younger crop gives the fatigued senior managers an energy boost.

We make 2 years and 5 years plans. The plans may be augmented according to changes. We always try to have contingent plans and strategies.

As Firm A's profile becomes more renowned, Firm A undertakes more prominent projects. It used to be that managers only need to hand down jobs; now, senior managers are much more involved.

KL was a subsidiary, but evolved to be independent due to different needs and the different strategies to confront the needs. Both offices realized that the KL office cannot have a wholesale transplant of Firm A (Singapore)'s model because of the different idiosyncrasies and nuances.

A Director of Firm A in Penang shared:

We started off as a contact office and there was only one person. At that time, we had quite a sizeable project in mainland Malaysia and Thailand. Thus, we started a head office here and hired more people. Now, we have five permanent staff.

A senior technical manager of Firm B in Singapore shared:

New graduates and new technology. Young architects can be innovative, or have learnt new things in their universities, have new ideas of things.

The greatest technological change in the industry is the 3-dimensional computer-aided design (CAD). It has created a rapid transformation in the industry and in our work.

A senior Vice-President of Firm C in Shanghai shared:

We cut down the dependency (on our HQ) down to almost insignificant level, meaning that we are quite independent in terms of delivering our services. When we started in 1999, the business development people here have no resources to do anything, except a brain of track record used to sell our services so we have to make sure that HQ could meet up with what is stated in contract. In 2001, we set up legal entity and started to recruit people up to 80 people.

We used to be a representative office. Now, we are a design office. We have also gained a lot of local knowledge. For example, we have familiarized ourselves with playing "Cha Bian

Qiu". It used to be "us" and "them" for expatriate staff and local staff, but now, we do not have such a sense of segregation anymore.

A business development manager of Firm C in HCM City shared:

Clients might have invested a hefty sum of money, so they tend to want to talk and communicate with consultants on a daily basis. Our Singaporean staff used to fly in and out of Ho Chi Minh City, but later, the company decided to change the strategies because we had a big project from a client. They are an international-level and sophisticated developer, and they demanded their consultants to be fast and efficient, to have a sophisticated consultant team in Ho Chi Minh City.

A senior associate of Firm C in HCM City shared:

We have eradicated quite a bit of bureaucracy to become more streamlined. We are using less paperwork, and more straightforward and direct emails. We have improved on our speed of doing things.

The Chairman of Firm D shared:

This year is our 40 plus year since establishment so we were around since the 1960s. As we are around, we cannot divert from the spirit. Today is a different structure from when we were first founded. We can even perhaps suggest that there are 4 different periods of happenings as we enter into a very interesting period now. We basically divide the growth of Firm D into four periods. Every decade there is a momentum that pushes us to another level and that includes the current crisis. This is certainly an interesting aspect. Every period of this, there is a crisis. Maybe in certain periods, the crisis is not as serious but could be longer for example Asian financial crisis, oil crisis, recession and so on.

A senior associate of Firm D in Shanghai shared:

Deliverance was more important than quality during the economic and construction boom. Now, with fewer projects, "speed" has become less important. We can focus on doing a good job.

An associate of Firm D in Shanghai shared:

Firm D has an office here because of coordination. It is hard to coordinate a project from Singapore. It gradually changed from taking up projects here and doing it in Singapore to taking up projects here and doing it here.

We had at one point, between 1999 and 2000, thirty over staff. However, we had difficulties sustaining the firm. Projects were difficult to get. We reduced our staff-count to cut down on overheads and employment costs here. Now, our staff-count here is ten. We have shifted our design operations to Suzhou again. Now, our staff here do feasibility studies, research, administrative work and business development.

Our Singaporean office has more than 600 staff. We were getting a little inefficient due to our growth and expansion. Our organizational structure had too many levels. Then, we implemented ISO and things improved. The ISO system introduced more standards and procedures into the organization, something that design firms never used to pay attention to.

A Vice-President of Firm F in Singapore shared:

We have to re-evaluate our position from time to time. The organization is like a big tree – everyone will have to contribute. The rethinking process might be cascaded down, so that everyone can chip in some suggestions on how to improve the company.

Market forces are the biggest agents of change. When demand changes, firms have to react with new business strategies.

Firm F is also looking at how to use technology to enable consultant to do their work more competitively. This is the evolution of services provided by Firm F, to make service more relevant to market. We have acquired new capabilities, and we are providing many forms of services that we were not in the past.

The General Director of Firm F in Vietnam shared:

In the company, we encourage learning and knowledge-transfer. For example, we have the learning series. It is a series of seminars or talks by senior staff, or people with experiences in foreign markets to give presentations to other staff.

We have evolved from public sector and moving into the private market... The training program that we have has been gradually changed as we are trying to gather more cross-boundary information to guide our staff and face the fact that we are becoming a globalized company.

Other than Singaporean A/E firms, the Managing Director of a quantity surveying firm in Shanghai shared:

The firm also has to keep changing to keep up with the changing environment and conditions. "Today" will become "Yesterday" tomorrow.

10.8 Synthesis of Findings and Themes

Although the economic interconnections between different locations across the globe are expanding at a rapid pace, it has been observed that the state of the world remains far from approaching spatial liquefaction. Instead, major cities in the world continue to expand, contrary to a commonly held view that new transportation and communication technologies are beginning to subvert urbanization processes (Krugman 1991; Taylor 2004). Such as phenomenon can be explained with the Gravity model (Isard and Peck 1954) and the Central Place Hierarchy Theory (Christaller 1933).

The Gravity model (Isard and Peck 1954) mimics the Newtonian Law of Gravity which considers physical sizes of and distance between objects to suggest that the more populated and proximate cities tend to have a higher intensity of mutual attraction of people, ideas and commodities. The model helps to anticipate traffic, telephone calls, transportation of goods and mails and other types of movement between places, and can be used to compare the gravitational attraction between continents, countries, states and even to neighbourhoods (Rosenberg 2004).

At the same time that firms are agglomerating in central places. Firms would be inclined to position their higher-value organizational activities such as leadership, finance, marketing, research and development in central and core cities but arrange lower-value or routine activities in periphery locations. A core location is disposed to draw in much of the economic potential in the region around it, but its neighboring cities could suffer from the back-wash effects of its success, even though these nearby periphery locations may benefit from lower-ordered spillages from the core locations.

10.8 Synthesis of Findings and Themes

The Spatial model amalgamates the Gravity model (Isard and Peck 1954) and the Central Place Hierarchy Theory (Christaller 1933), and put forward that there is a hierarchy of cities in a region, in terms of the roles they play, due to these cities' spatial/geographical properties. The integrated model illustrates how gravitational distance between two markets, assuming that the home-city is a core city, compresses the attractiveness and perceived viability of business opportunities from the core city to the foreign host city. It is suggested that the synthesized model (i) improves the ability of the Gravity model to estimate the power of attraction or interaction between two cities by considering the global or regional mosaics of the world; (ii) adds dynamism (distance) to the Central Place Hierarchy Theory; and (iii) provides a realistic reflection of how the size of a market is influenced by that market's distance away from a core location.

The figure shows how geography causes distance-rooted changes in business environments and firms' spatial interactions with overseas markets. It is postulated that these in turn has a profound implication on firms' choices of business strategies and organization designs. It is suggested in this research that the Spatial model helps to explain how the flight-time (proxy for intervening geographical distance) between a firm's home and host markets influences gravitational distances and the host city's hierarchical rank in the system of cities in the region, and in turn, influences the internationalizing firm's choice of organization design in an overseas city. The Spatial model is further authenticated by findings from the Content Analysis and Statistical Analysis which will be discussed below.

10.8.1 Generalization of Findings from Content Analysis

Figures 10.10, 10.11, 10.12, 10.13, 10.14, 10.15, 10.16 and 10.7 show the perception of similarities between factors by interviewees whose offices are in Singapore, KL, Penang, HCM City, Hanoi, Shanghai, Beijing and Tianjin respectively, using classical scaling. The distance between the two smaller opaque circles in each figure indicates the level of perceived relationship between the encircled factors: geographical distance and organization structure. The larger dotted circle surrounds "organization structure" and indicates how organization structure is perceived to be more related to factors that are located around it in each city. The size of the dotted circle is arbitrarily drawn to illustrate the proximity of factors to an internationalizing A&E firm's organization structure.

In Fig. 10.10, it is shown that A&E professionals whose offices are in Singapore perceive that organization structure is closely related to "cultural ownership", "socio-demographical distance", "agglomeration and localization", "cultural location" and "cultural complementary". This suggests that the organization design of an A&E firm in Singapore tends to face cultural influences due to the firm's ownership qualities, locational qualities and complementary industries, and the agglomeration and localization of economic activities and A&E talents. The firm's ownership qualities include its brand-name, core competencies, work

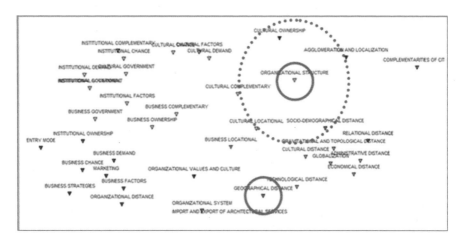

Fig. 10.10 Similarities between factors perceived by interviewees whose offices are in Singapore

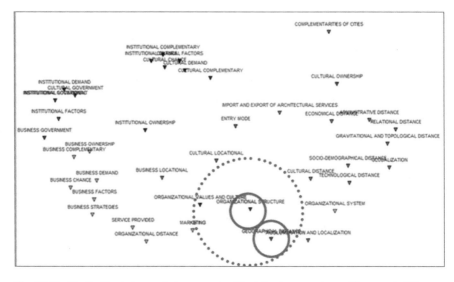

Fig. 10.11 Similarities between factors perceived by interviewees whose offices are in KL

systems, staff number, et cetera. Agglomeration and localization of economic activities and A&E talents in Singapore have also allowed a favorable condition for the A&E firm to set the organization's head-quarters in the city.

In Fig. 10.11, it is shown that A&E professionals whose offices are in Kuala Lumpur perceive that organization structure is closely related to "organizational values and culture" and "geographical distance". This suggests that the organization design of a Singapore-based A&E firm in Kuala Lumpur tends to be influenced by the company's organizational values and culture, and the proximity of the

10.8 Synthesis of Findings and Themes

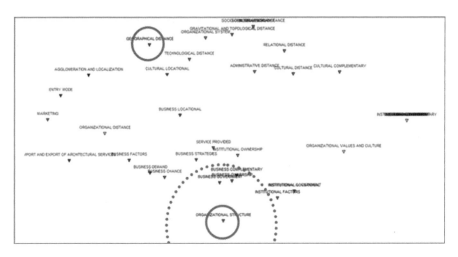

Fig. 10.12 Similarities between factors perceived by interviewees whose offices are in Penang

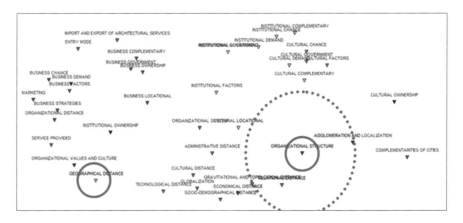

Fig. 10.13 Similarities between factors perceived by interviewees whose offices are in HCM City

branch-office to Singapore. The finding on organizational values and culture agrees with the McKinsey 7S Framework (Peters and Waterman 1980) which suggests that a firm's Strategy, Structure, Systems, leadership Style, Skills, Staff and Shared values affect one another. The finding on geographical proximity agrees with the Gravity model (Reilly 1931; Tinbergen 1962) and suggests that an A&E firm's branch-office in an overseas market is influenced by the intervening distance between the firm's home and host markets.

In Fig. 10.12, it is shown that A&E professionals whose offices are in Penang perceive that organization structure is closely related to "business government", "business ownership" and "business complementary". This suggests that the Singapore-based A&E firm in Penang organizes the branch-office according to (i) governmental regulations; (ii) the firm's characteristics and experiences; and

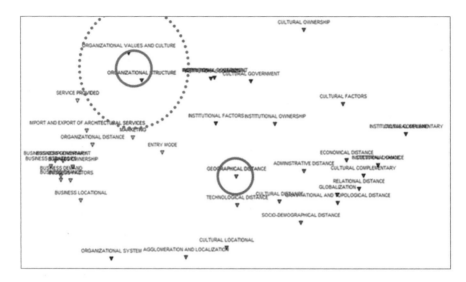

Fig. 10.14 Similarities between factors perceived by interviewees whose offices are in Hanoi

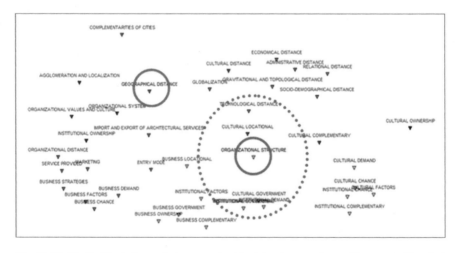

Fig. 10.15 Similarities between factors perceived by interviewees whose offices are in Shanghai

(iii) influences from supporting and complementary firms. This finding agrees with the concept of isomorphism, which emphasizes the role of conformity and convention as a response to environmental pressures exerted on organizations (DiMaggio and Powell 1983).

In Fig. 10.13, it is shown that A&E professionals whose offices are in HCM City perceive that organization structure is closely related to "relational distance" and "agglomeration and localization". The finding on relational distance suggests that the Singapore-based A&E firm in HCM City organizes the branch-office so that

10.8 Synthesis of Findings and Themes

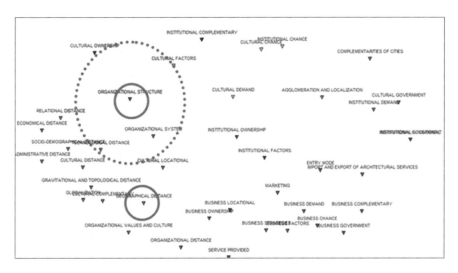

Fig. 10.16 Similarities between factors perceived by interviewees whose offices are in Beijing

relationships can be managed properly. This could be a hint that business networks are important in the city. The finding on agglomeration and localization reflects that HCM City is starting to attract more transnational companies and global talents. This suggests that there could be more development and construction, which translate to more projects opportunities for the A&E firm.

In Fig. 10.14, it is shown that A&E professionals whose offices are in Hanoi perceive that organization structure is closely related to "organizational values and culture". The finding on organizational values and culture is similar to that of Kuala Lumpur. It should also be noted that only one factor appears to influence the firm's organization structure. This could be a suggestion that Singapore-based A&E firms do not have many reasons to set up branch-offices in Hanoi.

In Fig. 10.15, it is shown that A&E professionals whose offices are in Shanghai perceive that organization structure is closely related to "cultural location", "technological distance", "cultural government", "institutional demand" and "institutional government". It should be noted that there are five factors that appear to influence the firm's organization structure, more than the two factors that appeared for Kuala Lumpur, three for Penang, two for HCM City, one for Hanoi, three for Beijing and none for Tianjin. It has also been observed that these numbers seem to reflect the complexity of A&E firms' organizational designs, such as organization structure and size.

In Fig. 10.16, it is shown that A&E professionals whose offices are in Beijing perceive that organization structure is closely related to "organizational systems", "cultural factors" and "technological distance". If we compare Beijing and Shanghai, we would notice that there are lesser factors around the vicinity of organization structure. This suggests that Beijing is a less attractive host-location than Shanghai for Singapore-based firms to set up branch-offices, and that Beijing tends to have a simpler organization structure than Shanghai.

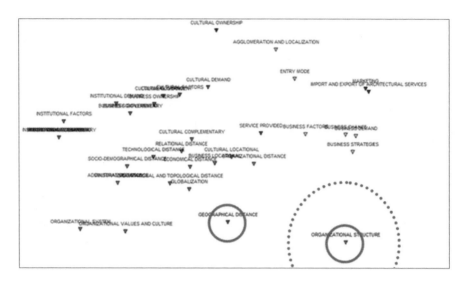

Fig. 10.17 Similarities between factors perceived by interviewees whose offices are in Tianjin

In Fig. 10.17, it is shown that A&E professionals whose offices are in Tianjin perceive that there are no factors closely related to organization structure. This is reflected by the observation that not many Singapore-based A&E firms have ventured into Tianjin. The finding agrees with the concept of Core and Periphery System of Cities (Myrdal 1963; Krugman 1991; Taylor 2004). This is probably because Shanghai and Beijing are still the preferred host-locations in China for internationalizing A&E firms. Tianjin, being too close geographically to Beijing, incurs back-washes effects due to the concentration of economic and commercial activities in Beijing.

It is observed that A&E professionals working for Singaporean A&E firms, but operating in different cities perceived different levels of similarities between factors. This appears to be the case because different countries or cities have varied business climates and cultures, which influence how people think, talk and behave. It is also possible that when Singaporean firms exit their national borders, they see things from other perspectives. Furthermore, the A&E firm may encounter constraints when it seeks to establish itself in a foreign market due to increasing geographical distance away from the home-country, which in turn affects a multitude of distance-rooted factors, such as the firm's access to home-based location-specific resources and its understanding of the overseas market.

The figures show how geography causes changes in business environments and firms' spatial interactions with overseas markets. These in turn has a profound implication on firms' choices of business strategies and organization designs. It is suggested in this paper that the Spatial Model helps to explain how the intervening geographical distance between a firm's home and host markets influences gravitational distances and the host city's hierarchical rank in the system of cities in the region, and in turn, influences the internationalizing firm's choice of organization design in an overseas city.

10.8.2 Generalization of Findings from Statistical Analysis

The statistical analysis found that transnational A/E firms tend to have a network that enables the sharing and access of resources, networks and markets. The survey respondents also believed that flight-time is irrelevant as a factor of consideration for the transnational A/E firm. However, this contradicts with how they thought geographical could affect the firm, even though flight-time can be a proxy for geographical distance, or that discontinuities and sap of access to location-specific resources due to boundaries and distance are insignificant or negligible. This is probably because the respondents have not considered flight-time as a meditational factor, can indirectly affect the internationalizing A/E firm. For instance, flight-time or geographical distance cause internationalizing firms to incur additional transportation, freight, communications and training costs. Flight-time or geographical distance are also likely to increase the A/E firm's transaction costs, reduce revenue and value, cause losses of information, miscommunications, problems in coordination and inefficiencies in cooperation. Furthermore, shuttling between cities is perceived as physically and mentally demanding and tiring, and takes up a considerable amount of time, and is considered to be an inconvenient aspect of transnational work. Internationalizing A/E firms would have to internalize distance-rooted changes, such as applying different architectural designs and engineering technologies to suit the demands of the overseas markets. The respondents also thought that the availability of direct flights could affect the A/E firm's decision to set up an office in a location. In addition, A/E firms venturing overseas are exposed to internationalization risks and face more difficulties and uncertainties, which in turn influence the internationalizing A/E firm's choice of business strategies and management.

10.9 Decision-Support Systems and Management Information Systems

Information can make the difference between success and failure for an internationalizing firm. This is because information changes the balance of power, gives choices and leverage in negotiations, a long-term future and potential to be big in Asia (Backman and Butler 2004). However, due diligence in most of Asia is not easy. The environment is besieged with ambiguity. The transnational firm in Asia also try to avoid "paralysis by analysis" – the paralysis of the firm due to too much analysis.

The CBR-DSS set up by the study therefore seeks to ease the informational load on the management team by offering preliminary guidance, advice and recommendations to firms venturing overseas. Decision-Support Systems and Management Information Systems are useful to internationalizing firms because (i) expert consultancy is expensive; and (ii) limitations imposed by human information processing capability, rushed pace of business and required decision making (Parker 1989).

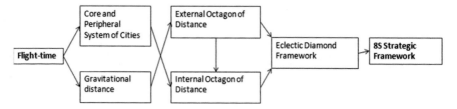

Fig. 10.18 Synthesis of major themes of the study

The CBR-DSS generally inquires about the qualities of the firm and the characteristics of the host market, and is able to prescribe recommendations pertaining to the firm's entry mode, organization structure, centralization (control from HQ), supervision, formalization, incentive system, leadership style, delegation, empowerment, skills of firm, skills of staffs, number of staffs, type of staffs, corporate culture and supply-chain networks. In this section, interviewees have shared on their firms' business strategies, organization designs, organization systems, leadership styles, firms' skills, staffs' characteristics, shared values and supply-chains.

10.10 Summary

Singapore's A/E firms are seeking markets abroad to solve the problem of an inherent lack of an incubational market and a cyclical market. Generally, there are four motivations for firms to internationalize: market-seeking, resource-seeking, efficiency-seeking and strategic-asset seeking. It has been observed that Singapore's A/E firms tend to venture into South-east Asian, Chinese, Indian and Middle-eastern cities in search of markets. These markets are not only geographically and culturally proximate, but also administratively, economically, technologically, socio-demographically and relationally close to Singapore. These help to shorten the organizational distance between overseas offices in these cities and the home-office in Singapore. The study proposes using the Eclectic Diamond Framework, a combination of Dunning's Eclectic Paradigm (Dunning 1988) and Porter's Diamond Framework (Porter 1990), to devise strategies to internalize the conditions the firm would come to face. The strategic and internalization framework is embodied by the study's 8S Model, which comprises of Strategy, Structure, Systems, Style of leadership, Skills, Staff, Shared values and Supply-chain. This chapter is thus a synthesis of all the above stated themes.

The synopsis of the research is reiterated in Fig. 10.18. The study asserts that distance is multi-faceted and not one-dimensional. The central premise of the investigation suggests that flight-time (a proxy for flight-distance and therefore geographical distance), influences a city's hierarchical rank in the System of Cities and gravitational distance, which in turn affects the other aspects of distance, embodied by the study's Double Octagon of Distances. The study then uses the

Eclectic Diamond Framework to analyze the macro, micro and task environment that the A/E firm would come to face or faced in the overseas market, to devise appropriate organization designs for the A/E firm's overseas office, pertaining to strategy, organizational structure, organization system, style of leadership, skills of firm, staff, shared values and supply-chain.

References

Aaker D, Mascarenhas B (1984) The need for strategic flexibility. J Bus Strateg 5(2):74–82
Aharoni Y (1966) The foreign investment decision process. Division of Research, Graduate School of Business Administration, Harvard University, Cambridge, MA
Ashby WR (1958) Requisite variety and its implications for the control of complex systems. Cybernetica (Namur) 1(2):53–99
Backman M, Butler C (2004) Big in Asia – 25 strategies for business success. Palgrave Macmillan, Basingstoke
Barlett CA, Ghoshal S (1998) Managing across borders: the transnational solution, 2nd edn. Harvard Business School Press, Boston
Baumol WJ (1959) Business behavior, value and growth. Macmillan, New York
Baumol WJ, Quandt RE (1964) Rules of thumb and optimally imperfect decisions. Am Econ Rev 54:23–46
Bergman E, Feser E (1999) National industry cluster templates: a framework for applied regional cluster analysis. Reg Stud 34(1):1–19
Björkman I, Forsgren M (2000) Nordic international business research. Int Stud Manag Organ 30(1):6–25
Blainey G (1977) Tyranny of distance: how distance shaped Australia's history. Sunbooks, Melbourne
Bogardus ES (1926) Social distance in the city. Proc Publ Am Sociol Soc 20:40–46
Bon R, Crosthwaite D (2000) The future of international construction. Thomas Telford, London
Bowman C (2003) Formulating strategy. In: Campbell A, Faulkner D (eds) Oxford handbook of strategy – vol 1: a strategy overview and competitive strategy. Oxford University Press, Oxford, pp 404–436
Braybrooke, D, Lindblom CE (1963) A strategy of decision. The Free Press, New York
Cairncross F (1997) The death of distance. Harvard Business School Press, Boston
Christaller W (1933) The central places of southern Germany. Prentice Hall, Englewood Cliffs
Coase RH (1937) The nature of the firm. Economica 4(16):386–405
Conley TG, Ligon E (2002) Economic distance and cross-country spillovers. J Econ Growth, Springer 7(2):157–187
Cyert R, March J (1963) A behavioural theory of the firm. Prentice-Hall, Englewood Cliffs
Diamond J (1997) Guns, germs and steel: the fate of human societies. Norton, New York
DiMaggio PJ, Powell WW (1983) The iron cage revisited: institutional isomorphism and collective rationality in organizational fields. Am Sociol Rev 48:147–160
Dunbar R (1996) The trouble with science. Harvard University Press, Cambridge
Dunning JH (1988) The eclectic paradigm of international production: a restatement and some possible extensions. J Int Bus Stud 19(1):1–31
Fiedler FE (1967) A theory of leadership effectiveness, McGraw-Hill, New York
Firat CE, Huovinen P (2005) Entering regional construction markets in Russia. In: Kahkonen K, Porkka J (eds) Global perspectives on management and economics in the AEC sector. Technical Research Centre of Finland and Association of Finnish Civil Engineers, Helsinki, pp 57–68
Friedman T (2005) The world is flat. Straus and Giroux, New York

Ghemawat P (2001) Distance still matters: the hard reality of global expansion. Harv Bus Rev 2001:137–147

Ghoshal S, Barlett C (1999) Managing across borders. Harvard Business School, Boston

Goh CT (2001) New Singapore. Prime Minister Goh Chok Tong's National Day Rally Speech at the University Cultural Centre, National University of Singapore on Sunday, 19th August 2001. Singapore Government Press Release, Media Division, Ministry of Information and the Arts

Goodnow JD, Hansz JE (1972) Environmental determinants of overseas market entry strategies. J Int Bus Stud 3(Spring):33–50

Hotelling H (1929) Stability in competition. Econ J 39(153):41–57

Huff DL (1963) A probabilistic analysis of shopping center trade areas. Land Econ 39:81–90

Hunger JD, Wheelen TL (2007) Essentials of strategic management, 4th edn. Pearson Prentice Hall, Upper Saddle River

Hymer SH (1976) The international operation of national firms: a study of direct foreign investment. MIT Press, Cambridge, MA

Isard W (1956) A general location principal of an optimum space-economy. Econometrica 20:406–430

Isard W, Peck MJ (1954) Location theory and international and interregional trade theory. J Econ 68:97–114

Johanson J, Mattson LG (1988) Internationalization in industrial systems – a network approach. In: Hood N et al (eds) Strategies in global competition. Croom Helm, London, pp 287–314

Johanson J, Wiedersheim PF (1975) The internationalisation of the firm – four Swedish cases. J Manag Stud 12(October):305–322

Katona G (1951) Psychological analysis of economic behavior. McGraw-Hill, New York

Kirkpatrick SA, Locke EA (1991) Leadership; do traits matter? Acad Manag Exec 5(2):48–60

Kotler P (2005) Marketing management: analysis, planning, implementation and control, 12th edn. Prentice Hall, Upper Saddle River

Krugman P (1991) Geography and trade. MIT Press, Cambridge, MA

Lawrence P, Lorsch J (1967) Differentiation and integration in complex organizations. Admin Sci Q 12:1–30

Lewin K (1951) Field theory in social science. Harper & Row, New York

Lojeski KS, Reilly RR (2007) Multitasking and innovation in virtual teams. In: Proceedings from the 40th Annual Hawaii International Conference, Big Island, HI, 3–6 January 2007

Majkgard A, Sharma DD (1998) Client-following and market-seeking strategies in the internationalization of service firms. J Bus Bus Mark 4(3):1–41

Masters WA, McMillan MS (2001) Climate and scale in economic growth. J Econ Growth 6(3):167–186

McGuinness T (1994) Markets and managerial hierarchies. In: Thompson G et al (eds) Markets, hierarchies and networks. Sage, London, pp 66–81

Montgomery CA (1995) Of diamond and dust: a New look at resources. In: Montgomery CA (ed) Resource-based and evolutionary theories of the firm. Kluwer Academic, Boston, pp 251–268

Myrdal G (1963) Economic theory and underdeveloped regions. Methuen, London

Ng TWH and Feldman DC (2010) The effects of organizational embeddedness on development of social capital and human capital. J Appl Psychol 95(4):696–712

Niels GN, Harzing A (2003) The country-of-origin effect in multinational corporations: sources, mechanisms and moderating conditions. Manag Int Rev 43(Special Issue 2):47–66

Ohmae K (1999) The borderless world: power and strategy in the interlinked economy – revised edition. Collins, London

Ojala A, Tyrvainen P (2006) Market entry and priority of small and medium-sized enterprises in the software industry: an empirical analysis of cultural distance, geographical distance, and market size. J Int Mark 15(3):123–149

Olson GM, Olson JS (2000) Distance matters. Hum Comput Interact 15:139–179

Parker C (1989) Management information systems – strategy and action. McGraw-Hill, New York

Penrose ET (1959) The theory of the growth of the firm. Blackwell, Oxford

Perlmutter HV (1969) The multinational firm and the future. Ann Am Polit Soc Sci 403(9):139–152

References

Peters T, Waterman R (1980) In search of excellence. Harper & Row, New York
Porter ME (1990) The competitive advantage of nations. Free Press, New York
Posner MV (1961) International trade and technical change. Oxford Economic Papers
Predoehl A (1928) The theory of location in its relation to general economics. J Polit Econ 36:371–390
Reilly WJ (1931) The Law of retail gravitation. Knickerbocker Press, New York
Rosenberg MT (2004) Gravity model: predict the movement of people and ideas between two places. http://geography.about.com/library/weekly/aa031601a.htm. Accessed Aug 2004
Sanchez R (2003) Analyzing internal and competitor competences: resources, capabilities, and management processes. In: Campbell A, Faulkner D (eds) Oxford handbook of strategy – vol 1: a strategy overview and competitive strategy. Oxford University Press, Oxford, pp 344–371
Seeley IH (1995) Building technology, 5th edn. Palgrave, Basingstoke
Taleb NN (2007) The black swan: the impact of the highly improbable. Random House, New York
Tallman SB (1992) A strategic management perspective on host country structure of multinational enterprises. J Manage 18(3):455–471
Taylor PJ (2004) World city network: a global urban analysis. Routledge, London
Tihanyi L, Griffith D, Russell C (2005) The effect of cultural distance on entry mode choice, international diversification, and MNE performance: a meta-analysis. J Int Bus Stud 36:270–283
Tinbergen J (1962) Shaping the world economy: suggestion for an international economic policy. The Twentieth Century Fund, New York
Tobler W (1970) A computer movie simulating urban growth in the Detroit region. Econ Geogr 46(2):234–240
Weber A (1929) Theory of the location of industries. The University of Chicago Press, Chicago
Williamson OE (1975) Markets and hierarchies: analysis and antitrust implications. The Free Press, New York

Chapter 11
CBR-DSS and Validation

11.1 Introduction

This chapter provides details on how the study, its validation, the CBR-logic and the CBR-DSS's efficacy in terms of accuracy and usefulness was undertaken. The copious factors of consideration set at the research's initial stages had been trimmed by selections from the Content Analysis and Statistical Analysis. Three supplementary factors – (i) the number of staff; (ii) embedded-ness of the firm; and (iii) isomorphism (mimetic, institutional and coercive) of firms were added to make up a more manageable list of 20 significant determinants (which would affect the strategic choice of an organization design) to be inputted into the CBR-DSS. The characteristics of the firms were summarized, tabled, and then used to establish the relationships between the independent variables (determinants) and the dependent variables (strategic choices of organization design). The weights of factors were derived through a re-run of the Content Analysis, using co-occurrences between key factors (with their related phrases and words) to determine the levels of significances (and thus the weights) to be allocated. The steps taken for the validation exercise is illustrated below in Fig. 11.1.

11.2 Management of an A/E Firm

Kotler (2005) recommended different strategies for different industries. A/E firms should not be managed like general firms. Moreover, A/E professionals may not be the best managers because of their inclination to specialize and focus on design and technology. It is therefore suggested that a CBR-DSS can assist A&E firms to internalize the myriad of environmental and business factors by drawing on accumulated knowledge and experiences to facilitate and improve decision-making in the choice of organization design when they export their services overseas.

A firm's business strategies, organization structures, organization systems, leadership style, skills, staff, shared values and supply-chain should be managed

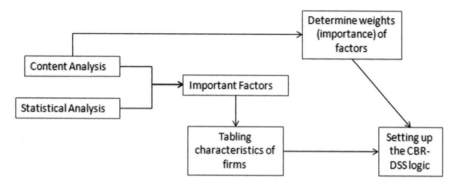

Fig. 11.1 Steps taken for the CBR-logic and the CBR-DSS's efficacy in terms of accuracy and usefulness

according to the firm's values, mission, objectives et cetera. These can be complicated by the nature of the architect's job. An architect from Firm D described:

> My work-scope ranges from making presentations, documentations; liaisons with clients, partners-at-work and suppliers; know clients' requirements, the product and basic pricing due to budget; coordinating design, color and materials; elaborating product specifications and textures, as well as physically going down to construction sites for inspections and coordination. We can see the color and etc. in the brochure but nothing beats going down personally to look at the samples. Moreover, some things have to be conveyed directly to the site as documents may not be able to document certain aspects fully.

An architect's work does not focus entirely on efficiency and profit-maximization. This finding agrees with Aharoni's (1966) Behavioural Theory. A senior architect from Firm B opined:

> Architecture is like a gastronomic creation – you need time to have good designs.

Architects are designers, and designers are, rightly or wrongly, known for their odd temperaments. A Director of Firm A noted an architect's motivation and role in a construction project:

> Architects are egoistic and independent. They are like Indian chiefs, to have to control other participants involved in the project. Architects must be able to discern and make judgments from mixed signals.

A senior associate of Firm A shared her views on how managers in A/E firms are different from managers in other types of firms:

> Architects do not make the best managers because they are often more design-oriented than business and management-oriented.
> The architect does not want to be a number in a game or a pawn in chess. An architect is a professional who is self-motivated and does not work only for money.
> Being business-oriented is being rudimentary, to get things done, is not challenging.

The organization and management of an A/E firm is not entirely based on efficiency and profit maximization. The 8S Framework advocates that strategic and organizational dimensions, namely: Strategy, Structure, Systems, Style of leadership, Skills, Staff, Shared Values and Supply chain are inter-related. It was therefore postulated in the study that an A/E firm, being unique in terms of its skills, staff, values and supply-chain, would have to be strategically managed and organized differently from general firms. Conventional wisdom pertaining to business strategies, management and organization design should be re-evaluated and adapted for an A/E firm.

11.3 Sharing and Learning from Others in the Industry

Learning and understanding is not so straight-forward. It is complicated, as a senior Vice-President of Firm C gave an example of learning about and understanding China:

> There are three stages of learning and understanding China. During the first stage, you try to learn and pick up things. During the second stage, you think you are getting to understand the contexts. But at the third stage, you realize that you are like a blind man touching an elephant and trying to describe it.

An organic firm learns from its mistakes or tries to improve as time goes by. This is also true for an A/E firm. A senior technical manager of Firm B shared how organizational learning within a firm benefits the firm during and after every project:

> We have a lot of sharing sessions. Due to regular meetings, we often settle the problems we face as a group and during the meetings, a lot of people learn from their mistakes. So far, it works
> Most of the time, whenever every project is finished, we will conduct a review and see where we can improve, despite success or failure. We will look at our success factors and what lead to our failures, learning from our mistakes. So over the years, we have actually improved and this routine have became natural for us now.

Sometimes, lessons can be acquired from elsewhere. A Vice-President of Firm F shared:

> We need not commit mistakes, and then learn to avoid such mistakes in the future. We can learn from other peoples' mistakes from a lot of case studies in the market. In a way, our management allows us to review other people's mistakes.

It is, however, important that context should be considered, and that firms should be discerning, and not follow blindly what other firms have implemented or advocated. An architect from Firm B shared:

> Everybody works differently; every company is different. We need to improvise and personalize. Firms can heed the general rules, logic, guide-lines, critical success factors and models, but must change and adapt the settings.

The architect from Firm B gave an example of why a firm should not conform indiscriminately to industry's practices or conventional wisdom for its choice of organization structure. He shared:

> Firms are different sized, have different needs and will need different organizational structures. What is important is that the company is efficient, productive, gets their work done, and is able to guarantee customer's satisfaction.

There are also limitations in the sharing-and-learning process. Some firms are reserved about teaching and imparting their valuable knowledge to other firms. Notwithstanding that, sharing-and-learning has enormous benefits. A senior technical manager of Firm B shared:

> There are things that you will share and things you won't. In general, we still share more than we keep definitely. Every firm will keep to a certain extent for fields that they are stronger in, but we have quite a few seminars whereby we will share with the rest of the firms in the industry. It helps and opens up our minds to look at things in different angles. Whatever you see, you have to analyze it. For example, we recently conducted a study trip to London and met up with quite a few architecture firms and it was then you observed a lot of things. I shared with the offices our experiences and we analyzed what is beneficial for the firms.

11.4 Discussion on Findings in Content Analysis and Statistical Analysis

Table 11.1 shows a summary of the findings from the Content Analysis, in terms of (i) frequency of cited factors according to their related words and phrases; (ii) sequences between factors; (iii) co-occurrences between factors; (iv) proximities between factors; and lastly (v) similarities between factors. These different methods or techniques of content analysis help to provide different perspectives and ways to interpret qualitative information. Table 11.2 shows the summary of the findings from the study's Statistical Analysis, in terms of the top factors ranked according to their average means, as well as unranked factors.

The Content Analysis suggested that:

(i) When transnational A/E firms internationalize, they are concerned mostly about Organizational distance, Business strategies and Business chances;
(ii) Organizational structure is dependent on Organizational distance, Business strategies and Service provided; Organizational structure affects Organizational distance, Business strategies, Business factors and Business chances; Geographical distance affects Organizational distance, Business strategies and Business factors; Geographical distance is often discussed in the context of Organizational distance, Business strategies and Service provided; and
(iii) Both Geographical distance and Organization structure are often discussed along-side with Organization distance, Business strategies, Business chances, Institutional Ownership, Organization systems, Organization values and cultures, Globalization, Business location, and Marketing.

11.4 Discussion on Findings in Content Analysis and Statistical Analysis

Table 11.1 Summary of findings from content analysis

No.	Categories	Factors
1	Frequently cited factors (and their related words and phrases) during the interviews	1. Organizational distance; 2. Business strategies; and 3. Business chances
2	Sequence	Organization structure follows: 1. Organizational distance; 2. Business strategies; and 3. Business factors
		Organization structure precedes: 1. Organizational distance; 2. Business strategies; and 3. Service provided
		Geographical distance follows: 1. Organizational distance; 2. Business strategies; and 3. Business factors
		Geographical distance precedes: 1. Organizational distance; 2. Business strategies; and 3. Business factors
3	Co-occurrences	Geographical distance mostly co-occurs with: 1. Organizational distance; 2. Gravitational and topological distance; and 3. Globalization
		Organization structure mostly co-occurs with: 1. Organizational distance; 2. Service provided; and 3. Organization systems
4	Proximities (equal to relationships or links)	Organization structure is most proximate to: 1. Institutional ownership; 2. Organization system; and 3. Organization values and culture
		Geographical distance is most proximate to: 1. Globalization; 2. Organizational distance; and 3. Business location
5	Similarities between factors	Geographical distance is most similar to: 1. Economical distance; 2. Gravitational and topological distance; and 3. Relational distance

(continued)

Table 11.1 (continued)

No.	Categories	Factors
		Organization structure is most similar to:
		1. Organization systems;
		2. Organizational distance
		3. Organization values and culture

Table 11.2 Top 3 grouped factors in terms of mean and the unranked factors

No.	Top 3 factors	Unranked factors
1	Psychic distance	(i) Discontinuities due to borders
2	Organization structure	(ii) Discontinuities due to distances
3	Risks and its influence on business strategies	(iii) Communications
		(iv) Time-zones/time differences
		(v) Control
		(vi) Networks
		(vii) Friction
		(viii) Factor conditions
		(ix) Demand conditions
		(x) Related and complementary industries
		(xi) Government intervention
		(xii) Chances
		(xiii) Ownership qualities
		(xiv) Difficulties of integrating work

The Statistical Analysis suggested two findings:

(i) The unranked factors (namely: Discontinuities due to borders, Discontinuities due to distances, Communications, Time-zones/time differences, Control, Networks, Friction, Factor conditions. Demand conditions, Related and complementary industries, Government intervention, Chances, Ownership qualities, and Difficulties of integrating work) were disregarded by transnational A/E firms when they internationalize; and

(ii) Transnational A/E firms were most mindful of their understanding of the foreign market, and how they should internalize business risks through the arrangement of organization structure and business strategies.

11.5 The CBR-Logic

CBR is broadly construed as the process of solving new problems based on the solutions of known facts or similar past problems (Nunez 2005). Therefore, it is postulated in this paper that the CBRDSS can be used by A&E firms as an affordable solution that provides comprehensive check-lists and easy-to-use toolkits for A&E consultancy firms to make rational decisions on appropriate business strategies and organizational structures that may be adopted as part of the organizational-learning based model. This is in coherence with Cyert and March's (1963) submission that when confronted with a problem, organizations tend to start their search for solutions among alternatives that are close to solutions that have been tried before.

The study integrated known facts, similar past problems, and solutions implemented by Singapore's A/E firms when they ventured into regional markets. Figure 11.2 lists the 20 questions that the CBR-DSS would inquire, and in turn, the 15 recommendations the CBR-DSS could provide for the user. The questions pertain to the macro, micro and task-environment of the target-market for the internationalizing firm.

The recommendations of the organization design essentially cover Strategy, Structure, System, Style of Leadership, Skills of Firm, Staff, Shared Values and Supply-Chain. The A/E firms' strategic considerations and organization design traits in various cities are summarized in Tables 11.3 and 11.4 respectively. In Table 11.3, the first example from the left shows that the firm is a private A/E firm in KL, has high risk averseness and an average amount of international exposure etc. In Table 11.4, a circle (o) denotes a "yes" while a cross (x) denotes a "no". An asterisk (*) denotes "unsure" because these overseas offices are one or two persons teams. Therefore, it does not make sense to categorize some of the firms' organization parameters. From Table 11.4, it is shown that the same office demonstrated the traits of: all staff are permanent staff, autocratic leadership, delegation of responsibilities and direct supervision by the management. Table 11.5 shows the CBR-logic and relationships between the determinants and the strategic choices of organization design. In Table 11.5, it is shown that a firm which has a high level of risk averseness, high level of embeddedness, with no or little international experience etc. is likely to take up a simple organization structure when they venture overseas and set up an office abroad.

The weights of factors were derived by re-running a Content Analysis's Co-occurrences search, and then using the frequency of the factor which co-occurred most regularly with the specified dimension of organization design as a denominator, to obtain the weights of the factors (refer to Table 11.6). These weights would rationalize how much each aspect of organizational design is influenced by independent factors.

11.6 Step-by-Step Demonstration of the CBR-DSS

Figures 11.3, 11.4, 11.5, and 11.6 shows a step-by-step demonstration of how the CBR-DSS works, complete with step-by-step screen-shots, by using a hypothesized example – Firm X planning to venture into Beijing, China for the first time. The descriptions of Firm X's and Beijing are provided below:

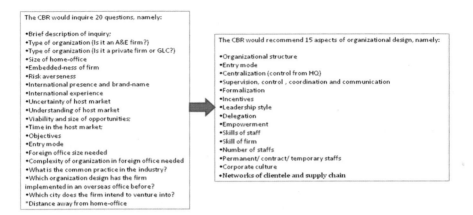

Fig. 11.2 CBR-DSS's inputs and outputs

1. Complexity of organization required – Medium;
2. Risk averseness of Firm X – Medium;
3. Size of potential market in Beijing – Large;
4. Firm X's length of presence in Beijing – Not in the market yet;
5. Firm X's understanding of Beijing – Medium;
6. Firm X's international presence and experience – Low;
7. Firm X's embeddedness in home-market – Medium;
8. Level of market uncertainty in Beijing – Medium;
9. Firm X is a Singaporean A/E firm;
10. Firm X prefers to set up a functional office in Beijing;
11. Firm X's main objective – Market-seeking;
12. Industrial practice – Singaporean A/E firms with offices in Beijing tend to be functional offices;
13. Firm X intends to place 10 staff in Beijing;
14. The level of hostility in Beijing – Medium;
15. Size of Firm X in Singapore – More than 30;
16. Firm X is a private A/E firm;
17. Firm X plans to venture into Beijing, China; and
18. Firm X does not have any overseas offices.

Figure 11.3 shows the screen-shot of the CBR-DSS when Firm X starts to conduct a new CBR-DSS search. Figure 11.4 shows Firm X putting in the description "Beijing entry mode" in the search criteria to initiate a case-find. A case-find locates, from the CBR-DSS's database, a similar case and its recommendations. The short-boxes shown in Fig. 11.5 facilitate the retrieval of similar cases and their recommendations for Firm X's plan to venture into Beijing. In this case, the CBR-DSS may retrieve cases such as "Firm A's entry mode in Beijing" and "Firm B's entry strategy in Beijing" for Firm X's assessment. Figure 11.6 shows that the CBR-DSS advises that Firm X should start by exporting to Beijing. Then, as Firm X

Table 11.3 Strategic concerns of firms for their overseas offices[a]

		A (KL)	A (PN)	A (SH)	A (SP)	B (SP)	C (BJ)	C (HCM)	C (SH)	C (SP)	C (TJ)
1	Description	Description is what is typed in by the user to initiate the case-find in the CBR-DSS									
2	A&E firm?	Yes	Yes	Yes	Yes	Yes	Yes	Yes	Yes	Yes	Yes
3	Genre	Private	Private	Private	Private	Private	Government-linked company	Government-linked company	Government-linked company	Government-linked company	Government-linked company
4	Name of firm	A	A	A	A	B	C	C	C	C	C
5	City of consideration	KL	PN	SH	SP	SP	BJ	HCM	SH	SP	TJ
6	*City (nearest flight)-	This is a "dumdum variable" to be answered only in the case when Question 5 cannot be answered accurately									
7	Size of home-office	>30	>30	>30	>30	>30	>30	>30	>30	>30	>30
8	Embeddedness	Low*	Low*	High	High	High	Medium	Medium	Medium	Medium	Medium
9	Risk averseness	High	High	High	High	High	Medium	Medium	Medium	Medium	Medium
10	International presence and experience	Medium	Medium	Medium	Medium	Low	High	High	High	High	High
11	Implemented	E.g. for entry modes, user would type of entry mode most commonly implemented by the firm (i.e. exp)									
12	Objective	Market + Efficiency + Resource + Strategic asset	Market + Efficiency	Market	Home-office	Home-office	Market	Market + Efficiency	Market + Efficiency + Resources + Strategic asset	Home-office	Market
13	Viable market size	Medium	Small	Large	Large	Large	Large	Medium	Large	Large	Medium
14	Hostility of Market	Low	Low	Low	Low	Low	Low	Low	Low	Low	Low
15	Uncertainty of Market	Low	Low	Medium	Low	Low	Medium	Medium	Medium	Low	Medium
16	Understanding	High	Medium	Medium	High	High	Medium	Medium	Medium	High	Low
17	Required complexity	Medium	Medium	Low	High	High	Low	Medium	Medium	High	Low
18	Industry's common practice	E.g. for entry modes, user would type in type of entry mode most commonly implemented by firms in the Indus)									
19	Size of overseas office	Medium	Medium	Small	Large	Large	Small	Medium	Large	Large	Small
20	Entry mode	WOS*	Export	Representative office	Home-office	Home-office	Representative office	Export	Representative office	Home-office	Export

[a]Only Firms A, B and C are shown here for the figure to be readable

Table 11.4 Traits of firm's offices in various locations[a]

	A (KL)	A (PN)	A (SH)	A (SP)	B (SP)	C (BJ)	C (HCM)	C (SH)	C (SP)	C (TJ)
All permanent staffs	o	o	x	o	o	x	o	o	o	o
Autocratic leadership	o	x	*	x	x	*	x	x	x	*
Delegated responsibilities	o	o	o	o	o	o	o	o	o	o
Democratic leadership	x	o	*	o	o	*	o	o	o	*
Direct supervision	o	o	*	x	x	*	x	x	x	*
Empowered	x	x	*	x	x	*	x	x	x	*
Ethnocentric corporate culture	x	x	o	o	o	x	o	x	x	x
Ethnocentric networks	x	x	x	o	o	x	x	x	x	x
Export	x	x	x	x	x	x	x	x	x	x
Formalized control and coordination	x	x	*	x	x	*	x	o	o	*
Functional structure	o	o	x	x	x	x	o	x	x	x
General oversight and review	x	x	*	o	o	*	o	x	x	*
Generalized skills for firm	x	x	x	x	o	x	x	x	x	x
General skills for staffs	o	o	x	x	x	x	o	x	x	x
High centralization	x	x	x	o	o	x	x	x	o	x
High formalization	x	x	x	x	x	x	x	o	o	x
Joint venture	x	x	x	x	x	x	x	x	x	x
Large number of staffs	x	x	x	o	o	x	x	o	o	x
Low centralization	o	o	x	x	x	x	o	o	x	x
Low formalization	x	x	o	x	x	o	x	x	x	o
Matrix structure	x	x	x	o	o	x	x	o	o	x
Medium centralization	x	x	o	x	x	o	x	x	x	o
Medium formalization	o	o	x	o	o	x	o	x	x	x
Medium number of staffs	o	o	x	x	x	x	o	x	x	x
Mix of staffs	x	x	o	x	x	o	x	x	x	o
Multidisciplinary firm	x	x	x	x	x	o	o	o	o	o
Niche firm	o	o	o	o	x	x	x	x	x	x
No/little delegation	x	x	*	x	x	*	x	x	x	*
Not empowered	o	o	*	o	o	*	o	o	o	*
Polycentric corporate culture	o	o	x	x	x	o	x	x	x	o
Polycentric networks	x	o	o	x	x	o	x	x	x	o
Procedural incentives	o	o	o	o	o	o	o	o	o	o
Regioncentric/geocentric culture	x	x	x	x	x	x	x	o	o	x
Regioncentric/geocentric networks	x	x	x	x	x	x	o	o	o	x
Representative office	x	x	o	x	x	o	x	x	x	o
Results-based incentives	x	x	x	x	x	x	x	x	x	x
Simple structure	x	x	o	x	x	o	x	x	x	o
Small number of staffs	x	x	o	x	x	o	x	x	x	o
Specialized skills for staffs	x	x	o	o	o	o	x	o	o	o
Wholly-owned subsidiary (technical o&$$$;	*	*	x	x	x	x	o	o	x	x
Unique situation	*	*	x	x	x	x	x	x	x	x

Circle (o) denotes a "yes" while a cross (x) denotes a "no". Asterisk (*) denotes "unsure" because these overseas offices are one or two persons teams

[a]Only Firms A, B and C are shown here for the figure to be readable

Table 11.5 CBR-logic and relationships between the determinants and the strategic choices of organization design[a]

Domain/s	Risk averseness	Embeddedness	International experience and presence	Market size and viability of opportunities	Objectives	Environment, barriers and restrictions	Entry mode	Size of office and Genre of organization	Isomorphism (norms)	Flight-time (h)	Recommended Organizational Design
Organization structure	High	High	No/little	Small/medium	Market seeking	High complexity, high uncertainty, high equivocality, high hostility	Business seedling/ Representative office	Size < 5 (small)	Simple configuration	2–3	Simple configuration
	Medium	Medium	Little/adequate	Medium/large	Market seeking/efficiency seeking	Low equivocality, low uncertainty, low complexity	WOS (technical office)	5 < size <50 (medium)	Functional configuration	1, 3–6	Functional configuration
	Low	Low	Experienced	Large	Market seeking/resource seeking/ efficiency seeking/ strategic-assets seeking	High equivocality, high complexity	WOS (design office)	Size > 50 (large)	Matrix configuration	1, 5–6	Matrix configuration
Entry mode	High	High	No/little	Small	Market seeking	High complexity, high uncertainty, high equivocality, high hostility	NA	No	Exporting only (including project office)	1–6	Exporting only (including project office)
	High	High	No/little	Medium/large	Market seeking	High complexity, high uncertainty, high equivocality, high hostility	NA	Small	Representative office or Business seed	5–6	Representative office or Business seed
	Medium	Medium	Little/adequate	Large	Market seeking/resource seeking/ efficiency seeking/	High equivocality	NA	Medium or large	Joint venture (JV)	1, 3–6	Joint venture (JV)

[a]Only organization structure and entry mode are shown here for the figure to be readable

Table 11.6 Co-occurrences and weights between factors[a]

	Background information	Centralization	Complexity of organization required	Corporate culture and values	Delegation	Embeddedness of firm	Empowerement
Background information	961	26	16	40	12	353	16
	10	0.27055	0.16649	0.41623	0.12487	3.67326	0.16649
Centralization	26	41	2	5	0	17	2
	6.34146	10	0.4878	1.21951	0	4.14634	0.4878
Complexity of organization required	16	2	48	0	2	2	0
	3.33333	0.41667	10	0	0.41667	0.41667	0
Corporate culture and values	40	5	0	72	1	34	2
	5.55556	0.69444	0	10	0.13889	4.72222	0.27778
Delegation	12	0	2	1	22	6	5
	5.45455	0	0.90909	0.45455	10	2.72727	2.27273
Embeddedness of firm	353	17	2	34	6	375	11
	9.41333	0.45333	0.05333	0.90667	0.16	10	0.29333
Empowerment	16	2	0	2	5	11	30
	5.33333	0.66667	0	0.66667	1.66667	3.66667	10
Entry mode	76	1	4	2	1	16	1
	8.94118	0.11765	0.47059	0.23529	0.11765	1.88235	0.11765

Example: Weight of "Embeddedness" on Entry mode = 1.88 (derived from table above) + 10 (base weight; The base weight is the recommended default weight of the CBR-DSS software) = 11.88

[a]Only part of the whole table is shown here for the figure to be readable

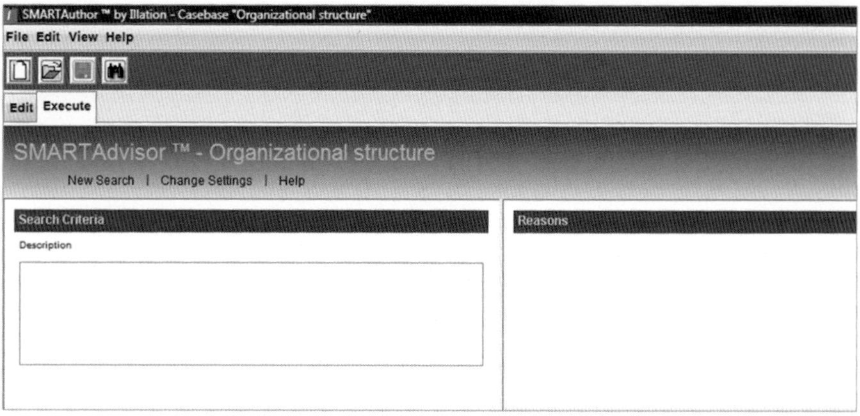

Fig. 11.3 A new CBR-DSS search (User's screenshot)

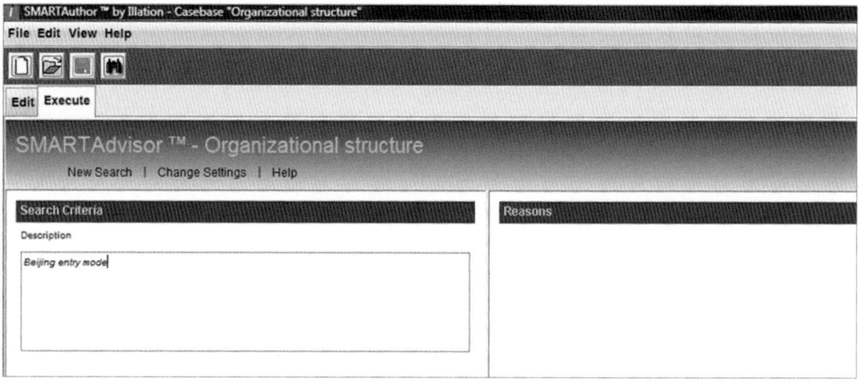

Fig. 11.4 Search criteria of the CBR-DSS (User's screenshot)

understands more about the market in Beijing, establishes more contacts and clinches more projects, it may choose to expand its scope and size.

11.7 Validation

Validation is an important process of knowledge inquiry because it tests the reliability of the research findings. The validation of the CBR-DSS was conducted between October 2009 and November 2009. Four firms were chosen for the validation, out of which two had participated as the research's case-studies. The CBR-logic and the efficacy of the CBR-DSS were validated by a senior practitioner in each of these four firms. Their profiles are shown in Table 11.7. After the

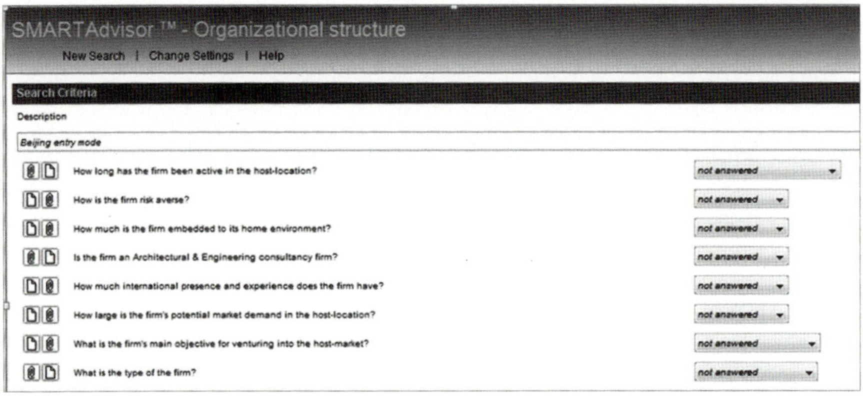

Fig. 11.5 Short boxes to facilitate case-find (User's screenshot)

Fig. 11.6 CBR-DSS for Firm X (User's screenshot; Only 7 out of the 20 questions are shown here for the figure to be readable; Long period of time is defined as a period of time that is more than 5 years. Any period of time less than that is defined as medium/short period of time)

Table 11.7 Profile of respondents for validation exercise

No.	Designation	Firm	Characteristics
1	Senior Vice President	Firm C	Firm C in other cities
2	Associate Director	Firm D	Firm D in other cities
3	Senior Advisor	Firm Y	Government-linked A/E firm
4	Chairman	Firm Z	Private A/E firm

researcher explained and demonstrated the CBR-DSS to them, these senior practitioners were told to try out the CBR-DSS based on their firms' (i) international experiences; and (ii) future endeavors. These senior practitioners were then asked to feedback on the CBR-DSS (refer to Appendix C).

11.7 Validation

11.7.1 Feedback

These senior practitioners attested to the validity of the CBR-logic and the CBR-DSS's applicability in terms of effectiveness and efficiency. These senior practitioners shared their views below.

When asked on what other factors he thought the DSS should include into consideration, and how the DSS can be improved, the senior Vice-President of Firm C opined:

> *I think there can be two types of hostility – business and culture. Maybe the system can consider differentiating them.*

> *The CBR-DSS is quite a good tool-kit for A/E managers to get recommendations and advices on business strategies and organization. However, there should be more guidance, like in terms of definitions and to make it easier to understand.*

The Associate Director of Firm D supported the use of the CBR-DSS as a useful toolkit and checklist by an internationalizing A/E firm to obtain preliminary guidance, advices and recommendations on business strategies and organization designs:

> *The CBR-DSS should be useful for firms with less or little international experiences, or for international managers who do not have adequate knowledge of an overseas market. Firms can also use the questions and options in the CBR-DSS as a checklist to evaluate the operating conditions and the firm's characteristics, before deciding on the appropriate business strategies and organization design to implement in the overseas market.*

The Chairman of Firm Z shared:

> *We do not run our firms like normal businesses. Furthermore, management consultancy firms may not know so much about our work, and would not be in a good position to advise us. Architectural firms sometimes look on top of prices and monies. For example, even if the firm is offered a low fee to redesign the Istana, we will take it without qualms, because it is a once-in-the-lifetime type of project. On top of that, we gain a lot of satisfaction from doing good designs and improving on our designs. Therefore, I still think it is the best that architects or engineers manage their own firms. It is better that an architect who is interested in management to learn to manage an A/E firm.*

> *More importantly, we need them to help us get accountants and legal firms to tell us more about the operational and legal frameworks of those places, like for example, how much set-up capital do we need, what are the taxation laws, how can we circumvent around these restrictions. Therefore, perhaps the DSS should try to incorporate these elements to be truly useful to an internationalizing firm.*

The senior advisor of Firm Y commented:

> *The most important consideration (for a firm's overseas office's organization structure) would be its business case. The firm would have to consider its vision, mission, local laws, market conditions, and the fundamentals of business management and organization. One of the key decisions would be whether to have an overseas office at all. For business, we always start small.*

> *A firm would probably need to be sufficiently big enough to be able to venture overseas. By that, I mean the firm size should be more than 30. At least 3 employees would have to pay attention to an export market. It is the same for a representative office – you may station 1*

Table 11.8 Recommendations and modifications to CBR-DSS

No	Recommendations	Actions/modifications
1	Differentiate types of hostilities	No modifications because the CBR-DSS seeks to perform the role of a Decision Support System but not an informational database
2	Provide clear definitions and guidance	Definitions have been tagged to technical jargons
		A glossary of terminologies has been built
		A guide has been constructed to explain how each dependent factor could be influenced by some variables
		Illustrations have been created to improve users understanding of the CBR-DSS system and its logic
3	Include operational and legal framework	No modifications because the operational and legal frameworks have been considered in other variables

staff there, but you would also need 2 other support staff in the home-office. A firm would have to have at least 6 staff in a technical office. Some of them would have to be from Singapore. 30 is an ideal, for a Small Medium Enterprise (SME). There are firms that had ventured out despite having only 4 or 5 staff, but they did it more out of no choice.

These practitioners were also asked to complete a feed-back survey pertaining to the CBR-DSS. Their feedback was as follows:

1. Organization design is important to a firm and its overseas offices;
2. Artificial Intelligence (AI) or Decision Support Systems (DSS) is useful for managerial decisions (e.g. decisions on internationalization);
3. CBR-DSS is accurate in reflecting the actual business strategies and organization design implemented (or to be implemented) by the firm's offices in overseas markets; and
4. CBR-DSS is seen as a useful toolkit and/or checklist for firms to obtain preliminary guidance, advices and recommendations on business strategies and organization designs for an internationalizing firm.

11.7.2 Recommendations and Modifications

Table 11.8 shows the recommendations from the validation exercise and the actions taken to improve the CBR-DSS. No rectifications were taken to differentiate the various types of hostilities because (i) the level of hostility in the overseas market has been aggregated; and (ii) the different types of hostilities have been taken into account in other variables. No actions were taken to include information on foreign markets' operational and legal frameworks in the CBR-DSS because (i) the CBR-DSS seeks to perform the role of a Decision Support System but not an informational database; and (ii) the operational and legal frameworks have been considered in other variables. However, the CBR-DSS has been improved by adding a guide, glossary and illustrations so that user would be able to (i) navigate around the programme; (ii) understand the technical jargons used in the system; and (iii) fully utilize the potential of this software.

11.8 The Completed CBR-DSS Prototype

Following the validation exercise, this section explains how the CBR-DSS prototype was ultimately set up. Figure 11.7 shows how the CBR-DSS is initiated. Figure 11.8 shows the set of questions that the user would be asked to answer.

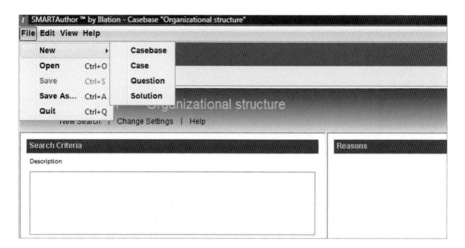

Fig. 11.7 Start to set up the CBR-DSS (Administrator's screenshot)

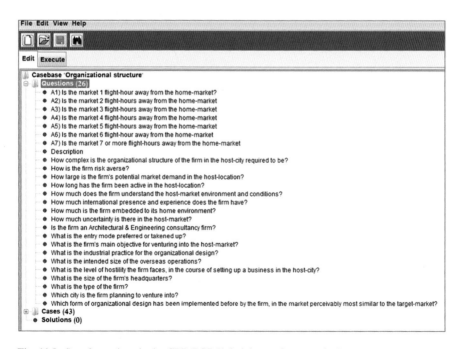

Fig. 11.8 Set of questions in the CBR-DSS (Administrator's screenshot)

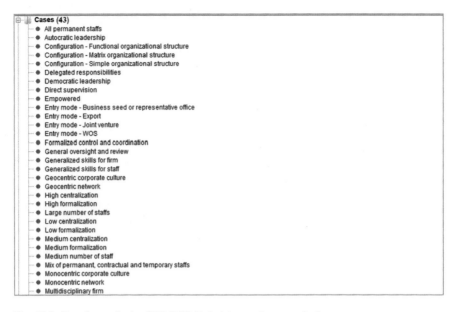

Fig. 11.9 Set of cases in the CBR-DSS (Administrator's screenshot)

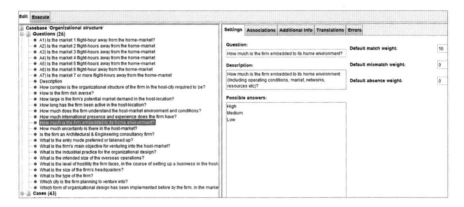

Fig. 11.10 Settings of possible answers to questions in the CBR-DSS (Administrator's screenshot)

Figure 11.9 shows the set-up of cases, or possible recommendations that the system could generate. Figure 11.10 demonstrates how possible answers are tagged to the questions asked – for example, the question "How much is the firm embedded in its home environment?" could elicit either a "High", "Medium" or "Low" response from the user. It is also shown in the figure that the default weight of an element has been set at base = 10. As explained in Table 11.6, the weight of a factor is determined by its co-occurrences with a particular aspect of organization design,

11.9 Conclusion from Validation

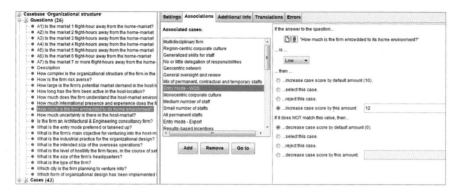

Fig. 11.11 Settings of associations in the CBR-DSS (Administrator's screenshot)

and the base-weight. Figure 11.11 shows how associations are set up in the CBR-DSS. For instance, entry mode is determined by many factors, one of these being the level of embeddedness of the firm to its home environment.

Figure 11.11 shows that when the firm's embeddedness to its home environment is low, the system is more inclined (rounded to the nearest number to 12 points) to recommend the firm to choose to establish a wholly-owned subsidiary as its entry mode into a foreign market. The user may choose to ignore or skip a question if he is unsure of its answer. Figures 11.12 and 11.13 show how the user can get supplementary information pertaining to definitions and recommendation in the CBR-DSS by clicking on the icons. For example, in Fig. 11.14, the CBR-DSS recommends that the firm should take up exporting as its entry mode into Beijing, China.

It should also be noted that CBR may be less effective with complex tasks (Leake 1996), and can be misled by common or coincidental similarities between cases, and thus fail to recognize important matches that may make the difference between case-selection and case-rejection (Wagman 2003). Therefore, human judgement is still required to alleviate the risks of installing structural errors in the CBR build-up. The CBR can be a useful tool to support the decision-making processes of an internationalizing A/E firm. This solution offers the merits of both the efficiency of artificial intelligence to extract information from a rich database and the discernment of human judgment.

11.9 Conclusion from Validation

A/E firms are exposed to altered conditions when they venture overseas. An internationalizing firm has to carefully devise appropriate business strategies and organization designs to internalize the risks of internationalization. However, firms are likely to have bounded knowledge and rationality of the appropriate business strategies and organization designs to implement when their firms intend to

Fig. 11.12 Example of supplementary information to guide users on how to use the CBR-DSS (User's screenshot)

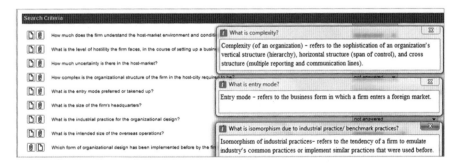

Fig. 11.13 Definitions of terms included in the CBR-DSS (User's screenshot)

internationalize into markets abroad. This is especially so when the company is a newcomer to the overseas environment (Root 1998). This problem is exacerbated for an A&E firm, because A&E professionals may not be the best managers due to their inclination to specialize and focus on design and technology.

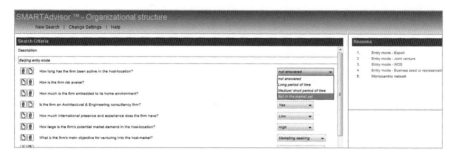

Fig. 11.14 Recommendations from the CBR-DSS (User's screenshot)

Another significant barrier impeding the internationalization of A/E firms is the lack of strategic and organizational know-how to internationalize. Whereas large multinational firms may engage management consultants to analyze their organizations, recommend new strategic directions and business strategies, streamline their operations et cetera, A/E firms may have an aversion to approach professional consultancy services because (i) the firm may not want to reveal too much of its businesses to external consultants; (ii) such services are expensive and time-consuming; (iii) A/E businesses are project-based and unique; and (iv) management consultants who are not architecturally or engineering trained may not fully appreciate the concerns of an A/E business.

It was therefore suggested that a CBR-DSS can assist A/E firms to internalize the myriad of environmental and business factors by drawing on accumulated knowledge and experiences to facilitate and improve decision-making in the choice of organization design when they export their services overseas. It was also postulated that the CBRDSS can be tailored to consider significant factors that influence the choice of organization design, to provide affordable solutions, comprehensive check-lists and easy-to-use tool-kits for A/E consultancy firms.

Through validation, the CBR-DSS has been ascertained to be a useful instrument to solve new problems based on known facts or solutions from precedent-problems. Furthermore, the CBR-DSS is also able to retrieve, reuse, revise and retain cases for future references and support. This means that new decisions would reconcile with existing knowledge and case-bases, and adapt themselves to fill gaps in the database for storage and future usage. Hence, the CBR-DSS is recommended as a useful toolkit and/or checklist by an internationalizing A/E firm to obtain preliminary guidance, advices and recommendations on business strategies and organization designs.

References

Aharoni Y (1966) The foreign investment decision process. Division of Research, Graduate School of Business Administration, Harvard University, Cambridge, MA

Cyert R, March J (1963) A behavioural theory of the firm. Prentice-Hall, Englewood Cliffs

Kotler P (2005) Marketing management: analysis, Planning, implementation and control, 12th edn. Prentice Hall, Upper Saddle River

Leake DB (1996) CBR in context: the present and future. In: Leake DB (ed) Case-based reasoning: experiences, lessons & future directions. AAAI Press/MIT Press, Menlo Park, pp 3–30

Nunez S (2005) SMART author user's guide. Illation Ltd., Singapore

Root FR (1998) Entry strategies for international markets, Revised edn. Jossey-Bass, San Francisco

Wagman M (2003) Reasoning processes in humans and computers: theory and research in psychology and artificial intelligence. Praeger, Westport

Chapter 12
Conclusion

12.1 Introduction

Ever since former Prime Minister Mr. Goh Chok Tong and current Prime Minister Mr. Lee Hsien Loong urged that Singapore's home-grown firms should not stay satisfied to be comfortably embedded in Singapore, but have to see the world as their oysters, and exhorted Singapore's firms to take advantage of the country's geographical and cultural proximity to thriving markets in the region, many indigenous firms have taken the recommendation, and ventured abroad with market-seeking, resource-seeking, efficiency seeking or strategic assets seeking objectives. These nearby markets, because of their proximity from Singapore, were suggested to impose less logistical constraints and sap of access to strategic home-based location-specific resources for these firms' endeavors. In addition, these locations are likely to share historical, cultural and language affinities with Singapore. It was thus put forward that Singapore's firms are more cognizant of these business environments, and incur less uncertainty and risks for their overseas forays into these locations.

Many of these firms' overseas ventures have succeeded, but many have also failed. There seem to have scores of Critical Success Factors pertaining to the internationalization of firms. Indigenous and transnational firms domiciled in Singapore have need of sound strategic management and organization when they export or extend their operations or services to these neighboring countries or cities. The firms' organization designs are of particular importance for their offices and staff in separate locations to stay connected and congruent to common goals, build resilient relationships between them, synchronize and monitor work in a spatially distributed environment (Thompson 1967). Corporate-level, business-level, and functional-level business strategies and organization implemented by offices in different cities also have to be well-balanced and harmonized by the transnational firm to avert from problems and inefficiencies in coordination, cooperation and communication.

The lack of a critical mass or substantial home demand has spurred many Singapore's A/E firms to attempt to export of their consultancy services to regional markets such as Kuala Lumpur, Penang, Ho Chi Minh City, Hanoi, Shanghai, Beijing and Tianjin. This study therefore aimed to (i) appraise the competitiveness of Singapore's A/E consultancy firms in these regional markets; (ii) find out what are the preferred business strategies of A/E firms when they venture overseas; (iii) compare and contrast the internationalization efforts of private and government-linked A/E firms; (iv) evaluate the discontinuities in environment and access to home-based resources due to national borders and geographical distances; (v) examine if distance changes the A/E firm's risk perceptions and decisions due to bounded rationality (satisfying with sequential decisions) due to the increasingly complex and uncertain environment; (vi) analyse the relationship between flight-time (proxy for geographical distance) and organization structures adopted by Singapore-domiciled A/E consultancy firms when they export their services; (vii) test if business strategies or organization structures could be extrapolated according to the flight-time away from Singapore; and (viii) develop a Case-based Reasoning (CBR) Decision Support System (DSS), or in short, CBR-DSS, that would assist companies to decide on, and formulate appropriate business strategies and organization designs when they internationalize.

This study started by hypothesizing that flight-distance could be the causal factor for the differences in a spectrum of factors, such as climate, time-zone, bodily adjustments, cultural distance, administrative distance, geographical distance, economical distance, technological distance, socio-demographical distance, relational distance and organizational distance. Organizational distance could in turn, manifest itself as changes, spill-over, time-lag, time-differences, psychic distance, networks, communications, net costs-benefits, and control (Sect. 1.5). Concepts such as Localization and Agglomeration were then introduced to elucidate the phenomena of Core and Periphery Locations, and the System of Cities in the world today, and to explain Singapore's A/E firms' market selections and their corresponding choices of entry modes, strategic management and organization when they internationalize. The research is a synthesis of these knowledge areas.

12.2 Major Contributions of the Study

This section presents the major contributions of the study in four parts, namely: (i) important findings of the research; (ii) validation of hypothesis; (iii) contribution to knowledge; and (iv) contribution to industry. The research was contemplated in the first place because of the knowledge gap that while Singapore-domiciled A/E firms have been venturing overseas, it was unclear what were the entry modes adopted by these firms to gain the all-important beach-heads and footholds, and then the policies, strategies and management techniques implemented subsequently to expand the overseas ventures; and how these firms organize themselves structurally and systematically in these overseas cities. It was also unclear if there is a relationship between flight-time (as a proxy for geographical distance), business

12.2 Major Contributions of the Study

strategies and organization design. The purpose of this study was to provide answers to this lacuna in knowledge as well as to develop a framework for organizational learning through a CBR-DSS.

12.2.1 Major Findings of the Study

12.2.1.1 Competitiveness of Singapore's A/E Firms in Regional Markets

The research identified the most important constituents of Singapore's A/E firms' strengths, weaknesses, opportunities and threats in regional markets. Using the study's Eclectic Diamond Framework-SWOT Analysis Matrix, Table 12.1 highlights the competitiveness of Singapore's A/E consultancy firms in regional markets. In general, Singapore's A/E firms are considered to be very strong in terms of A/E capabilities and good-value for money in the region, and are in a favorable position to tap into market opportunities in the vicinity because of the geographical and cultural proximities between Singapore and these regional markets. However, Singapore's A/E firms are considered to be weaker than top A/E firms from USA, Europe, Japan and Australia, in terms of design capabilities.

12.2.1.2 Strategies Adopted by Singaporean A/E Firms When They Venture Overseas

From the case studies, interviews and questionnaire surveys, the study detected the corporate, business and functional-level strategies devised or implemented by Singapore's A/E firms for internationalizing into regional markets. Table 12.2 presents 25 commonly applied strategies by Singapore's A/E firms, stratified into the three main stages of an A/E firm's internationalization process, namely: preparation, entry and operations. As a general rule, Singapore's A/E firms try to build competitive advantages and promote their brand-names at preparation stage, take up entry modes that require less commitment and investments at entry stage, and provide customer-focused value-for-money services at operations stage.

12.2.1.3 Comparisons Between Overseas Offices of Private and Government-Linked A/E Firms

Table 12.3 underscores how Singapore's A/E GLCs have generally evolved after their privatization. Table 12.4 highlights the differences between Singapore's private and government-linked A/E firms. These two observations draw on the study's 8S (or 7S + S) Framework, adopted from the McKinsey 7S Strategic Toolkit, to analyze the strategic parameters of the organizations in order to be organized in a holistic and effective way (Pascale and Athos 1981). The 8S

Table 12.1 Eclectic Diamond Framework-SWOT analysis matrix of Singapore's A/E firms

Eclectic Diamond Framework	Strengths	Weaknesses	Opportunities	Threats
Factor	Concentration of A/E firms and talents in the region	Lack of substantial home demand	Export of services to fast-developing locations in the region	Host-city's local competitors are catching up in terms of knowledge and technology, and are asking for much lower professional fees
Demand	Above average in terms of sophistication of demand	Few iconic/landmark projects (often designed by internationally renowned firms instead)	Technology transfer to regional cities	Host-city's local clients are more concerned about prices than quality of design and services
Complementary services	Agglomeration of professional activities in Singapore	Firms are individualistic and do not form Keiretsu like Japanese firms. For Chinese markets, Singapore's firms do not network as well as firms from Hong Kong and Taiwan, thus losing project opportunities to them in the process	Enter foreign markets with fellow Singaporean partners, or as a consortium	Problems of communication, coordination and cooperation between firms of different work cultures and backgrounds
Strategy (due to competition)	Experiences in selling their niches along with geographical diversification	Have not ventured into developed markets in USA and Europe, and thus have not gained from the vibrancy of the industries there	Green and sustainable buildings; Multi-disciplinary one-stop services	Many international A/E firms already have presences in the region's top cities
Government	Architecture of FTAs and good bilateral or multilateral ties	Firms may lack initiative and tend to look to the government for "answers"	IESingapore, set up by the Ministry of Trade and Industry, informs Singapore's firms of project opportunities abroad	Restrictions imposed by host authorities

12.2 Major Contributions of the Study

Chance	Singapore has historical and cultural affinities with, and enjoy geographical proximity to South-east Asia, China and India	Mostly relying on word-of-mouth recommendations- not enough marketing	Business seedlings, representative offices to find new businesses	Risks of defaults on payments by home-city's local clients
Ownership	Brand-name of Singapore and of firm	Reputation not as stellar as USA, European, Japanese and Australian A/E firms	Brand-name may get advertized if overseas jobs are well-done	Brand-name may get tainted if overseas jobs are botched
Location	Geographical proximity to markets	No hinterland for more growth stimulus	Fast-developing economies in the region	Taiwan and Hong Kong's A/E firms are vying for Chinese markets, and they share even closer cultural affinities and are located more proximate geographically
Internalization	Making use of cultural and geographical proximity	Lack of flexibility or inability to maneuver around restrictions	Venturing into regional markets, especially in South-east Asia, China and India.	Competition between A/E firms is intense, may lead to cut-throat price-wars

Table 12.2 Strategies adopted by Singapore's A/E firms

Action	Stage	Purpose
Adding and improving competencies and capabilities[a]	Preparation	Improve work, Attract talents, Develop niches
Building brand-name by winning awards and competitions[a]		Improve reputation, Build up firm's and staff' confidence
Building up project references (both overseas and in Singapore)[a]		Improve firm's profile, Develop competencies
Using both Singapore's and firm's brand-name[a]		Marketing
Making use of alliances and networks	Entry	Partner with clients
Consortium		Benefit from one another's strengths
Diversifying in terms of geographical markets		Diversify into new markets, Acquire knowledge of markets
Exporting		Enter to understand new market
Business seedling or representative offices		Seek new market opportunities
Due diligence on prospective clients		Risks management
Ethnocentric work culture and management	Operations	Quality control and portrayal of image
Customer-relationship management		Retain clients
Strategic advice/consultancy		Value-added services
Collaborating with local design institutes		Satisfy regulations and to learn about market
Enhancing IT infrastructure within the organization		Enhance efficiency of virtual collocation and enabling sharing of informational resources
Training and sharing of knowledge		Human resource development
Multi-disciplinary one-stop services		Provide convenience and synergy
Niche		Forte
Iconic design		Win bid-for-project by design
International-level service at regional-level prices		Value-for-money
Hedging currencies or stipulation of contractual terms on payment		Financial strategy
Localization		Lower operational costs/to become sustainable in a foreign market
Setting up a RHQ abroad to manage a few offices in the region		Heightened awareness of businesses'/projects' conditions in region
Outsourcing		Firms outsource non-critical and non-core activities so that they can focus on their core competencies.
Incrementalism		Firms incrementally internationalize into markets which are geographically further away, or/and incrementally increase their commitment in these overseas markets

[a]Strategies do not stop at preparation stage

12.2 Major Contributions of the Study

Table 12.3 Re-posturing and realignment of strategies and organization designs by A/E GLCs

McKinsey (7S + "S")	Comparison (previously)	GLC (now)
Strategy	To provide public goods and services;	Target segments and foci are different;
	Did not internationalize;	Diversification of markets through internationalization;
	Did not pay attention to marketing	Marketing (7P – product, price, place, promotion, people, process and physical evidence)
Structure	Ownership: Government;	Ownership: Corporatized or privatized;
	Hierarchical organization;	Matrix organization;
	More rigidity in terms of work allocation	Firms are more flexible, and teams are often formed to work on projects
System	More centralized;	Decentralized;
	More formalized;	Less formalization
	Promotion and remuneration very much based on seniority in the organization	Staff (including top management) are more likely to be employed from outside the organization;
		Communications and reporting have been made easier and more efficient with the introduction of intranet portals and e-communication systems
Style of leadership	More bureaucratic	More empowerment of authority and delegation of responsibilities
Skills	Functional silos as governmental boards or agencies	Have a wider range of expertise due to cross-over of staff from other GLCs
Staff	Bureaucrats	Promotional prospects and remuneration based on meritocracy;
		Top management may be talent-hunted from the private sector, even though senior bureaucrats are still routinely promoted to the board/top management;
		Cross-over of staff between GLCs has become common
Shared Values	Ethnocentric	More region-centric or even geocentric
Supply-chain networks	Mostly projects from governmental agencies or for public goods and services	More region-centric or even geocentric; Have to compete for projects

Framework adds "Supply-chain" to the existing model of Strategy, Structure, System, Style, Staff, Skills and Shared Values popularized by Peters and Waterman (1980). It was found that A/E GLCs are likely to re-posture themselves and realign their business strategies and organization designs when they corporatized or privatized. Private and GLCs tend to cater to different target segments and have different organization structures.

Table 12.4 Strategic differences between Private and Government-linked companies when they venture overseas

McKinsey (7S + "S")	Private	GLC	Comparison
Strategy	Niche	Multi-disciplinary	Target segments and foci are different
Structure	Mostly Simple, or Functional	Mostly Functional, or Matrix	Organization structures are more complex in GLCs
System	Centralized decisions from HQ More flexible and direct	Decentralized decisions from HQ May be more hierarchical, with more formalization	GLCs are more likely to have fully-functional design offices abroad
Style of leadership	Singaporean expatriate staff assume more leadership and are more empowered	Singaporean expatriates are not as empowered as in the private sector	Leadership is more democratic in private firms
Skills	Commercial projects	Master-planning, Township-planning, Institutional projects, etc.	GLCs have wider range of expertise GLCs have better track records/project references due to their heritages as nation-building agencies before they were corporatized
Staff	Less staff	More staff	GLCs employ more staff
Shared values	Ethnocentric	Region-centric	Private firms tend to transfer design-based work to home-offices
Supply-chain networks	More ethnocentric	More region-centric or geo-centric	GLCs collaborate with host-city's local institutional clients more

12.2.1.4 Discontinuities in Environment and Access to Resources due to Geographical Distances

The study puts forward that flight-time (a proxy for geographical distance) could influence a plethora of other factors or issues that would affect a firm's internationalization efforts (i.e. business strategies and organization design). It is espoused in the study that flight-time, as an independent variable, affects mediator variables (climate, time-zones, geography, gravitational relationship, culture, administration, economy, technology, demography and historical links between two cities, which in turn influence the organization design of a firm, a dependent variable.

Figure 12.1 illustrates a Double-octagonal Perspective of Distance. It espouses that these manifestations of distance are mediator variables between flight-time and organization design. The First Octagon (on the left) considers how the actual or perception of a regional market could be affected by Cultural distance,

12.2 Major Contributions of the Study

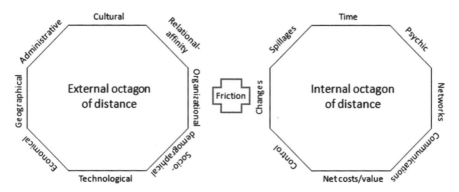

Fig. 12.1 Double-octagonal perspective of distance

Administrative distance, Geographical distance, Topological distance, Gravitational distance, Economical distance, Technological distance, Socio-demographical distance and Organizational distance. The Second Octagon (on the right) considers how these forms of distance influence dimensions of organizational distance, including Changes, Spillages, Time-differences and lags, Psychic distance, Networks, Communications, Net Value-Costs and Control (or parent-subsidiary relationship). The Double-octagonal Perspective of Distance describes and warns of how companies routinely overestimate the attractiveness of foreign markets while ignoring the friction, costs and risks of doing business in a new market. It is suggested in this study that an explicit consideration of the Double-octagonal perspective of distance can change an A/E firm's outlook on overseas market and rethink about its strategic options.

12.2.1.5 Implications of Distances on Risk Perception and Bounded Rationality of Decisions

The Uppsala Model (Johanson and Wiedersheim 1975) suggests that firms abstain from being overly entrenched with commitments and investments when they internationalize into farther away markets, and even more so when they do not have much experiences of internationalization. This is mainly due to the firm's (or the management's) lesser knowledge and familiarity of the foreign market that is further away from the firm's home-market. The study found that the flight-time (as a proxy for distance), affects the size of viable markets for the firm and the risk perception of these markets by the firm, which subsequently affects the choice of the firm's business strategies and organization design. Figure 12.2 highlights the relationships between flight-time, market size, attractiveness of market, opportunity-risk consideration, and the firm's consequent choice of business strategies and organization design. It also shows how the book is pieced together.

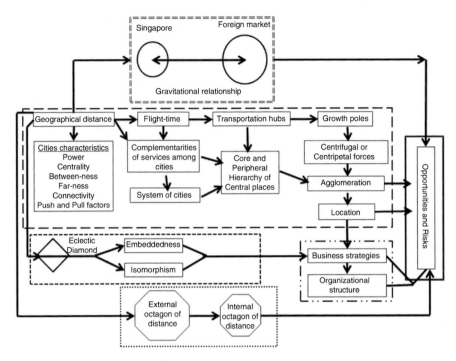

Fig. 12.2 The influences of distance. The different themes of which this community of factors belong to are boxed differently – Gravitational relationship boxed in *doubled dotted lines* (= =), Core and Peripheral System of Cities boxed in *long single dotted lines* (– –), Eclectic Diamond Framework boxed in *short single dotted lines* (———), Business strategies and Organization boxed in *single lines and dots* (—·—··—), Opportunities and Risks boxed in *single lines* (—), and the Double-octagonal Perspectives of Distance boxed in *single dots* (·····)

12.2.1.6 The Relationship Between Flight-Time and Organization Structures

The study was able to discover and ascertain the relationship between flight-time (proxy for geographical distance) and organization structures adopted by Singapore-domiciled A/E consultancy firms when they export their services into regional markets. Two concepts, namely: Core and Periphery Locations, and Gravitational distance, are pivotal to underpinning the relationship. It is established that the market size of a city profoundly hinges on its geographical distance away from a central or Core location. The market size in turn influences the internationalizing A/E firm's organization design. It is also suggested that the attractiveness of a foreign market hinges on its gravitational distance from the home-market, which takes into account the geographical distance away from the home-market, and the size of the opportunity or market abroad. Figure 12.3 shows how flight-time sway preferences in the entry modes and organization structures of overseas offices.

12.2 Major Contributions of the Study

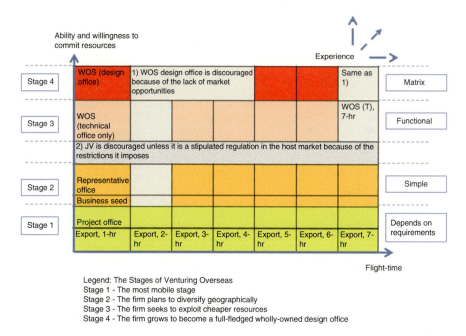

Fig. 12.3 Guide on entry mode for Singapore's A/E firms when venturing overseas

Grey boxes in the figure point out that the options are not desirable because (i) there is a general lack of demand for A/E consultancy services; or (ii) the option has many restrictions. On the other hand, the other coloured boxes point to the four stages of an internationalizing A/E firm in an overseas market or the type of choices that the firm is recommended to take up. Typically, an A/E firm's involvement in an overseas market begins with the exporting of its services to the foreign market via an export entry mode. Subsequently, the firm assigns business development personnel to build contacts and networks in the market or sets up a representative office. Then, as the firm have accumulated sufficient knowledge of the market, it seeks to establish a Wholly-owned subsidiary in the market.

12.2.1.7 Extrapolation of Organization Structures According to the Flight-Time Away from Singapore

A validation study was conducted to test the findings on the relationships between flight-time, business strategies, strategic management and organization design of Singapore's transnational A/E firms in regional markets, based on case studies, interviews and questionnaire surveys conducted in Singapore, Kuala Lumpur, Penang, Ho Chi Minh City, Hanoi, Shanghai, Beijing and Tianjin. The results suggested that A/E consultancy firms from Singapore could extrapolate to get a

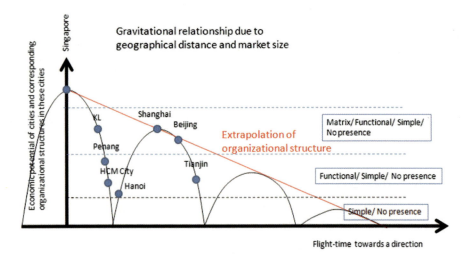

Fig. 12.4 Extrapolation of organization structures

recommended organization structure, as shown in Fig. 12.4. In the figure, it is suggested that the economic potential of a city first falls, but then rebounds and increases with increasing flight-time away from a core location (in this case, Singapore). It should however, be noted that the relationship could also be affected by (i) the power of the core city (in this case, Singapore) and the host city in the region; (ii) the between-ness of both the home and host cities; (iii) the proximity of both home and host cities to other markets; (iv) the complementarities of cities in the region; (v) the centrality of the home and host cities; (vi) the connectivity of the home and host cities; and (vii) industry's prospects in the host city.

12.2.1.8 Development of a CBR-DSS on Business Strategies and Organization Designs for Internationalizing A/E Firms

The common factors that could affect an A/E firm's choice of organization design when it ventures overseas are shown in Table 12.5. These components are categorized under: internal factors, interface, and external environments, and grouped in accordance with the Eclectic Diamond Framework: Factor conditions, Demand, Strategy due to competition, Related and supporting industries, Chance, Governmental intervention, Ownership qualities, Locational qualities and Internalization. These factors contributed to the development of the study's CBR-DSS on business strategies and organization designs for the internationalizing A/E firm. The CBR-DSS can assist Singapore's A/E consultancy firms to make informed decisions when they contemplate to internationalize into foreign markets.

12.2 Major Contributions of the Study

Table 12.5 List of factors for consideration in the choice of organization design

Eclectic Diamond Framework	Internal factors	Interface	External environment
Factor		Strategic fit (for efficiency, effectiveness and viability)	Barriers of entry or internationalization
Demand			Market size in overseas city
Strategy due to competition	Objectives (strategic asset seeking, efficiency seeking, resource seeking or market seeking); Entry mode		
Related and supporting industries		Whether the firm already have a beach-head in the overseas market	
Chance		Type and range of work and its requirements on communication and reporting lines	Opportunities and chances of clinching projects, considered with opportunity costs
Government intervention			Government restrictions
Ownership	Type of firm (Government-linked or Private); Presence of firm and its brand-name in overseas markets; Staff characteristics (Number of staff, skill-sets, behavior etc.)		
Locational	Embeddedness; International experience	Distance and location	Culture
Internalization	Risk averseness; Access to home-based resources and availability of resources; Mimetic, institutional and Coercive Isomorphism influence on the organization	Costs of maintaining structure	

12.2.1.9 Recommendations for Singapore's A/E Firms

The study recommends that Singapore's A/E firms should be forward-looking and aim to be world-class A/E firms. To run the next lap, Singapore's A/E firms should the following:

(i) Internalize distances – Singapore's A/E firms should not only view distance as a force of deterrence/costs/risks, but should see it as an opportunity;
(ii) Be distinctively/uniquely Asian to tap into Asian markets (including Asian clients in other continents);
(iii) Singapore's A/E firms should not only consider lucrative markets like China, India and the Middle-east. It can enter into other strategic (both consumption and production) sites in the Asia-Pacific, Europe, Africa, Americas etc. Singapore's A/E firms should also establish more regional offices and branch-offices, and set up networks between them to facilitate and integrate resource-sharing;
(iv) Merger with and acquisition of US or European A/E firms;
(v) Strategic alliances/collaborate more often with top A/E firms to learn from them;
(vi) Employ and attract international talents with top dollars;
(vii) To adopt geocentric corporate values, human resource management, networks etc.;
(viii) Branding and marketing the firm (e.g. through advertising);
(ix) Excellence in design and management. Singapore's A/E firms should be proud of their designs and be firm on the quality of implementation of their designs; and
(x) Work on revolutionary/iconic projects (e.g. in terms of design, technology) and larger-sized projects

12.2.2 Validation of Hypotheses

It was hypothesized that, using Singapore Changi International Airport as the point of origin, there is a relationship between flight-time (proxy for geographical distance) and organization structures adopted by Singapore-domiciled A/E consultancy firms when they export their services abroad. The sub-hypotheses were (i) flight-time affects actual or perceived institutional risks, business risks and cultural risks – the three cruxes of an environmental scan, and these in turn influence organization design of A/E firms when they venture overseas; and (ii) the behaviour of transnational firms in various overseas markets could be conjectured by their positions in imaginary concentric rings with progressive distances away from the home-city, such that firms in separate rings would have to formulate and execute different strategies to attenuate augmented problems due to reduction in understanding of the foreign markets and sapping of access to home-based resources.

12.2 Major Contributions of the Study

The in-depth survey of Singapore's A/E firms in KL, Penang, HCM City, Hanoi, Shanghai, Beijing and Tianjin has attested that flight-time (as a proxy for geographical distance) has a symbiotic relationship with organization structures. However, the study opined that to be more precise, it should be gravitational distance that would affect the choice of an appropriate organization structure in the foreign market. The gravitational distance (R) could be understood as R = (size of market A × size of market B)/(distance between A and B)^2. Gravitational distance was found to be a crucial factor that would influence the perception of a foreign market's attractiveness to the internationalizing firm.

It is acknowledged in the study that a firm's sensitivity to flight-time can be influenced by the firm's mobility, the relativity of flight-time/distance, and the attractiveness of the overseas market. It has also been corroborated that flight-time could be a causal factor to cultural distance, administrative distance, geographical distance (including topological distance and gravitational distance), economical distance, technological distance, socio-demographical distance, relational and affinity distance and organizational distance, and these in turn affect institutional risks, business risks and cultural risks to be faced by the A/E firm.

The supposition that the behaviour of transnational firms in various host markets could be surmised by their positions in progressive imaginary concentric rings away from the home-market with their corresponding forms of strategic management and organization has been tested and ascertained to be true. This is possibly because according to Tobler's (1970, p. 234) First Law of Geography, "Everything is related to everything else, but near things are more related than distant things." Therefore, markets which are positioned in the same ring might be more alike to one another, and are more suited to be applied the same type of business strategies and organization designs as one another.

However, the preposition of a linear relationship between flight-time and organization structure has been refuted. Instead, the relationship is of a cosine-sine curve, which stems from a location's market prospect or market size due to its distance away from a Core location. With market-seeking objectives as of the utmost priority for most Singapore's internationalizing A/E firms, organization structure, construed to be a function of market size, seems to fluctuate orderly with flight-time or flight-distance. However, the study noted that market size does not necessarily equate to construction opportunities. A/E consultancy firms have also inclined to concentrate around production sites such as New York and London, or consumption sites or "hot-spots" such as Shanghai and Beijing (Ren 2005).

12.2.3 Contribution to Knowledge

- The Eclectic Diamond Framework for Competitiveness of Firms is formulated by combining Dunning's (1988) Eclectic Paradigm and Porter's (Porter 1990) Diamond Theory. The framework suggests that the two models add value to each other by addressing what the other lacks. It postulates that a firm uses different

strategies to internalize its factor conditions, demand conditions, related and supporting industries, government intervention, chance, ownership qualities and locational factors, in the way that the fit is efficient, effective and valid. The Eclectic Diamond Framework is then used to (i) evaluate the competitiveness of Singapore's transnational A/E firms in regional markets; and (ii) catalogue the list of factors to be considered by the A/E firm for its business strategies and organization designs in overseas markets.
- The study's 8S Strategic Framework is improvised from McKinsey's 7S Toolkit to reflect the growing importance of a firm's upstream and downstream activities to its strategic management and organization. The framework therefore adjoined "supply chain" to strategy, structure, system, style, staff, skills and shared values. The 8S Strategic Framework is then applied to understand (i) how Singapore's government-linked A/E firms have evolved; and compare (ii) Singapore's private and government-linked A/E firms.
- The study contributes to knowledge on Economic Geography and Corporate Geography because no one has so far attempted to establish the relationship between flight-time with business strategies and organization designs. It also contributes knowledge to the study of proxemics, the study of spatial proximity and its effects on human behaviour, communication and social interaction because it probes into how distance could affect environments, internationalization strategies, strategic management and organization.
- Theories from Economic Geography, Internationalization, Strategic management, and Organization of firms are synthesized. This study epitomizes how interdisciplinary studies could be fused together to create synergy across various fields and new knowledge in a specialized area.
- The information consolidated and the logic set-up established in the CBR-DSS is a contribution to knowledge. The CBR-DSS on internationalization modes, business strategies and organization structures of Singapore's A/E firms would offer useful insight of how the CBR-DSS could be utilized for other study areas.

12.2.4 Contribution to Practice

- The construction industry in Singapore is fraught with limitations due to the rhythmic peaks and troughs, and lack of a critical mass of home-demand within a small domestic market. To continue to grow, A/E firms should foray into regional markets to ride on the growing business opportunities in these countries or cities. This study presents useful information and recommendations on the strategic management and organization of A/E firms when they venture overseas. Furthermore, the internationalization efforts of Singapore's A/E GLCs were examined to better understand how they re-postured themselves and realigned their business strategies and organization designs when they export their services overseas into regional markets. Then, these government-linked A/E firms are compared with private A/E firms so that they can learn from each other.

12.2 Major Contributions of the Study

- The study elucidates Singapore's A/E firms' experiences in regional markets. The pre-requisites, CSFs, competitiveness of firms, opportunities, threats, business strategies and organization designs are explicated in general, and also for the various cities, namely KL, Penang, HCM City, Hanoi, Shanghai, Beijing and Tianjin. It is expounded that self-awareness and learning from the experience of other companies is imperative to help shorten the learning curve. Like what Cyert and March (1963) contended, when confronted with a problem, organizations tend to start their search for solutions that have been tried before. The experiential knowledge garnered from the "first-movers" can provide invaluable business intelligence to those following suit later.
- The study presents a holistic perspective of distance and their push-and-pull effects on the internationalizing firm. These different forms of distance have often been forgotten, or ignored by firms until considerable problems crop up, when firms are already too severely entrenched into the quandaries. The Double-octagonal Perspective of Distance reminds firms of how cultural distance, administrative distance, geographical distance, topological distance, gravitational distance, technological distance, socio-demographical distance and organizational distance, in the form of change, spillage, time-differences and time-lags, communication, psychic distance, networks, net value-cost and control can complicate their overseas ventures. The Double-octagonal Perspective of Distance describes and warns of how companies routinely overestimate the attractiveness of foreign markets while ignoring the costs and risks of doing business in a new market. It is also postulated in this study that an explicit consideration of the Double-octagonal perspective of distance can change an A/E firm's outlook on overseas market and rethink about its strategic options.
- The established CBR-DSS enables the filtering and sharing of recommendations, advices, concerns, information, and intelligence for reference and adaptation by companies for their future endeavours. The CBR-DSS draws attention to the difficulties of venturing into a particular market and suggests how to circumvent around them to compete and participate more competently. This will help firms to avoid the pitfalls previously encountered by other firms, aid to facilitate upgrading across the board (for Singapore's A/E firms), as well as forge better relationships between fellow A/E firms through learning and collaboration. Furthermore, the study also lays down the foundation of CBR-DSS for other forms of exports or markets beyond the 7-h frontier.

12.2.5 Innovations of the Study

- The competitiveness of Singapore's A/E consultancy firms was appraised using the study's Eclectic Diamond Framework which merges Dunning's (1988) Eclectic Paradigm with Porter's (1990) Diamond Theory. The Eclectic Diamond Framework combines the strengths of both models as they complement each other.

- The differences between a Private and Government-linked firm were evaluated using the study's 8S-model, an improved version of the McKinsey 7S Framework. It introduces "Supply-chain" as the new "S" to the existing 7S, namely – Strategy, Structure, Systems, Style, Staff, Skills and Shared Values, because businesses cannot operate in isolation by themselves, but have to interact with other partners in the supply chain.
- The research scrutinized how flight-time or flight-distance is a causal factor for other aspects of distance (geographical distance, topological distance, gravitational distance, cultural distance, administrative distance, technological distance, socio-demographical distance, relational and affinity distance, and organizational distance), and the ramifications they have on business strategies and organization designs.
- Theories/concepts on Gravitational distance, Agglomeration, System of Cities, Core and Periphery Locations, Spatial Economics and Corporate Geography are applied in the study to advocate that organization structure, construed to be a function of market size, seem to fluctuate orderly with flight-time or flight-distance, as distance increases from a Core location.

12.3 Limitations of the Research

- Thirty completed questionnaires were collected in total. The sample size was adequate for a reliable statistical test to be conducted using the student's t-test, to generalize statistics for the population. However, the sample size was insufficient for a two-sample unpaired t-test or multiple-samples ANOVA test, which could have been applied to compare findings between private and government-linked firms, or between individual firms, or between different cities.
- Content Analysis is a purely descriptive research method. It does not explain observed phenomena, and is limited by the availability and subjectivity of materials. It is also very much influenced by the choice of associated or related keywords that were inputted into the program. Moreover, the Long-tail Syndrome and description of business strategies and organization structures can be subjective and hard to define.
- CBRs are less impressive in complex tasks, as they can often be misled by common or coincidental similarities between cases (Leake 1996). This limitation has however been reduced in the study because the factors of causes and effects were filtered and weighted through the statistical and content analyses.
- Efforts were taken to apportion the source of information via questionnaire surveys and interviews, so that a senior person in the top echelon, a middle manager, and an entry-level professional in each city could share their knowledge of the local industry and of their offices. However, that was not always permissible in the different cities because of time-tabling and schedule constraints.
- Design-oriented and commercial-oriented A/E firms are two different genres of firms with different preferences and approaches in strategic management and

organization. The study selected larger firms with the view that they are considerably more successful and have a higher probability of venturing overseas than smaller firms. These larger firms tend to be more commercial-oriented. Other firms may prefer different *modus operandi*.
- The study examined Singapore's A/E firms' business strategies and organization designs when they venture into Kuala Lumpur, Penang, Ho Chi Minh City, Hanoi, Shanghai, Beijing and Tianjin. Findings from the fieldwork conducted in these cities were used to deduce and infer the relationship between flight-time away from Singapore and organization design. It should be noted that the research did not explore into other cities or locations.

12.4 Recommendations for Future Research

- This study presented analyses and recommendations for Singapore's A/E consultancy firms' endeavors in regional markets that are within 7-h flight-radius away from Singapore in the North-East direction, with reference from Singapore, towards Kuala Lumpur, Penang, Ho Chi Minh City, Hanoi, Shanghai, Beijing and Tianjin. Future works can probe into:
    (i) Other industries or other types of firms;
    (ii) Other directions with reference from Singapore, i.e. in the North-West direction towards India, the Middle-east and Europe; or in the South-East direction towards Indonesia, Australia and New Zealand, to underpin the consistency of the flight-distance-business strategies and organization design phenomenon; and
    (iii) An extended flight-range to beyond 7-h.
- The research considered from the Core-Periphery system of cities' perspective, a core city – Singapore, as the reference point-of-origin. As a result, the economic potential of nearby to farther away locations tends to drop, bottom-out, and rebound. Future researches can look into the effects of flight-time or geographical distance, from a semi-core or periphery city, or from another country or city.
- The different facets of distance can be investigated to better understand the interrelationships between these dissimilar manifestations of distance, and the extent these factors affect an internationalizing firm.
- The extent of how much mobility of firms, relativity of distance and attractiveness of markets can influence firms' sensitivities to flight-time can be explored. A study can also be conducted to investigate what are the other factors that may affect the transnational firm's sensitivities to flight-time.
- The CBR-DSS can be further developed to perform more thorough diagnoses and precise recommendations on business strategies and organization designs for transnational firms. The CBR-DSS can also be made more informative and user-friendly.

References

Cyert R, March J (1963) A behavioural theory of the firm. Prentice-Hall, Englewood Cliffs

Dunning JH (1988) The eclectic paradigm of international production: a restatement and some possible extensions. J Int Bus Stud 19(1):1–31

Johanson J, Wiedersheim PF (1975) The internationalisation of the firm – four Swedish cases. J Manage Stud 12:305–322

Leake DB (1996) CBR in context: the present and future. In: Leake DB (ed) Case-based reasoning: experiences, lessons and future directions. AAAI Press/MIT Press, Menlo Park, pp 3–30

Pascale R, Athos A (1981) The art of Japanese management. Penguin, London

Peters T, Waterman R (1980) In search of excellence. Harper & Row, New York

Porter ME (1990) The competitive advantage of nations. Free Press, New York

Ren XF (2005) World cities and global architectural firms: a network approach. In: Paper presented at the social organization of urban space workshop, University of Chicago, Chicago, 3 November

Thompson JD (1967) Organizations in action. Transaction Publishers, New Brunswick

Tobler W (1970) A computer movie simulating urban growth in the Detroit region. Econ Geogr 46(2):234–240

Appendix A: Internationalization of Architectural and Engineering (A/E) Firms

Background

Interviewee's information
Company
Designation
Name
Role
Years of experience
Contact
Telephone number
Email address
Interview
Location
Time

Discussions

Please note that *The Organization* refers to the collective units of main and field-offices while *The firm* refers to the branch office which is away from the headquarters.

S/no	Questions and aims	Reference (and rationale)
Internalization and Strategic models		
1	Please describe your organization and firm's background in terms of ownership, locational and internalization (OLI) factors. How does flight-distance influence OLI factors?	*Dunning's Eclectic Paradigm (OLI and distance)*

(continued)

(continued)

S/no	Questions and aims	Reference (and rationale)
2	Please describe your organization and firm's strategies and structures due to rivalry, factor and demand conditions, supporting and related industries, government intervention and chances. How does flight-distance influence the Diamond's factors?	Porter's Diamond Theory (Diamond and distance)
3	Please describe your organization and firm's strategic management model and strategic thrusts. Discuss isomorphism of firms Discuss embeddedness.	McKinsey 7S (Change in strategies due to distance)

Internationalization: Reasons for overseas venture and where, when, what, why, who, how

4	Discuss agglomeration and localization effects Discuss centrality of cities in the world	Krugman's Agglomeration economics
5	In which countries and cities does your organization have offices? When were these country and branch-offices formed? What were the reasons for these overseas ventures? Why were these countries/cities chosen? What were their qualities? How familiar is the firm with the environment, its regulations and markets? What type of entities are these offices? How are the experiences of the firm in internationalizing? Who are the managers of these offices? How are the experiences of the managers in internationalization? What varieties of services do these offices provide? How are these services similar or different from those provided by the main office or headquarters? How much control does the headquarters have over the overseas offices or how much independence each overseas office has? How are the resources available different or similar? How are the businesses integrated? How did the firm decide on these strategies?	Ghoshal and Barlett's Transnational Organization

Organizational structures and business/entry strategies – from vision to implementation

6	What are the firm's vision, mission, objectives, investment horizon and pay-back considerations, policies, programs, plans, culture and values?	Waterman and Peters's Excellent Company

(continued)

Appendix A: Internationalization of Architectural and Engineering (A/E) Firms

(continued)

S/no	Questions and aims	Reference (and rationale)
7	Please describe the organization structure, processes and culture of the organization, headquarters and overseas office?	Mintzberg's Strategic Management (Company's organizational structure)
8	What was the spearheading/entry strategy when the firm entered the particular geographical market? Did the firm consider and apply varied entry strategies in different countries/cities? How did the firm prepare itself for the particular overseas venture? How were the decisions made? What were the sequence and steps of considerations? What were the entry modes?	Root's Entry Strategy (Company's entry strategy)
9	What were/are the instructions for the overseas office – from setting-up to present? What are the costs break-down for an overseas posting and assignment?	Theory of the firm -Value-costs evaluation
10	What are the competitive strengths of the firm? How competitive is the firm? Did venturing abroad impose discontinuities and erode comparative and competitive advantages?	Hamel and Prahalad's Core Competencies (Core competence and distance)
11	Does the firm take a region-centric, ethnocentric, polycentric or geocentric approach in management? Please give some examples. (region-centric – approach based on regional environment; ethnocentric – approach solely based on home environment; polycentric – approach based on individual country/city; geocentric – integrated approach)	Geocentric model of management and marketing
12	How does your firm manage internationalization and distance's implications on inconveniences, control, psychic and cultural distances, communications, value and costs, sap of resources, time-differences, time-lags, and physical changes which may require assimilation training for A&E specialists, networks, spill-over, friction etc.?	Octagonal + 2 factors (Internationalization and distance)
13	What are the main risk considerations by the organization? What are the social interactions that affect risk assessment? Why is the firm concerned about these risks? How are they different or similar in each city? How is the risk adverseness of the firm towards commitment and investment in each city? What are the firm's goals of risk management? How are risks managed? Political, legal and contractual, project and operational, management, financial, cultural, etc.	Risk-returns evaluation (risk and distance)

(continued)

(continued)

S/no	Questions and aims	Reference (and rationale)
	How does the firm perform risk evaluation? What were the techniques used?	
	How does risk management benefit the organization?	
14	What are the critical success factors (CSF) and possible pit-falls in each city?	CSF and Pit-falls
	What are the pre-requisites for internationalizing construction firms? Is the Singapore-brand helpful?	Pre-requisites
15	What were some of the problems regarding organizational design encountered by the firm and how were they solved?	Problem-solving (problem solving and distance)
	What were some of the problems regarding business strategies encountered by the firm and how were they solved?	
	How were conflicts resolved?	
16	How have the organizational structures of (A) of the organization evolved? And (B) of the branch-office evolved?	Collin's Organic Evolution of the Firm (Evolution of strategies and distance)
	How have the business strategies of (A) of the organization evolved? And (B) of the branch-office evolved?	
17	What is the value chain of the organization and branch-office? Does the firm have alliances or collaboration with other firms or institutions to enable overseas ventures?	Networking (Networking and distance)
18	Is there localization in resource management? What are the procurement assessment criteria and options?	Resource Management
19	What are some important lessons from previous internationalizing experiences?	Experience and learning (Experience, learning and distance)
	How can organizational learning and experiences aid to improve decision making for these instances?	
20	What are your experiences with transnational work?	Flight-time/distance and travel
	What do you think of flight-distance and availability of flight and their impact on internationalization?	
	What do you think of "time-space compression" and "virtual collocation"	
	Does distance sap resources?	

Appendix B: Internationalization of Architectural and Engineering (A/E) Firms

Survey on Organizational Structures in Architectural and Engineering (A/E) Consultancy Firms

Part 1: General information of your firm
1 Does your company have overseas branch-offices? If yes, how many does it have and where are these offices situated?
2 What is the organizational structure of the firm?
3 What is the nature of your organization's businesses and services?
4 How are the services provided by the overseas branch-offices similar or different to those provided by the headquarters?
5 What are the business strategies of the organization? Are they different at the overseas branch offices?
6 Financial turnover of organization
7 Age and evolution of the organization
8 Permanent/contractual/temporary employees in organization

To what extent does the following best describe your assessment? Please circle your assessment, based on a specific city, like the example shown above.

Part 2: Internationalization	
Proximity and access to resources, networks and markets	
1 Our foreign office have accesses to resources from our Singapore head-quarters/regional head-quarters	1 2 3 4 5 6 7
2 Our foreign offices have accesses to networks from Singapore	1 2 3 4 5 6 7
3 Our foreign offices are patronized by our Singaporean business partners	1 2 3 4 5 6 7
	(continued)

(continued)

	Part 2: Internationalization	
4	Our Singapore office has access to the host resources	1 2 3 4 5 6 7
5	Our Singapore office has access to the host networks	1 2 3 4 5 6 7
6	Our Singapore office has access to the host markets	1 2 3 4 5 6 7

Discontinuities

7	Our foreign office's access to organizational resources, networks and markets could be discontinued at city boundaries (e.g. office in Boston not receiving adequate support from RHQ in New York)	1 2 3 4 5 6 7
8	Our foreign office's advantages due to access to home's resources, networks and markets are discontinued at national boundaries	1 2 3 4 5 6 7
9	Our foreign office's advantages due to access to home's resources, networks and markets erode with cultural distance	1 2 3 4 5 6 7
10	Our foreign office's advantages due to access to home's resources, networks and markets erode with attributional/institutional distance	1 2 3 4 5 6 7
11	Our foreign office's advantages due to access to home's resources, networks and markets erode with geographical distance	1 2 3 4 5 6 7
12	Our foreign office's advantages due to access to home's resources, networks and markets erode with economical distance	1 2 3 4 5 6 7

Compression of time-space dimensions, Virtual collocation and Global-interconnectivity

13	The organization is multinational (each subsidiary is independent)	Yes/No
14	The organization is global (universal approach)	Yes/No
15	The organization is international (retaining much of the characteristics of the parent firm/HQ)	Yes/No
16	The organization is transnational (fully integrated and taking the strengths of each location)	Yes/No
17	The offices are well-interconnected with one another – there is significant time-space compression and virtual collocation	1 2 3 4 5 6 7

Part 3: Location of overseas offices or operations		

Flight-time/geographical distances, Agglomeration and Location

18	Flight-time/geographical distance is an important consideration to select location of offices overseas	1 2 3 4 5 6 7
19	Availability of direct flights is a consideration to select setting up of offices overseas	1 2 3 4 5 6 7
20	Shuttling between cities/countries (including preparations, transit/transfers and flight-time) is physically or mentally demanding and tiring; it takes up a considerable amount of our working time and is an inconvenient aspect of transnational work	1 2 3 4 5 6 7
21	Long term overseas posting (more than 1 year) will help to improve on work efficiency in the foreign office	1 2 3 4 5 6 7
22	Geographical distance is a consideration to select location of overseas offices	1 2 3 4 5 6 7
23	Geographical distance is a consideration to select procurement and allocation of resources	1 2 3 4 5 6 7
24	Geographical distance is a consideration to select networks abroad	1 2 3 4 5 6 7
25	Geographical distance is a consideration to select overseas markets	1 2 3 4 5 6 7
26	Geographical borders is a consideration to select setting up of offices	1 2 3 4 5 6 7
27	Geographical borders is a consideration to select procurement of resources, choice of networks and choice of markets overseas	1 2 3 4 5 6 7
28	Accessibility to clients and partners is an important determinant to the location of the overseas office	1 2 3 4 5 6 7

(continued)

(continued)

Part 3: Location of overseas offices or operations	
29 Accessibility to amenities is an important determinant to the location of the overseas office	1 2 3 4 5 6 7

Cost-value evaluation

30 The organization incur significant transportation and freight costs due to air-travel/air-mails and packages	1 2 3 4 5 6 7
31 The organization incur significant communications costs due to the need to set up infrastructural network	1 2 3 4 5 6 7
32 The organization incur significant training costs to inculcate values and assimilate to host environment	1 2 3 4 5 6 7
33 The organization incur training costs because of the need to inculcate local staff with the company's values and culture	1 2 3 4 5 6 7
34 Geographical distance increases operating costs	1 2 3 4 5 6 7
35 Geographical distance reduces potential value	1 2 3 4 5 6 7
36 Geographical distance affects net value-costs.	1 2 3 4 5 6 7

Communication

37 There are losses of information	1 2 3 4 5 6 7
38 There are miscommunications	1 2 3 4 5 6 7
39 There are problems of coordination with overseas counterparts/colleagues	1 2 3 4 5 6 7
40 There are problems of cooperation with our overseas counterparts or colleagues (sometimes, familiarity and trust are absent)	1 2 3 4 5 6 7
41 There are problems of reporting	1 2 3 4 5 6 7
42 There are problems and undesirable time-lags in decision-making due to geographical separation of the offices	1 2 3 4 5 6 7

Psychic distances

43 The cultures between the cities are different	1 2 3 4 5 6 7
44 The organizational cultures between the offices are different	1 2 3 4 5 6 7

Spill-over and the Core to the Periphery

45 The location of regional offices are determined by spill-over and influences from the headquarter/Singapore's resources, networks and markets	1 2 3 4 5 6 7
46 The political environment in the host and home markets are similar	1 2 3 4 5 6 7
47 The economical environment in the host and home markets are similar	1 2 3 4 5 6 7
48 The socio-cultural environment in the host and home markets are similar	1 2 3 4 5 6 7
49 The demographical environment in the host and home markets are similar	1 2 3 4 5 6 7
50 The technological environment in the host and home markets are similar	1 2 3 4 5 6 7
51 There are commonalities in demand in the host and home markets	1 2 3 4 5 6 7

Time-zones and time-lags

52 We contact and communicate with our overseas counterparts/colleagues during our working hours which do not coincide with their working hours	1 2 3 4 5 6 7
53 We contact and communicate with our overseas counterparts/colleagues during their working hours which do not coincide with our own working hours	1 2 3 4 5 6 7
54 The differences in time-zones affect our work	1 2 3 4 5 6 7
55 We often have to wait for longer to receive our overseas offices' counterparts/colleagues' replies to continue with our work	1 2 3 4 5 6 7

Sociological and physical change

56 Training is required to assimilate and educate staff because of socio-cultural changes	1 2 3 4 5 6 7

(continued)

(continued)

Part 3: Location of overseas offices or operations	
57 There are climate differences between the host and home cities	1 2 3 4 5 6 7
58 Physical changes necessitates different technologies	1 2 3 4 5 6 7
59 Physical changes necessitates different designs	1 2 3 4 5 6 7
60 Training is required to re-educate and assimilate staff because of the difference in the physical environment	1 2 3 4 5 6 7
Control	
61 The overseas branch-office is controlled by the headquarters	1 2 3 4 5 6 7
62 There is a control and autonomy paradox: Control is desired by the headquarters while Autonomy is preferred by the branch-offices	1 2 3 4 5 6 7
Networks	
63 Networks are important for businesses/operations overseas	1 2 3 4 5 6 7
Friction	
64 Friction in the form of bounded knowledge and rationality, and sequential actions increases with geographical distances	1 2 3 4 5 6 7
65 Telecommunications, technology and globalization have deemed distance irrelevant	1 2 3 4 5 6 7
66 Physical/personal presence and contact is becoming more important in modern business	1 2 3 4 5 6 7
Part 4: Factor, Demand, Complementary and related industries, Government, Chance, Ownership and Locational factors	
Factor	
67 Changes in environment are huge and require the firm to switch business strategies and organizational design	1 2 3 4 5 6 7
68 Changes in accessibility require the firm to switch business strategies and organizational design	1 2 3 4 5 6 7
69 Diminished knowledge of overseas market requires the firm to switch business strategies and organizational design	1 2 3 4 5 6 7
70 The firm adapts well to environmental changes	1 2 3 4 5 6 7
Demand	
71 The host market is more sophisticated than the home market	1 2 3 4 5 6 7
72 The firm is capable of meeting the expectations of the host market	1 2 3 4 5 6 7
Related and supporting industries	
73 Related and supporting industries in the host environment are critical to the success of the firm in the overseas market	1 2 3 4 5 6 7
74 The overseas branch-office relies on local business partners more than home business partners	1 2 3 4 5 6 7
Government	
75 The firm is able to turn statutory restrictions by the home government into opportunities	1 2 3 4 5 6 7
76 The firm is able to turn statutory restrictions by the host government into opportunities	1 2 3 4 5 6 7
77 The firm is able to make use of the benefits given by the home government	1 2 3 4 5 6 7
78 The firm is able to make use of the benefits given by the host government	1 2 3 4 5 6 7

(continued)

Appendix B: Internationalization of Architectural and Engineering (A/E) Firms

(continued)

Part 4: Factor, Demand, Complementary and related industries, Government, Chance, Ownership and Locational factors	
Chance	
79 The firm is aware of the opportunities available	1 2 3 4 5 6 7
80 Our intelligence are accurate and useful to inform us of the opportunities around	1 2 3 4 5 6 7
81 The firm is concerned about the long-term sustainability of the firm in the overseas market	1 2 3 4 5 6 7
Ownership	
82 The foreign office has autonomy and is not controlled excessively by the head-quarters	1 2 3 4 5 6 7
83 The managers delegate to and empower the subordinates	1 2 3 4 5 6 7
84 The organization is Singaporean	1 2 3 4 5 6 7
Locational	
85 The city is conducive for business	1 2 3 4 5 6 7
86 There are commonalities in the home and host markets	1 2 3 4 5 6 7
87 It is difficult to coordinate work with a distant colleague	1 2 3 4 5 6 7
88 It is difficult to integrate work with a distant client	1 2 3 4 5 6 7
89 It is difficult to integrate work with a distant business partner	1 2 3 4 5 6 7
90 It requires extra efforts to integrate work with more distance	1 2 3 4 5 6 7
91 Deception is more common when distance increases	1 2 3 4 5 6 7
92 Physical distance changes the cultural, attributional/institutional, geographical and economical aspects of the business environment	1 2 3 4 5 6 7
Part 5: Risk management	
Risks	
93 The firm has a structured and elaborate risk management plan	1 2 3 4 5 6 7
94 Risk is an important consideration for overseas ventures	1 2 3 4 5 6 7
95 The firm is risk adverse (low threshold towards risks)	1 2 3 4 5 6 7
96 The firm seeks to minimize uncertainty by gathering intelligence and conducting due diligence	1 2 3 4 5 6 7
97 The firm uses framing of possible scenario to manage risk	1 2 3 4 5 6 7
98 The firm makes decision based on anticipation of regret/opportunity costs	1 2 3 4 5 6 7
99 The firm seeks to minimize risks by avoidance	1 2 3 4 5 6 7
100 The firm seeks to minimize risks by reduction	1 2 3 4 5 6 7
101 The firm seeks to minimize risks by transference	1 2 3 4 5 6 7
102 The firm seeks to retains risks	1 2 3 4 5 6 7
103 Political risks are significant in this particular country/city	1 2 3 4 5 6 7
104 Legal risks are significant in this particular country/city	1 2 3 4 5 6 7
105 Market and industry risks are significant in this particular country/city	1 2 3 4 5 6 7
106 Financial risks are significant in this particular country/city	1 2 3 4 5 6 7
107 Socio-cultural risks are significant in this particular country/city	1 2 3 4 5 6 7
108 Management risks are significant in this particular country/city	1 2 3 4 5 6 7
109 Technological/engineering and project risks are significant in this particular country/city	1 2 3 4 5 6 7
110 Design risks are significant in this particular country/city	1 2 3 4 5 6 7
111 Risk perception of foreign market is influenced by cultural distance	1 2 3 4 5 6 7

(continued)

(continued)

	Part 5: Risk management	
112	Risk perception of foreign market is influenced by administrative and political distance	1 2 3 4 5 6 7
113	Risk perception of foreign market is influenced by geographical/flight distance	1 2 3 4 5 6 7
114	Risk perception of foreign market is influenced by access due to transportation and communications infrastructure	1 2 3 4 5 6 7
115	Risk perception of foreign market is influenced by economic distance	1 2 3 4 5 6 7
116	Risk analysis is an important component of value-costs evaluation	1 2 3 4 5 6 7
117	The choice of business strategies and management is influenced by the perception of risks	1 2 3 4 5 6 7
118	The choice of organizational design is influenced by the perception of risks	1 2 3 4 5 6 7
	Part 6: Organization design	
	Organizational structure (− Please provide organizational chart)	
119	Organizational design follows business strategies – Please choose 1; or Business strategies follow organizational design – Please choose 5	1 2 3 4 5 6 7
120	The relationship between organizational design and business strategies is dynamic	1 2 3 4 5 6 7
121	Business strategies are organic and dynamic; it evolves with time and situations. It is a contingency/situational model that is flexible to deal with complexity	1 2 3 4 5 6 7
122	The organizational structure is organic and dynamic; it evolves with time and situations. It is a contingency/situational model that is flexible to deal with complexity	1 2 3 4 5 6 7
123	Value-costs evaluation influences business strategies and organizational design	1 2 3 4 5 6 7
124	The structure (reporting, communication, coordination, cooperation, authority and responsibility) can be flexible	1 2 3 4 5 6 7
125	The organizational structure is efficient and effective	1 2 3 4 5 6 7
126	The firm is a learning organization	1 2 3 4 5 6 7
127	The lines and processes of reporting are efficient	1 2 3 4 5 6 7
128	The lines of communication are top-down – Please choose 1; or bottom-up – Please choose 5; or Please choose 3 if it is both ways	1 2 3 4 5 6 7
129	The lines of coordination and cooperation are efficient	1 2 3 4 5 6 7
130	The set-out of authorities and responsibilities are effective	1 2 3 4 5 6 7
131	Power distance (preferential treatment to senior management) is large	1 2 3 4 5 6 7
132	Masculinity/manliness traits is preferred (vs. feminity and emotionality)	1 2 3 4 5 6 7
133	Staff have a short term time orientation (vs. long)	1 2 3 4 5 6 7
134	There is uncertainty avoidance	1 2 3 4 5 6 7
135	The staff practices individuality (vs. collectivity)	1 2 3 4 5 6 7
136	Decision making is autocratic (vs. democratic and with consensus) and centralized (vs. empowerment)	1 2 3 4 5 6 7
137	The firm encourages employee movements across offices	1 2 3 4 5 6 7
138	The firm tends to promote from within the organization (instead of employing senior staffs from "outside")	1 2 3 4 5 6 7

(continued)

(continued)

Part 6: Organization design	
139 Employees share common values	1 2 3 4 5 6 7
140 The office is fully functional, equipped to handle, e.g. procurement, financial, technology, networking, human resource, service, marketing and other aspects of a normal organization in entirety	1 2 3 4 5 6 7
Part 7: Background	

Interviewee's information
 Company
 Designation
 Name
 Role
 Years of experience
Contact
 Telephone number
 Email address

Appendix C: Validation Form

Please help us to evaluate the Case-Based-Reasoning-Decision-Support-System (CBR-DSS) on Internationalization, Business strategies and Organization design of Architectural and Engineering (A/E) firms when they venture overseas.

1. Do you think organization design is important to a firm and its overseas offices?
   Important ( )   Moderately important ( )   Unimportant ( )
2. Do you think Artificial Intelligence (AI) or Decision-Support-Systems (DSS) is useful for managerial decisions (e.g. decisions on internationalization)?
   Useful ( )   Moderately useful ( )   Not useful ( )
3. Do you find the CBR-DSS easy to use?
   Yes ( )   No ( )
4. Do you think the CBR-DSS accurately reflects the actual business strategies and organization design implemented (or to be implemented) by the firm's offices in overseas markets?
   Accurate ( )   Moderately accurate ( )   Inaccurate ( )
5. Do you think the CBR-DSS is an easy-to-use useful toolkit and/or checklist for you to obtain preliminary guidance, advices and recommendations on business strategies and organization designs for an internationalizing firm?
   Useful ( )   Moderately useful ( )   Not useful ( )
   Other comments?

Bibliography

Aamodt A, Plaza E (1994) Case-based reasoning: foundational issues, methodological variations, and system approaches. AI Commun 7(1):39–52

Abe JM, Dempsey PE, Bassett DA (1998) Business ecology – giving your organization the natural edge. Butterworth Heinemann, Boston

Adair J (1990) Understanding motivation. Talbot Adair Press, Guildford

Agarwal S, Ramaswami NS (1992) Choice of foreign market entry mode: impact of ownership, location and internalisation factors. J Int Bus Stud 23(1):1–28

Allen TJ, Hauptman O (1994) The influence of communication technologies on organizational structure: a conceptual framework for future research. In: Allen TJ, Morton MSS (eds) Information technology and the corporation of the 1990s – research studies. Oxford University Press, New York, pp 475–483

Andrews PH, Herschel RT (1996) Organizational communication – empowerment in a technological society. Houghton Mifflin, Boston

Argyle M, Dean J (1965) Eye-contact, distance and affiliation. Sociometry 28(3):289–304

Argyris C, Schön D (1978) Organizational learning. Addison-Wesley, Reading

Ariff M (1988) A financial management perspective. In: Ariff M, Thynne I (eds) Privatisation Singapore's experience in perspective. Longman, Singapore, pp 83–100

Balign HH (2006) Organization structures – theory and design, analysis and prescription. Springer, New York

Barlett CA, Ghoshal S (1996) Building structures in managers' minds. In: Mintzberg H, Quinn JB (eds) The strategy process – concepts, contexts, cases, 3rd edn. Prentice Hall, Upper Saddle River, pp 375–381

Barnard C (1948) Organization and management. Harvard University Press, Cambridge, MA

Barnard C (1968) The functions of the executive. Harvard University Press, Cambridge

Barron D (2003) Evolutionary theory. In: Campbell A, Faulkner D (eds) Oxford handbook of strategy – vol 1: a strategy overview and competitive strategy. Oxford University Press, Oxford, pp 74–97

Baumohl B (2005) The secrets of economic indicators – hidden clues to future economic trends and investment opportunities. Wharton School Publishing, Upper Saddle River

Benito G, Gripsrud G (1995) The internationalization process approach to the location of foreign direct investments: an empirical analysis. In: Green MB, McNaughton RB (eds) The location of foreign direct investment – geographic and business approaches. Averbury, Aldershot, pp 43–58

Bennis W, Nanus B (2003) Leaders: strategies for taking charge. Collins, New York

Bergsten CE (1997) Open regionalism. World Econ 20(5):545–565

Berry B, Pred A (1961) Central place studies: a bibliography of theory and application, vol 1, Bibliography series. University of Pennsylvania, Regional Science Research Institute, Philadelphia

Blake R, Mouton J (1964) The managerial grid. Gulf Publishing, Houston

Blanchard K, Johnson S (2000) The one-minute manager. HarperCollins Business, London

Bleeke J, Ernst D (1996) Collaborating to compete. In: Mintzberg H, Quinn JB (eds) The strategy process – concepts, contexts, cases, 3rd edn. Prentice Hall, Englewood Cliffs, pp 362–366

Bonoma TV (1991) Making your marketing strategy work – revised. In: Dolan RJ (ed) Strategic marketing management. Harvard Business School, Boston

Bosworth DL (2005) Determinants of enterprise performance. Manchester University Press, Manchester

Bowles P (2007) Capitalism. Pearson, London

Brakman S, Garretsen H, Marrewijk CV (2001) An introduction to geographical economics. Cambridge University Press, Cambridge

Braunerhjelm P, Lipsey R (1998) Geographical specialization of US and Swedish FDI activity. In: Braunerhjelm P, Ekholm K (eds) The geography of multinational firms. Kluwer, Boston, pp 33–58

Bridges W (2002) Managing transitions: making the most of change. Nicholas Brealey, London

Burke R (2003) Project management – planning and control techniques. Wiley, Chichester

Burns JM (1978) Leadership. Harper & Row, New York

Burns JM (2003) Transforming leadership: the pursuit of happiness. Grove Press, New York

Burton RM, Obel B (2004) Strategic organizational diagnosis and design, 3rd edn. Springer, New York

Campbell A (2003) The role of the parent company. In: Campbell A, Faulkner D (eds) Oxford handbook of strategy – vol 2: corporate strategy. Oxford University Press, Oxford, pp 72–94

Cantwell J (2004) Globalization and the location of firms. Elgar, Cheltenham

Carlton J (1997) Apple: the inside story of intrigue, egomania, and business blunders. Random House, New York

Chabuk T, Seifter M, Salasin J, Reggia J (2006) Integrating knowledge-based and case-based reasoning. University of Maryland, College Park. TR-CS-4821, UMIACS-TR-2006-38

Champy J, Hammer M (2004) Reengineering the corporation – revised edition. Collins, New York

Chang PL (2006) Trade, foreign direct investment and regional competition: the case of Singapore. In: Koh WTH, Mariano RS (eds) The economic prospects of Singapore. Pearson, Singapore

Chemers MM (1997) An integrative theory of leadership. Erlbaum, Mahwah

Child J (2002) Theorizing about organization cross-nationality. In: Warner M, Joynt P (eds) Managing across cultures: issues and perspectives, 2nd edn. TJ International, Padstow, pp 26–58

Child J (2003) Organizational learning. In: Campbell A, Faulkner D (eds) Oxford handbook of strategy – vol 1: a strategy overview and competitive strategy. Oxford University Press, Oxford, pp 437–465

Christensen C (2003) The innovator's dilemma; when new technologies cause great firms to fail – revised edition. HarperBusiness, New York

Christensen CM, Overdorf M (2000) Meeting the challenge of disruptive innovation. Harv Bus Rev 78(2):66–76

Collins J, Porras J (1994) Built to last. Collins, New York

Cooper D, Schindler P (1998) Business research methods. McGraw-Hill, Boston

Covey S (1989) The seven habits of highly effective people. Simon & Schuster, New York

Crainer S (1998) Business the Murdoch way. Capstone, Oxford

Cuervo CA (2002) Firm transformation through the co-evolution of resources and scope. Academy of Management Annual Meeting, Denver, CO, August 11

Cullen JB (1999) Multinational management: a strategic perspective. South-Western College Publishing, Cincinnati

Dalton DR, Todor WD, Spendolini MJ, Fielding GJ, Porter LW (1980) Organization structure and performance: a critical review. Acad Manag Rev 5(1):49–64
Davenport TH (2001) Knowledge work and the future of management. In: Bennis W, Spreitzer GM, Gummings TG (eds) The future of leadership – today's top leadership thinkers speak to tomorrow's leaders. Jossey-Bass, San Francisco, pp 41–58
Davis S, Meyer C (1999) Blur: the speed of change in the connected economy. Capstone, Oxford
De Bono E (1967) Lateral thinking. Penguin Books, London/New York
De Geus A (2002) The living company: habits for survival in a turbulent business environment. Harvard Business School Press, Boston
Deal T, Kennedy A (2000) The new corporate cultures. Texere, London
Del Gaizo ER et al (2004) Secrets of top performing salespeople – selling with a customer focus. McGraw-Hill, New York/London
Deming WE (1982) Out of the crisis. MIT Centre for Advanced Engineering Study, Cambridge, MA
Dolan RJ, Silk AJ (1991) Marketing planning and organization – revised. In: Dolan RJ (ed) Strategic marketing management. Harvard Business School, Boston
Drucker P (1942) The future of industrial man. Greenwood, Westport
Drucker P (1969) The age of discontinuity. Butterworth-Heinemann, Oxford
Drucker P (1989) The new realities: in government and politics in economics and business, in society and world view. HarperCollins, New York
Drucker P (1999) Challenges for the 21st century. Butterworth-Heinemann, Oxford
Ekholm K (1998) Proximity advantages, sale economies, and the location of production. In: Braunerhjelm P, Ekholm K (eds) The geography of multinational firms. Kluwer, Boston, pp 59–76
Ensign PC (1995) An examination of foreign direct investment theories and the multinational firm: a business/economics perspective. In: Green MB, McNaughton RB (eds) The location of foreign direct investment – geographic and business approaches. Averbury, Aldershot, pp 15–28
Ericsson S, Henricsson P, Jewell C (2005) Understanding construction industry competitiveness: the introduction of the hexagonal framework. In: Porkka J, Kahkonen K (eds) Global perspectives on management and economics in the AEC sector. Technical Research Centre of Finland and Association of Finnish Civil Engineers, Helsinki, pp 188–202
Etzioni A (1975) A comparative analysis of complex organizations. Free Press, New York
Fang DP, Li MG, Fong SW, Shen LY (2004) Risks in Chinese construction market – contractors' perspective. ASCE J Constr Eng Manag 130(6):853–861
Faulkner D (2003) International strategy. In: Campbell A, Faulkner D (eds) Oxford handbook of strategy – vol 2: corporate strategy. Oxford University Press, Oxford, pp 159–182
Fayol H (1984) General and industrial management. In: Newton N et al (eds) Business – the ultimate resource – new edition. A&C Black, London
Follett MP (1982) Dynamic administration. Buccaneer Books, New York
Ford H (2000) My life and work – revised edition. Ayer Company, North Stratford
Fors G (1998) Locating R&D abroad: the role of adaptation and knowledge-seeking. In: Braunerhjelm P, Ekholm K (eds) The geography of multinational firms. Kluwer, Boston, pp 33–58
Foss NJ, Knudsen C, Montgomery CA (1995) An exploration of common ground: integrating evolutionary and strategic theories of the firm. In: Montgomery CA (ed) Resource-based and evolutionary theories of the firm. Kluwer Academic, Boston, pp 1–18
Freud S (1985) Group psychology and the analysis of the ego. Civilis Soc Relig 12:91–178
Friedman M (1976) Price theory. Aldine Transaction, Chicago
Frisk P (2006) Marketing genius. Capstone, Chichester
Fujita M, Thisse JF (2000) The formation of economic agglomerations – old problems and new perspectives. In: Huriot JM, Thiss JF (eds) Economics of cities. Cambridge University Press, Cambridge, MA, pp 3–73

Galbraith JR (1996) Strategy and organization planning. In: Mintzberg H, Quinn JB (eds) The strategy process – concepts, contexts, cases, 3rd edn. Prentice Hall, Upper Saddle River, pp 322–330

Ganslandt MR (1998) Strategic location of production in multinational Firms. In: Braunerhjelm P, Ekholm K (eds) The geography of multinational firms. Kluwer, Boston, pp 171–194

Gates B (1999) Business @ the speed of thought. Penguin, London/New York

Gehrig T (2000) Cities and the geography of financial centers. In: Huriot JM, Thiss JF (eds) Economics of cities. Cambridge University Press, Cambridge, pp 415–445

Gerber M (1995) The E-myth revisited: why most small businesses don't work and what to do about it. Harper Collins, New York

Gladwell M (2001) The tipping point. Abacus, London

Glaser B (1992) Basics of grounded theory analysis. Sociology Press, Mill Valley

Goold M, Alexander M, Campbell A (1994) Corporate-level strategy. Wiley, New York

Grant RM (2003) The knowledge-based view of the firm. In: Campbell A, Faulkner D (eds) Oxford handbook of strategy – vol 1: a strategy overview and competitive strategy. Oxford University Press, Oxford, pp 47–73

Graves RH (1934) The triumph of an idea: the story of Henry Ford. Doubleday, Garden City

Greenhut M (1952) Integrating the leading theories of plant location. South Econ J 18(4):526–538

Gripsrud G (1990) The determinants of export decisions and attitudes to a distant market: Norwegian fishery exports to Japan. J Int Bus Stud 21(3):469–486

Hague MS (1997) Recent changes in Asian public service in the context of privatisation. In: IIAS and the United Nations (ed) Public administration and development. IOS Press, Washington, DC, pp 43–66

Hall RH (1996) Organizations: structures, processes and outcomes. Simon and Schuster, New York

Hammer M (2001) The agenda. Random House Business Books, London

Hammond KJ, Burke R, Schmitt K (1996) A case-based approach to knowledge navigation. In: Leake DB (ed) Case-based teasoning – experiences, lessons & future directions. AAAI Press/MIT Press, Menlo Park, pp 125–136

Hampden-Turner CM, Trompenaars F (2002) A mirror-image world: doing business in Asia. In: Warner M, Joynt P (eds) Managing across cultures: issues and perspectives, 2nd edn. TJ International, London/Boston, pp 143–167

Handy C (2001) A world of fleas and elephants. In: Bennis W, Spreitzer GM, Gummings TG (eds) The future of leadership – today's top leadership thinkers speak to tomorrow's leaders. Jossey-Bass, San Francisco, pp 29–40

Hansen N (1975) An evaluation of growth-centre theory and practice. Environ Plann A 7(7):821–832

Haynes KE, Dinc M (2000) Globalization and the borderless economy: perspectives for a 21st century regional science. Edward Elgar, Boston

Helsley RW, Strange WC (1990) Matching and agglomeration economies in a system of cities. Reg Sci Urban Econ 20(2):189–212

Henderson V, Becker R (2000) Political economy of city sizes and formation. J Urban Econ 48:453–484

Herzberg F, Mausner B, Snyderman BB (1959) The motivation to work. Wiley, New York

Hollensen S (2001) Global marketing: competing in the global marketplace, 4 edn. Prentice Hall

Hymer SH (1970) The efficiency (contradictions) of multinational corporations. Am Econ Rev Pap Proc 60:441–448

Hymer SH (1972) The multinational corporation and the law of uneven development. Macmillan, London

Israel L (1985) Estee Lauder: beyond the magic: an unauthorized biography. Random House, New York

Jackson S (1983) J.P. Morgan, a biography. Stein and Day, New York

Jain SC (1990) Marketing planning & strategy, 3rd edn. South-Western Publishing, Cincinnati

Jiang R, Beamish PW (2002) Entry strategies and subsequent foreign expansion: Japanese firms in China. In: Inaugural conference of Chinese management research, Beijing

Jiang HB, Low SP (2004) Estimation of international construction performance: analysis at the country level. Constr Manag Econ 22(3):277–289

Johanson J, Vahlne JE (1990) The Mechanism of Internationalization. Int Mark Rev 7(4):11–24

Kanter RM (1995) World class: thriving locally in the global economy. Simon & Schuster, New York

Kaplan R, Norton D (1996) The balanced scorecard: translating strategy into action. Harvard Business School Press, Boston

Kay J (1993) Foundations of corporate success. Oxford University Press, Oxford

Kenney M, Florida R (1995) The transfer of Japanese management style in two us transplant industries: auto and electronics. J Manage Stud 32(6):789–802

Kerr S (2001) Boundaryless. In: Bennis W, Spreitzer GM, Gummings TG (eds) The future of leadership – today's top leadership thinkers speak to tomorrow's leaders. Jossey-Bass, San Francisco, pp 59–66

Kim WC, Mauborgne R (2005) Blue ocean strategy – how to create uncontested market space and make the competition irrelevant. Harvard Business School Press, Boston

Knoben J (2008) Firm mobility and organizational networks: innovation, embeddedness and economic geography. Edward Elgar, Cheltenham

Koch R (1998) The 80/20 principle: the art of achieving more with less. Bantam, New York

Koh WTH, Mariano R (2006) The economic prospects of Singapore. Addison-Wesley, Singapore

Kolodner JL, Leake DB (1996) A tutorial introduction to case-based reasoning. In: Leake DB (ed) Case-based reasoning – experiences, lessons & future directions. AAAI Press/MIT Press, Menlo Park, pp 31–66

Kotabe M, Mol MJ (2006) Introduction. In: Kotabe M, Mol MJ (eds) Global supply chain management, vol 1. Edward Elgar, Cheltenham, pp xi–2

Kotler P (1999) Kotler on marketing: how to create, win, and dominate markets. Free Press, New York

Kotov A (1971) Think like a grandmaster (trans: Cafferty B) Batsford, London

Kotter J (1996) Leading change. Harvard Business School Press, Boston

Krikorian DH, Lee JS, Chock M, Harms C (2000) Isn't that Spatial?: Distance and communication in a 2-D virtual environment. J Comput Mediat Commun 5(4), pp 0

Krugman P (1992) Does the new trade theory require a new trade policy? World Econ 15(4):423–442

Kwa CG (2007) Asean-China relations – ties shaped by history and social memories. For The Straits Times. Singapore Press Holding Limited, Singapore, 21st Feb 2007

Kwok CCY, Arpan J, Folks WR (1994) A global survey of international business education in the 1990s. J Int Bus Stud 25:605–623

Lane JE (1997) Introduction: public sector reform: only deregulation privatization and marketization? In: Lane JE (ed) Public sector reform – rationale, trends and problems. Sage, London, pp 1–16

Latan B, Liu JH, Nowak A, Bonevento M, Zheng L (1995) Distance matters: physical space and social impact. Pers Soc Psychol Bull 21(8):795–805

Laulajainen R, Stafford HA (1995) Corporate geography – business location principles and cases. Kluwer, Dordrecht

Lee HL (2001) Economic review committee report. Ministry of Trade and Industry, Singapore

Lee MTG (2007) World conquest in progress – what happens when Singapore companies Internationalise. Marshall Cavendish, Singapore

Lenin V (1948) Imperialism, the highest stage of capitalism. Lawrence and Wishart, London

Leonard D, Straus S (1997) Putting your company's whole brain to work. In: Harvard business review on knowledge management. Harvard Business School Press, Boston, pp 109–136

Levitt T (1962) Innovation in marketing. McGraw-Hill, New York

Levitt SD, Dubner SJ (2005) Freakonomics. HarperCollins, New York

Li H (1996) The organization structure of strategy. Discussion paper series, no. 185. School of Economics and Finance, The University of Hong Kong, Hong Kong

Likert R (1961) New patterns of management. McGraw-Hill, New York

Lipsey RE, Weiss MY (1984) Foreign production and exports of individual firms. MIT Press

Litvak IA, Banting PM (1968) A conceptual framework for international business arrangements. In: King RL (ed) Marketing and the new science of planning. American Marketing Association, 1968 Fall conference proceedings, Chicago, pp 460–467

Low L (1991) The political economy of privatisation in Singapore. McGraw-Hill, Singapore

Low SP, Jiang HB (2004) Domestic issues, international construction and lessons in international project delivery systems for Singapore. In Shuzo F (ed) Proceedings of the 20th symposium of building construction and management of projects, perspective: construction markets and construction management for east Asian countries. Architectural Institute of Japan and Kyoto University, 22–24 July, Kyoto Science Park, Kyoto, Japan, pp 65–74

Low SP, Rashid AAA (1993) Competitive and marketing strategies for the global construction industry. Trade Link Media, Singapore

Low SP, Yeo KK (1994) Sun Tzu's art of war: applications for leadership qualities and client-project manager relationship. Manage Dev J Singapore 4(1):10–30, Management Development Institute of Singapore

Lowenatein R (1996) Buffet. Doubleday, New York

MacEwan A (1999) Neo-liberalism or democracy? Economic strategy, markets and alternatives for the 21st century. Zed Books, London/New York

Maddox RC (1993) Cross-cultural problems in international business – the role of the cultural integration function. Quorum Books, Westport/London

Maister DH (1996) Balancing the professional service firm. In: Mintzberg H, Quinn JB (eds) The strategy process – concepts, contexts, cases, 3rd edn. Prentice Hall, Upper Saddle River, pp 669–677

Makridakis S (1990) Forecasting, planning, and strategy for the 21st century. Free Press, New York

Maslow A (1987) Motivation and personality, 3rd edn. Harper & Row, New York

Mason RB (2007) The external environment's effect on management and strategy: a complexity theory approach. Manage Decis 45(1):10–28

Mayo E (1946) The human problems of an industrial civilization. Harvard University Press, Cambridge, MA

McGregor D (1960) The human side of enterprise. McGraw-Hill, New York

McKenna R (1993) Relationship marketing. Perseus Books, Reading

McLuhan M (1962) The Gutenberg galaxy. Routledge & Kegan Paul, London

Meyer S, Qu T (1995) Place-specific determinants of FDI: the geographical perspective. In: Green MB, McNaughton RB (eds) The location of foreign direct investment – geographic and business approaches. Averbury, Aldershot, pp 1–14

Mintzberg H (1979) The structuring of organizations. Prentice Hall, Englewood Cliffs

Mintzberg H (1994) The rise and fall of strategic planning. Prentice Hall, Englewood Cliffs

Mintzberg H (1999) Managing quietly. Lead Lead 12(Spring):24–30

Mintzberg H (2005) How to plan a strategy. In: Mintzberg H (ed) Strategy bites back. Prentice Hall, Harlow

Mintzberg H, Ahlstrand B, Lampel J (2001) Strategy safari – a guide tour through the wilds of strategic management. Prentice Hall, London

Moden KM (1998) Patterns of foreign direct investment into Sweden. In: Braunerhjelm P, Ekholm K (eds) The geography of multinational firms. Kluwer, Boston, pp 135–156

Moon Y (1998) The effects of distance in local versus remote human-computer supported cooperative work. Computer supported cooperative work 1999, Copenhagen, Denmark, pp 159–178

Morabito J, Sack I, Bhate A (1999) Organization modeling – innovative architectures for the 21st century. Prentice Hall, Upper Saddle River

Morill R, Symons J (1977) Efficiency and equity aspects of optimum location. Geogr Anal 9(3):215–225
Morita A (1989) Made in Japan: Akio Morita and Sony. Dutton, New York
Naisbitt J (1984) Megatrends. Warner Books, New York
Nalebuff B, Brandenburger A (1997) Co-opetition. Profile Business, London
Nielsen JU, Madsen ES, Pederson K, Peterson M (1995) International economics: the wealth of open nations. McGraw-Hill, London
Nilsson J, Dicken P, Peck J (1996) The internationalization process: European firms in global competition. Paul Chapman, London
Ohmae K (1991) The mind of the strategist; the art of Japanese business – revised edition. McGraw-Hill, New York
Ouchi W (1981) Theory Z. Addison-Wesley, Reading
Oz O (2001) Source of competitive advantage of Turkish construction companies in international markets. Constr Manage Econ 19:135–144
Pahl G, Beitz W, Wallace K (1984) Engineering design. Design Council, London
Parson T (1956) Suggestions for a sociological approach to the theory of organizations. Adm Sci Q 1(1):63–85
Pascale R (1990) Managing on the edge: how successful companies use conflict to stay ahead. Simon & Schuster, New York
Peng MW (1995) Foreign direct investment in the innovative-driven stage: towards a learning option perspective. In: Green MB, McNaughton RB (eds) The location of foreign direct investment – geographic and business approaches. Averbury, Aldershot, pp 29–42
Pfeffer J (1998) The human equation: building profits by putting people first. Harvard Business School Press, Boston
Porter ME (1996) How competitive forces shape strategy. In: Mintzberg H, Quinn JB (eds) The strategy process – concepts, contexts, cases, 3rd edn. Prentice Hall, Englewood Cliffs, pp 75–82
Priem RL, Butler JE (2001) Is the resource-based theory a useful perspective for strategic management research? Acad Manage Rev 26(1):26–40
Pugh DS, Hickson D (2002) On organizational convergence. In: Warner M, Joynt P (eds) Managing across cultures: issues and perspectives, 2nd edn. TJ International, Padstow, pp 7–12
Quinn JB, Hilmer FG (1996) Core competencies and strategic outsourcing. In: Mintzberg H, Quinn JB (eds) The strategy process – concepts, contexts, cases, 3rd edn. Prentice Hall, Englewood Cliffs, pp 63–73
Ramachandran M, Mangano D (2004) Knowledge based reasoning for software architectural design strategies. ACM Sigsoft Softw Eng Notes 29(3):1–4
Rosenthal SS, Strange WC (2003) Geography, industrial organization, and agglomeration. Rev Econ Stat LXXXV(2):377–393
Rowntree L, Lewis M, Price M, Wyckoff W (2008) Globalization and diversity – geography of a changing world, 2nd edn. Prentice Hall, Upper Saddle River
Rugman AM (2007) Internalization is still a general theory of foreign direct investment. Rev World Econ 121(3):570–575
Schein E (1980) Organizational psychology. Prentice Hall, Englewood Cliffs
Schein EH (1994) Innovative cultures and organizations. In: Allen TJ, Morton MSS (eds) Information technology and the corporation of the 1990s – research studies. Oxford University Press, New York, pp 125–146
Schein E (1997) Organizational culture and leadership, 2nd edn. Jossey-Bass, San Francisco
Schermerhorn JR (1996) Management, 5th edn. Wiley, New York
Schonberger RJ (1990) Building a chain of customers. Free Press, New York
Segal-Horn S (2003) Strategy in service organizations. In: Campbell A, Faulkner D (eds) Oxford handbook of strategy – vol 1: a strategy overview and competitive strategy. Oxford University Press, Oxford, pp 466–500

Selznick P (1957) Leadership in administration: a sociological interpretation. Row, Peterson, Evanston
Shapiro A (2003) Creating contagious commitment: applying the tipping point to organizational change. Lighting Source, London
Shee PK (2003) East Asian new regionalism: toward economic integration. Ritsumeikan Int Aff 1:57–87
Singh K (2007) The limited relevance of culture to strategy. Asia Pac J Manage 24:421–428
Slater M (2003) The boundary of the firm. In: Campbell A, Faulkner D (eds) Oxford handbook of strategy – vol 1: a strategy overview and competitive strategy. Oxford University Press, Oxford, pp 47–73
Stake R (1995) The art of case study research. Sage, Thousand Oaks
Stewart T (1998) Intellectual capital: the new wealth of organizations. Doubleday, New York
Stinchcombe AL (1965) Social structure and organizations. In: Handbook of organizations. Rand McNally, Chicago
Stöttinger B, Schlegelmilch BB (2000) Psychic distance: a concept past its due? Int Mark Rev 17(2):169–173
Strauss A (1987) Qualitative analysis for social scientists. Cambridge University Press, Cambridge/New York
Subcommittee on Domestic Enterprise (2002) Construction group report. Economic Review Committee, Singapore
Svennson R (1998) The choice of entry mode in foreign direct investment: market structure and development level. In: Braunerhjelm P, Ekholm K (eds) The geography of multinational firms. Kluwer, Boston, pp 157–170
Svensson G (2001) "Glocalization" of business activities: a "glocal" strategy approach. Manage Decis 39(1):6–18
Tallman SB (1992) A strategic management perspective on host country structure of multinational enterprises. J Manage 18(3):455–471
Tan AHH (2006) The economic challenges facing Singapore. In: Koh WTH, Mariano RS (eds) The economic prospects of Singapore. Pearson, Singapore
Tay F (2007) Which market, what entry strategy. Singapura Management Pte Ltd. http://www.singapura-management.com/Downloads/MIF-Singapore.pdf
Taylor FW (1998) The principles of scientific management. Dover, Mineola/New York
Thynne I (1988) A framework for analysis. In: Thynne I, Ariff M (eds) Privatisation: Singapore's experience in perspective. Longman, Singapore, pp 1–18
Tier M (2004) The winning investment habits of warren buffet and George Soros – harness the investment genius of the world's richest investors. Inverse Books, Hong Kong
Toyoda E (1987) Toyota: fifty years in motion. Kodansha International, Tokyo
Tukey JW (1977) Exploratory data analysis. Addison-Wesley, Reading
Tung RL (2002) Managing in Asia: cross-cultural dimensions. In: Warner M, Joynt P (eds) Managing across cultures: issues and perspectives, 2nd edn. TJ International, London, pp 137–142
Turnbull M (2002) The tyranny of proximity: Australia in the 21st century. Vice Chacellor's Sesqui, Centenary Lecture Series, Sydney
Tussie D (1992) Trading in fear? US hegemony and the open world economy in perspective, New international political economy. Lynne Riener, Buenos Aires
Tzu Sun (6th Century BC) The art of war, Rev edn (translated by Griffith SB 1971). Oxford University Press, Oxford
Vecchio RP (1995) Organizational behaviour, 3rd edn. The Dryden Press, New York
Venables AJ (1996) Equilibrium locations of vertically linked industries. Int Econ Rev 37(2):341–359
Vries KD, Miller D (1990) The neurotic organization. Jossey-Bass, San Francisco
Waldrop M (1992) Complexity. Simon & Schuster, New York

Watson T Jr (2003) A business and its beliefs: the ideas that helped IBM, Rev edn. McGraw-Hill, New York

Weber M (1964) The theory of social and economic organization. Free Press, New York

Welch J (2001) Jack: straight for the gut. Warner, New York

Wendell RE, Hurter AP Jr (1973) Location theory, dominance, and convexity. Oper Res 21(1):314–320

Wheeler JO, Muller PO, Thrall GI, Fik TJ (1998) Economic geography, 3rd edn. Wiley, New York

Whittington R (2003) Organizational structure. In: Campbell A, Faulkner D (eds) Oxford handbook of strategy – vol 2: corporate strategy. Oxford University Press, Oxford, pp 319–348

Wild JJ, Wild KL, Han J (2006) International business: the challenges of globalization, 3rd edn. Pearson, Upper Saddle River

Yin R (1994, 2003) Case study research: design and methods. Sage, Thousand Oaks

Yuan LT, Lee TY (1991) Growth triangle: the Johor-Singapore-Riau experience. Institute of Policy Studies, Singapore

Zhao H, Luo Y, Suh T (2004) Transaction cost determinants and ownership-based entry mode choice. J Int Bus 35:524–544